COLLEGE READING SKILLS

Lettie J. Austin

in collaboration with

Alice W. Grant
Chloe A. Morrison
Joan B. Murrell
Eleanor W. Traylor

Alfred · A · Knopf, Publisher

New York

L. C. catalog number: 65–11959

THIS IS A BORZOI BOOK,

PUBLISHED BY ALFRED A. KNOPF, INC.

FIFTH PRINTING

To Dr. Charles H. Thompson
whose counsel and encouragement helped to make this book a reality

PREFACE

This book is designed to help anyone who wishes to read better. Through a unified approach to reading, it offers instruction for readers of varying abilities. Generally speaking, its unified method grows out of three steps: presentation, illustration, and application. First, the principles of the English language are presented as they are related to the reading process. These explanations are then followed by models which illustrate the principles at work. And finally, exercises are provided so that the reader himself may apply each concept and test its effectiveness in his hands.

Because the authors believe that good reading and clear thinking are inseparable, they have selected provocative materials. From these readings, questions are deliberately phrased to elicit thoughtful answers. This emphasis on reflective answers discourages the mere recall of facts as an adequate test of comprehension. Moreover, the use of reasoning spurs the reader to develop criteria for making intelligent, discriminating evaluations of what he has read. In the final analysis it is this ability that differentiates the active, critical reader from the passive, parrotlike one.

Stated simply, the underlying philosophy of the book is this:

1. Learning to read well is an acquired skill.
2. Improvement in reading is related to general proficiency in the use of language.
3. Growth in reading occurs more quickly when the reader understands theoretical principles and learns to use them in a meaningful context.
4. Thinking logically is an integral part of effective reading.
5. Enjoyment of literature depends upon knowing how to read.

Two broad sections, subdivided into chapters, make up the structure of this text. Part One deals with the fundamentals of reading: words, sentences, paragraphs; integration of these elements; development of techniques for critical appraisal. Part Two deals with the reading of imaginative literature; increasing the speed of reading comprehension; and improvement of reading skills for gainful study.

The two parts are closely interrelated. Mastery of the principles of Part One prepares the reader for handling the materials of Part Two. In the chapters of Part One the organization is cumulative. A principle is introduced and explained in detail. It is followed by a model sentence, paragraph, or essay which is analyzed in the light of the preceding discussion. Exercises then engage the reader in careful application of the principles to which he has just been exposed.

Having improved his ability to read, the student begins Part Two. In contrast to the general foundation of Part One, this section has specialized materials. Chapter IV, for example, is concerned with the reading of imaginative literature for recreation. Indirectly, the authors also have another purpose: through their choice of selections they hope to whet the appetite of the reader with limited literary experience and, thus, to help him cultivate a taste for reading works of merit. A brief commentary introduces the essentials of the literary types to be considered and offers guide questions to aid the reader in comprehension.

The next chapter in this section deals with rate of reading. It shows the reader how he can improve his speed without sacrificing depth of comprehension. Selections from fiction and nonfiction, arranged according to length, are each followed by a comprehension and vocabulary test.

The last chapter points out the relationship between reading and studying. Performance in college frequently depends on the student's ability to show his instructors how well he has mastered the content of what he has read. The authors have, therefore, included outlining and notetaking as organization skills related to the reading of textbooks. This chapter ends with advice on the taking of examinations.

Although the materials in both Parts One and Two are arranged sequentially, each chapter is complete within itself. Thus, the teacher or student will easily be able to isolate units for review or to omit those that are not pertinent to the needs of the user.

We have not included a separate section on vocabulary. Instead, vocabulary is treated as an essential aspect of the discussions and exercises. We strongly believe that a consistent pattern of vocabulary development is more beneficial than isolated units of drill and that the reader becomes more sensitive to the power of words if he sees them in action. Moreover, this continuous reference to words and their functions aids the reader in his progress from a level of mere acquaintance to one of familiarity and control.

One final point should be mentioned. This book reflects the combined experiences of a trained staff, each of whom is a specialist in English or Linguistics, Psychology, or Education. Credit is also due to hundreds of college students whose names do not appear. Their reading deficiencies motivated the Howard University Reading Staff to envision these units and to develop and use them in the classroom. Again, it was the performance of students which made it obvious that revisions were necessary and which thus shaped the final form of the manuscript. The book, then, is truly the result of a cooperative effort between students and teachers.

It is a pleasure to make grateful acknowledgments here to Dr. Ivan E. Taylor, Dr. Charles G. Hurst, Jr., Mrs. Marjorie Hooper, Miss Bertha McNeill, and Mrs. Marguerite Marshall for their valuable suggestions and assistance. We wish also to express our indebtedness to the editors at Alfred A. Knopf, Inc., for their critical comments that improved the content and make-up of the book.

Special thanks for their help in the preparation of the original manuscript must go to Mrs. Faith Barlow and Mrs. Marjorie Edwards, who were members of the Reading Staff when the idea of this book was conceived.

CONTENTS

NOTE TO THE STUDENT

Whatever the reason for your opening this book —coercion, suggestion, or curiosity—there probably lurks within you the question of whether you absorb fully the various kinds of reading material to which you are exposed. This question of your ability—or lack of it—is a healthy one, for the awareness of a need must precede the satisfaction of it; the identification of a problem must precede its solution. If you feel at all uneasy when you approach certain types of reading, you should do something about it. Be assured, however, that if you have a problem, you are not at all unique. Indeed, it was the awareness of the growing number of students who need help with reading that prompted the authors to write this book.

There are, of course, many causes of reading poorly—from astigmatism to brain damage—but we are convinced that, barring the need for physical or psychic repair, there are two principal causes:

a less than adequate familiarity with the workings of the English language and insufficient practice in critical thinking. It is to these two areas of achievement that this book is addressed.

Because of students' varying abilities and study situations, we have designed this text for use in a formal reading course as well as for independent study. In either case, for the fullest benefit from the text, constant application is necessary. Apply yourself daily to the exercises; review the materials in each chapter periodically; direct your attention to each new or vaguely understood word; check your progress weekly with the teacher's help, if it is available.

The first chapter, "Sentence Analysis," begins with a short reading selection in which the words are broken in odd places. Try to read the selection by re-grouping the letters so that they form recognizable words.

Good luck.

Part **1**

The Fundamentals of Reading

Chapter I

SENTENCE ANALYSIS

INTRODUCTION

This is a story about an old Arab. See if you can read it.

a Nol Dara Bwasve ryclo setod yinghe call edtog eth er hi sthr ee sonstot ell the mab outh owhe wis hedtod ivi dehisfor tunea mon gthem he tol dtheol dest tha this par twou ldbe on ehal fofhi spos sessio nsheto ldthes econ dsonth athi spa rtwo uldbea thir dand to t hey oun gestso none ninth aft eraw hil eth efat herd iedan dthes ons camet oget her toat ten dtot hedi visi onoft hepro pert yast hefat herhad wi she dat fir st t he red idno tsee mtob eany pro ble mbu tsooni twa sneces sary todi vid eth ecam elsthef ath erle ft 17 an umb er im poss ibletod ivi de by tw oth re eo rni ne the ycal ledin awi sema noft hevil lagetoa skad vic ehef oun das oluti ontoth eirpro ble mhe had theca mel slin edup bef oreh imandad ded hi sow nca meltot helin ethe n hes aidtot hebro the rsle tea choneta kehi spar tthe fir stonet ookni neth esec onds ix they oun gest twot hey we ream azeda tthew isdo moft heol dman.*

As you tried to decipher this jumbled text, you looked for some clues with which to get started, and then you began to read, as best you could, by moving from the most rudimentary steps in the reading process to the more complicated. In order to get meaning from the text, you had to rely on an instinctive familiarity with the language and on certain kinds of knowledge about it:

1. You had to know what the words were. You looked first for any combinations of letters that seemed familiar. Second, you seized upon a combination that recalled any known syllable, and then you looked for others. You recognized as meaningful structures such combinations as /the/ f ath er/ le ft/ n umb er/. You rejected, without thinking about it really, such combinations as /Bwasve/ gthem/ because in our language they seem unpronounceable. The meaningful portions, however, triggered immediate responses; they recalled items of experience in our language. They were *words* to you.
2. You had to know the denotations of the words. Such words as *very, told, an, camel* have

certain prescribed meanings. Either they denote an impression or experience which can be accurately described, or they serve as function words to indicate a particular aspect of the word associated with it (*an* old man, *very* close).

3. You had to know the connotations of some of the words. Some words called to mind additional associations or colorings. The connotation is the significance a word may carry apart from its explicit meaning. "Old," in reference to the Arab, may connote "experienced," "ripe," or "full of wisdom," rather than "feeble," "decrepit," "weak," or "full of years." The former connotations are in keeping with the tone of the story.

Once you were able to isolate the words out of which the language is structured, you felt then that you could *read* the text.

4. You had to be aware of implications of diction. The choice of words used by the author enabled you, as the reader, to get an accurate picture of what he had in mind. For instance, "close to dying" suggests—more clearly than "ill" or "very sick"—the condition of the father at the beginning of the story.
5. You had to group these words into meaningful units. Your inherent sense of the structure of the English language determined these units for you. You were aware that such a grouping as /an old man/ or /an impossible number to divide/ formed workable language units which, when put together in certain patterns, formed message units expressing complete thoughts.
6. You had mentally to "punctuate" the units to identify them. Instinctively you *read* into the text the short and long pauses and the full stops which indicated where punctuation marks should go. What word groups should be read as a whole, which should be separated— these matters you ascertained by "inserting" marks of punctuation.

---

* Adapted from *Nathan the Wise* by Gotthold E. Lessing in *Library of the World's Best Literature, Ancient and Modern,* ed. G. D. Warner (Warner Co., 1897).

7. You had to be aware of the normal order of words. Your knowledge of normal word order in English gave you additional clues in forming these message units. The usual sentence pattern of the subject-verb-and/or object or complement led you to catch easily the swing of the first three sentences. After the word *called,* you knew that an object—in this case a naming word—had to follow. In quick succession you read: "*He called* together

subj.   verb

his three sons. . . ." For what reason did he

dir. obj.

call? Without hesitating, you continued to read "*to tell* them how he wished to divide

infin.   indir.   dir.
          obj.   obj.

his fortune among them." The third and fourth sentences are similar: "*He told* the *oldest*

subj.   verb   indir. obj.

that his part would be half of his possessions.

direct object

He told the second *son* that his part would

subj. verb   indir. obj.   dir.
                                      obj.

be a third."

From these examples you should see that in our language words are patterned in a particular way. These patterns were built into your nervous system from the moment you learned to parrot phrases when you were a toddler.

8. You had to know the function of certain words (parts of speech). The order of words in a sentence is determined by the functions of all the words included. You needed to know whether the words in the text *named,* or *indicated* or *connected,* or *modified* something.

9. You had to recognize the important words in a message unit in order to recognize a complete thought. Only then were you able to understand the relationship of the words to each other. This meaningful relationship was recognized because you understood how the basic sentence elements worked together to express complete thoughts.

In addition to knowing how to get the meaning from a sentence, you needed to know how a sentence is structured, the means by which it expresses many ideas of varying importance. You also needed to be responsive to the qualities of unity, coherence, and emphasis, which make it possible for words to give special meanings and subtleties to man's thoughts.

All of these steps, which were necessary in order to get meaning from the scrambled text, make up

the process of reading. It is this process, a graduated analysis beginning with the study of words and ending with the complexities of a sentence, which this chapter applies to sentence reading. The intensive analysis of sentences leads to ease in comprehension. The exercises, therefore, are designed to help you understand what a sentence says as you follow the steps outlined below:

I. Understanding words
   A. Knowing their denotative meanings
   B. Knowing their connotative meanings
   C. Seeing the relationship of selective diction to meaning
II. Understanding the relationship of punctuation to meaning
III. Understanding the normal word order in our language and its relation to meaning
IV. Understanding the functions of words in a sentence (parts of speech)
V. Understanding the basic elements of a sentence as they combine to express complete thoughts
VI. Understanding the structure of sentences and how structure relates to complexity of thought
VII. Being familiar with the devices of unity, coherence, and emphasis

Needless to say, the first requirement for the proper study of words is a good dictionary. The unabridged *Webster's New International Dictionary* and the *Oxford English Dictionary*—found in most college libraries—are invaluable references. But every student should have a dictionary in his personal library for reference on meanings, usage, denotations, and connotations of words—not only for English, but also for other courses. The establishment of a strong dictionary habit will be a mainstay in later life as well as in college and graduate school. Especially recommended are up-to-date, shorter reference works such as the *Webster's New Collegiate Dictionary* (G. & C. Merriam Co., Springfield, Massachusetts) or the *American College Dictionary* (Random House, New York). The latter is the principal reference for the exercises in this textbook.

UNDERSTANDING WORDS

This figure represents or "stands for" a cat. It is not itself a real cat. In the same way, the word "c-a-t" represents the idea of a real cat, and is not itself a cat. Words are symbols *for* things or ideas. We can add lines and markings to the above crude sketch of a cat in order to say something more about it. If we wish to convey to the viewer a cat in high spirits, we can add a large grin to the face. Or if we want to portray a rather malicious cat, we can add a frown to its forehead. In like manner, descriptive words which precede or follow the word *cat* give a more specific picture of the cat, as in the phrases used above: "a cat in high spirits," or "a rather malicious cat."

The English language, however, involves more than "adding to" its word symbols to convey various impressions; it is as subtle and rich as the minds and needs of its users, and words often have meanings and power in themselves which are not dependent on modifying words or phrases.

Word Meanings: Denotation and Connotation

Word meanings may be either denotative or connotative. Denotative meanings are those agreed upon in the communication of the majority of educated and linguistically responsible people — these are the dictionary definitions. More precisely, a denotative meaning indicates a direct referral to an object or an idea — a one-to-one relationship in which nothing more than the object or idea is suggested by the word. Thus, the denotative meaning of *cat* is: "a carnivorous mammal *(Felis catus)* long domesticated; any of the cat family *(Felidae)*." About this meaning there is no dispute and no variety of interpretations. The denotative meanings of abstract words such as *good* and *evil*, *equality* and *justice* are more difficult to establish. Too often these words have meanings *relative* to the user and his particular loyalties.

Connotative meanings are special, suggestive meanings a word acquires through use in a particular way. Inherent qualities of the referent itself; the sound of the word; personal experience, which creates a private attitude toward a word; historical associations, which create general attitudes toward a word; literary associations and conventions; and special usage — these are some of the sources of connotative meanings. Poetry and fiction make frequent use of the rich suggestiveness of certain words.

For example, the word *rose* literally means a flower, but, when used suggestively, connotes beauty, love, and romance. Similarly, the word *lamb* carries with it, when used suggestively, the connotations of gentleness and innocence and the image of Christ. To compare a man to a fox is to imply he is crafty, stealthy, agile, surreptitious; *red* may imply valor, love, or passion; *blue* has

been used to suggest melancholy or sadness, nobility, and loyalty. Sometimes words, by their very sounds or length, are more connotative than virtual synonyms. In the phrase "the murmuring of innumerable bees," *innumerable* is far richer than *many* or *a great number,* and *murmuring* does much to suggest the actual sound the bees make; *multitudinous,* in Shakespeare's "the multitudinous seas incarnadine," is far more suggestive of size and dimension than *vast, many,* etc. In each case, however, it is important to note the context of a word; connotative meanings are more often determined by their special usage than by implicit meaning.

Knowing the connotative meanings of words as well as the denotative meanings is imperative in grasping ideas in reading.

Word Power: Diction

The power of a word depends on the skill of the user — through proper selection and apt placement — to provide levels of understanding, moods, nuances, and emphases. Awareness of why an author chose a particular word provides an important clue to reading comprehension. The English language offers its users many choices between words that may have similar denotations but quite different connotations: *stubborn, firm, obstinate,* and *pigheaded,* for example. The choice of one of these words over the other three would depend on the attitude of the author and the effect he wished to produce. To read well, you must become aware of the intended meaning.

Exciting interpretations can arise from the selection of a word rich in emotion or color: "To *wanton* with the Sun." A calculated ambiguity can come from the use of a word that is understood on one or more levels, as Hamlet's "A little more than *kin* and less than *kind,*" or words that are reminiscent of other words, as in most puns: "They went and *told* the sexton and the sexton *tolled* the bell." Then, too, a precise or concrete word will curtail the possibility of misinterpretation and can evoke an image so clear and precise that the alert reader shares immediately the experience and perception of the author. Note how well the words of Hamlet and Horatio evoke the mood and "climate" on the platform, as they wait for the ghost to make its appearance: "The air bites shrewdly," and "It is a nipping and an eager air."

The following exercises provide practice in understanding denotation, connotation, and diction.

EXERCISE 1: DENOTATION

Mount McKinley National Park, nearly two million acres in extent, contains the highest mountain on the North American continent, large glaciers of the Alaska Range, and a [1]*concourse* of North Country wildlife scarcely to be found anywhere else from Newfoundland to the Aleutians. Wolves are the commonest [2]*predators* here. Within the [3]*bounds* of the park these animals [4]*wreaked* the most [5]*havoc* amongst the [6]*ungulates*—mountain sheep, moose, and, most spectacularly, the caribou herds. Congress passed a law making it [7]*mandatory* to destroy the wolves in the park. Although this law has not as yet been fully [8]*complied* with, we today find the caribou herds so numerous that they are seriously reducing the available [9]*forage,* and we are threatened with large losses from starvation.

In Yosemite, the deer have been [10]*unmolested* for years. As a consequence, the oak-grass parklands in the floor of the valley are producing no young oaks at all to replace those older ones that suffer the usual [11]*vicissitudes* of age. The deer have simply eaten these young [12]*saplings* as soon as they appeared. Bears have become so numerous as to be an absolute nuisance in many spots within the park.

Yellowstone is faced with much the same trouble regarding bears as Yosemite. It is true that their [13]*antics* are both [14]*intriguing* and comical to the [15]*transient* visitor, but the bears can be extremely destructive, and occasionally quite dangerous to persons not familiar with their [16]*quirks*.

There are many more problems that [17]*beset* the administrators of our National Park System. [18]*Poaching* within the confines of the park is increasing. Engineers interested in water storage programs are constantly striving to [19]*inundate* large areas within the parks. Mining promoters press to obtain [20]*franchises* inside the limits. Grazing and use permits for other activities are consistently sought. [21]*Skirmishes* for these and other [22]*encroachments* are yearly occurrences. Most of them are defeated, but just enough sneak by to cause trouble. Artillery ranges, testing grounds, grazing permits, access roads, utility lines—all bring about a never-ceasing [23]*attrition* of the true purpose of the park.*

PART I

DIRECTIONS: Using your dictionary, find the definition for each of the following words, and write it below. If there is more than one definition, select the meaning which most accurately suits the context.

1. concourse

2. predators

3. bounds

4. wreaked

* From "Nature out of Balance," by Clark C. Van Fleet, *The Atlantic,* February, 1961. By permission of author.

5. havoc

6. ungulates

7. mandatory

8. complied

9. forage

10. unmolested

11. vicissitudes

12. saplings

13. antics

14. intriguing

15. transient

16. quirks

17. beset

18. poaching

19. inundate

20. franchises

21. skirmishes

22. encroachments

23. attrition

PART II

DIRECTIONS: Reread the text, inserting a synonym in place of each of the italicized words. What differences do the inserted word or words make, if any? Does the writer seem to have a particular reason for choosing the words that he did?

PART III

DIRECTIONS: Write a sentence for each of the pairs of synonyms listed below. Use each synonym in an appropriate context.

1. bounds

   frontier

2. havoc

   ruin

3. intriguing

   complicating

4. transient

temporary

5. beset

harass

6. poaching

stealing

7. franchise

license

8. battle

skirmish

9. encroach

trespass

EXERCISE 2: DENOTATION

Plainly, the central idea of secession is the essence of anarchy. A majority held in restraint by constitutional checks and limitations, and always changing easily with deliberate changes of popular opinions and sentiments, is the only true sovereign of a free people. Whoever rejects it does, of necessity, fly to anarchy or to despotism. Unanimity is impossible; the rule of a minority, as a permanent arrangement, is wholly inadmissible; so that, rejecting the majority principle, anarchy or despotism in some form is all that is left.*

DIRECTIONS: Certain words in this passage, of which anarchy and despotism are the most notable, are keys to Lincoln's thesis. Without understanding the meanings of these words, the reader cannot receive the full import of the message. The reader may have a nodding acquaintance with a few others, such as sovereign and sentiments, but if he is not careful, he will miss their range of meanings as used here. Define those words you need to know in order to understand fully this passage, and be prepared to explain how each word is used in this context.

1. secession

2. anarchy

3. constitutional checks

4. sentiments

5. sovereign

6. despotism

7. unanimity

8. inadmissible

* From "First Inaugural Address," by Abraham Lincoln, March 4, 1861.

EXERCISE 3: DENOTATION

PART I

DIRECTIONS: Using your dictionary, review the meanings of the following words. Be careful; some have a number of different meanings. Then, in the blanks below, write a suitable word from the list.

alliance	macrocosm
arbitrator	mellifluous
blazer	noxious
cant	opportunism
daguerreotype	pellucid
efficacious	plebeian
façade	quixotic
gazebo	respite
harangue	scratch
immolation	tackle

1. The freshman, donning his college _____ and cap for the first time, feels undeniable pride in being a part of the campus fellowship.

2. Among the most important rituals of primitive peoples of all countries is the _____ of both human beings and animals for the appeasement of tribal gods.

3. Although according to the Constitution _____ interests are served equally by the three branches of the government, the onus of responsibility falls most heavily upon Congress, for its members are elected to represent the fifty states.

4. In one area of medicine, dermatology, research has produced many _____ salves and pills.

5. In no other gathering does one find the political _____ used as effectively as it is in national conventions for the nomination of a party's presidential and vice-presidential candidates.

6. In the early dramas of the century, villains customarily spoke in _____ tones to lure the innocent heroine.

7. The current trend toward nuclear warfare has made the promotion of the international _____ and rigid adherence to its terms an absolute necessity for the member nations.

8. Although it is comparatively unknown in the United States, the Russians have for years enjoyed the pleasures of the _____ at their country houses.

9. E. B. White's many essays for New Yorkers have been admired for being _____ in style, witty, and thought-provoking.

10. Crewmen in the exciting sailing contests of the America's Cup Series, waged annually between Britain and America, demonstrate rigid training, including every aspect of handling ship's _____.

11. The thoughtful citizen learns to evaluate the _____ of politicians for its truthfulness and its hypocrisy.

12. The adjective _____, which has come into the English vocabulary to characterize a temperamental person who fluctuates in moods and feelings, is derived from the famous hero of Cervantes' novel.

13. The battle of the conservationists focuses on many issues: preserving our national forest lands, controlling wildlife, and preventing the pollution of our rivers and streams by _____ wastes, the by-products of industry.

14. Photography has been so revolutionized since 1839 that the inventor of the _____ would hardly recognize his contribution.

15. Interpreting the vast _____ to their satisfaction occupied the interests of the philosophers and scholars of the Middle Ages.

16. Sports car racing in the United States is a contest of tough endurance and highly skillful driving in which contestants have little or no _____ from start to finish.

17. Although the politician is commonly accused of _____, there is hardly a profession that doesn't have those who seek advantages for themselves.

18. The task of beginning a business from _____ is such a herculean one for a person without sufficient experience or training that the odds are heavily weighted against his success.

19. The role of the _____ is especially important in this area of national government: settling wage, hour, and profit disputes between business and labor in order to avoid or terminate strikes.

20. Neuroticism is the price many apparently successful men pay for maintaining a _____ of wealth and prestige.

PART II

DIRECTIONS: Match each word with its appropriate meaning by placing the letter which stands for the meaning in the blank before the word.

_____ 1. *ad hoc*	a. to charge, often under law
_____ 2. dithyramb	b. seething or overflowing
_____ 3. impugn	c. to penetrate or pass through the mass
_____ 4. fatuous	d. to send to an obscure position or place
_____ 5. adept	e. Eskimo hunting craft
_____ 6. juvenescent	f. to harass, torment
_____ 7. relegate	g. apparently good or right without merit
_____ 8. nonage	h. eager desire to possess something, greed
_____ 9. adjure	i. to direct to one side
_____ 10. specious	j. for this special purpose
_____ 11. permeate	k. dominance, leadership
_____ 12. quire	l. one competent to pass critical judgment in an art
_____ 13. badger	m. set of 24 uniform sheets of paper
_____ 14. shard	n. foolish, unconsciously silly
_____ 15. hegemony	o. to allow as a discount
_____ 16. rebate	p. fragment of broken earthenware
_____ 17. cupidity	q. Greek choral song of wild character
_____ 18. kayak	r. becoming youthful
_____ 19. connoisseur	s. employed, disposed of
_____ 20. ebullition	t. call in question
	u. period of legal minority
	v. academic requirement
	w. well-skilled, proficient

PART III

DIRECTIONS: Select the word or phrase which is most nearly a synonym of the italicized word in the left-hand column. Put the letter of your answer in the blank.

_____ 1. a *tenable* theory
    a. capable of being held
    b. easily refuted
    c. inconclusive

_____ 2. to *thwart* his plans
    a. to carry across
    b. to resound
    c. to oppose successfully

_____ 3. to *transcend* his wildest dreams
    a. to excel
    b. to cross over
    c. to change

_____ 4. an *unctuous* merchant
    a. very bland
    b. unduly suave
    c. thrifty

_____ 5. his *unwonted* ways
    a. unorthodox
    b. unhealthy
    c. unaccustomed

_____ 6. the *vernal* rains
    a. tropical
    b. springlike
    c. flooding

_____ 7. a *prolific* author
    a. lewd
    b. productive
    c. careful

_____ 8. to *winnow* truth from falsehood
    a. to make up
    b. deduce
    c. separate

_____ 9. a *candid* opinion
    a. secret
    b. sincere
    c. unpleasant

_____ 10. to *languish* in prison
    a. to pine or suffer
    b. to labor
    c. to repent

EXERCISE 4: CONNOTATION

PART I

DIRECTIONS: Though it is often difficult to tell the precise connotations of a word without knowing the context in which it is used, words do suggest, inherently, attitudes and meanings far different from those of their apparent synonyms. Examine the different connotations for each of the following groups of words or phrases. Briefly explain the differences in each group. (Webster's Dictionary of Synonyms, **an excellent source for distinguishing the meanings of words, should prove of help in this exercise.)**

1. died

   passed away

   gave up the ghost

   bit the dust

   was promoted to glory

2. punish

   imprison

   chastise

   excommunicate

3. barter

   swap

trade

bargain

4. beat

thrash

pummel

whip

5. idle

supine

lethargic

inert

6. fat

obese

chubby

gross

7. lenient

   merciful

   soft

   indulging

PART II

DIRECTIONS: **Underscore the word which, according to the context of the sentence, is most appropriate.**

1. The religious (enthusiasm, fanaticism) which culminated in witch-burning is a sore point in the history of New England.
2. The long summer in that secluded cabin high in the Berkshires enabled her to establish real (communication, rapport) with nature.
3. His conscious acceptance of his family's long ownership of the historic textile mills rendered him a very (considerate, attentive) employer.
4. The custom among some present-day aborigines of abandoning the aged, the weak, and the sick to die is a (primitive, barbaric) survival of their early harsh tribal life.
5. The transition from one idea to another in a paragraph should be as (liquid, fluid) as possible.

PART III

DIRECTIONS: **Construct sentences showing the difference in meaning between the words in each group.**

1. to barter — to bargain

2. rebellious — recalcitrant

3. wrest — pry

4. mock — scorn

5. crowd — mob

EXERCISE 5: CONNOTATION

DIRECTIONS: In the series of synonyms that follow, notice the common general meaning shared by the members in each group. (Check your dictionary!) Point out the differences in shades of meaning. Write original sentences for all the words in each group, showing clearly how each word is most appropriate for its sentence context.

1. humane, benevolent, kind

2. blame, condemn, censure

3. pilfer, steal, filch

4. hit, strike, slug

5. slow, dull, stupid

6. praise, laud, acclaim, extol

7. sharp, keen, shrewd

8. share, part, portion

9. stimulate, rouse, excite

10. steady, reliable, dependable

11. sudden, quick, instantaneous

12. astonish, amaze, dumbfound, flabbergast

EXERCISE 6: CHOICE OF WORDS

PART I

DIRECTIONS: **Replace the bracketed word(s) with more vivid, concrete words or phrases.**

Lying stretched on her bed, Therese listened to the [noise] . . . _____ of china being put away in the kitchen. The afternoon was [gloomy] _____. The furniture feebly reflected back the dull light. The day was pursuing its usual course. The noise of cars and lorries reached her ears, the [noise] _____ of brakes and the [loud] _____ cries of children at play—an audible reminder that humanity was still busy reproducing itself. The chair mender came round, sounding his [little] _____ horn. . . .

The afternoon [ended] _____. Cars [made noises] _____ at one another at the intersections. . . . In a moment of sudden quiet a bird [called out] _____ and fell silent. . . . Just after six o'clock she heard the front-door bell, and then a man's voice, followed by Marie's [funny] _____ laugh.*

PART II

DIRECTIONS: **Put vivid words in the spaces provided. Note what part of speech each word should be.**

I noticed at luncheon that he was eating _____ (adv.), his eyes staring _____ (adv.) in front of him. There is nothing lovelier than the remoteness which belongs to certain young people, the air they have of being somewhere else, with their minds intent on some _____ (adj.) dream. So _____ (pred. adj.) did he appear that I felt free to watch him without taking my usual precautions. But so _____ (pred. adj.) did he seem to be that I couldn't, in spite of myself, help feeling somewhat _____ (pred. adj.). I followed the direction of his gaze, and what was my amazement when I discovered that by some trick of reflection (the dining room was full of mirrors) it was me at whom he was looking! His expression was so _____ (pred. adj.) that I felt quite _____ (pred. adj.). I lowered my eyes quickly so that he should not see that I had discovered what he was doing. He continued to stare at my reflection with an air of mingled _____ (noun) and _____ (noun). †

---

* Adapted from *Thérèse,* by François Mauriac, trans. Gerard Hopkins (N.Y.: Farrar, Straus & Co. and London: Eyre & Spottiswoode, 1947). By permission of the publishers.

† *Ibid.*

EXERCISE 7: CHOICE OF WORDS

PART I

DIRECTIONS: Specific and concrete words evoke more definite responses than general words. A failure to be specific usually reflects conscious or unconscious evasion on an author's part. In the blank spaces provided for each grouping below, number the most specific word "a," the next "b," and the most general word "c." Note the different effects!

1. ____ man	____ soldier	____ corporal
2. ____ steak	____ meat	____ porterhouse steak
3. ____ painter	____ artist	____ Cezanne
4. ____ travels	____ goes	____ hikes
5. ____ fat	____ large	____ 230 pounds
6. ____ defeat	____ landslide	____ loss
7. ____ business	____ U.S. Steel	____ corporation
8. ____ mistake	____ felony	____ murder
9. ____ parched	____ dry	____ withered
10. ____ dispute	____ conflict	____ Korean War

PART II

DIRECTIONS: The most important advantage of an extensive vocabulary is that it provides one with the ability to speak and write with accuracy, subtlety, and imagination. In the following phrases the italicized words are dull, trite, and vague. Select a more subtle and discriminating word to replace each one.

1. a *watery* grave

2. *blissfully* happy

3. *budding* genius

4. *burning* questions

5. *checkered* career

6. *finer things* of life

7. *herculean* efforts

8. *promising* future

9. *proud* possessor

10. *red-letter* day

11. *ruling* passion

12. *sneaking* suspicion

13. *troubled* times

14. *undying* faith

15. *vanished* glory

PART III

DIRECTIONS: The language in the following paragraph is general, colorless, and unimpressive. Rewrite the passage, enlivening it with more specific and descriptive words.

Watching small children play is very interesting. They seem able to stick to one thing for a long time, and, unlike adults who are easily bored, their attention does not wander. Give a little boy an eggbeater and he will think of many things to do with it and stay happy for hours. A little girl can find equally as many things to do with a clothespin doll. Perhaps we don't give children enough credit. We should give them more and more chances to learn instead of limiting them.

PUNCTUATION AND MEANING

Familiarity with the word as a single unit must be followed by familiarity with words in meaningful groups. Punctuation helps greatly in determining this grouping. These marks are signals to the reader, signals that, rightly interpreted, suggest the writer's intonation pattern, tone, and emphasis. They aid the author in putting into print as close as possible a representation of the thought in his own mind.

End Marks

• **The period** is the most common marker for the end of a sentence. In normal discourse, the voice follows a certain pattern of rising and falling pitches, ending in a full stop when a thought is completed. The period is the marker for this full stop. It occurs most frequently in expository writing, whose function it is to present clear explanations, directions, and definitions. These are often conveyed in simple declarative statements. Technical writing, which is largely expository, relies mainly on factual sentence statements.

In fiction writing, too, the declarative sentence is effective. Because of its versatility the writer can employ it to describe persons, places, and things in detail. He can use it to set the stage for his cast of characters, to depict minutely their expressions, inner feelings, and the play of one character against another. Although the reader may not be consciously aware of the frequency of the declarative statement, it is this kind of sentence that carries the weight of the narrative, provides insight into character, and shifts the reader from one emotion or mood to another.

The following paragraph illustrates the striking results that may be achieved through the use of declarative sentences. Note how a series of random reminiscences is accomplished by short, reflective statements.

When the short days of winter came dusk fell before we had well eaten our dinners. When we met in the street the houses had grown somber. The space of sky above us was the colour of ever-changing violet and towards it the lamps of the street lifted their feeble lanterns. The cold air stung us and we played till our bodies glowed. Our shouts echoed in the silent street.*

The author wants the reader to grasp, one at a time, the recalled details of some period of the narrator's life. Each sentence is fairly short, and its contents are capable of being taken in at a glance. A complete description is skillfully presented by a succession of images: the short days of winter, the

coming of dusk, the somber cast of the houses, the deepening sky overhead. The five declarative sentences move swiftly from picture to picture, disclose the nostalgia of the narrator and make a vivid appeal to the reader's senses of sight, sound, and feeling.

All of this is accomplished purposely without any punctuation signals other than the period at the end of each sentence. As a result of this, and of the careful choice of words, Joyce creates a steady rhythm that enables the reader to begin each sentence in the pattern of normal speech. In other words, he starts at medium pitch level, rises to high at the main point of the sentence, falls to the lowest pitch, and comes to a full stop at the period.

Other end mark signals are used when the pace is quickened, when excitement is forthcoming, and when the author wants to attract the reader's attention for some particular reason.

" " Quotation marks indicate dialogue or conversation. They are also used to quote passages exactly from another source, to denote special (usually ironic) emphasis, and to indicate titles of short works (poems, essays, or stories) contained within a larger volume.

! The exclamation point indicates expression of strong feeling or emphasis.

? The question mark indicates that the speaker asks of the listener, or perhaps of himself, a question. This question may or may not require a verbal response on the part of the listener.

Notice the end marks in the following passage and how they affect meaning.

"I see it! I see it!" shrieked Beatrice. "It is my father's fatal science! No, no, Giovanni; it was not I! Never, never! I dreamed only to love thee and be with thee a little time, and so to let thee pass away, leaving but thine image in mine heart. For, Giovanni, believe it, though my body be nourished with poison, my spirit is God's creature and craves love as its daily food. But, my father, —he has united us in this fearful sympathy. Yes; spurn me, tread upon me, kill me! Oh, what is death after such words as thine?" †

Internal Marks

When the sentence structure becomes more complex, certain internal punctuation marks may aid the reader in isolating meaningful clusters and associating related ideas.

• **The colon.** These two dots within a sentence signal to the reader that what follows has

---

* From "Araby," by James Joyce in *Dubliners* (The Viking Press). By permission of publisher.

† From "Rappaccini's Daughter," by Nathaniel Hawthorne.

been singled out for emphasis. *The colon* throws the emphasis forward upon the words that follow it.

1. It may direct the reader's attention to a formal list, or an explanation, or a long quotation at the end of a sentence.

The following students should report to Miss Greene at once: George Adams, Carol Benton, and Charles Wood.

After only a hurried investigation of the damage and a few local inquiries, the answer was clear: raccoons.

Alexander Pope sharply satirizes the man who knows many facts but probably cannot apply them:

> The bookful blockhead, ignorantly read,
> With loads of learnèd lumber in his head.

2. It may separate two main clauses when the first one is explained or amplified in the second clause.

Dostoyevski's novel *The Brothers Karamazov* presents an extraordinarily broad spectrum of characters: it ranges from the gentle Alyosha to the passionate Dmitri, and from the perverse Smerdyakov to the wise and humane Father Zossima.

His performance confirmed what we had long suspected: Gerald's real talent was for the comic.

3. It is used after the salutation in a business letter.

Dear Sir:
Gentlemen:
Dear Dean Downing:

4. It is used to separate chapter and verse indications in citing Biblical references.

Luke 4:17
Genesis 1:12

5. It is used to indicate the minute following the hour in stating the time.

promptly at 4:12
arriving on track 14 at 6:10

;   The semicolon. When two independent clauses are closely related in thought, the author may want to include them in the same sentence. He uses a *semicolon* to separate them. If a connecting word or conjunctive adverb *(besides, however, nevertheless,* etc.) is used, a comma follows it.

History is not discontinuous; the frontiers of change remain blurred.

The language of art may be complex and varied; understanding may require an experience shared with the artist.

He is no longer a member of our chapter; in fact, he has been ousted from the national body.

The semicolon is used instead of a comma to separate very long coordinate clauses and phrases

such as this one; phrases where the use of the comma would be ambiguous; and in series of words or phrases where extreme distinctness is desired.

The only ones there were John; my son, Harry; the neighbor's boy, Joe; and the barber.

The most important books on the subject are A. I. Oparin, *The Origin of Life on Earth;* David Forsyth, *How Life Began;* and G. Ehrensvärd, *Life: Origin and Development.*

—   The dash is often used carelessly by writers. They let it trail the reader off into meaningless space or they use it interchangeably with the comma.

In her day—
She deserved something better than that—far better.
Yet that was not the end—a circle is endless.

The dash properly marks an unexpected turn of the thought or a sudden change in the construction or direction of the sentence. In narratives it may indicate faltering speech. It may indicate that a summing-up follows. Used in pairs, dashes may set off interpolations, something repeated for emphasis, or parenthetical matter. Notice how their use is distinguished from that of the comma and how they avoid ambiguity in sentences with comma series.

James Delmore, Jennifer West, and William McCaffrey—pedestrians at the scene of the crash—volunteered to give evidence.

Margaret read in the corner—placid, her head deeply bowed, lost—never noticing Bill's entrance.

"Do you—I mean do you really believe in predestination?" he asked.

italics   If the writer wants to call the reader's attention to something in a special way, he may use marks of punctuation whose special functions are to *emphasize.* The equivalent of printed italics in handwriting or typing is underlining; this is the conventional sign to the printer to print the words in italic type.

Notice the following examples:

For the Western visitor to Africa two things come upon him with surprise: *the discovery that all of Africa is not a jungle but has certain cities as cosmopolitan as New York, Rome, or Paris; the further discovery that some countries have a cultural heritage pre-dating that of the early Egyptians.*

In the preceding sentence, the two discoveries which are surprising to Westerners are italicized for special emphasis. The italics here have the effect of reinforcing for the reader the element of dumbfounded surprise. Use italics sparingly for special emphasis; their use can become an easy substitute for careful sentence structure and emphatic word order.

Foreign words and phrases, titles of books and magazines, letters of the alphabet, words receiving special emphasis, and words referred to as such are italicized.

"You mean the manuscript is with the printer already?" "Yes, the book is virtually a *fait accompli.*"
J. D. Salinger's three books—*Nine Stories, The Catcher in the Rye,* and *Franny and Zooey*—establish clearly his understanding of the problems of sensitive young people.
These endings, *d, t, ed, n,* and *en,* are common signs of the past participle of the regular verb.
The book did not tell us *how* to write essays, only *how we should not.*
The words *Scotch, Scot,* and *Scottish* vary in usage according to locality: *Scotch* comes from the dialect of the Midlands of Southern England; *Scot* and *Scottish* are preferred in Northern England and Scotland.

Certain words or phrases chosen for special emphasis should be enclosed in quotation marks rather than italicized. For these the emphasis is not so much a singling out for a special effect but rather a calling of the reader's attention to words or phrases which are being used apart from their normal significance.

I was born only a short distance from what Ozarkers—but only Ozarkers—call "mountains," the Boston Range in Arkansas.
Any political statement that is "farther out" than the context demands is open to question.
When the musicians "got in the groove" and "went to town," the audience at the Birdland jumped for joy.

In the last example, the writer uses quotation marks to indicate to the reader that he considers "got in the groove" and "went to town" to be colloquial or slang expressions, not normally used in formal writing.

, The comma is an important marker. One of the most frequently used internal marks of punctuation, it permits the writer to clarify his meaning, and aids the reader to understand the intentions of the writer.

Presented below are a few of the basic principles concerning the uses of the comma. Broadly speaking, these principles fall into two groups: (1) those in which the comma is used "to separate" and (2) those in which it is used "to enclose." It should be noted, however, that in journalistic writing and among writers in general, practices will vary. For you, the college student, understanding and application of the following rules will enhance your reading and writing.

Commas to Separate

1. The comma usually separates independent clauses[a] joined by one of the connecting words or coordinating conjunctions *and, but, or, nor, for, yet.* (When the clauses are short and closely related in meaning, or when the subject is the same in both, the comma is often omitted before the connecting word.)

London in 1851 inaugurated the tradition of the world's fair, and after more than one hundred years New York carries on the tradition with its fair of 1964–65.
[The comma precedes *and;* note the change of subject.]

Science has devised means of destroying the world, but the humanities must find ways of preserving man's heritage.
[The comma appears before *but.*]

Strauss wrote "Wiener Blut" and the Viennese rejoiced.
[Both independent clauses are brief and the connection between them is very close.]

I tried to understand but I failed.
[The subject remains the same.]

2. Where a dependent adverbial clause precedes an independent clause, it is customarily set off by a comma unless the clause is extremely short. Generally, if the independent clause comes first, no comma is used.

Although the Eiffel Tower survived to become the symbol of France's city after the World's Fair of 1889, at that time many Parisians became enraged at its ugliness and demanded that it be torn down.
[This rather long adverbial clause of concession introduces the sentence and a comma precedes the main idea.]

The students were asked to move near the front of the lecture room because there was equipment in the back.
[Note that the adverbial clause comes after the independent clause and that the comma is omitted.]

3. Three or more words, phrases, or clauses in a series are separated by commas.

Transportation to cut down cases of exhaustion include the short monorail, the thrilling Swiss cable car, leisurely guided tours, and jaunty strollers for children.
[The comma appears after each item in this series

[a] A clause is a group of words containing both a subject and a predicate. There are two kinds of clauses: (1) independent, main, or principal, and (2) subordinate or dependent. A writer may introduce a subordinate clause by the use of a subordinating conjunction (such as *when, than, because, while, since, unless, if*) or by a relative pronoun *(who, which, that).* Functioning as an adjective, adverb, or noun, dependent or subordinate clauses rely upon the rest of the sentence for their meaning.

of nouns with modifiers. Note that the comma before the conjunction is retained. Although some writers omit the comma before the connective, in formal writing the present practice is to use it.]

The purpose of the meeting is to anticipate difficulties, to avoid misunderstanding, and to plan the agenda.
[A series of infinitive phrases is used to complete the meaning of the subject.]

The ribbon was cut, the crowd surged forward, the exhibit was open.
[This series of independent clauses, limited in length and in meaning, is punctuated with commas. Notice, however, that the conjunction is omitted.]

4. Commas are used to separate coordinate adjectives that precede the noun they modify.

Relics of ancient, pre-Mosaic times are being uncovered today in Israel.
[By substituting *and* between the adjectives, you can test whether they are equal in rank. Also if you can change the order of the adjectives, you can determine whether they are coordinate. Note that the comma is never used after the last adjective.]
Falstaff is frequently depicted as a jolly fat man.
[In this example it would be unnatural to say "a jolly and fat man." The two adjectives are so closely related that they are not coordinate.]

5. Commas are used to prevent misreading of sentence elements.

When the Dean called Mary, Jane also left the dormitory.
[The order of this sentence can be changed to avoid confusion.]
Father bought some fertilizer, for the soil had been affected by the drought.
[The comma is used before *for* to avoid its being mistaken as a preposition.]
Before starting to eat, Gregory said the grace his mother had taught him.
[The noun *Gregory* might be mistaken as the object of the infinitive if a comma were not placed after *to eat.*]

6. Commas are used after an introductory modifying phrase that contains a verb form.

Possessing the drive of a dynamo and the vision of a Biblical prophet, the late John F. Kennedy made young Americans eager to give of themselves.
[The phrase "possessing . . . prophet" consists of an -ing form of the verb plus objects and modifiers. It is called an adjective or participle phrase and modifies the noun *John F. Kennedy*. Since it precedes the subject, it is set off from the rest of the sentence.]
The game being over, the students slowly left the stadium.

[The introductory phrase consists of a noun plus a participle. Although it modifies the entire sentence and not a particular word, it is set off by a comma.]

7. Commas are used to separate contrasting sentence elements.

One of man's chief problems today is communication, not transportation.
[The word *not* with the comma preceding it points to the contrast between communication and transportation.]
The more money we Americans make, the less satisfied we seem to be.
[These two contrasting clauses do not make sense alone, but together they form a complete idea.]

8. Commas are placed after mild interjections and sentence adverbs when they appear at the beginning of a sentence.

Goodness, I could hardly believe a writer would use that plot.
[Note comma after the word *goodness.*]
Yes, the college enrollments in this country are soaring, yet slightly more than a third of our high school graduates get to college.
[Note the comma after *yes,* a responsive word appearing at the beginning of a sentence.]

9. To separate numbers of four or more digits that do not designate years, telephone numbers, and house numbers, commas are used.

On some American television programs $375,000 is spent in less than a month.
If you telephone Taylor 1903, you will learn that the census figures for our city are 4,560,842.

Commas to Enclose

10. Commas are used to enclose *nonrestrictive* clauses and phrases within a sentence. They are not used to enclose *restrictive* clauses and phrases.

The Unisphere, which was built and presented to the World's Fair of 1964–65 by U.S. Steel, is made of 470 tons of stainless steel and is twelve stories high.
[The "which clause" of the first sentence is considered by the writer to be nonrestrictive and is, therefore, set off by commas. Its meaning is not essential to one's understanding of the independent clause or the sentence; it can even be eliminated without affecting the basic idea of the statement.]
As an example of the intricacies that construction of the Unisphere required, engineers solved with high-speed computers one problem that required 670 simultaneous equations.
[The "that clauses" are thought of by the writer as restrictive and are not set off by commas. Their

meanings are essential to one's understanding of the total sentence. They cannot be eliminated without affecting the meaning of the word *intricacies* and the basic idea of the independent clause beginning with *engineers*.]

The law school building, located on the east corner of the campus, was recently dedicated.
[Nonrestrictive]

The building located on the northwest corner of the campus is the library.
[Restrictive]

My brother Bill was there.
[Restrictive: I have two brothers.]

My brother, Bill, was there.
[Nonrestrictive: I have only one brother.]

11. Commas are customarily used to enclose words in apposition.

James Brown, the laboratory technician, has received a fellowship to study at the University of Heidelberg.
[James Brown is further identified by the word *technician*. Because this is additional information, it is set off by commas.]

The word *appositive* is a noun or pronoun used to limit, qualify, or supplement a preceding noun or pronoun.
[Note that commas do not enclose *appositive* because it is so close to the noun that the two are read as a unit.]

Any technical subject, for example, physics, should be read carefully for full comprehension.
[The appositive *physics* is introduced by *for ex-*

ample, which is enclosed by commas. Other words commonly used to introduce appositives are *that is, namely, for instance, such as*. With the exception of the latter, which is not followed by a comma, all of the words are usually enclosed by commas.]

12. Commas are used to enclose parenthetical elements of a sentence. Any expression that breaks the train of thought and does not materially affect the meaning is parenthetical.

Will you, if possible, make that reservation for the Philadelphia Symphony Concert early in September?
[Note commas before and after *if possible*.]

13. Commas are used to enclose nouns of direct address.

Never lose faith in your ability to learn something, Marjorie.
[At end of sentence]

We have witnessed, my fellow countrymen, a great tragedy.
[Within the sentence]

14. Commas are used to set off dates, addresses, and titles.

Every American will long remember Friday, November 22, 1963.

Mail the yearbook to the graduate who lives at 47 Wickersham Road, Mount Pleasant, New York 12457.

The guests featured on the program are James Olds, Ph.D., and Frank Carlyle, M.D.

EXERCISE 8: THE COLON AND SEMICOLON

PART I

DIRECTIONS: Each sentence makes correct use of the colon and semicolon. Study them carefully. What rules govern their use?

1. I thought a great deal about that decision; it was the right one for the family to make.

2. Before I knew all of the students in the class, I was frightened whenever I recited; but now, after three months and after making several friends, I find it easier to speak.

3. Strikes in the United States during the past decade are the subject of three novels: *Wild-Cat* by Carl Moses (1954); *Labor Marches On* by Robert Wyn (1960); and *The Pickets* by June Hooper (1964).

4. No one knew of the great loss of morale but Walter; he alone, therefore, could accurately record the results.

5. The parade of characters is long and sad: an adolescent estranged from his parents; a neurotic business-man; a psychiatrist who feels isolated from the world; and a co-worker who is hopelessly in love with him.

6. Skirting sentiment, the dramatist has created unique characters who have universal qualities; thus the play provides the audience with an entertaining and provocative evening.

7. At the end of the visit one of the students summed up the evening: we have learned more in three hours than we did in four years.

8. The elite will provide the following alternatives: bloodless revolution, immediate imprisonment, or instant death.

9. Foreigners often view American life as being topsy-turvy; therefore, tourists who go abroad should be aware of the image they create.

10. His conclusion is convincing: the population explosion must be controlled.

PART II

DIRECTIONS: Write in the colon and/or the semicolon correctly in the following sentences.

1. The editors are distinguished scholars their comments are timely and informative.
2. Most native families in South Africa spend all of their meager earnings their economic deprivation and the government's repressive measures produce hostility and rebellion.
3. The colonial record of the British and French in Africa is not all bad indeed, some of it is to be commended.
4. The body of Kierkegaard's thought is difficult for the beginning college student hence, his works are usually recommended to the advanced student.
5. In the Preface to the *Lyrical Ballads,* Wordsworth comments "Poetry is the breath and finer spirit of all knowledge it is the impassioned expression which is in the countenance of all Science."
6. The reader of this book can arrange the sections in whatever order he wishes the contents provide a wealth of information and entertainment.
7. The students have a real grievance the registration procedure is too time-consuming and unnecessarily complicated.
8. This is the theme of the book the soundest political instrument for any new nation depends upon the educational level of its populace.
9. The idea that the earth was once covered by water is an old one both Herodotus and Xenophanes had accounted for the remains of marine animals on dry land.
10. Conflict between Russia and China is not new a study of the relationships between the two nations will bring many revealing facts to light.

EXERCISE 9: ALL INTERNAL PUNCTUATION

DIRECTIONS: In the following passage, certain marks of punctuation are numbered. In the space provided below it, explain the use of these punctuation marks.

The *Transcript*[1] was celebrating its one hundredth anniversary when I went to work there. Its roster included upwards of a hundred persons under the heading Editors and Reporters, although on examination this category was found to include office boys,[2] telephone operators, and a fair number of individuals entirely unknown to the active news staff. In this latter group was a man who had contributed for several decades an anonymous column of witticisms which appeared weekly[3] — it may have been semiweekly —[3] on the editorial page. It had a title of its own, "Facts and Fancies,"[4] and it was a thoroughly competent piece of work,[5] but it is the simple truth that none of us had ever laid eyes on its author or heard his name;[6] the editor who had taken him on in the first place was long dead and gone,[7] and the "Facts and Fancies"[8] man,[9] who transacted his business with the cashier and never asked for a raise, was as near to a genuine nonentity as an active contributor to a daily metropolitan newspaper could be.*

1.

2.

3.

4.

5.

6.

7.

8.

9.

* From "The Boston Evening Transcript," *The Atlantic,* January, 1961. Copyright 1961 by Charles W. Morton, with his permission.

WORD ORDER

Having discovered the power of words and how punctuation clarifies word groupings, you must become aware of the structural relationships words can have to each other, inasmuch as a sentence is no more than words expanded into greater meaning through structure.

"I am living in a house white" should sound strange to you. Yet to place the adjective without stress after the noun it modifies is the regular pattern of Romance languages. And as Germanic in origin as English is, you will find quite peculiar "I will your children to the movie take," which is the normal pattern for German sentences.

The English language, like any other, adheres to certain conventions in its structure. A conscious or unconscious familiarity with this structure is necessary if you are to derive meaning from the sentence and be sensitive to any emphasis the writer has made. Variations in meaning can be achieved by structural variations, such as shifts in *word order*.

Not only do you unconsciously anticipate the position of adjectives and verbs, but you also are aware of shifts in meanings when words are rearranged:

She has plenty of money.
Money she has plenty of.
Plenty of money has she.

The first of these three sentences offers no problem of interpretation or emphasis. This is normal word order. The second suggests that she has plenty of money but probably nothing else. This word order is for emphasis and shift in meaning. The third seems to be constructed for its sound or rhythm rather than for any particular emphasis in the message it conveys; it might appear in a jingle.

The exercise that follows will help you become aware of shifts in meaning obtained by varying the word order.

EXERCISE 10: WORD ORDER

DIRECTIONS: Examine these groups of sentences. What changes in emphasis or meaning are effected by changing word order?

1. We gave Mother an electric blanket for her birthday last year.
    Last year, we gave Mother an electric blanket for her birthday.

2. "Black is the color of my true love's hair."
    My true love's hair is black.

3. Impudent is what she was.
    She was impudent.

4. While he was in training, he followed all the health rules religiously.
    He followed the health rules religiously while he was in training.

5. She has just come to the city for the conference.
    She has come to the city just for the conference.

6. He prepared lesson plans for only three of his classes.
    He prepared lesson plans only for three of his classes.

7. Only he prepared the lesson plan for his class.
    He only prepared the lesson plan for his class.

8. Often he and I used to sit here and read poetry to each other.
    He and I used to sit here often and read poetry to each other.

9. Personally, I don't want to insist on his continuing the violin lessons.
    I *personally* don't want to insist on his continuing the violin lessons.

10. A member of a family much honored in the community, she is beautiful, witty, and talented, too.
    A member of a family much honored in the community, she is too beautiful, witty, and talented.
    A member of a family much honored in the community, she too is beautiful, witty, and talented.

PARTS OF SPEECH AND MEANING

You have seen that words in sentences have denotations and connotations, and that the arrangement of the words signals particular meaning. But an obstruction to comprehension can be caused by the inability to determine the function of these words. It is of no avail to know that *work* means "useful or gainful employment" if you come across the expression *work shoes*. Does that mean shoes that are useful employment? That nonsense could never occur to you because you realize that in such an expression *work* is *saying something about* the shoes. In other words, the meaning of the noun *work* is different from that of the adjective *work*. *Work shoes* are thus those *used in* useful or gainful employment.

Knowing what the parts of speech are and that a word may be any part of speech depending upon *how it is used* is a good part of understanding the English language, which, in turn, is the whole of reading English.

Note the following sentences; without knowing what they mean, you are able to detect the functions of many nonsense words.

1. Let's dollobak the frest kolik.
2. They bekoved the minal on the skor slavon.
3. Panavy, they mulited the snates with roms.
4. In the freger, we snare our wegen because the storen bigs cnadon.
5. If the bakar dolds, we will pandu.

This is what we can gather about sentence 1:

a. You and I (and perhaps others) are to do something.
b. The something we are to do or the action we are to perform is *dollobak*.
c. The action is to be performed on the kolik.
d. The kolik is a frest kolik.
e. We are to dollobak now.

You can see that our knowledge of the structure of the language helps us in determining the function of words or their parts of speech. How does this help you in reading the following poem?

love is more thicker than forget*
E. E. CUMMINGS

love is more thicker than forget
more thinner than recall
more seldom than a wave is wet
more frequent than to fail

*Copyright, 1940 by E. E. Cummings. Reprinted from his volume, *Poems 1923–54*, by permission of Harcourt, Brace & World, Inc.

it is most mad and moonly
and less it shall unbe
than all the sea which only
is deeper than the sea

love is less always than to win
less never than alive
less bigger than the least begin
less littler than forgive

it is more sane and sunly
and more it cannot die
than all the sky which only
is higher than the sky

E. E. Cummings seems to take great delight in experimenting with language. He achieves artistic effects not only by disregarding conventional punctuation and spelling but also by using his own system of word classification. The very first line sounds strange to us:

love is more thicker than forget.

Whether we know the grammar of the sentence or not, we are aware of the fact that some words in this first line behave in a way quite different from what one normally expects. The word has a sense which is dependent on the way it is used—a contextual meaning. What is more, our ears are accustomed to certain word patterns in our language. Given the pattern,

love is more ____ than ____,

we can expect a relatively fixed number of responses. We could fill in two words such as *heartache/pleasure;* or *crying/sighing;* or *painful/pleasant.* After a verb such as *is,* there are only certain kinds of words which can complete the sentence correctly. The connecting link requires its joined members to be similar in function and structure. If it is intended to join *thicker* and *forget* in a comparative relationship, then we are given to understand that the two words belong to the same class. They perform the same function—that is, they name some quality of love. On the other hand, another pattern is possible.

love is more ____ than forget (is).

It is then possible to substitute such words as *durable, lasting,* or *eternal.*

Thus, we see how the parts of speech we use depends on the way in which the words are used in the sentence.

Naming Words: Nouns and Pronouns

Nouns name:

persons: Mr. Green, man, children, director, manager, saleslady, professor

places: New York, city, town, playground, America, house, Mt. Everest

things: books, pencils, radio, money, nickel

ideas: economy, conference, joy, freedom

actions: debate, exercise, walking, dancing, swimming (The -ing forms, called verbal nouns or gerunds, pattern in the same way as do concrete names for persons, places, things, and ideas. Notice:

The family is proud of her __.

The sentence can be completed by any one of the following: *managing, baking, acting, dancing, poise, talent, beauty.*)

Pronouns refer to:

person who speaks: I, me, my, mine, we, our, ours

person spoken to: you, your, yours

person or thing spoken about: he, her, it, him, its, his, hers, they, them, their, theirs

someone in the text immediately preceding: who, whom, that

something in the text immediately preceding: which, that

that which has been pointed out: these, those, this, that

indefinite reference: each, every, everyone, anybody, nobody, someone

Verbs: The Sentence Makers

Verbs:

tell what the subject does: go, begin, inform, write, shout, refer, exert, believe, elect

tell the condition or state of being of the subject: feel, seem, is, appear, become, grow

Describing Words: Adjectives and Adverbs

Adjectives: describe or modify nouns and pronouns answering:

what kind? red, solitary, ashen, gay, rotten, dressed, flattering

how many? much, less, dozen, few, lot, large

which one? in the red dress, near the fence[a]

[a] Prepositional phrases used as adjectives.

Adverbs: describe or modify adjectives, verbs, and other adverbs, answering:

how? carefully, in a hurry,[b] outwardly, decidedly

why? for the record,[b] for the baby[b]

where? in the yard,[b] at home,[b] under the table[b]

when? soon, often, in a minute,[b] tonight

to what degree? such, very, too

Connectives: Conjunctions, Prepositions, Interjections

Conjunctions: join sentence elements which are closely related.

Coordinate conjunctions join elements which are parallel in structure and in idea.

sugar, salt, *and* pepper

both boys *and* girls

over the river *and* through the woods

not my sister *or* my brother

not in terms of dollars *but* rather in terms of spiritual gains

we waited 'til she came *for* she was the one who invited us

Subordinate conjunctions make the logical connection between two elements in a sentence, one of which is dependent upon the other for complete thought and structure.

He will make the trip *although* his doctor advised him not to go.

We were reassured *because* his powerful sermon comforted our family.

Since he won't come to see us, we'll have to visit him.

Prepositions: form modifying sentence elements by connecting nouns or pronouns to the rest of the sentence. A prepositional phrase consists of the preposition and the following noun or pronoun called its object.

In the living room, *in* the room, *on* the table, *under* the chair, *near* the window, *beside* the hearth

Come *to* our house *for* a while.

Interjections: are usually introductory words showing strong feeling or emotion; they have no grammatical relationship to the other words in the sentence.

Oh! I can't believe that!

So, you want to be a teacher?

Heavens, I didn't imagine such a thing was possible!

[b] Prepositional phrases used as adverbs.

EXERCISE 11: PARTS OF SPEECH

DIRECTIONS: Note the italicized words in the following passage. How are they used in the sentences in which they appear? Enter them and their functions under the appropriate columns on the chart below.

Many people were shocked recently to learn that not all physicians are required to swear the ¹*Hippocratic* ²*oath* upon receiving their M.D. degrees. A ³*survey* of American medical ⁴*schools* showed that ⁵*about* one in four does not administer professional oaths of any kind. At a time when so many ethical problems, both old and new, are being hotly discussed in the field of medicine, is it possible that the Hippocratic oath has lost its value?

⁶*Certainly,* the ⁷*profession* appears to have grave doubts about the continued validity of the oath. In recent years, ⁸*there* have been many ⁹*attempts* to ¹⁰*modernize* or ¹¹*replace* it, ¹²*but* so far no alternative version has been able to command anything like general acceptance.

¹³*Despite* uncertainties about the authorship of the original oath (it is generally ascribed to Hippocrates, a famous Greek physician of the 5th and 4th centuries B.C.), ¹⁴*its* importance in the history of medical ethics is ¹⁵*acknowledged* by all. Here it is, in one of many translations:

¹⁶"*I* swear by Apollo Physician and Asclepius and Hygeia and Panacea and all the gods and goddesses, making ¹⁷*them* my witnesses, that I will fulfill according to my ability and judgment this oath and covenant:

"To hold him ¹⁸*who* has taught me this ¹⁹*art* as equal to my parents and to live my life in partnership with him, and if he is in need of money to give ²⁰*him* a share of mine, and to regard his offspring as equal to my brothers in male lineage and to teach them this art—if they desire to learn it—without fee and ²¹*covenant;* to give a share of precepts and oral instruction and all the other ²²*learning* to my sons and to the sons of him who has ²³*instructed* me and to pupils who ²⁴*have* ²⁵*signed* the covenant and taken an oath according to the medical law, but to no one else.

"I will apply ²⁶*dietetic* measures for the benefit of the sick according to my ability and judgment; I will keep them from harm and injustice.

"I ²⁷*will* neither ²⁸*give* a deadly drug to anybody if asked for it, nor will I make a suggestion to this effect. ²⁹*Similarly* I will not give to a woman an ³⁰*abortive* remedy. In purity and holiness I will guard my life and my art.

"I will not use the knife, ³¹*not* ³²*even* on sufferers from stone, but will withdraw in favor of such men as are engaged in this work.

³³"*Whatever* houses I may visit, I will come for the benefit of the sick, ³⁴*remaining* ³⁵*free* of all intentional injustice, of all mischief and in particular of sexual relations with both female and male persons, ³⁶*be* they free ³⁷*or* slaves.

"What I may see or hear in the course of the treatment or ³⁸*even* outside of the treatment in regard to the life of men, which on no account one must spread abroad, I will keep to myself, holding such things shameful to be spoken about.

"If I ³⁹*fulfill* this path and do not violate it, may it be granted to me to enjoy life and art, being honored with fame among all men for all time to come; if I ⁴⁰*transgress* it and swear falsely, may the opposite of all this be my lot."*

* From "Would Hippocrates Rewrite His Oath?" by Louis Lasagna, *The New York Times Magazine,* June, 1964. Copyright © 1964 by The New York Times Company. Reprinted by permission.

Word	Part of Speech	Function In Sentence
1. Hippocratic	adjective	tells what kind of oath
2. oath		
3. survey		
4. schools		
5. about		
6. certainly		
7. profession		
8. there		
9. attempts		
10. modernize		
11. replace		
12. but		
13. despite		
14. its		
15. acknowledged		
16. I		
17. them		

Word	Part of Speech	Function In Sentence
18. who		
19. art		
20. him		
21. covenant		
22. learning		
23. instructed		
24. have		
25. signed		
26. dietetic		
27. will		
28. give		
29. similarly		
30. abortive		
31. not		
32. even		
33. whatever		
34. remaining		

Word	Part of Speech	Function In Sentence
35. free		
36. be		
37. or		
38. even		
39. fulfill		
40. transgress		

EXERCISE 12: PARTS OF SPEECH

DIRECTIONS: The words below are selected from the passage in Exercise 11. Change each of them to another part of speech, identify its new function, and then use the new word in a sentence that demonstrates its meaning.

Word	New Word	Function	Sentence
1. survey	surveyed	verb	We surveyed the American medical schools and learned that about one in four does not administer a professional oath.
2. professional			
3. attempts			
4. acknowledged			
5. learning			
6. signed			
7. transgress			

EXERCISE 13: PARTS OF SPEECH

DIRECTIONS: Write original sentences in which the following words are used correctly.

1. shock *(noun)*

2. shock *(verb)*

3. command *(noun)*

4. command *(verb)*

5. regard *(noun)*

6. regard *(verb)*

7. art *(noun)*

8. art *(adjective)*

9. law *(noun)*

10. law *(adjective)*

11. original *(noun)*

12. original *(adjective)*

13. will *(noun)*

14. will *(verb)*

EXERCISE 14: PARTS OF SPEECH

DIRECTIONS: For the words given, supply derivative forms used as other parts of speech. (Some words may not have all forms.)

Verb	Noun	Adjective
teach		
require		
modernize		
administer		
violate		
fulfill		
continue		
command		
remain		
engage		

ELEMENTS OF THE SENTENCE

Once you become familiar with parts of speech, the next step, understanding elements of the sentence, is astonishingly simple although not at all unimportant. In reading, you search for meaningful units or groups of words in a sentence which seem to "go" together. The eye seeks out these units automatically. When confusion arises, it may not be difficulty with definitions but rather with determining the elements of the sentence that belong together and their subsequent relationship to another part. Punctuation can do some clarifying, as you have seen in "Punctuation and Meaning," pp. 27–31, but familiarity with sentence elements is equally helpful.

In the following "sentence" you should have no trouble defining the terms, but the meaning is obscure:

Snow sleep very always winter.

That obscurity is a result of your inability to relate in any meaningful way one word to another. No relationship can be established, however, until we know what we are looking for. What is the sentence about—the subject? What is being done to or by the subject—the verb? These and many other questions are automatic, if not articulated, when we read a sentence. To answer the question, we need to know the *basic sentence elements,* and, in turn, how they are related to each other.

Subject and Predicate

In English there are two basic elements of each sentence—the subject and the predicate. The subject is defined as the person, place, or thing that is discussed. It may be a noun, a pronoun, or a word-group (phrase or clause) that functions as a noun.

Students should study regularly.
[noun]
They attended class five days a week.
[pronoun]
To write a Broadway play was his dream.
[infinitive phrase]
That he traveled to many countries influenced his writing and reading interests.
[noun clause]

Though the subject varies in position, it is generally at the beginning of an independent or a dependent clause. Normal English word order places the subject before the verb, but often the verb comes before the subject, as in these sentences:

There must be twenty players on the reserve team.

[Declarative sentence with the subject–verb order inverted]
Get the professor a light for the lectern, please.
[Imperative sentence with the subject you omitted or understood]

Has he gone to the library for the book?
[Interrogative sentence with the subject separating the parts of the verb]
How lovely are the flowers!
[Exclamatory sentence with the subject–verb order inverted]

Subjects may be further classified into (1) the simple subject, composed only of the noun or its substitute, and (2) the complete subject, which includes the noun with its modifiers (adverbs and adjectives).

(A diligent college student) plans a program of study for the semester and follows the schedule.
[The simple subject is underscored; the complete subject is in parentheses.]

The predicate expresses something about the subject. It, too, may be divided into the simple predicate (the verb alone) and the complete predicate (the verb and its modifiers).

As an integral part of the predicate, the verb can be identified by these properties:

(1) Person
The form used to indicate the speaker, or first person (I *am,* I *think*); the person spoken to, or second person (you *are,* you *think*); the person spoken of, or third person (he *is,* he *thinks*).
(2) Number
The form of a verb that indicates one (singular) or more than one (plural). In English, except for the verb *to be,* the only verb ending which shows the property of person and number is that of the *s* added in the third person singular, present indicative. Of course, the subject, with which the verb always agrees, largely determines person and number.
(3) Mood
The property of a verb that shows how the writer or speaker views the action. English has three moods: *indicative, imperative,* and *subjunctive.*
The indicative mood states a fact or asks a question.
[School *began* the second Tuesday in September.]
The imperative mood expresses a command or request.
[*Ask* not what your country can do for you but what you can do for your country.*]

* From "Inaugural Address," by John F. Kennedy, January 20, 1961.

The subjunctive mood expresses doubt, a condition contrary to fact, a wish.

[He acts as if he *were* in a daze.]

(4) Voice

The property of a verb that indicates whether the subjects acts (active) or is acted upon (passive).

[I *drove* the Ford. (active voice)]

[The Chevy *was driven* by Ruth. (passive voice)]

(5) Tense

The property of the verb that denotes the time of the action. English has six tenses: *present, past, future, present perfect, past perfect, future perfect.*

Present tense indicates action is going on at present time.

[He *studies* and seldom *works* when school is in session.]

Past tense indicates an action completed in the past.

[Last summer the teacher *drove* to Boston for a vacation.]

Future tense indicates an action that will take place in the future.

[He *will appoint* the members of the committee at the next meeting.]

Present perfect tense indicates action started in the past and continuing into the present.

[The mathematics department *has worked* on the problem since last year, but *has* as yet not *presented* a solution.]

Past perfect tense indicates action started in the past and completed before some other past action.

[Last winter I saw a former classmate who *had graduated* the year before I did.]

Future perfect tense indicates action which will be completed before some future time.

[By the time this school term ends, they *will have written* ten papers.]

Generally speaking, verbs may also be classified according to their completeness of meaning in a given context. A transitive verb indicates action that goes from the verb to an object; an intransitive verb does not require an object.

Machiavelli broke the democratic traditions of the Greeks.
[Transitive]
With Machiavelli, the democratic traditions of the Greeks died.
[Intransitive]

Verbs that join two nouns or a noun and an adjective are called linking verbs. (See discussion of complements, pp. 55–56.) Those that *help* make the various forms of the main verb are auxiliary verbs. Together the auxiliary and the main verb constitute a verb phrase.

The students *were assembling* quietly in the auditorium to attend the memorial service.
[*were* is the auxiliary, *assembling* the main verb]

In every language, verbs have principal parts. The English verb has three principal parts: the *present tense* (present infinitive), the *past tense,* and the *past participle.* When you are in doubt about the principal parts of a verb, always consult your dictionary.

You will also note that in English, verbs are categorized according to whether they are regular or weak verbs, irregular or strong verbs. Regular verbs form their past tense and past participle when such endings as *d* or *ed* are added to the present infinitive:

to view — view, viewed, viewed

Fortunately, most new verbs that come into the English language are regular:

blitz, blitzed, blitzed
queue, queued, queued

Irregular or strong verbs form their past tense and past participle by internal vowel changes:

write, wrote, written
ring, rang, rung

A few irregular verbs have the same form for the three principal parts:

burst, burst, burst

Differentiation between Verbs and Verbals

Unless you are able to distinguish between verbs and verbals, your reading and writing will be seriously impaired.

Verbals are verb forms used chiefly as other parts of speech. They fall into three groups: the *infinitive,* the *gerund,* and the *participle.*

(1) The infinitive

The infinitive is the first principal part of a verb. It can stand alone, but it is usually preceded by the preposition *to.* It can serve as a noun, an adjective, or an adverb.

To eat is a great delight.
[As a noun, the infinitive here serves as subject of the sentence.]
To enjoy life is my only aim.
[As a noun, the infinitive here again serves as subject; at the same time it acts as a verb, taking the direct object *life.*]
I want *to go.* He can *go.*
[These are both infinitives serving as direct objects. After the verbs *can, may, must,* and sometimes *dare* and *need,* the infinitive is used as a direct object without the preposition *to.*]
I want something *to drink.*
[The infinitive is used here as an adjective modifying *something.*]

I came *to see* you.
[The infinitive here serves as an adverb, modifying *came,* and as a verb, taking *you* as direct object.]

Infinitives, like all verbals, have a time sense relative to the main verb of the sentence. The present infinitive indicates a time the same as, or future to that of, the main verb:

He planned *to see* you yesterday, but now he plans *to see* you tomorrow.

The perfect infinitive, which is formed by the infinitive of the auxiliary verb plus the past participle of the verb *(to have seen, to have been),* indicates a time previous to that of the main verb:

I am sorry *to have missed you* yesterday.

(2) The gerund
The gerund is the first principal part of a verb plus *-ing.* Because the present participle also ends in *-ing,* it and the gerund are frequently confused. But the participle functions only as an adjective and the gerund only as a noun. The gerund is used principally as a subject or an object.

Fishing is my favorite sport.
[subject]
I love *fishing.*
[direct object of the verb *love*]
The most fun *in fishing* is not always *in catching* fish.
[object of the preposition *in*]

(3) The participle
The participle has three forms: the *present,* the *past,* and the *perfect.* As an adjective, the participle can be modified by an adverb and can itself modify a noun or a pronoun. It sometimes functions also as a verb and can then take an object and be modified by an adverb.

The *trotting* horse paused as it neared the house.
[present participle, an adjective modifying *horse*]
A *shattered* cup lay on the floor.
[past participle, an adjective modifying *cup*]
Having fallen, the cup lay in pieces on the floor.
[perfect participle, followed by past participle *fallen*]

Hastily *driving* home, the student kept glancing at his watch.
[As an adjective, *driving* modifies *student;* as a verb, it is modified by the adverb *hastily*.]
A gourmet came *to inquire* about the exotic food the host served.
[An infinitive used as an adverb]

Complements

Within the predicate lie the verb and its complements, which we shall now consider in detail. The word *complement* actually means "to complete."

There are four kinds of complements: the direct object, the indirect object, the subjective complement (noun or adjective), and the objective complement.

(1) The direct object is the noun or pronoun following the verb that answers the question *what?* or *whom?* In other words, it names the receiver of the action of the main verb.

The Weddingtons sold their *house* only this morning.
One year from tomorrow we shall know *who will occupy the White House for the next four years.*
The family encourages *planning and working together.*

The italicized word, phrase, or clause completes the meaning of the main verb in each sentence. What did the Weddingtons sell? What shall we know? What does the family encourage? The word "house," the noun clause "who will occupy . . . years," and the phrase "planning and working together" are receivers of the action of the main verbs in their respective sentences.

Note where these parts appear in the frame below:

(2) The indirect object names, without the use of a preposition, *for whom* or *to whom* something is done. The indirect object always appears with a direct object, but the reverse is not true.

Give your country service.
         indir.   dir.
         obj.   obj.

I send you my best wishes for continued success.
     indir.   dir.
     obj.   obj.

Subject	Verb	COMPLEMENT Object
The Weddingtons	sold	house
We	shall know	who will occupy the White House
The family	encourages	planning and working together

(3) The subjective complement may be a noun, pronoun, or adjective. It completes the predicate and either renames or describes the subject.

The key date was *October 4, 1957.*

This change, in fact, became most *apparent* subsequent to Mr. Eisenhower's re-election.

Further, the problem for the candidates has become more *difficult* since Khrushchev came to visit.

The basic cause of the commander's frustration was the South's growing *reluctance* to see any aspect of slavery damaged.

He appeared *willing* to make a compromise.

The italicized words are clearly related to the subject in each sentence. October was the date; the change was apparent; the problem is a difficult one. After verbs such as *to be, to appear, to seem, to become* (called intransitive linking verbs), one

finds a word or group of words which are labeled the *predicate noun* or *predicate adjective.*

(4) The objective complement is a word or group of words that refers to the direct object.

The citizens elected Mr. Somers *Chairman* of the Grievance Committee.

Students in South America called him *foolish.*

The president made Jason *editor* of the newspaper.

The italicized words either rename or describe the object. After such words as *elect, choose, make, call, consider, appoint,* one frequently finds the objective complement. A comparison between the subjective complement and the objective complement can be made clear if one extracts the "key word" preceding the complement: *subject* or *object.*

Study the relationship between the parts of the frame:

Subject	Linking Verb	Predicate Noun	Predicate Adjective
The key date	was	October 4, 1957	
This change	became		apparent
The problem for the candidates	has become		difficult
The basic cause of the commander's frustration	was	the South's growing reluctance	
He	appeared		willing

Subject	Verb	COMPLEMENT	
		Object	Objective Complement
The citizens	elected	Mr. Somers	Chairman
Students in South America	called	him	foolish
The president	made	Jason	editor

The Predicate in Detail

By way of summary, let us look at a frame which presents the predicate in detail.

Subject	Verb	Object	Objective Complement	Predicate Nominative or Predicate Adjective
The parents	were			outraged
Our children	will be			good citizens
The results of this survey	are			encouraging
Speeding on the highway	causes	accidents		
We	painted	the chairs	green	
The student council	has appointed	Mary	secretary	

Phrases and Clauses as Sentence Elements

Expanding the simple subject or predicate is done through the use of related words, commonly called phrases and clauses. We have noted that a group of words without a subject and predicate is a phrase, and that one with the basic elements is a clause. You may also recall that prepositional and verbal phrases function as adjectives, adverbs, or nouns. Review these examples:

The building *with the dome* is the observatory.
[Prepositional phrase used as an adjective]

For an hour the orchestra played a modern symphony.
[Prepositional phrase used as an adverb]

The best time to concentrate is *in the morning.*
[Prepositional phrase used as a predicate noun]

To wonder about the glorious men and women of American history means that one has taken the first step in seeking knowledge of the past.
[Infinitive phrase used as subject of verb *means*]

Hearing again the familiar ring of his voice, one moves swiftly backwards in time to recapture the vitality and exuberance of the man.
[Participial phrase, modifying *one*]

Seeing their candidate appear on the flag-draped platform before them caused the delegates to come to their feet in a tumultuous ovation.
[Gerund phrase, subject of verb *caused*]

When the fire alarm was heard, the students did not stop *to pick up their books and papers.*
[Infinitive phrase, modifying the verb *did stop*]

In the same manner as phrases, dependent clauses augment the meaning of an idea. They also add to sentence variety and to emphasis. Study the following sentences, and, if necessary, refer to the footnote on p. 29.

My list, *which includes the Jefferson Memorial, the Lincoln Memorial,* and *the White House,* will guide you to memorials to the great presidents of American history.
[Adjective clause, modifying *list*]

That the work of Pierre L'Enfant and Benjamin Banneker in creating Washington, D.C., as the nation's capital has stood so well the passage of the years is the finest tribute to their vision and their skill.
[Noun clause, subject of verb *is*]

When one visits the re-created colonial town of Williamsburg, Virginia, one feels such a sense of awe at the forward sweep of history since the eighteenth century.
[Adverbial clause, modifying *feels*]

In longer sentences or more complex structures, the basic elements are not so evident. Other words intervene and momentarily delay the perception of the subject and the predicate. Study the following example and try your hand at analyzing it:

Nikos Kazantzakis was a Greek who knew as much about suffering and absurdity as those who carve the literary totem poles which celebrate those deities, but Kazantzakis was not himself a worshiper of revulsion and the dark: "My prayer is not the whimpering of a beggar nor a confession of love. My prayer is not the trivial reckoning of a small tradesman: Give me and I shall give you. My prayer is the report of a soldier to his general. . . ."*

* From "Jorge Guillén: A Poet of This Time," by Archibald MacLeish, *The Atlantic,* January, 1961. By permission of author.

EXERCISE 15: ELEMENTS OF THE SENTENCE

DIRECTIONS: The number of the sentence in the paragraph corresponds to the number in the exercises below. Follow each set of directions.

¹Summer is gone, and word comes to us from a lady at Squam Lake who found she had a sick hummingbird on her hands in October and—, ²well, this lady at Squam Lake had some success at luring and feeding hummingbirds in the warm months, and one of them didn't look quite right to her when it came to be fed, so she netted it and nursed it back to health. ³But by that time frost had arrived and all the other hummingbirds had gone South. ⁴This, however, was a determined lady. ⁵She put the hummingbird in a cardboard box with air holes in it and drove it over to the local airport. ⁶Here she found the pilot of a small plane that was about to take off for LaGuardia with a passenger list of three. ⁷She explained the situation to him and asked if he would be willing to turn the bird over to the chief pilot of a Florida-bound airliner. ⁸"Sure I will, lady," he said. ⁹"Those guys don't have much to do on that flight." ¹⁰She's certain the hummingbird arrived safely and got in touch with all its friends.*

PART I

DIRECTIONS: Select the subject, verb, and complements for each sentence in the paragraph above.

	Subject	Verb	Complement
1. a.			
b.			
2. a.			
b.			
c.			
3. a.			
b.			
4.			
5.			
6.			
7.			
8.			
9.			
10.			

* From "Birds," *The New Yorker,* Nov. 4, 1961. Reprinted by permission; © 1961 The New Yorker Magazine, Inc.

PART II

DIRECTIONS: List three clauses used as modifiers. Tell how they are used and what they modify.

1.

2.

3.

PART III

DIRECTIONS: List three prepositional phrases used as adverbs. What do they modify?

1.

2.

3.

EXERCISE 16: ELEMENTS OF THE SENTENCE

[1]The most obvious way to make a good impression, as everybody knows, is to adapt to the physical requirements of the particular culture at hand. [2]The cultural effect of eating other people's cooking—King George and the hot dog, Governor Rockefeller and the blintz—has long been understood, and the current study adds little to the pioneer thinking already done in this field. [3]The American abroad, however, may find himself presented with some pretty unpalatable concoctions, and *Working Effectively Overseas* does suggest some guidelines for dealing with such situations. [4]Under no circumstances should the American try, as one lady did, to stuff the food through cracks in the floor ("I was observed"). [5]If worse comes to worst, the PCV[c] may say that in our country fishheads are reserved for the ladies (if he is a man) or for the gentlemen (if the PCV is a woman). [6]This would be a low trick if an American of the opposite sex happened to be present, but the possibility isn't mentioned.

[7]Adapting to another culture may cost the traveler a good deal more than nausea. [8]"The American should adopt indigenous social forms and conventions when appropriate," we are informed, and customs, it turns out, can be just as difficult as fishheads to dispose of. [9]Sometimes, it is true, they can be fun—"The moments I enjoyed the most were those spent squatting down on my haunches Indian style"—but more often they raise prickly psychological and moral questions. [10]It's one thing to learn about a culture, or even to *seem* to appreciate it—steps that most handbooks, including those of the Army, suggest we take. [11]But it's quite another thing to get mixed up personally in native ways, as the more advanced texts would have us do. [12]For one thing, native ways are different. [13]"Fairness," for example, "is a function of each society's values." [14]Accordingly, "It may be fair to chop off a hand for stealing in one place." [15]Function or not, it's the sort of thing that could get a person down after a while, and though *Working Effectively Overseas,* like the studies that preceded it, throws in the towel when it comes to completely redoing the traveler's personality for his trip, it reminds him that he himself "will tend to judge others' behavior from his own cultural point of view."

[16]There are, however, certain merciful limits. [17]It is not necessary, for example, to permit a laborer to be beaten to death with a pole in your presence; nor in polygamous countries need one accede to the indigenous suggestion that he take on a few concubines. [18]In the latter case the American would do well to be ready with an "appropriate reason" for his refusal, since no good can come of compounding one rudeness with another.*

[c] PCV: Peace Corps Volunteer.

PART I

DIRECTIONS: Select from the above text an example for each sentence element requested below. Enter these in the appropriate spaces and tell how they function in the sentences in which they appear.

Element	Word(s) from Text	Sentence Number	Function in Sentence
1. Gerund			
2. Coordinate conjunction			
3. Infinitive			
4. Appositive			
5. Introductory adverbial clause			

* From "How to be an American Abroad," by Meg Greenfield, *The Reporter,* Dec. 7, 1961. Copyright 1961 by The Reporter Magazine Company.

Element	Word(s) from Text	Sentence Number	Function in Sentence
6. Intransitive linking verb			
7. Participial adjective			
8. Adjective clause			
9. Noun clause			
10. Prepositional phrase			
11. Conjunctive adverb			

PART II

DIRECTIONS: Select from sentences 1, 2, 4, and 8 the basic sentence parts and their modifiers.

Sentence Number	Subject	Modifiers of Subject	Verb	Modifiers of Verb
1				
2				
4				
8				

PART III

DIRECTIONS: Select from each sentence in the text listed below a complement of a main verb. Tell how it affects the meaning of the sentence.

Sentence Number	Complement	Function in Sentence
4		
5		
6		
7		
8		
9		
12		
13		
14		
15		

PART IV

DIRECTIONS: Select from each sentence in the text a connective which has the following functions:

Function	Connective	Sentence Number
To form compound direct object		
To join subject-predicate word groups to form compound sentence		
To include a subject-predicate word group within the sentence as a modifier		
To show alternative possibilities		

TYPES OF SENTENCES

Just as knowing the elements of the sentence helps you to know the relationship between one group of words and another, being able to identify certain types of sentences helps you to know the relationships between several complete ideas within one sentence.

When you wish to express an idea about one subject which is involved in one particular action or assertion, or about which one thing is said, this idea can be structured in what we call a simple sentence.

Consider the following sentences. (The subject has been underlined once, the verb twice.)

Our paths may never cross again.

My mother decided to have watermelon for dessert.

He is good at making a nuisance of himself.

Standing so close to the heat is dangerous.

Standing too close to the heat, he scorched his pants.

Now contrast these sentences with the following:

I am taking a job in India next year, and our paths may never cross again.

We had lots of ice cream in the refrigerator, but my mother decided to have watermelon for dessert.

Matthew gets on everybody's nerves; he is good at making a nuisance of himself.

In the first group of sentences, one thought was being expressed by the elements in each sentence. In the second group, each sentence combined two ideas into a logical unit. This type of statement which combines two or more similarly structured thoughts into a logical whole, is labeled a compound sentence. This combination usually results in a more effective expression of the ideas than if they are separated.

A third grammatical type of sentence, the complex, is one in which at least one complete sentence unit is made a subordinate element by means of special connectives.

Since (connective is a subordinate conjunction) I am going to take a job in India, our paths may never cross again.

Notice that what was once a complete sentence unit (I am going to take a job in India) becomes a dependent element with addition of the word *since*. Something must follow to give meaning to the condition now set forth.

Although (subordinate conjunction) we had lots of ice cream in the refrigerator, Mother decided to have watermelon for dessert.

Here again, the once complete unit becomes a subordinate element which depends on the rest of the sentence for completeness and meaning.

Sometimes an idea needs the expanse of a compound—complex sentence, which is simply a combination of the last two types.

Although we had lots of ice cream in the refrigerator, Mother decided to have watermelon for dessert, and watermelon is what we had.

It is unusual for Mr. Simms to be coming home at this hour; unless it's a holiday, he regularly takes the 4:30 train from Skyhill and gets into Rich Square at five.

The grammatical structure serves the writer as a means of ordering the ideas as he conceives them and wishes to express them. A simple sentence may suffice for many kinds of ideas and it need not necessarily be short.

Yes, I understand you completely.

I won't go!

This is madness!

I feel that this award was not made to me as a man but to my work—a life's work in the agony and sweat of the spirit, not for glory and least of all for profit.*

The compound sentence structure allows the writer to combine two or more closely associated ideas, usually parallel in structure, into one unit. Each part of the unit must be independent and must be able to stand alone under analysis.

The complex sentence provides a pattern for the subordination of elements in order to give importance to the main thought and balance to the structure. Study the following sentences:

Jim was rather quiet this evening. He didn't even play his new record.

Here the author intends that the force of Jim's mood be built up sentence by sentence.

Jim was unusually quiet this evening, for he didn't even play his new record.

The author now wants to show a causal relationship; one idea has bearing on another, and they can be fused into one unit successfully.

Since Jim didn't even play his new record this evening, I'm sure that there is some reason for his being so very quiet.

Here the subordinate conjunction *since* immediately establishes a causal relationship, and leads the reader to put more emphasis on Jim's quietness. Note how *quiet* is climactically placed at the end of the sentence.

* Adapted from William Faulkner's Nobel Prize Acceptance Speech. Reprinted from *The Faulkner Reader,* Copyright 1954 by William Faulkner (Random House, Inc.)

What is the difference in structure in each of the following? What is the effect of the structural difference on the idea?

1. I feel that this award was not made to me. It was made to my work.
   I feel that this award was not made to me but to my work.

2. Our tragedy today is a general and universal fear. This fear has been sustained so long that now we can even bear it.

   Our tragedy today is a general and universal fear so long sustained by now that we can even bear it.

3. He [the writer of today] writes not of love. He writes of lust. He writes of defeats in which nobody loses anything of value. He writes of victories without hope. He writes, worst of all, without pity or compassion. He writes not of love but of lust, of defeats in which nobody loses anything of value, of victories without hope and, worst of all, without pity or compassion.*

   * *Ibid.*

EXERCISE 17: RECOGNITION OF SENTENCE TYPES

DIRECTIONS: Write S for simple, C for compound, X for complex, CX for compound-complex in the blank space before each sentence. (Taken from William Faulkner's Nobel Prize Acceptance Speech.)

_____ 1. It will not be difficult to find a dedication for the money part of it [the award] commensurate with the purpose and significance of its origin.

_____ 2. But I would like to do the same with the acclaim too, by using this moment as a pinnacle from which I might be listened to by the young men and women already dedicated to the same anguish and travail, among whom is already that one who will some day stand here where I am standing.

_____ 3. . . . The young man or woman writing today has forgotten the problems of the human heart in conflict with itself which alone can make good writing because only that is worth writing about, worth the agony and sweat.

_____ 4. He must learn them again.

_____ 5. He must teach himself that the basest of all things is to be afraid; and, teaching himself that, forget it forever, leaving no room in his workshop for anything but the old verities and truths of the heart, the old universal truths lacking which any story is ephemeral and doomed—love and honor and pity and pride and compassion and sacrifice.

_____ 6. Until he does so, he labors under a curse.

_____ 7. His griefs grieve on no universal bones, leaving no scars.

_____ 8. He writes not of the heart but of the glands.

_____ 9. Until he learns these things, he will write as though he stood among and watched the end of man.

_____ 10. I believe that man will not merely endure: he will prevail.*

* _Ibid._

UNITY, COHERENCE, AND EMPHASIS

To struggle with the *idea* of a sentence is one thing—that's an intellectual challenge and one worthy of the keenest minds; but to struggle getting *to* the idea is quite another. Such a struggle discourages the reader and registers the writer's failure. A good writer can express the most complex idea, or convey the most subtle expression, so that the reader grasps precisely what he has in mind. The writer achieves such clarity by carefully relating each element in a sentence to all the other elements, and to the purpose of the sentence as a whole. The subordination of individual parts to a central purpose gives the sentence *unity;* the clear and logical relationship of one part of a sentence to the next gives the sentence *coherence;* and the relative importance or impact given to particular elements shows the use of *emphasis.* Though the well-wrought sentence will use these principles inseparably, it is helpful here to isolate them for close study. Chapters II and III will examine how these three principles operate in the paragraph and the whole work; here the concentration will be on their role within the individual sentence and the short passage.

Unity

A sentence shows unity when it is controlled by one dominant idea or impression. This singleness of purpose is achieved by the *elimination* of the irrelevant and the *subordination* of all relevant ideas and impressions to the central point. Unity depends upon consistent tone and appropriate diction.

Note carefully how everything in the following sentence contributes to the dominant idea.

During the whole of a dull, dark, and soundless day in the autumn of the year, when the clouds hung oppressively low in the heavens, I had been passing alone, on horseback, through a singularly dreary tract of country, and at length found myself, as the shades of the evening drew on, within view of the melancholy House of Usher.*

Dull, dark, soundless, autumn, clouds oppressively low, alone, singularly dreary, shades of evening—all of these words or phrases contribute to the eminently melancholy impression the House of Usher makes, and the touch of sadness and despair with which Poe wishes to begin his famous story. In writing, an author has an infinite number of *choices.* Poe might have chosen a brighter day, the springtime, or a more cheerful tract of country

with which to begin; clearly, such choices would have destroyed his unity, his singleness of effect. As a literary artist, Poe uses *images* to achieve consistent tone; but the prose of ideas requires an equally unifying effort, usually without the aid of such visual devices.

Note how each sentence in the following excerpt contributes to the unified focus of the whole:

We hold these truths to be self-evident, that all men are created equal, that they are endowed by their Creator with certain inalienable Rights, that among these are Life, Liberty, and the pursuit of Happiness. That to secure these rights, Governments are instituted among Men, deriving their just powers from the consent of the governed—That whenever any Form of Government becomes destructive of these ends, it is the Right of the People to alter or abolish it, and to institute new Government, laying its foundation on such principles and organizing its powers in such form, as to them shall seem most likely to effect their Safety and Happiness. †

In the first sentence, various statements that would otherwise have little relevance to each other are brought together as complements of the original statement, "We hold these truths to be self-evident." You will see the force of this unifying device if you rephrase the sentence without the word *that.* Notice how much of the impact is lost by having several short, loosely connected sentences, instead of a single, unified statement. The connection of the main idea to its subordinate elements is reinforced in the second sentence by the emphatic *that* which begins it; the unity of the two sentences is further established by their culmination in the final word, *Happiness*—the same word which ended the first sentence. Throughout the passage, subordination and repetition give unity to the thoughts being expressed.

In the following passage, note how the main idea, stated in the first half of the topic sentence in the form of a principle, is rephrased in the last half and illustrated in the second sentence by examples.

The practice of every art subjects the artists to some particular inconvenience, usually inflicting some malady on that member which has been overwrought by excess: nature abused, pursues man into his most secret corners, and avenges herself. In the athletic exercises of the ancient Gymnasium, the pugilists were observed to become lean from their hips downwards, while the superior parts of their bodies, which they overexercised, were prodigiously swollen; on the contrary, the racers were meagre upwards, while their feet acquired an unnatural dimension. ‡

The unity of these sentences depends upon the aptness of the illustrations. Clearly they demonstrate the initial principle.

* From "The Fall of the House of Usher," by Edgar Allan Poe.

† From *The Declaration of Independence.*
‡ Isaac Disraeli.

Unity is destroyed in a sentence when the central idea is not apparent, or when the sentence contains unrelated or irrelevant elements. Such flaws are often the product of incoherent relationships between the elements of a sentence.

Coherence

Note how the following sentences lack both unity and coherence. The product of their failure is ambiguity and obscurity.

John went to the store and he was eleven years old. [Which idea is central? Are the ideas related? *Could* they be combined in a unified, coherent sentence?]
My brother Bill came home for Thanksgiving and my sister Jane is a good tennis player.
[Note how the thoughts are neither related nor parallel. There is no logical connection between one idea and the next.]

The flexibility of our language allows for the use of various function words which help hold parts of the sentence together and show relationships between the parts. Coordinate conjunctions, for example, join together ideas of equal value to create the impression of:

1. Addition

    We waited *and* we worried.
    Then we all walked away, *and* we left your granddaddy there in his grave.

2. Contrast

    We won ten games this season, *but* last year we did not win any.
    Most of us went home for the vacation, *but* Frank had to remain and complete his experiments.

3. Alternation

    You're not to eat any fried foods, *nor* are you to have any chocolate.
    We can use this room to practice in, *or* we can go over to the studio.

Subordinate conjunctions, on the other hand, point out the relationship between sentence elements which are of unequal value. The less important ideas are subordinated by putting them into modifying phrases or clauses. Examples of words which indicate these relationships are:

Who

    We telephoned all the people *who* were on our lists.
    His grandfather, *who* had been a lumberman, would be missed by the boys at the camp.

When

    When Allen came into the room, suddenly everything became quiet.

Although

    We don't want a laundromat located in our neighborhood, *although* it may be a real convenience for some people here.

Because

    Because he was so insistent, we gave him permission to register a day later.

A gifted writer can manage the most complex relationships without obscuring his central purpose. Study the way in which Thoreau maintains coherent relationships between the various elements in this long, highly complex sentence.

Let us settle ourselves, and work and wedge our feet downward through the mud and slush of opinion, and prejudice, and tradition, and delusion, and appearance, that alluvion which covers the globe, through Paris and London, through New York and Boston and Concord, through Church and State, through poetry and philosophy and religion, till we come to a hard bottom and rocks in place, which we can call *reality,* and say, This is, and no mistake; and then begin, having a *point d'appui,* below freshet and frost and fire, a place where you might found a wall or a state, or set a lamp-post safely, or perhaps a gauge, not a Nilometer, but a Realometer, that future ages might know how deep a freshet of shams and appearances had gathered from time to time.*

Note first the way certain concepts and images have been combined in parallel constructions: *work* and *wedge; opinion, prejudice, tradition, delusion,* and *appearance; Paris, London, New York, Boston,* and *Concord; Church* and *State; poetry, philosophy,* and *religion,* etc. Then observe the visual movement of the sentence, downward until "we come to a hard bottom and rocks." This sentence is particularly brilliant in the way it translates places (Paris, London, etc.) into ideas by means of paralleling them to other ideas; and Thoreau often whimsically balances images in a series which appear to have little in common— *delusion* and *tradition, state* and *lamp-post*—as a way of implying ironic or real similarity. Most important for our purposes, without such *aids* to coherence as parallelism and consistent direction, this passage might have become unintelligible.

Emphasis

Authors give emphasis to words or ideas by strategically placing them in a sentence. Given the following details, for example—

* Henry David Thoreau.

He put on his uniform. He stepped into the yard. A little man was there. The man was sitting on the bench. He had white hair.

We can express these details in a variety of ways. Study the different emphases.

He put on his uniform and stepped into the yard. On the bench there he saw a white-haired little man.

After he had put on his uniform, he stepped into the yard where he saw, much to his surprise, a white-haired little man sitting on the bench.

The white-haired little man! There he was, sitting on the bench. I had just put on my uniform and stepped into the yard when I saw him again.

On the bench was sitting a white-haired little man. I had stepped into the yard after putting on my uniform, and there I saw him.

Study the emphases in each of the following pairs of sentences. Which, in each case, is more effective? Be able to explain why.

1. Not from chance but from art comes true ease in writing.
   True ease in writing comes from art, not chance.*
2. For fools rush in where angels fear to tread. †
   Where angels fear to tread fools will rush in.
3. It is divine to forgive, but it is human to err.
   To err is human, to forgive divine. ‡

The original version, in each of the above pairs, is a line of poetry. Note how stress and meter—the music of the line—affect emphasis.

* From "Essay on Criticism, II," by Alexander Pope.
† *Ibid.*
‡ *Ibid.*

EXERCISE 18: UNITY

The following passage is a purposefully distorted text. The sentence-unifying elements have been omitted. Notice how dull it is, how jerky the movement is from one idea to another, and how unity, coherence, and meaningful emphases are marred.

He sat with his grandfather in the yard on the white bench under the Camphor tree that summer. Now on this alien stone, the grandson remembered something. He remembered the first time he had known his grandfather. It was on a trip to Galveston. They went to Galveston to fish. The grandson was fourteen then. He was lonesome there with this little old graying limping stranger who was his grandfather. His grandfather was wild somewhere. The grandson could not surmise. He could only fear it. Who was this man tied to him by blood through his father? He strongly resembled his father. He seemed an alien. He did not seem a friend. The grandfather had sat on the rocks. He had drunk whiskey. The grandson fished. He did not talk much. The grandson felt that there was a constant toil of figuring going on in the old man. He looked out over the brown Gulfwater. His feet were bare. His shoes were on the rocks. One was crooked.*

PART I

DIRECTIONS: Here is the correct version of the text. See if you can explain the unifying effects of the italicized connectives.

[1]*As* he sat with his grandfather in the yard on the white bench under the Camphor tree that summer, and now on this alien stone, the grandson remembered *that* the first time he had known his grandfather was on the trip to Galveston *where* they went to fish — the grandson was fourteen — and how lonesome he was there with this little old graying limping stranger *who* was his grandfather and who was wild somewhere that the grandson could not surmise, only fear. [2]Who was this man tied to him by blood through his father *and* who, though he strongly resembled his father, seemed an alien, not even a friend. [3]The grandfather had sat on the rocks and drunk whiskey *while* the grandson fished; and *though* he did not talk much, the grandson felt *that* there was a constant toil of figuring going on in the old man *as* he looked out over the brown Gulfwater, his feet bare and his shoes on the rock, one crooked one by one good one.

*Sentence
Number*

1. As

   that

   where

   who

* Adapted from "Old Wildwood," by William Goyen, *The Kenyon Review,* Summer, 1955.

Sentence Number

2. and

3. while

though

that

as

PART II

DIRECTIONS: Select from this text the unifying devices listed below. Explain their effects. Refer to sentence numbers.

A. Subordination of a less important idea through the use of a subordinate clause.
B. Use of contrasting words and phrases.
C. Use of the semicolon to separate two structurally complete units which are closely related in thought.
D. Use of dashes to allow intrusion of a structurally irrelevant element which has a particular relevance to the sentence thought.
E. Use of adjective clause to include descriptive details.

A.

Sentence Number	Subordinate Ideas	Main Idea
1.	As . . . summer	the grandson remembered

B.

Sentence Number	Contrasting Words and Phrases

C.

Sentence Number	Semicolon to separate two related clauses

D.

Sentence Number	Dashes to allow for structural intrusions of ideas related to thought

E.

Sentence Number	Adjective clauses with descriptive details

EXERCISE 19: COHERENCE

DIRECTIONS: Include in a single, effective sentence each of the groups of facts below.

1. He sat down alone to read his letter. The postman had brought it an hour ago. It was in his mother's handwriting.

2. Grandfather's funeral was two days ago. The funeral was at home. There were many flowers.

3. He folded the letter and put it back in his pocket. He leaned back and settled himself on the stone steps. He thought about home and Grandfather.

4. His left leg was shorter than his right. That foot had some flaw in it. The shoe on it curled upwards.

5. It had been a long time since he had seen Grandfather. The last time was when he was on leave from the Navy. That was five years ago. He was twenty-one then.

EXERCISE 20: EMPHASIS

DIRECTIONS: Rewrite each sentence in Exercise 19 to emphasize the idea given below; put this idea in the main clause and subordinate the other ideas to it.

1. The postman had brought it an hour ago.

2. There were many flowers.

3. He thought about home and Grandfather.

4. The shoe on it curled upwards.

5. The last time was when he was on leave from the Navy.

REVIEW EXERCISE

DIRECTIONS: In the following exercise you will find sentences taken from a New York Times editorial.* As well as you can, analyze these sentences according to the principles previously discussed, and follow the directions given at the close of each statement.

PART I

Those who wrote the Magna Carta, and forced King John to seal it 750 years ago, labored better than they knew.

a. List the principal clause, the simple subject, and the simple predicate.

b. What are the subordinate clauses in the sentence?

c. What are the essential elements of each subordinate clause?

d. Comment on the internal punctuation marks in this sentence.

e. Describe this sentence as to grammatical type.

* From "Eternal Magna Carta," Editorial in *The New York Times,* June 27, 1965. © 1965 by The New York Times Company. Reprinted by permission.

PART II

Magna Carta was England's glory; but the barons, ecclesiastics and townsmen who drew up Magna Carta did not intend to be revolutionary, nor did they do anything but put down rights and privileges that had been accepted on behalf of "the community of all the land" for centuries.

a. List the principal clauses and each simple subject, simple predicate, and complement.

b. What are the subordinate clauses?

c. List the prepositional phrases and describe their use in the sentence.

d. Explain the phrase "the community of all the land."

e. Write a summary of the sentence.

PART III

They proclaimed no philosophy of liberty, except for their own rights.

a. List the simple subject, the simple predicate, and the complement.

b. What does this statement mean to you?

c. Describe this sentence as to grammatical type.

PART IV

Yet out of this document, so unexceptional in its terms for that age, came the parliaments, the jury systems, the constitutions, the determination to defy and overcome tyranny and bad government, and above all, the rule of law by which the free world lives.

a. List the principal clause and each simple subject, simple predicate, and complement.

b. What is the subordinate clause in the sentence?

c. Identify the verbals.

d. Comment on the internal punctuation marks in this sentence.

e. Write a summary of the sentence.

PART V

Here in the United States, our Constitution embodies principles that were in the Charter of 1215, and so does the United Nations Declaration of Human Rights.

a. List the principal clauses and each simple subject, simple predicate, and complement.

b. What is the subordinate clause?

c. What are the essential elements of the subordinate clauses?

d. Describe this sentence as to grammatical type.

e. Write a summary of the sentence.

PART VI

The men who met "in the meadow called Runnymede" put down at the end of the first clause that the "liberties written out below" were being granted "for us and our heirs forever."

a. Identify the principal clause and the subordinate clauses.

b. What is the function of each subordinate clause?

c. Explain the significance of the quotation marks.

d. What does this statement mean to you?

Chapter II

PARAGRAPH ANALYSIS

INTRODUCTION

If I do not forgive everyone, I shall be untrue to myself. I shall then be acting as if I were innocent of the same offenses, and I am not. I must forgive lies directed against me because so many times my own conduct has been blotted by lies. I must forgive the lovelessness, the hatred, the slander, the fraud, the arrogance which I encounter, since I myself have so often lacked love, and have hated, slandered, defrauded and been arrogant. And I must forgive without noise and fuss. In general, I do not succeed in forgiving fully; I do not get as far as being always just. But he who wishes to live by this principle, simple and hard as it is, will know the real adventures and triumphs of the soul.*

As you read the previous paragraph, its central thought should have been obvious to you. Although the thought is expressed in personal terms, it should also be evident that it applies to all humanity, not just to the author. However, if you discovered only these obvious aspects of the paragraph, your skills are not sufficient for effective, comprehensive reading. You should also be able to analyze its ideas, perceive its implications, recognize its pattern of development, and determine its tone. Only when you possess this complexity of reading skills will your reading efforts be rewarded with a thorough understanding of the author's thought and a clearer insight into his attitude toward the subject.

In the preceding chapter your concern was with analyzing sentences. Now you will be expected to build upon this knowledge to see how sentences interact in a paragraph to expand its thought. Later, as you progress to analysis of whole selections in which many paragraphs interact to expand and develop the theme, your mastery of the techniques of analyzing paragraphs presented in this chapter will be an indispensable aid to your more comprehensive reading.

In the following pages your guide to paragraph reading is divided into five steps: (1) Getting the Main Thought; (2) Recognizing the Principles of Unity, Coherence, and Emphasis in the Paragraph; (3) Understanding Types of Paragraphs; (4) Learn-ing Methods of Paragraph Development; and (5) Interpreting an Author's Tone. Facilitating your comprehension of these steps are explanations that include both definitions and illustrations. At the end of each section are exercises which will allow you to test your skill in applying what you have learned. Also included are supplementary activities that will enable you to relate the principles of paragraph reading to your writing.

ELEMENTS OF THE PARAGRAPH

What is a paragraph? The common (and a generally correct) reply is that a paragraph is a group of related sentences which express a complete thought. But if "express a complete thought" is taken to mean that the main thought is literally in one sentence or another, then such a definition is inadequate. Some paragraphs—narrative and descriptive, for example—may not conform to this definition. Such nonconforming types will be discussed later. But the fact that they do exist, and are frequently used, makes it obvious that a more inclusive definition of a paragraph is necessary. Let us rather think of a paragraph as a basic unit of thought, implied or stated, which employs related sentences as a vehicle of communication.

If you fail to recognize the main thought, or to gain clear concepts of what related sentences are, you will not really understand paragraphs. The ability to recognize main thoughts, topic sentences, and key words will help you to see clearly the role of supporting details. This power of comprehension is probably best acquired by an understanding of the definitions and functions of these elements, by an awareness of how they interact to unify and connect ideas; and finally, through exercises in which you apply this knowledge to the analytical reading of paragraphs.

Main Thought

If you were to enter a room in which your friends were conversing, you would most likely ask them

---

* From "Your Second Job," by Dr. Albert Schweitzer, as told to Fulton Oursler, *The Reader's Digest,* Oct., 1949. Copyright 1949 by The Reader's Digest Association.

what they were talking about. Once they had answered, you would still want to know the specific context of the subject under discussion before you joined the conversation. To be told, for example, that your friends were talking about politics would not be enough. Your comments on current political practices in America would be inappropriate if your friends were considering the politics of another country or another period. Therefore, you would need to know what was being discussed and in what context, in order to become familiar with the main thought of the conversation. Once these questions had been answered, you would be able to follow the details of the discussion with little difficulty.

This situation of discovering the main thought of a conversation is comparable to the one you face in reading, and to some extent may be solved in the same fashion. Whether you are reading a short unit of thought, such as a paragraph, or a larger unit, such as an essay or a chapter in a textbook, you can discover the substance of the unit by asking, "What is this about? How has the subject been limited, qualified, or defined?" The answer you receive through reading the unit is the main thought in its specific context. When you have grasped the thought and its context, you will be able to identify the elements of the unit and see how they function and interact to develop the thought.

Topic Sentence

After you have grasped the main thought of a paragraph, finding the topic sentence is relatively simple: merely ask yourself, "Which sentence best expresses this thought?" The one that answers this question is the topic sentence. Although many paragraphs have such a topic statement, some do not: narrative paragraphs, in which an incident is related; descriptive, in which a picture is painted; paragraphs in which the thought is implied; and the rare paragraphs which present a series of details or examples for the development of an idea mentioned in a previous paragraph. In addition, you may occasionally find a paragraph in which the topic sentence has been divided between two sentences, i.e., part of the thought appears in one sentence and the remainder in another.

Many writers prefer to begin with the topic sentence, with details following. Being aware of this preference will greatly aid you in developing rapid reading, though it should not be assumed that all paragraphs follow this order. For emphasis or effect, some writers occasionally place the details first, with the main thought appearing in a summarizing statement at the end. In a few instances the main thought may be expressed in the middle of the paragraph, or it may be divided so that part of the

thought appears near the beginning and the other part comes later. But these cases are rare. Most paragraphs will have the main thought expressed in the first or second sentence.

Key Words

Some words in a paragraph merely provide fluency and coherence to the thought; others, such as transitional words or phrases, connect specific ideas; but a few words are really vital to the thought. Such words as the subject, qualifiers, and complements that are essential to the thought of a sentence are called *key words*. Particularly important in a topic sentence, they are guideposts not only for communicating the main thought of the paragraph, but also for coordinating the other sentences. The ability to distinguish these words from the others in the sentence will assist you in seeing the relevancy of the supporting details. (Throughout this chapter, whenever key words are discussed, we will be referring to the key words of the topic sentence.)

Supporting Details

The sentences in a paragraph which develop the thought of the topic sentence supply the specific ideas or supporting details. These illustrative details reinforce the thought by allowing for more meaningful generalizations, offering evidence to support conclusions, or providing ways to apply the thought to other situations. To be relevant in a paragraph, the supporting details must develop the key words of the topic sentence. For recognizing the relationship of supporting details to the topic sentence, ask this question: "How do these details or ideas expand the main thought?"

Inferences

An inference is an idea which is not directly stated, but which you derive by reasoning from the given facts or premises, or by "reading between the lines." The author (or speaker) implies; the reader (or listener) infers. When we listen, the speaker's tone of voice and gestures often aid us in acquiring suggested ideas; when we read, the author's choice of words is our basis for gleaning them. An inference is often based on connotative meanings of words, or ideas suggested by an allusion, metaphor, or simile—since these are excellent devices for investing a comment with additional meaning. When Hamlet sharply replies to Claudius' "How is it that the clouds still hang on you?" by saying ". . . I am too much i' the sun," he implies many things. He may mean that he is *son* to too many people—his father, the dead king, and now his mother's new husband whom he fiercely dislikes; he may mean that there is too much light, too much scrutiny upon him and his acts; or he may mean that his thoughts are not "cloudy" but too bright and sharp. Sometimes, of course, we are led astray by an idea the writer did not intend to imply. This is a particular danger when interpreting imaginative literature. But we must chance the risk, for good comprehensive reading requires an understanding of both stated and implied ideas.

Conclusions

A conclusion is not a bald repetition of the main thought or the topic sentence; neither should it introduce a new thought. Though it may be stated or implied, a conclusion should be a natural summation or consequence of what has previously been developed; a conclusion is the logical result of all that has been said or implied in the whole unit about the main thought. If a conclusion has been explicitly stated, it is complete within itself; if the conclusion is implied, it is helpful to ask, "If this is true, what else does it tell me?"

Having briefly defined the elements of a paragraph and indicated the structural relationship existing between them, we are ready to attempt a critical analysis of the whole that these elements have produced. Surface interpretations will not suffice: we must delve deeply into the paragraph and find suggested or implied meanings or ideas. The following questions will serve as a guide for discovering both explicit and implicit content:

Main Thought	1. What is the main thought of the paragraph?
	2. How is this thought limited, qualified, or defined?
Topic Sentence	3. Is this thought expressed in one sentence?
	4. Which sentence best expresses it?
Key Words	5. What words are vital to this thought?
Supporting Details	6. What specific details contribute to the development of the thought?
Inferences	7. What inferences can we draw from the paragraph?
Conclusions	8. What conclusions are explicitly stated, and what conclusions can we reasonably draw?

To gain a better understanding of the relationship among the elements of a paragraph, you must practice paragraph analysis. The example below will show you how the above questions can be applied to the exercises which follow.

Although commonly thought to be one of man's greatest deep-sea enemies, the octopus is generally a harmless scavenging animal that rarely assaults man. There have been some incidents in which octopuses have attacked divers, but even these scattered accounts have been exaggerated. Victor Hugo is said to have originated the idea of the octopus being a dangerous predator. In his *Toilers of the Sea* he described how this devilfish eats a human being. The tale became so popular that other novelists, and later the movies, used episodes which depict a man struggling in the arms of this marine monster, and thus the misconception of the octopus as a vicious, merciless killer was spread.

ANALYSIS:

(Main Thought)

1. What is this about — most broadly conceived, the octopus
2. How is this thought limited? — confined to a discussion of the fallacy that the octopus is an enemy to man

(Topic Sentence)

3. Is this thought stated? — yes
4. Which sentence best states it? — the first

(Key Words)

5. What words are vital to this thought? octopus, generally, harmless, (to) man

(Supporting Details)

6. What specific details contribute to the development of the thought?
   (a) Those that narrow the topic idea (second sentence)
       (1) Incidents of attacked divers
       (2) Accounts greatly exaggerated
   (b) Those that give evidence about the fallacy (third and fourth sentences)
       (1) Originator, Hugo
       (2) Adoption and dissemination by other writers

(Content: Inferences)

7. What inferences may we draw?
   (a) That Hugo was a very effective writer
   (b) That Hugo and other writers were not sufficiently familiar with the habits of the octopus

(Content: Conclusions)

8. What conclusion may we reasonably draw? That if the writer is correct, we should stop thinking badly of the octopus.

A cursory glance at the paragraph would indicate that answers to questions about the main thought, topic sentence, key words, and supporting details came from explicit statements. But how we derived the inferences and conclusion may not be clear. Let us take these answers individually and go carefully through the paragraph in order to point out what *stated* information was useful.

Inference (a): that Hugo was a very effective writer. Even if you did not know from prior information that Hugo was a writer, the reference to Hugo's *Toilers of the Sea* should be an adequate index. Since Hugo is the only person named in this paragraph, the words "other novelists" tell you that Hugo himself was a novelist—or, as we phrased it, a writer. With regard to his effectiveness as a writer, this point is supported by noting the popularity of Hugo's story about a "vicious, merciless killer," the octopus. If Hugo launched this fallacy which is still accepted as fact, his effectiveness as a writer is still indisputable.

Inference (b): that Hugo and other writers were not sufficiently familiar with the habits of the octopus. The paragraph states that Hugo, other novelists, and later the movies helped to spread the misconceptions about the octopus. We also know from the first sentence that there was a dearth of knowledge about the true habits and nature of the octopus, for many people apparently believed what was written in stories about these marine creatures. Therefore, we may assume either that Hugo and the other novelists were also unfamiliar with the habits of the octopus or that they deliberately took advantage of the public's ignorance. Since we have no evidence of such deliberate attempts, we must infer that they were as ignorant of the facts as the general public was.

Conclusion: If the writer is correct, we should stop thinking badly of the octopus. First of all, we must qualify our conclusion by saying "*if* the writer is correct" because we have not been given any proof to substantiate the writer's claim. But if we grant that his source of information is more authoritative than Hugo's, a logical reaction to what he has written about Hugo and the octopus should be a change in attitude toward the maligned animal.

This paragraph about the octopus was relatively simple. If you were able to follow the analysis of it without undue difficulty, you may want to see this procedure used with textbook material similar to that you are frequently assigned to read. Let us take a more complex paragraph from a biological science textbook and apply this analysis to it.

Metamorphosis occurs most conspicuously also among the amphibians, where an aquatic stage gives way to the terrestrial mode of life. In the frogs and toads, this involves replacement of gills with lungs, of a swimming tail with leaping legs, of herbivorous or omnivorous habits and a long, much coiled intestine, with carnivorous habits (and extensile tongue, improved vision and other sensory changes) and a shortened intestine, and many more fundamental alterations in physiological mechanisms and structural details. In newts and salamanders the changes are less pronounced, but like the frogs and toads, the acquisition of adult characteristics includes not only functional reproductive organs and related behavior, but also the development of a characteristic pattern in the pigmentation of the skin.*

ANALYSIS

(Main Thought)

1. What is this about?—metamorphosis
2. How is this thought limited?—confined to a discussion of metamorphosis among amphibians; specifically, toads, frogs, newts, and salamanders.

(Topic Sentence)

3. Is this thought stated?—yes
4. Which sentence best states it?—the first

(Key Words)

5. What words are vital to this thought?—metamorphosis, amphibians

(Supporting Details)

6. What specific details contribute to the development of the thought?
   (a) Metamorphic process in frogs and toads
       (1) Replacement of aquatic organs with terrestrial organs (sentence 2)
       (2) Other fundamental alterations (sentence 2)
   (b) Metamorphic process in newts and salamanders
       (1) Change less pronounced (than in frogs and toads)
       (2) Acquisition of adult characteristics (sentence 3)

(Content: Inferences)

7. What inferences may we draw?
   (a) That metamorphosis occurs among some organisms other than amphibians
   (b) That frogs, toads, newts, and salamanders are amphibians
   (c) That young frogs and toads in the aquatic stage bear little or no resemblance to the way they will look in adulthood
   (d) That there is a relationship between eating habits and the length of the intestine

(Content: Conclusions)

8. What conclusion may we reasonably draw? That metamorphosis involves internal and external changes which result in a significant difference between an adult organism and its young.

* From *The Biotic World and Man* by Louis J. Milne and Margery J. Milne. © 1958. Prentice-Hall, Inc., Englewood Cliffs, N.J.

In case these inferences and conclusions are still puzzling you, here is an explanation of how they were drawn from the paragraph:

Inference (a): that metamorphosis occurs among some organisms other than amphibians. We may infer this because the first statement tells us that "metamorphosis occurs most conspicuously *also* among the amphibians." The "also" is the basis for our knowing that metamorphosis is not restricted to amphibians.

Inference (b): that frogs, toads, newts, and salamanders are amphibians. The justification for including details about frogs, toads, newts, and salamanders in this paragraph is that they are amphibians and undergo a conspicuous metamorphosis during their transition from the aquatic stage to a terrestrial mode of life.

Inference (c): that young frogs and toads in the aquatic stage bear little or no resemblance to the way they will look in adulthood. According to the paragraph, the maturing frogs and toads will make noticeable changes in such overt characteristics as structure, coloring, and behavior. Since these are the prime bases for resemblance, radical changes in them will eliminate any external similarities between an adult of a species and its young.

Inference (d): that there is a relationship between eating habits and the length of the intestine. We may infer this because the paragraph states that during the aquatic stage when the frogs and toads are herbivorous or omnivorous, they have a long much-coiled intestine; when, in the terrestrial stage, they are carnivorous, they have a shortened intestine. Since the changes in eating habits and the length of the intestine occur at the same time, this relationship suggests that the need for a particular type of intestine is dependent upon the kind of food that will be required for existence, or vice versa. (Likewise, as the frogs and toads adopt carnivorous habits, the appearance of an extensile tongue, improved vision, and other sensory changes points to a relationship.)

Conclusion: Metamorphosis involves internal and external changes which result in a significant difference between an adult organism and its young. Although this paragraph is restricted to metamorphosis among certain amphibians, it provides a basis for ascertaining that metamorphosis occurs conspicuously in organisms other than amphibians — inference (a). It also gives a clear description of the extensive changes that are considered conspicuous. When we put these facts about metamorphosis together, we can conclude that whenever it takes place, the result is a marked physiological and structural change in the organism.

If you are a science or mathematics student, you may think that this kind of analysis will not work with paragraph reading in your more advanced textbooks. But it will! As a matter of fact, because of the inherently technical character of such books (i.e., about chemistry, physics, zoology, algebra, calculus, etc.), generally the main thought is clearly stated in an introductory clause or phrase, or in a topic sentence; often this main idea is italicized. The details which are also given with equal clarity are frequently numbered.

In the exercises which follow, you will analyze paragraphs on literary and scientific topics. Since the exercises are arranged according to levels of difficulty, you should read the paragraphs carefully, answer the questions, and check your results before proceeding. If necessary, reread the two examples included in this chapter and review the procedures for determining the main thought, details, inferences, and conclusions.

EXERCISE 1: THE MAIN THOUGHT

(LEVEL OF COMPREHENSION: EASY)

DIRECTIONS: Below each of the following paragraphs are questions about the main thought. Indicate your answer by circling the letter you think is correct.

PART I

The most remarkable weapon invented by primitive man was the boomerang, used by the natives of Australia. It is made of hard wood bent into a curve over a bed of hot coals. It is from two to four feet long, flat on one side and rounded on the other, with a sharp edge. There are several kinds of boomerangs—for war, for hunting and for amusement—varying in size and proportion. The well-known "return" boomerang is chiefly used as a toy. Instead of going straight forward, it slowly rises in the air, whirling around and around in a curved line until it reaches quite a height, when it begins to fly back again and, sweeping over the head of the thrower, falls behind him. This surprising motion is produced by the action of the air on the bulging side of the boomerang. The other types are effective weapons because of their size and irregular motion, but they do not return to the thrower. The natives show remarkable skill in the use of this weapon; it is said that with it they can cut a small animal almost in two at ranges within 400 feet.*

1. The main thought of this paragraph is:
   (a) the natives of Australia are remarkable
   (b) the boomerang is a remarkable weapon
   (c) primitive man invented many weapons
   (d) the boomerang is an excellent toy

2. The thought is limited to:
   (a) a discussion of the natives of Australia
   (b) the uses of the boomerang in hunting
   (c) weapons invented by primitive man
   (d) a description of the boomerang and its uses

3. The topic sentence is:
   (a) the first
   (b) the last
   (c) the second
   (d) implied

4. The subject of the first sentence is:
   (a) weapon
   (b) man
   (c) boomerang
   (d) natives

5. The key words are:
   (a) remarkable weapon
   (b) primitive man
   (c) boomerang
   (d) all of the above

6. The supporting details offer:
   (a) a description, and the uses of the boomerang
   (b) details of how to make a boomerang
   (c) details of how the boomerang is used in war
   (d) a description of native life in Australia

* From *Experiences in Reading and Thinking* by Stella S. Center and Gladys L. Persons, copyright 1940 by The Macmillan Company.

7. According to the paragraph:
    (a) all boomerangs return to the thrower
    (b) the "return" boomerang is used in hunting
    (c) boomerangs vary in proportion
    (c) all of the above

8. The irregular motion of the boomerang is caused by:
    (a) the bending of the hard wood
    (b) the varying sizes and proportion of boomerangs
    (c) the whirling of the wind on the sharp edge
    (d) the air acting on the rounded side

9. We may infer that:
    (a) the boomerang cannot be used in ranges of less than 400 feet
    (b) the boomerangs used for hunting and those used for war differ in size and proportion
    (c) the boomerang is the only weapon invented by primitive man
    (d) the natives of Australia have no other weapons

10. We may conclude that:
    (a) the irregular motion of the boomerang makes it a remarkable weapon
    (b) the skill the natives show in using the boomerang makes it a remarkable invention
    (c) the wood used for making the boomerang is found only in Australia
    (d) only the "return" boomerang has an irregular motion

PART II

Geometry is the branch of mathematics which deals with the properties of space. It is one of the principal branches of mathematics. The word "geometry" is derived from the Greek and means "earth measurement." It is in the application of the subject, as illustrated by its name, that the science originated. The Egyptians had to determine boundary lines which were washed away by the frequent floods of the Nile River and for this purpose invented a crude sort of surveying. Discovery of Babylonian inscriptions and Egyptian papyri has extended our knowledge of early geometry. As early as 1700 B.C., Ahmes, an Egyptian scribe, wrote a mathematical treatise containing a number of geometric rules. The Greeks did a great deal to advance the science of geometry by developing many of the famous proofs. For many years Greeks went to Egypt to study and when they returned home they created a great interest in the study of geometry. New truths were discovered, a system developed and geometry became a science.*

1. The main thought is about:
    (a) the Egyptians
    (b) Ahmes
    (c) Geometry
    (d) the Greeks

2. The thought is limited to:
    (a) the early Egyptian civilization
    (b) the mathematical treatise of Ahmes
    (c) the meaning and origin of geometry
    (d) the flooding of the Nile River

3. The topic sentence is:
    (a) the first
    (b) the last
    (c) the second
    (d) the third

* Adapted from *Mathematics*, Encyclopaedia Britannica Home Reading Guide. By permission of publisher.

4. The key words are:
   (a) mathematics, properties of space
   (b) truths, system, science
   (c) principal, mathematics
   (d) "earth measurement," application

5. How do the supporting sentences contribute to this thought?
   (a) They give the origin of mathematics.
   (b) They describe the early civilization of Egypt.
   (c) They illustrate some of the proofs of geometry.
   (d) They give the history of the invention and development of geometry.

6. Geometry was invented by:
   (a) the Greeks
   (b) the Egyptians
   (c) the Babylonians
   (d) Ahmes

7. We may infer that:
   (a) geometry was invented prior to 1700 B.C.
   (b) the Egyptians did not have a name for geometry
   (c) the Greeks had no practical need for geometry
   (d) all of the above

8. We may also infer that:
   (a) the Egyptians were already familiar with some mathematical principles
   (b) there may be some historical connection between Egypt and Babylon
   (c) surveying involves the application of geometric principles
   (d) all of the above

9. The passage definitely states that:
   (a) the Egyptians went to Greece to study
   (b) the Babylonians went to Egypt to study
   (c) the Greeks developed many of the geometric proofs
   (d) all of the above

10. We may conclude that the establishment of a science requires:
   (a) an illustrative application of the subject
   (b) discovery of ancient inscriptions and treatises
   (c) the development of rules, truths, proofs, and a system
   (d) all of the above

PART III

It is in Germany that the art-song reached its greatest development. After the Reformation, secular music in Germany did not play a very large role until the 18th century. A number of composers had written songs before this time, among them Telemann, Agricola, Reichardt, and Johann Sebastian Bach's son, Karl Philipp Emanuel Bach, but the real outburst of song did not come until it was inspired by the poetry of Goethe and Schiller. Haydn, Mozart and Beethoven all wrote songs, but it was not in this form of music that they showed their greatest genius. With the publication of the *Erlkönig* (Erl-King) in 1815, by Franz Schubert, then a boy of 18, the lyrical song reached a perfection which many critics say has never been surpassed. Schubert has been called the greatest song writer of all ages and his settings to the poems of Goethe, Müller and Heine are known and loved everywhere.*

---

* Adapted from *Appreciation of Music,* Encyclopaedia Britannica Home Reading Guide. © 1965. By permission of publisher.

1. This paragraph is about:
   (a) Germany
   (b) the art-song
   (c) Schubert
   (d) Goethe

2. The main thought is limited to:
   (a) a definition of the art-song
   (b) a description of the art-song
   (c) the story of the *Erlkönig*
   (d) the development of the art-song

3. The topic sentence is:
   (a) the first
   (b) the last
   (c) the third
   (d) implied

4. The key words are:
   (a) Reformation, development
   (b) Schubert, secular music
   (c) art-song, development
   (d) Goethe, lyrical song

5. The development of the art-song was inspired by:
   (a) Schubert's *Erlkönig*
   (b) the poems of Schiller and Goethe
   (c) the Reformation
   (d) the genius of Haydn, Mozart, and Beethoven

6. According to the paragraph, Haydn, Mozart, and Beethoven:
   (a) inspired Goethe, Müller, and Heine to develop the poetic form
   (b) were 18th-century poets
   (c) showed unsurpassed genius in writing lyrical songs
   (d) made their greatest contributions in other musical forms

7. According to the paragraph, Franz Schubert is primarily known as:
   (a) a poet
   (b) a composer
   (c) a writer
   (d) a critic

8. It can be inferred that:
   (a) the Reformation occurred before A.D. 1700
   (b) the *Erlkönig* was written during the Reformation
   (c) there were no songs before the Reformation
   (d) Karl Philipp Emmanuel Bach showed his greatest genius as a poet

9. We may infer that the art-song
   (a) is a type of secular music
   (b) was developed by Goethe and Schiller
   (c) played a large role in Germany during the Reformation
   (d) was perfected by Johann Sebastian Bach

10. We may conclude that Germany:
    (a) was not affected by the Reformation
    (b) abounded in artistic genius during the 18th and 19th centuries
    (c) did not allow secular music to be played until the 18th century
    (d) all of the above

EXERCISE 2: SUPPORTING DETAILS

DIRECTIONS: The supporting sentences in a paragraph should develop the main thought, which is often clearly expressed in a topic sentence. But if the paragraph is a dialogue or narrative which does not have its main thought explicitly stated, then the supporting sentences should be limited to the specific time, event, and characters mentioned. In each of the exercises below, you are given the opening sentence of a paragraph. Following it are possible supporting sentences. Put an R before those that are relevant to the main thought in the topic sentence (or to the specific time, event, and characters in an opening narrative sentence); put an N before those that are not relevant.

1. Corporations exist only by authority of some state legislation.

   _____ State laws require that stockholders' meetings be held at least once a year.

   _____ Each share of stock is entitled to one vote at the annual meeting.

   _____ It was at first the practice for the state legislature to grant a separate franchise to each corporation.

   _____ As this form of business organization became more common, the legislature passed general corporation laws, under which corporations could be formed by complying with the provisions of the statute.

   _____ The stockholder signs the proxy and returns it to the secretary of the company.

   _____ This is known as voting by proxy.

   _____ The directors of a corporation elect the officers of the corporation.

   _____ A corporation is formed only through process of law, by a number of persons associating themselves for the purpose of conducting a legal business.

   _____ A corporation is a being, or entity, distinct from its stockholders, individually or collectively.

   _____ Three is the usual number prescribed by law as the minimum number of persons who may form a corporation.*

2. The collective farmer [in Russia] finds that his farm must pay taxes to the state and, in addition, he must sell the state a fixed quota of crops and livestock products at prices well below those on the free market.

   _____ The price difference is actually a tax.

   _____ There is no estate, or inheritance, tax in Russia.

   _____ It was abolished in 1942.

   _____ And his quota is based not on his output, but on the size of his farm.

   _____ For many Russians, however, the family "estate" may consist largely of holdings of state savings bonds.

   _____ Normally, the bonds cannot be cashed until they mature—and maturity dates can be, and are, put off as they approach.

   _____ If his chickens do not lay enough eggs to meet his quota, he has to go into the free market to buy eggs, then deliver them to the state at a loss.

   _____ Russians pay many other taxes, and, typically, the taxes also are designed to guide or restrict the lives of the individuals.

   _____ If the Russian goes to a lecture on Marxism, it's tax-free.

   _____ Other lectures are taxed at 5 percent of the admission price. †

* Adapted from *Elementary Accounting for Colleges* by Fayette H. Elwell, published by Ginn and Company, owners of the copyright, 1945. Used with permission.

† Adapted from "Russian Income Tax to Go—But Biggest Taxes Stay On," from a copyrighted article in *U.S. News & World Report,* May 16, 1960.

3. Sauntering near the quay, Chrysis passed the famous sculptor Demetrios, who watched her graceful walk.

_____ Demetrios, meeting her lovely eyes, found himself trembling.

_____ He declared his love for her, but found himself unexpectedly and fiercely resisted.

_____ In the evening Chrysis was the first to arrive at her friend's house.

_____ Bacchis was one of the wealthiest courtesans in Alexandria and was famous for the entertainment offered in her splendid house.

_____ He promised anything in order to gain her affection.

_____ The statue of the goddess Aphrodite appeared in the moonlight as though living.

_____ When the desecration of Aphrodite became known, the cup brimmed full and the populace went berserk.

_____ Encouraged by his passion, Chrysis made three outrageous demands.

_____ Demetrios was to procure the silver mirror belonging to the noted courtesan Bacchis, the comb of carved ivory in the possession of the High Priest's wife, and the seven-row necklace of pearls hanging about the neck of Aphrodite.

_____ Demetrios was depressed but softly said, "Tomorrow thou shalt have them."*

4. The type of adjustment found within a given field-structure situation represents an equilibrium of a great many forces.

_____ Particular latent elements within the personality make it difficult for the individual to confront and acknowledge certain conditions of realistic social change.

_____ These elements we refer to as _latencies_.

_____ Latencies are behavioral practices that the individual is unable or reluctant to abandon.

_____ Thus, every adjustment is the nodal point of a number of confluent forces which have entered into the adjusted state.

_____ The distinction between individual and group latencies is one primarily of scope and complexity.

_____ Latencies represent prior states of social equilibrium.

_____ He should ask whether the needs of the habituated attitude are likely to be fulfilled or thwarted.

_____ Such states of equilibrium in highly differentiated societies like ours are precarious; they display constant flux and change.

_____ Each equilibrium is formed by individual attitudes, social and cultural pressures, and physical circumstances—all joining at a common meeting point of internal balance.

_____ If we recognize that the social and cultural conditions of a given situation impose a frame of reference, we may then regard such conditions as limiting our social activities. †

EXERCISE 3: THE MAIN THOUGHT

(LEVEL OF COMPREHENSION: STANDARD)

DIRECTIONS: Below each of the following paragraphs are questions about the main thought. Indicate your answer by circling the letter you think is correct.

PART I

Edgar Allan Poe (1809–1849) occupies a unique position in the history of the short story. It is not accurate to say that he was the father of the short story, but he first defined and helped to popularize a genre, most of the current practitioners of which have disowned him. Reviewing Hawthorne's *Twice-Told Tales* in 1842, he declared that a short story should aim at a single effect and that everything in it must contribute to "one pre-established design." Under the influence of Chekhov and others, the later development of the short story has been in a different direction; nevertheless, Poe performed an important service in giving form to a class of fiction that before him was too often loose and digressive.*

1. This paragraph is concerned with:
   (a) Hawthorne's *Twice-Told Tales*
   (b) Chekhov's influence on the short story
   (c) the establishment of a genre
   (d) Poe's contribution to the short story

2. The topic sentence is:
   (a) the first
   (b) the last
   (c) the second
   (d) implied

3. The key words are:
   (a) father, short story
   (b) Poe, genre
   (c) Poe, short story
   (d) Chekhov, short story

4. The supporting sentences:
   (a) define the short story
   (b) trace the development of the short story
   (c) delineate Poe's role in the development of the short story
   (d) summarize Hawthorne's *Twice-Told Tales*

5. It is stated in the paragraph that Poe:
   (a) reviewed Hawthorne's *Twice-Told Tales*
   (b) helped to popularize a genre
   (c) gave form to the short story
   (d) all of the above

6. According to the paragraph, Poe:
   (a) was influenced by the work of Chekhov
   (b) was the father of the short story
   (c) was the first to define the short story
   (d) wrote the first short story

* From *The Rinehart Book of Short Stories*, ed. C. L. Cline (Holt, Rinehart and Winston, Inc., 1952). Copyright and permission by editor.

7. We may infer from the passage that:
   (a) though Poe is not the father of the short story, he early gave form to a previously loose genre
   (b) the short story was a well-developed literary form even before Poe's time
   (c) Hawthorne's *Twice-Told Tales* did not have a "pre-established design"
   (d) Chekhov's stories were loose and digressive

8. We may infer that:
   (a) the short story is a class of fiction
   (b) Poe's short stories each had one pre-established design
   (c) Chekhov wrote in a later time period than Poe
   (d) all of the above

9. The paragraph definitely states that:
   (a) many current short story writers have disowned Poe
   (b) current short stories are loose and digressive
   (c) Chekhov was instrumental in popularizing the short story
   (d) all of the above

10. We may conclude that Poe:
    (a) got his idea of "one pre-established design" from reading the works of Chekhov and Hawthorne
    (b) contributed more to the early development of the short story than any other writer
    (c) wrote short stories that were often loose and digressive
    (d) all of the above

PART II

In this fashion was the theory of unending evolution presented by the *Origin of Species*. Contrary to popular belief, however, Darwin did not originate the evolutionary theory. The idea is older than Aristotle and Lucretius. Such brilliant minds as Buffon, Goethe, Erasmus Darwin (Charles' grandfather), Lamarck and Herbert Spencer had supported the doctrine. Charles Darwin's contribution was noted in two directions. First, he accumulated more indisputable evidence to show the *fact* of evolution than had ever been offered before. Secondly, he advanced his famous theory of natural selection as a reasonable explanation for the *method* of evolution.*

1. This paragraph is primarily concerned with:
   (a) pre-Darwinian theories of evolution
   (b) the fact of evolution
   (c) the method of evolution
   (d) the *Origin of Species* by Charles Darwin

2. The thought is confined to:
   (a) statements of the writer's opinion of the theory of evolution
   (b) statements concerning evolution already known to the average man
   (c) proofs that Darwin was the father of the evolutionary theory
   (d) statements explaining Darwin's part in establishing the theory of evolution

3. The topic sentence is:
   (a) the first
   (b) the second
   (c) the fourth
   (d) divided

* From *Books That Changed the World* by Robert Downs.

4. The key words are:
   (a) Darwin, *Origin of Species*
   (b) Aristotle, Lucretius, evolutionary theory
   (c) fact, method, evolutionary theory
   (d) Darwin, evolutionary theory

5. According to the paragraph, Charles Darwin:
   (a) was older than Lucretius
   (b) originated the theory of evolution
   (c) gave more evidence to prove the fact of evolution than ever before
   (d) all of the above

6. It is also stated in the paragraph that:
   (a) Charles Darwin was the son of Erasmus Darwin
   (b) the idea of natural selection is older than Aristotle
   (c) Charles Darwin explained the method of evolution
   (d) none of the above

7. The writer of the paragraph implies that the theory of evolution:
   (a) was originated by Aristotle and Lucretius
   (b) is an old theory dating back to no one known person
   (c) did not have any support before Charles Darwin
   (d) is a lot of unsupported ideas in need of proof

8. We may infer that:
   (a) Charles Darwin originated the theory of natural selection
   (b) Erasmus Darwin accumulated the evidence that Charles Darwin used
   (c) the *Origin of Species* was written to disprove the evolutionary theory
   (d) none of the above

9. It may be further inferred that:
   (a) Darwin and Aristotle were contemporaries
   (b) Aristotle and Lucretius did not support the theory of evolution
   (c) Darwin wrote the *Origin of Species*
   (d) all of the above

10. We may conclude that:
    (a) Charles Darwin contributed more to the development of the theory than any other person
    (b) Charles Darwin had little to do with the theory
    (c) it is well known that Darwin did not originate the theory
    (d) Erasmus Darwin, rather than Charles, was responsible for the development of the theory of evolution

PART III

The basis for color is a disturbance of or a departure from a "white" spectral energy distribution. Various optical phenomena are responsible for color. Color may be created by dispersion; by selective absorption, reflection, and scattering; by interference; and by polarization. Each of these phenomena is of considerable interest in adding to our knowledge of the nature of light, and each has been applied in ways of great practical value.*

1. This paragraph is about:
   (a) energy
   (b) color
   (c) disturbance
   (d) dispersion

* Adapted from *College Technical Physics* by Robert L. Weber, Marsh W. White, and Kenneth V. Manning. Copyright 1947. McGraw-Hill Book Company, Inc. Used by permission.

2. The thought is limited to:
   (a) the disturbance of spectral energy
   (b) the dispersion of energy
   (c) the absorption of color
   (d) the creation of color

3. The topic sentence is:
   (a) the first
   (b) the second
   (c) the fourth
   (d) divided

4. The key words are:
   (a) basis, color
   (b) disturbance, departure
   (c) energy, distribution
   (d) all of the above

5. The supporting sentences give:
   (a) a definition of color
   (b) the uses of color
   (c) a definition of energy
   (d) details of the creation of color

6. According to the paragraph, color is produced by:
   (a) the nature of light
   (b) "white" spectral energy
   (c) various optical phenomena
   (d) all of the above

7. The disturbance of a "white" spectral energy distribution is:
   (a) the nature of light
   (b) the dispersion of color
   (c) the basis for color
   (d) polarization

8. We may infer that polarization is:
   (a) the nature of light
   (b) the basis for color, dispersion, and interference
   (c) an optical phenomenon
   (d) the basis for "white" spectral energy

9. We may also infer that optical phenomena which create color:
   (a) are responsible for spectral energy
   (b) are the basis for "white" spectral energy distribution
   (c) create and distribute the nature of light
   (d) disturb or depart from "white" spectral energy distribution

10. We may conclude that a "white" spectral energy distribution is:
    (a) the absence of any light
    (b) a composite from which all colors can be created
    (c) a departure from polarization
    (d) the basis for interference

EXERCISE 4: THE MAIN THOUGHT

(LEVEL OF COMPREHENSION: DIFFICULT)

DIRECTIONS: Below each of the following paragraphs are questions about the main thought. Indicate your answer by circling the letter you think is correct.

PART I

Again, we can never free ourselves from the need of something outside us for the preservation of our being, and we can never live in such a manner as to have no intercourse with objects which are outside us. Indeed, so far as the mind is concerned, our intellect would be less perfect if the mind were alone, and understood nothing but itself. There are many things, therefore, outside us which are useful to us, and which, therefore, are to be sought. Of all these, none more excellent can be discovered than those which exactly agree with our nature. If, for example, two individuals of exactly the same nature are joined together, they make up a single individual, doubly stronger than each alone. Nothing, therefore, is more useful to man than man. Men can desire, I say, nothing more excellent for the preservation of their being than that all should so agree at every point that the minds and bodies of all should form, as it were, one mind and one body; that all should together endeavor as much as possible to preserve their being, and that all should together seek the common good of all. From this it follows that men who are governed by reason—that is to say, men who, under the guidance of reason, seek their own profit—desire nothing for themselves which they do not desire for other men, and that, therefore, they are just, faithful, and honorable.*

1. This paragraph is about:
   (a) the mind
   (b) man
   (c) faith
   (d) justice

2. The thought is limited to:
   (a) the powers of the mind
   (b) the dependence of man
   (c) the influence of faith
   (d) the desire for justice

3. The topic sentence is:
   (a) the first
   (b) the last
   (c) the sixth
   (d) implied

4. The key phrase in the paragraph is:
   (a) we can never free ourselves
   (b) the need of something outside us
   (c) the preservation of our being
   (d) objects which are outside us

5. According to the passage, the most useful thing to man is:
   (a) objects outside us
   (b) the perfection of our minds
   (c) the preservation of our being
   (d) man himself

* From "Foundations of the Moral Life," by Baruch Spinoza in *The World's Great Thinkers, Man and Spirit: The Speculative Philosophers*, eds. Saxe Commins and Robert N. Linscott (Random House, Inc., 1947).

6. The paragraph also states that the mind:
   (a) understands nothing but itself
   (b) would be less perfect if it were alone
   (c) is the most useful thing to us
   (d) all of the above

7. The author apparently believes in:
   (a) a life within the mind
   (b) the brotherhood of man
   (c) the survival of the fittest
   (d) isolationism

8. The author concludes that the best solution for the preservation of our being is:
   (a) to live in such a manner as to have no intercourse with objects outside ourselves
   (b) for the intellect to be made more perfect
   (c) for men to act as one mind and one body
   (d) all of the above

9. It may be inferred from the passage that:
   (a) through the union of minds, the greatest good for all may be accomplished
   (b) a union of minds does not deter man from seeking his own good
   (c) men governed by reason do not need something outside themselves
   (d) the being can be preserved only through finding those things which exactly agree with our nature

10. We may conclude from the paragraph that:
   (a) man is complete and independent only in his mind
   (b) man cannot free himself of selfish aims
   (c) the aim of man is to protect himself from the outside
   (d) man is by nature dependent upon others for his preservation

PART II

Just as there are philosophers dissatisfied with the processes of analysis and discursive knowledge who place greater reliance on immediate and direct insight or intuition, so there are those who, applying this general attitude to the problems of supernaturalism, distrust all argumentation and all authority as well, in favor of an alleged immediate insight into the reality of the supernatural. By no means have all mystics interpreted their mystical experiences as evidence for a *supernatural* reality. Among those who have, the number of non-philosophic or lay mystics is relatively large, and includes many who were subsequently canonized as saints. There are also many who look to the insight of mystics as supplementary to, rather than as opposing, theistic argumentation.*

1. The main thought is concerned with:
   (a) mystics and insight
   (b) philosophers and discursive knowledge
   (c) saints and theistic argumentation
   (d) mystical experiences

2. The thought is limited to:
   (a) the uses by mystics of insight into supernaturalism
   (b) the reliance of philosophers upon discursive knowledge
   (c) proof of the existence of a supernatural reality
   (d) examples of unusual cases of intuition and insight

* From *Philosophy: An Introduction* by John H. Randall, Jr. and Justus Buchler (Barnes & Noble, Inc., 1942).

3. The topic sentence is:
   (a) the first
   (b) the last
   (c) the second
   (d) implied

4. The key words are:
   (a) philosophers, knowledge
   (b) insight, supernaturalism
   (c) saints, argumentation
   (d) evidence, supernatural reality

5. The supporting sentences offer:
   (a) a definition of insight
   (b) an illustration of mystical experiences
   (c) a differentiation of the uses of insight by mystics
   (d) arguments to disprove the existence of a supernatural reality

6. According to the passage, many mystics:
   (a) are opposed to philosophy and philosophers
   (b) rely on immediate insight as evidence of a supernatural reality
   (c) are dissatisfied with reality
   (d) rely on the processes of analysis and discursive knowledge

7. The passage definitely states that:
   (a) greater reliance should be placed on direct insight or intuition
   (b) many lay mystics have been canonized as saints
   (c) mystics oppose theistic argumentation
   (d) there is evidence of a supernatural reality

8. It may be inferred that:
   (a) philosophers place greater reliance on intuition than do mystics
   (b) philosophers do not believe in a supernatural reality
   (c) mystics are considered to be a type of philosophers
   (d) philosophers do not have mystical experiences

9. We may infer from the use of the word *alleged* that the writers:
   (a) feel that mystical experiences are proofs of a supernatural reality
   (b) do not believe that mystics actually have had peculiar experiences
   (c) have some doubts as to the validity of immediate insight into a supernatural reality
   (d) consider all mystics to be insane

10. We may conclude that the methods by which philosophers obtain knowledge are:
    (a) more reliable when direct insight or intuition is used
    (b) not as exact as in scientific investigation
    (c) valid only when argumentation is used
    (d) the same as in all areas of investigations

PART III

But, in the same way that turning the time axis means physically that the space separation of two events has different values . . . when viewed from a moving vehicle, turning the space axis would mean that the time separation of the two events observed from a moving vehicle differs from the time separation of the two events when observed from a stationary point on the ground. Thus, if the bank robbery and plane crash were 15 minutes apart by the City Hall clock, the time interval registered by the wrist watch of a bus passenger would be different—not because the two timepieces move at different rates as the result of mechanical imperfections, but because time itself flows at different rates in vehicles moving at different speeds, and the actual mechanism that records it is correspondingly slowed, though, at low speeds of bus travel, this retardation is so negligible as to be imperceptible.*

1. This paragraph is about:
   (a) timepieces
   (b) time separation
   (c) space separation
   (d) bus travel

2. The thought is limited to:
   (a) the inaccuracies of timepieces
   (b) the differences in space separation
   (c) the differences in time separation
   (d) the effects of low speeds of bus travel

3. The topic sentence is:
   (a) the first
   (b) the last
   (c) implied
   (d) divided

4. The key words are:
   (a) space separation, differs
   (b) time separation, differs
   (c) timepieces, imperfections
   (d) bus travel, low speeds

5. The supporting sentences offer:
   (a) a definition of time
   (b) a definition of space
   (c) an illustration of space separation
   (d) an illustration of time separation

6. According to the passage, time rates:
   (a) are perceptible at low speeds
   (b) vary in vehicles moving at various speeds
   (c) are accelerated at low speeds
   (d) are stationary

7. The paragraph also states that two timepieces move at different rates:
   (a) because of mechanical imperfections
   (b) because time is imperceptible
   (c) in vehicles which are stationary
   (d) in vehicles moving at different speeds

* From *One, Two, Three . . . Infinity* by George Gamow (The Viking Press).

8. We may infer that the greater the speed:
   (a) the more imperceptible the time retardation
   (b) the more imperceptible the time acceleration
   (c) the more perceptible the time retardation
   (d) the more perceptible the time acceleration

9. We may further infer that the rate of flow of time on a spaceship in interplanetary travel would be:
   (a) accelerated
   (b) slowed
   (c) imperceptible
   (d) the same as on earth

10. We may conclude that:
    (a) speed makes timepieces mechanically imperfect
    (b) there is an inverse relationship between rate of speed and flow of time
    (c) a clock on a stationary object is more reliable than a wrist watch in a moving vehicle
    (d) the time separation between two events as registered in a moving vehicle depends upon the direction in which the vehicle is traveling

SUPPLEMENTARY ACTIVITIES: PARAGRAPH WRITING

It is possible to learn much about the structure and development of paragraphs by actually writing them; as you are forced to make choices and to plan strategically your development, you will learn not only to write better yourself but also to appreciate the skill of fine writers.

PART I

DIRECTIONS: Select three of the following subjects and write a cogent paragraph on each. Underline the topic sentence of each paragraph. Then classify the supporting sentences you have used according to the ones which have limited, qualified, or defined your topic, and those which offer evidence that supports your statement of the main thought in your paragraph.

1. Moral commitment and moral apathy in one important Civil Rights issue
2. The possible intellectual apathy television produces in children (You may quarrel with this assertion.)
3. Purposes for studying the humanities (literature, philosophy, history)
4. One religious quarrel with the theory of evolution
5. One argument for [or against] students marrying while still in college

1.

2.

3.

PART II

DIRECTIONS: The following statements have been taken from the works of established authors. Choose three and, using each as a topic sentence, develop a supporting paragraph. The quotation need not be your first sentence.

    1. A man is rich in proportion to the number of things which he can afford to let alone. *
    2. The civilized man has built a coach, but has lost the use of his feet. †
    3. Whoso would be a man, must be a nonconformist. ‡
    4. The best way to prove the clearness of our mind, is by showing its faults. §
    5. It is not easy to find a man who has studied for three years without aiming at pay. ‖

1.

* Henry David Thoreau.
† Ralph Waldo Emerson.
‡ *Ibid.*
§ Jonathan Swift.
‖ Confucius.

2.

3.

RECOGNIZING THE PRINCIPLES OF UNITY, COHERENCE, AND EMPHASIS IN THE PARAGRAPH

A discussion of paragraph comprehension would not be complete without some reference to the principles of unity, coherence, and emphasis. It has been demonstrated how these principles operate in the shortest unit of thought, the sentence, and you will see later how they occur in a longer unit. By definition these principles do not vary in the different thought groups, but as the units become larger, their roles become more apparent and more important. The interdependence of sentences in a paragraph makes it essential that each contribute to the unity, coherence, and emphasis of the main thought. Likewise, in longer units of discourse, interdependence of paragraphs is necessary to achieve the same results.

Unity

We have shown previously that a paragraph should convey one main thought and that supporting sentences should contribute to its development. This singleness of purpose which all of the sentences share is called unity. It is established in a paragraph by the stated or implied topic sentence giving the main thought, and the supporting sentences furnishing relevant information to complement that thought. Without this singleness of purpose to unify the sentences, the paragraph becomes confusing and ineffective.

The following paragraphs will further clarify the role of unity in a paragraph. In the first one irrelevant sentences have been added; the second one is the correct version. Note how the exclusion of the irrelevant sentences gives the second paragraph a "oneness" of thought:

[1] So powerful was the invasion of scientific ideas and of the scientific habit of reliance upon proved facts that the Protestant churches—which numbered in their membership five out of every eight adult church members in the United States—were broken into two warring camps. [2] Psychology was king. [3] Those who believed in the letter of the Bible and refused to accept any teaching, even of science, which seemed to conflict with it, began in 1921 to call themselves Fundamentalists. [4] The newspapers were giving columns of space to inform the people of the latest scientific discoveries. [5] A new dictum from Albert Einstein was now front-page stuff. [6] The Modernists (or Liberals), on the other hand, tried to reconcile their beliefs with scientific thought; to throw overboard what was out of date, to retain what was essential and intellectually respectable, and generally to mediate between Christianity and the skeptical spirit of the age. [7] The general public was captivated by the theories of Freud, Adler, Jung, and Watson*

* Adapted from *Only Yesterday* by Frederick Lewis Allen (Harper & Brothers).

[1] So powerful was the invasion of scientific ideas and of the scientific habit of reliance upon proved facts that the Protestant churches—which numbered in their membership five out of every eight adult church members in the United States—were broken into two warring camps. [3] Those who believed in the letter of the Bible and refused to accept any teaching, even of science, which seemed to conflict with it, began in 1921 to call themselves Fundamentalists. [6] The Modernists (or Liberals), on the other hand, tried to reconcile their beliefs with scientific thought; to throw overboard what was out of date, to retain what was essential and intellectually respectable, and generally to mediate between Christianity and the skeptical spirit of the age.

It is obvious that both of these paragraphs are about the impact of science on American life in the 1920's, but one paragraph cannot say all that there is to say about the subject. The first paragraph attempts to say too much and the result is a jumble of ideas. The topic sentence in both paragraphs (sentence 1) avoids this confusion by limiting the discussion to the effect that science had on the Protestant churches. Thus only the sentences which have the single purpose of showing the impact of science on the Protestant churches are relevant. By eliminating the irrelevant sentences (numbers 2, 4, 5, and 7) of the first paragraph, we derive the second paragraph in which all of the statements are essential to the development of the topic sentence. In this manner, the second paragraph achieves unity.

Coherence

Probably the easiest principle to recognize in a paragraph is coherence. Certainly the lack of it would be conspicuous. As we have already seen in Chapter 1, coherence is achieved by a clear, logical arrangement of ideas so that the flow within a sentence or between several sentences will be smooth and even. This orderly sequence enables the reader to follow the development of the thought.

In addition to the arrangement of sentences, certain classes of words and phrases, which are generally called transitional devices, contribute to the coherence of the paragraph. They facilitate the even movement of the thought from one sentence to another. Examples of these devices are listed below.

Coherence through transitional words and phrases:

1. To show succession of thought from one sentence to another: *and, also, besides, but, finally, for example, for instance, furthermore, in addition, inasmuch as, in other words, in short, moreover, of course.*

2. To show continuity or agreement of time: *afterwards, here, later, meanwhile, in the meantime, now, soon, subsequently, then.*

3. To show cause or effect: *accordingly, as a result, because, consequently, for this* (or *that*) *reason, hence, so, therefore, thus.*

4. To show comparison of ideas: *in the same fashion, in like manner, likewise, similarly.*

5. To show a contrast of ideas: *but, however, nevertheless, on the other hand, on* (or *to*) *the contrary, or, still, yet.*

Coherence through sentence construction:

1. Repetition of an important word or idea from one sentence to the following one, as:

The term *Renaissance* is usually taken to mean the rebirth of learning, or literary and artistic re-use of classical antiquity at the close of the Middle Ages. But the Renaissance was much more than this.*

2. Use of pronouns to refer to key word of the main thought or topic sentence, as:

The person of Pope is well known not to have been formed by the nicest model. *He* has, in *his* account of the "Little Club," compared *himself* to a spider, and by another is described as protuberant behind and before. *He* is said to have been beautiful in infancy, but *he* was of a constitution originally feeble and weak, and as bodies of a tender frame are easily distorted, *his* deformity was probably in part the effect of *his* application. *His* stature was so low that, to bring *him* to a level with common tables, it was necessary to raise *his* seat. But *his* face was not displeasing, and *his* eyes were animated and vivid.† [Italics authors'.]

3. Repetition of phrases, clauses, or sentences of identical or similar words in order to show parallelism between ideas of equal importance, as:

Rebecca had beauty, brains, and breeding.
[Parallelism of single words]

From the North, from the South, from the East, from the West, the men came to answer the call to arms.
[Parallelism of phrases]

When Barbara was leaving for college, she promised her mother that she would not cut classes, that she would submit all assignments on time, and that she would study at least three hours each day.
[Parallelism of clauses]

The people wanted freedom, but there was no freedom.
The people wanted justice, but there was no justice.
[Parallelism of sentences]

A combination of several of these devices for making the thought logical and coherent may be found in a well-written paragraph. By themselves

* From *History of Art* by Jean Anne Vincent (Barnes & Noble, Inc. 1955).
† From "Pope" by Samuel Johnson.

these devices may seem very minor to you, but their importance to the coherence of the thought will be more evident when you see how choppy and disjointed a paragraph can be when they are omitted.

To illustrate the importance of coherence, the following paragraph is shown first with its sentences scrambled and transitional words and phrases omitted; then it is shown with its sentences in a logical order and its appropriate transitional devices restored. The thought of the paragraph deals with the events which led to the Scopes Trial (or, as popularly called, the "Monkey Trial" of Tennessee) in which William Jennings Bryan, a famous orator, former Secretary of State, and three times a presidential candidate, debated with Clarence Darrow, an equally famous lawyer and agnostic, over the right to teach the theory of evolution in public schools. Compare the effectiveness of these two paragraphs:

This law [prohibiting the teaching of evolution] had been placed upon the books. A little group of men in the sleepy town of Dayton, Tennessee, decided to put it to the test. William Jennings Bryan volunteered his services to the prosecution; Rappelyea wired the Civil Liberties Union in New York and secured for Scopes the legal assistance of Clarence Darrow, Dudley Field Malone, and Arthur Garfield Hays; the trial was set for July, 1925. Dayton discovered that it was to be put on the map with a vengeance. Their motives were mixed; it was characteristic of the times that (according to so friendly a narrator of the incident as Arthur Garfield Hays) Rappelyea declared that their action would put Dayton on the map. The illegal deed was perpetrated and Scopes was arrested. George Rappelyea, a mining engineer, was drinking lemon phosphates in Robinson's drug store with John Thomas Scopes, a likable young man of twenty-four who taught biology at the Central High School, and two or three others. Rappelyea proposed that Scopes should allow himself to be caught red-handed in the act of teaching the theory of evolution to an innocent child, and Scopes — half serious, half in joke — agreed. ‡

This law [prohibiting the teaching of evolution] had no sooner been placed upon the books than a little group of men in the sleepy town of Dayton, Tennessee, decided to put it to the test. George Rappelyea, a mining engineer, was drinking lemon phosphates in Robinson's drug store with John Thomas Scopes, a likeable young man of twenty-four who taught biology at the Central High School, and two or three others. Rappelyea proposed that Scopes should allow himself to be caught red-handed in the act of teaching the theory of evolution to an innocent child, and Scopes — half serious, half in joke — agreed. Their motives were apparently mixed; it was characteristic of the times that (according to so friendly a narrator of the incident as Arthur Garfield Hays) Rappelyea declared that their action would put Dayton on the map. At all events, the illegal deed was shortly

‡ Adapted from *Only Yesterday, op. cit.*

perpetrated and Scopes was arrested. William Jennings Bryan forthwith volunteered his services to the prosecution; Rappelyea wired the Civil Liberties Union in New York and secured for Scopes the legal assistance of Clarence Darrow, Dudley Field Malone, and Arthur Garfield Hays; the trial was set for July, 1925, and Dayton suddenly discovered that it was to be put on the map with a vengeance.

Notice how the illogical arrangement of sentences in the first paragraph could lead you to several erroneous conclusions. The paragraph seems to imply that Bryan and Darrow were among the group of men who decided to test the law against teaching evolution; later it also seems to say that the illegal deed Scopes committed was the drinking of lemon phosphates in Robinson's drugstore. There are places, too, where the first paragraph does not seem to make any sense. The second paragraph, however, with its logic and coherence restored, is clear and dispels any misconceptions or faulty conclusions you may have drawn.

Transitional devices not only relate sentences in a paragraph, but also connect the ideas of a longer unit. Some paragraphs themselves are virtually transitions in that they join the thought of a preceding paragraph to the one which follows.

Emphasis

The principle of emphasis involves the strategic placement, for stress and accent, of particular words, phrases, and sentences within the paragraph. Here again the topic sentence is important, but from the standpoint of its position. Where a writer places this key statement depends on his purpose, subject, and audience. Frequently, he chooses the first and last positions because of their psychological impact on the reader: the main thought at the beginning or end of a paragraph usually attracts attention and is therefore more easily remembered.

In the following examples, the same paragraph appears with only the position of the topic sentence changed. Either version is correct, but in the second one a dramatic effect is achieved by the shift of the topic sentence.

Jonathan was an honorable man. In his business, Jonathan adhered to a firm ethical code which compelled him to be honest and fair in his dealings with friends or rivals. In his home, he was a faithful, considerate husband and a just and loving father. His religious and social life was also exemplary, and left nothing to be desired.

In his business, Jonathan adhered to a firm ethical code which compelled him to be honest and fair in his dealings with friends or rivals. In his home, he was a faithful, considerate husband and a just and loving father. His religious and social life was also exemplary, and left nothing to be desired. Jonathan was an honorable man.

Emphasis is also achieved by repetition of a phrase or idea. Note the hammering effect and sharply satiric emphasis placed on the word "Facts" in this opening passage of Dickens' *Hard Times:*

"Now, what I want is, *Facts.* Teach these boys and girls nothing but *Facts. Facts* alone are wanted in life. Plant nothing else, and root out everything else. You can only form the minds of reasoning animals upon *Facts:* nothing else will ever be of service to them. This is the principle on which I bring up my own children, and this is the principle on which I bring up these children. Stick to *Facts,* Sir!"

Note also the way "Facts" is placed in the emphatic position of the sentences in which it occurs: first or last.

Now we are ready to apply our knowledge of the principles of unity, coherence, and emphasis to further analysis of paragraphs.

EXERCISE 5: UNITY

DIRECTIONS: Unity in the following paragraphs has been destroyed by the insertion of irrelevant details. Read each paragraph and write the number of the topic sentence in blank (a); in (b), mark the numbers of the related sentences.

PART I

¹You might imagine that [on an Arctic iceberg] we dread the winter most, with its darkness, below-zero temperature, and wind howling around the trailers. ²But it is the summer that presents the most problems. ³People who live at the equator probably think winter presents the most problems. ⁴These people must prefer summer's heat to winter's cold. ⁵When the weather warms, the ice begins to drop, and we wade around in slush. ⁶The airstrip is too soft for planes to land, and parachuted supplies must be dragged laboriously into camp. ⁷We are always glad when the first breath of winter starts to harden the ice. ⁸Personally, I prefer temperate regions where extremes in weather seldom occur.*

(a) _____   (b) _____

PART II

¹Pro-football crowds seem to be about as "early middle-aged" as baseball crowds, but they are not as surly to referees or among themselves. ²As a game, pro-football has everything college football has, plus the two-platoon system, wide-open play, and the strategic field goal. ³Platoon specialists, offensively and defensively, make the game a thing of excellence and beauty. ⁴Baseball has run short of talent, and boxing has already run out of talent. ⁵Horse-racing crowds are massive, but the sport itself is hardly a "game." ⁶The open play—long passes, spread formations, and wide runs—not only permits fans to see what is going on, but also makes them feel truly that every play is a potential touchdown, just as every charge of the bull is a potential goring. ⁷Bull-fighting is the leading sport in Mexico and Spain. ⁸Recently, several Americans have gone to these countries to take up the cloak of the matador. ⁹The field goal (in pro-football, goal posts are placed on the goal line, instead of ten yards back as in college football) makes the 40–yard line dangerous scoring territory and gives meaning to every series of downs even at mid-field. †

(a) _____   (b) _____

PART III

¹As the Gothic cathedral towers over the small provincial town that forms its setting, so the church towers over mediaeval Europe. ²The reason for this is clear. ³When the Roman Empire, which had included all the western civilized world within its boundaries, collapsed, no strong political power was left in western and central Europe. ⁴The Roman Empire had greatly expanded under the rule of Julius Caesar. ⁵Countries now known as France and Belgium were once part of the Roman Empire, and even England today still shows remnants of the Roman conquests. ⁶The fall of Rome thus affected much of the then known world. ⁷The church, already possessing a good system of organization that had been patterned after the organization of the empire, stepped into the vacuum left by the state and seized upon this opportunity to enhance its power.‡

(a) _____   (b) _____

---

* Adapted from "My Life on an Iceberg," by Gery Cabaniss, *Parade,* Feb. 28, 1960.
† Adapted from "The Wham in Pro Football," by Thomas B. Morgan, *Esquire,* Nov., 1959.
‡ Adapted from *Interior Decoration,* Encyclopaedia Britannica Home Reading Guide. © 1965.

PART IV

[1]"Rock-and-Roll," so popular among teen-agers in this country, has spread its appeal to such far points as Japan and Russia. [2]The American Negro has furnished the United States with its most widely known type of folk-song. [3]The talent and enthusiasm of the Negro for music has resulted in a large group of folk-songs, which can be classified into spirituals, work songs, the "blues" and social songs. [4]The spirituals are the best known Negro songs, and they are spontaneous outbursts of deep feeling and intense religious fervor with a strong rhythmic appeal. [5]The words of the spirituals are not particularly important, and often one simple phrase taken from the stories of the Bible is repeated over and over to make a whole song. [6]Negro music, especially some of the best-known spirituals, is permeated with poignant sadness, but is at the same time full of hope and confidence in better times to come. [7]Marian Anderson is best-loved for her renditions of favorite spirituals. [8]The work songs were sung by Negroes as they performed tasks of manual labor, particularly when there was a group of workers together, and the tasks performed called for rhythmic movements. [9]The "blues" are the melancholy songs of personal troubles in strongly syncopated rhythm which were one of the chief sources of modern jazz.*

(a) _____   (b) _____

PART V

[1]Newton's third law expresses the observation that for every force there is a force of reaction equal in magnitude and opposite in direction. [2]Hooke's law is concerned with the proportion of stress to strain. [3]When an object not free to move is acted upon by an external force, it is pushed or pulled out of its natural shape. [4]As a consequence it exerts an elastic reaction in an attempt to resume its normal shape. [5]Newton's first law of motion is also known as the law of inertia. [6]His second law deals with force and acceleration. [7]On the other hand, the action of a force upon a free object results in an acceleration. [8]The object exerts an inertial reacting force upon the agent of the accelerating force. [9]Sir Isaac Newton also formulated the law of gravity. †

(a) _____   (b) _____

* Adapted from *Appreciation of Music, op. cit.*
† Adapted from *College Technical Physics, op. cit.*

EXERCISE 6: COHERENCE

PART I

DIRECTIONS: In the following paragraphs some of the devices to achieve coherence are italicized and numbered. Read each paragraph, and in the blanks that correspond to the numbered words, identify the device. Wherever a key word is referred to, write it on the same line.

A. Therefore whosoever heareth these sayings of mine, and doeth them, I will liken ¹*him* unto a wise man, which built his house upon a rock. ²*And* the rain descended, and ³*the floods came,* and ⁴*the winds blew,* and beat upon that house; and ⁵*it* fell not, for it was founded upon a rock. ⁶*And* every one that ⁷*heareth these sayings of mine,* and doeth them not, shall be likened unto a foolish man ⁸*which built his house upon the sand.* ⁹*And the rain descended, and the floods came, and the winds blew, and beat upon that house; and it fell, and great was the fall of* ¹⁰*it.**

1. _____   6. _____
2. _____   7. _____
3. _____   8. _____
4. _____   9. _____
5. _____   10. _____

B. The term growth is not confined to physical changes in structures and physiological functions. The ¹*term* is ²*also* applied to the behavior and achievement of children. ³*Thus,* motor sequences such as crawling, standing, walking, and running are a part of the study of ⁴*growth.* ⁵*Similarly,* the changes that occur in a child's ability to act in relation to others in family, neighborhood, and community groups may be described as social ⁶*growth.* †

1. _____   4. _____
2. _____   5. _____
3. _____   6. _____

PART II

DIRECTIONS: The coherence in each of the following paragraphs has been impaired by the illogical arrangement of the sentences. Rewrite the paragraphs, putting the sentences in a logical, coherent order.

A. One day I was studying my lesson in the room next to the kitchen. No one except myself had entered the room. Who was to blame for the damage? The maid had put Miss Lambercier's combs in front of the fireplace to dry. When she came back to fetch them, she was surprised to find the teeth of one of them broken off. On being questioned, I denied that I had touched the comb. This matter was considered serious, as indeed it deserved to be. Mr. and Miss Lambercier both began to admonish, to press, and to threaten me—but all to no avail; I obstinately persisted in my denial; the appearances were so strong that they overshadowed all my protestations, although this was the first time that I had been found to lie so boldly. ‡

* From the *Sermon on the Mount.*
† From *Child Development* by Willard C. Olson (D.C. Heath and Company).
‡ Adapted from *Confessions,* Book I, by Jean Jacques Rousseau (London: The Aldus Society, 1903).

B.   As it happened, we weren't in the house a week when Johnny broke his arm. On Tuesday she gave him a Davy Crockett button. I asked him recently what ever happened to Cleo and he replied solemnly, "I don't know, but I hear she's going to have to sit in a corner for the rest of her life." We've learned what happens to young boys. Everybody warned us that we could expect a lot of broken bones the moment the lads started to clamber over the balcony and out among the gargoyles. It didn't happen here, though — it happened in nursery school. Clearly this girl means business, and I think Johnny should keep . . . away from her. On Wednesday she pushed him into a box and broke his arm in two places. And good enough for her, too. On Monday she gave him a penny. A four-and-a-half-year-old blonde named Cleo had had her eye on Johnny.*

* From *Please Don't Eat the Daisies* by Jean Kerr. Copyright © 1957 by Jean Kerr. Reprinted by permission of Doubleday & Company, Inc.

EXERCISE 7: EMPHASIS

DIRECTIONS: Read each of the following paragraphs and note the position of the topic sentence. As a basis for evaluating the emphasis in each paragraph, answer the questions listed below:

1. What is the main thought of this paragraph?
2. Where has the emphasis been placed?
3. What is the effect of having the emphasis placed here?
4. Could the emphasis have been placed elsewhere without affecting its coherence?
5. If so, would the effect created by this change differ from the original effect?

PART I

The beach is not the place to work; to read, write or think. I should have remembered that from other years. Too warm, too damp, too soft for any real mental discipline or sharp flights of spirit. One never learns. Hopefully, one carries down the faded straw bag, lumpy with books, clean paper, long over-due unanswered letters, freshly sharpened pencils, lists, and good intentions. The books remain unread, the pencils break their points, and the pads rest smooth and unblemished as the cloudless sky. No reading, no writing, no thoughts even—at least, not at first.*

1.

2.

3.

4.

5.

PART II

Through these turbulent seas, not far from the trenches of Korea, plowed a considerable formation of American warships. A battleship and two cruisers, accompanied by fourteen destroyers to shield against Russian submarines, held steady course as their icy decks rose and fell and shivered in the gale. They were the ships of Task Force 77 and they had been sent to destroy the communist-held bridges at Toko-ri. †

1.

2.

3.

4.

5.

* Adapted from *Gift from the Sea* by Anne Morrow Lindbergh (Random House, Inc.), Pantheon © 1955.
† From *The Bridges at Toko-ri* by James A. Michener (Random House, Inc.) © 1953.

PART III

Change is the first law of growth. The organism is never static. It is an energy system with constant intake and output. The change that occurs in the balance between intake and excretion is described as growth. The growth process is characterized by both regularity and rhythm. In broad outline each individual passes through the same successive stages in very much the same sequence. In some the physiological time clock is running rapidly, and the sequences are compressed into a narrower portion of the life span. In others, physiological time is slower, and the sequence of events is stretched out over a longer period. As will be seen in later discussions of the stimulation and retardation of growth, the individual himself and the adults about him have little control over physiological time; wise nurture, therefore, in both physical care and education, makes no attempt to alter the individual's rate of growth and development.*

1.

2.

3.

4.

5.

PART IV

Out here? Out here is a sky so gentle
Five stars are ventured on it. I can see
The sky's pale belly glowing and growing big,
Soon to deliver the moon. And I can see
A glittering smear, the snail-trail of the sun
Where it crawled with its golden shell into the hills.
A darkening land sunken into prayer
Lucidly in dewdrops of one syllable,
Nunc dimittis. I see twilight, madam. †

1.

2.

3.

4.

5.

* From *Child Development, op. cit.*
† From Act II of *The Lady's Not for Burning* by Christopher Fry. Copyright 1949, 1950 by Christopher Fry. Second ed., rev., 1952. By permission of Oxford University Press.

TYPES OF PARAGRAPHS

A writer's purpose will determine the type of paragraph he writes and the method of development he uses. The skillful writer, conscious of his purpose, will first have become acquainted with the forms of discourse and the patterns of development he has available. Having completed this step, he will choose the vehicles which are most apt for his purpose. As readers, therefore, we should be familiar with the choices of form and development which lie before the writer. First, let us examine the various types of paragraphs.

Paragraphs may be divided into four categories: Narrative, Expository, Descriptive, and Argumentative. No one of these types is found exclusively in a reading selection; a combination of them is in every well-written, integrated work. Some paragraphs themselves even show an overlapping of types. But for the purpose of examining the characteristics of each type, let us define and illustrate them separately; after that we will be ready to study some of the subtle overlappings of types that often occur.

Narrative

A paragraph which tells an anecdote, incident, or story—whether real or imagined—is called a narrative. As a dominant type in novels, short stories, and plays, the narrative paragraph usually contains three essentials: *what* happened, *who* or *what* was involved, *where* an incident occurred. Some writers also include *why, how, when* an episode took place. To order the events in a narrative paragraph, most authors select a chronological sequence, though a combined time and logical order is frequently employed to connect several incidents.

Point of view is the perspective from which the action is observed. It is important in the narrative paragraph because with this element the writer controls his reader's interest. To tell a story a writer frequently chooses one of three viewpoints: first person, third person or omniscient, or shifting. An author utilizing the first person identifies with one of the characters and relates the events as they occur, or he creates a spokesman who is not personally involved in the action. In the third person, the narrative is told with the writer standing on the outside looking in at his characters and the situation with an "all-knowing" attitude. From the shifting point of view the writer moves from one vantage point to another as he reveals different parts of the story. Regardless of the point of view employed, the reader should identify it and analyze its relationship to the content of the narrative.

Study the following examples. Although the point of view in each is different, there are similarities in purpose and development.

There was an old man named Pierre, whose duty it was to bring the meat from the store-room for the men. Old Pierre, in the kindness of his heart, used to select the fattest and the best pieces for his companions. This did not long escape the keen-eyed *bourgeois,* who was greatly disturbed at such improvidence, and cast about for some means to stop it. At last he hit on a plan that exactly suited him. At the side of the meat-room, and separated from it by a clay partition, was another apartment, used for the storage of furs. It had no communication with the fort, except through a square hole in the partition; and of course it was perfectly dark. One evening the *bourgeois,* watching for a moment when no one observed him, dodged into the meat-room, clambered through the hole, and ensconced himself among the furs and buffalo-robes. Soon after, old Pierre came in with his lantern; and, muttering to himself, began to pull over the bales of meat, and select the best pieces, as usual. But suddenly a hollow and sepulchral voice proceeded from the inner room: "Pierre, Pierre! Let that fat meat alone. Take nothing but lean." Pierre dropped his lantern, and bolted out into the fort screaming, in an agony of terror, that the devil was in the store-room; but tripping on the threshold, he pitched over upon the gravel, and lay senseless, stunned by the fall. The Canadians ran out to the rescue. Some lifted the unlucky Pierre; and others, making an extempore crucifix of two sticks, were proceeding to attack the devil in his stronghold, when the *bourgeois,* with a crestfallen countenance, appeared at the door. To add to his mortification, he was obliged to explain the whole strategem to Pierre, in order to bring him to his senses.*

I resolved to have a horse to ride. . . . In the afternoon I brought the creature into the plaza, and certain citizens held him by the head, and others by the tail, while I mounted him. As soon as they let go, he placed all his feet in a bunch together, lowered his back, and then suddenly arched it upward, and shot me straight into the air a matter of three or four feet! I came as straight down again, lit in the saddle, went instantly up again, came down almost on the high pommel, shot up again, and came down on the horse's neck—all in the space of three or four seconds. Then he rose and stood almost straight up on his hind feet, and I, clasping his lean neck desperately, slid back into the saddle, and held on. He came down, and immediately hoisted his heels into the air, delivering a vicious kick at the sky, and stood on his fore feet. And then down he came once more, and began the original exercise of shooting me straight up again.

The third time I went up I heard a stranger say: "Oh, *don't* he buck, though!" †

Both paragraphs have these points in common: first, the purpose of each is to tell a story—one in the first person, the other in the third; second, the

* Adapted from *The Oregon Trail* by Francis Parkman.
† From *Roughing It* by Mark Twain.

details of the incidents are arranged in a natural time sequence; and third, the sentences of both share equally in revealing the story; that is, no *one* sentence tells the story, but rather, *all* are needed for the whole account. As we have already noted, point of view, the *what, who,* and *where* essentials, and the effective ordering of events are the main characteristics of narrative paragraphs.

A common variation of the narrative paragraph is *dialogue.* You may question the grouping of dialogue under narrative paragraphs, reasoning that dialogue represents a conversation between two or more people in which each verbal exchange may seem to be a distinct paragraph. However, do not let the system of indentation used in printing dialogue confuse you. If you accepted our original definition of a paragraph—a unit of thought, implied or stated, which consists of related sentences as a vehicle of communication—then it is not difficult to see how dialogue conforms with this definition. Think of the topic of conversation as the main thought, and the exchange of ideas by the conversationalists as the related sentences. Thus, as long as the conversation follows one topic, the dialogue itself represents a unit of thought, or paragraph. When the topic changes, a new paragraph begins.

Let us see how the following example clarifies the idea that dialogue is a form of narration:

Then they went down the steep bank and across the stream, climbing over and around the boulders and up the other bank, pulling up by some projecting roots, and along it until they found where the lion had been trotting when Macomber first shot. There was dark blood on the short grass that the gun-bearers pointed out with grass stems, and that ran away behind the river bank trees.

"What do we do?" asked Macomber.

"Not much choice," said Wilson. "We can't bring the car over. Bank's too steep. We'll let him stiffen up a bit and then you and I'll go in and have a look for him."

"Can't we set the grass on fire?" Macomber asked.

"Too green."

"Can't we send beaters?"

Wilson looked at him appraisingly. "Of course we can," he said. "But it's just a touch murderous. You see we know the lion's wounded. You can drive an unwounded lion—he'll move on ahead of a noise—but a wounded lion's going to charge. You can't see him until you're right on him. He'll make himself perfectly flat in cover you wouldn't think would hide a hare. You can't very well send boys in there to that sort of show. Somebody bound to get mauled."

"What about the gun-bearers?"

"Oh, they'll go with us. It's their *shauri.* You see, they signed on for it. They don't look too happy though, do they?"

"I don't want to go in there," said Macomber. It was out before he knew he'd said it.

"Neither do I," said Wilson very cheerily. "Really no choice though." Then, as an afterthought, he glanced at Macomber and saw suddenly how he was trembling and the pitiful look on his face.

"You don't have to go in, of course," he said. "That's what I'm hired for, you know. That's why I'm so expensive."*

In this passage, the topic of the conversation (main thought) is the trapping and killing of a wounded lion. This topic has been restricted to a discussion of what should be done and who should do it. Notice that none of the sentences serves adequately as a topic sentence, but rather that all of them contribute equally to relating an incident. Also notice that the author's purpose is to relate with vivid immediacy, in this case a dramatic incident. These features are consistent with our understanding of a narrative paragraph.

Your analysis of the dialogue should further reveal that there are several inferences that can be drawn, namely: (a) the wounded lion is hiding in thick brush; (b) Wilson is an experienced lion hunter; (c) Macomber is inexperienced; (d) Macomber is afraid to go after the lion; and (e) their predicament is due to Macomber's failure to kill the lion with his first shot. We can also draw a conclusion, namely: it is much more dangerous to trap a wounded lion than an unwounded one. Thus, a careful reading of dialogue will yield the same kinds of information about the content that you have discovered in other paragraph readings. Except for indentation and quotation marks, dialogue is essentially like other narrative paragraphs.

Expository

An expository paragraph is the type that you will most often encounter, for it is used in textbooks, magazine articles, and prose works in general. The major characteristic of this type is that it explains or discusses facts and ideas, or tells how to do something. Neither the time sequence nor the point of view is an important determinant here. Instead, the purpose, form, and subject matter will distinguish it from a narrative paragraph. In an expository paragraph the purpose is to give a logical explanation of some fact or idea, whereas in a narrative paragraph the purpose is to relate a story. This difference, as well as those of form and subject matter, will be more apparent if we study the following expository example:

A struggle for existence inevitably follows from the high rate at which all organic beings tend to increase.

Every being, which during its natural lifetime produces several eggs or seeds, must suffer destruction during some period of its life, and during some season or occasional year, otherwise, on the principle of geometrical increase, its numbers would quickly become so inordinately great that no country could support the product. Hence, as more individuals are produced than can possibly survive, there must in every case be a struggle for existence, either one individual with another of the same species, or with the individuals of distinct species, or with the physical conditions of life. It is the doctrine of Malthus applied with manifold force to the whole animal and vegetable kingdoms; for in this case there can be no artificial increase of food, and no prudential restraint from marriage. Although some species may now be increasing, more or less rapidly, in numbers, all can not do so, for the world would not hold them.*

The purpose of this paragraph is to discuss the struggle for existence. It should be obvious that the procedure is to state the idea in a topic sentence and then use supporting sentences to explain or discuss the concept. In this example the procedure clearly differs from that in a narrative paragraph.

When a paragraph tells how to do something, such as "How to Build Model Airplanes," it is a form of exposition. Its purpose is to explain the method of accomplishing a specific task. Though in purpose it is like other expository paragraphs, in procedure it resembles narrative paragraphs in that all the sentences are needed to develop the main thought. In paragraphs that tell how to do something, the main thought is an explanation of the method being discussed. Note the purpose and form in this example:

HOW TO READ A BOOK

How should we read a book? Clearly, no answer that will do for everyone; but perhaps a few suggestions. In the first place, a good reader will give the writer the benefit of every doubt; the help of all his imagination; will follow as closely, interpret as intelligently as he can. In the next place, he will judge with the utmost severity. Every book, he will remember, has the right to be judged by the best of its kind. He will be adventurous, broad in his choice, true to his own instincts, yet ready to consider those of other people. This is an outline which can be filled in at taste and at leisure, but to read something after this fashion is to be a reader whom writers respect. It is by the means of such readers that masterpieces are helped into the world. †

Descriptive

A descriptive paragraph describes something. Its purpose is to paint a verbal picture, and, as in

narrative paragraphs, no one sentence singly expresses the thought (the picture) but all contribute. In descriptive paragraphs there is a directional or spatial order, that is, the specific features of the picture are given in a logical pattern (from head to toe, left to right, north to south, east to west, front to back, etc.) rather than in a desultory fashion. The subject matter in these paragraphs is confined to objects that can be perceived through the senses. This type of paragraph is found as frequently in fiction as in factual writing. The following examples will help to clarify the characteristics of descriptive paragraphs:

Jade has a special sensuous quality that other polished gems lack. It is not a perfect sphere as a pearl is, but it is pleasantly rounded, without sharp angles or jagged edges. It is firm and cool, but it does not have the harsh, cold hardness of a diamond. Its rich green color suggests a softness that is refreshing and relaxing. The round, cool firmness of jade makes it exceptionally gratifying to the sense of touch. It is not surprising that some primitive societies believe that these qualities make a piece of jade a cure for a pain in the side.

The interior of these [Shinto] monasteries is very splendid. On a platform is a gilded statue of the Buddha with attendant Bodhisattvas, above which hangs an elaborate canopy with angels carrying musical instruments. The timbers are decorated with vermilion, blue, and green, and with gilding and lacquer; the walls are covered with frescoes representing the paradise of Amida Buddha. The rich color harmony adds to the mystic calm of the Buddha, so that the whole effect suggests a plastic representation of the paradise seen in the T'ang paintings. ‡

These paragraphs have the same purpose—to describe something; each, however, attains its purpose in a different manner. The first deals with the feel of an object; the second, with the look, or arrangement of an object. Each, designed to evoke an image of jade or Shinto monasteries, is descriptive in form. As with these examples, all descriptive paragraphs share the same purpose, to help you explore and appreciate the physical world by appealing to your senses of smell, taste, sight, touch, and sound.

Argumentative

A paragraph which attempts to change or alter our beliefs or actions is argumentative. Such a paragraph may persuade us to follow a certain course of thought or behavior, or to dissuade us from taking a particular action. Or, an argumentative paragraph may defend or attack an opinion,

---

* From *The Origin of Species* by Charles Darwin.
† From "How Should One Read a Book?" by Virginia Woolf in *The Second Common Reader* (Harcourt, Brace & World, Inc.).

‡ From *Art Through the Ages* by Helen Gardner (1936 edition). Reprinted by permission of Harcourt, Brace & World, Inc.

decision, policy, or law. Although the writer's purposes in using argument are manifold, one characteristic unites them: he makes a logical, systematic effort to persuade the reader to accept his views. The most common use of argumentation is in magazine or newspaper editorials, but many articles of argumentative character deal with the pros and cons of current issues.

The following paragraphs are examples of argumentative writing. The first illustrates argument in which a policy is being attacked; the second illustrates argument in which an opinion is being defended.

Darwin's horrid doubt was unjustified. The human mind is free, and the creature of no single instinct. It can discover a truth, as it can create a lie. It can paint a Madonna, as it can arrange a battle. It can conceive of a brotherhood of man, as it can envision a community of death. It can postulate treaties or symphonies, massacres or gas-chambers, songs in the morning or dirges at night. It can probe the margins of a new enlightenment, or it can perpetuate the delusions of a romantic fallacy.*

I heartily accept the motto, "That government is best which governs least"; and I should like to see it acted up to more rapidly and systematically. Carried out, it finally amounts to this, which also I believe — "That government is best which governs not at all"; and when men are prepared for it, that will be the kind of govern-

* From *African Genesis* by Robert Ardrey. Copyright © 1961 by Literat S.A. Reprinted by permission of Atheneum Publishers.

ment which they will have. Government is at best but an expedient; but most governments are usually, and all governments are sometimes, inexpedient. The objections which have been brought against a standing army, and they are many and weighty, and deserve to prevail, may also at last be brought against a standing government. The standing army is only an arm of the standing government. The government itself, which is only the mode which the people have chosen to execute their will, is equally liable to be abused and perverted before the people can act through it. Witness the present Mexican war, the work of comparatively few individuals using the standing government as their tool; for, in the outset, the people would not have consented to this measure. †

In these argumentative paragraphs, Ardrey has chosen to attack Darwin's "horrid doubt" that if man had indeed evolved from natural selection his mind could not be considered "free," and Thoreau has defended Jefferson's dictum for minimal government. Although each writer has made his personal views clear, the validity of their respective arguments is determined by the soundness of their reasoning, and the aptness of their examples. This soundness of reasoning is what we as readers should look for before accepting or rejecting a writer's argument.

The following exercise will test your ability to recognize the four types of paragraphs as part of your analytical skills in paragraph reading.

† From "Civil Disobedience," by Henry David Thoreau.

EXERCISE 8: TYPES OF PARAGRAPHS

DIRECTIONS: Answer the questions below each paragraph to check your understanding of its content.

PART I

Capital punishment is, in my opinion, morally wrong. It has a bad effect on everyone, especially those involved in it. It gives a false sense of security to the public. It is vastly expensive. Worst of all it beclouds the entire issue of motivation in crime, which is so importantly relevant to the question of what to do for and with the criminal that will be most constructive to society as a whole. Punishing—and even killing—criminals may yield a kind of grim gratification; let us all admit that there are times when we are so shocked at the depredations of an offender that we persuade ourselves that this is a man the Creator didn't intend to create, and that we had better help to correct the mistake. But playing God in this way has no conceivable moral or scientific justification.*

1. What is the subject of this paragraph?

2. What type of paragraph is it?

3. What is the explicit thesis of this paragraph?

4. Does the author give valid reasons for his position?
   What reason does the author feel is most important?

5. What may we infer is the author's attitude on "motivation in crime"?

PART II

There is no other great English writer in whom the satiric element is so predominant as it is in [Jonathan] Swift. His three principal works, *The Battle of the Books*, *A Tale of a Tub*, and *Gulliver's Travels*, are all satires; his verse is prevailingly satirical, and the best of his miscellaneous writings are also satirical. The satire is generally tinged with irony, and sometimes it is irony pure and simple. The general standpoint is revealed in a sentence which has been quoted again and again from a letter to [Alexander] Pope: "I hate and detest that animal called man, although I heartily love John, Peter, Thomas, and so forth." The hatred can hardly be disputed by any reader of the loathsome *Voyage to the Houyhnhnms,* and the love is attested by the history of Swift's relations with men like Pope and Arbuthnot, and by his charities as Dean of St. Patrick's—his secret pension to Mrs. Dingley, for example. There is not much personality in his satire. He "exposed the fool and lash'd the knave, not as individuals, but as types. . . .†

1. What is the subject of this paragraph?

2. How may we classify it as to type?

3. What does this paragraph attempt to demonstrate?

* From "Verdict Guilty—Now What?" by Karl Menninger, *Harper's*, Aug., 1959.
† From *English Satire and Satirists* by Hugh Walker (J. M. Dent & Sons, Ltd.).

4. a. What is the purpose of the quotation from the letter to Pope?

b. What does this quotation reveal about the general standpoint in Swift's satires?

c. How does the last sentence help to clarify this standpoint?

5. How does the author justify his initial statement?

PART III

When I was a child of seven years old, my friends, on a holiday, filled my pocket with coppers. I went directly to a shop where they sold toys for children; and, being charmed with the sound of a *whistle,* that I met by the way in the hands of another boy, I voluntarily offered and gave all my money for one. I then came home, and went whistling all over the house, much pleased with my *whistle,* but disturbing all the family. My brothers, and sisters, and cousins, understanding the bargain I had made, told me I had given four times as much for it as it was worth; put me in mind what good things I might have bought with the rest of the money; and laughed at me so much for my folly, that I cried with vexation; and the reflection gave me more chagrin than the *whistle* gave me pleasure.*

1. What is the subject of this paragraph?

2. How may we classify it as to type?

3. What does the author mean by "filled my pocket with coppers"?

4. Observe how the author repeatedly emphasizes the whistle. In the light of this emphasis, what may we infer about the whistle?

5. What may we further infer is the purpose of this paragraph?

PART IV

In our country, before the War between the States, most stock and bond trading was for future delivery. A trader might buy or sell stock for delivery in 30, 60 or 90 days. This method, still used in England, allowed speculation without undue complication. Today a man who sells stock that he does not have must borrow it and make delivery within four days. If a dividend is declared in the stock while he is "short" of it, he must make good that dividend. But when, in the last century, he merely sold a promise to deliver in 90 days, no actual stocks were involved and no dividends had to be made good.†

1. What is the subject of this paragraph?

---

* From "The Whistle," by Benjamin Franklin.
† From *The Sophisticated Investor* by Burton Crane. Simon and Schuster, Inc. Copyright © 1959 by the author.

2. How may we classify it as to type?

3. What is the purpose of this paragraph?

4. a. According to the paragraph, what is the difference between trading in England and in America?

   b. What is the difference between trading in mid-nineteenth-century America and mid-twentieth-century America?

5. a. What may we infer is the meaning of being "short" of a stock?

   b. What may we infer about speculation in today's trading?

   c. What advantage does the stockholder of today have over his counterpart of the pre-Civil War era?

PART V

Mr. Robinson is really an uncommonly nice looking young fellow. He must, one thinks, be the jeune premier; for it is not in reason to suppose that a second such attractive male figure should appear in one story. The slim, shapely frame, the elegant suit of new mourning, the small head and regular features, the pretty little moustache, the frank clear eyes, the wholesome bloom on the youthful complexion, the well brushed glossy hair, not curly, but of fine texture and good dark color, the arch of good nature in the eyebrows, the erect forehead and neatly pointed chin, all announce the man who will love and suffer later on. And that he will not do so without sympathy is guaranteed by an engaging sincerity and eager modest serviceableness which stamp him as a man of amiable nature. . . .*

1. What is the subject of this paragraph?

2. How may we classify it as to type?

3. What may we infer is the purpose of this paragraph?

4. On what does the author base his judgment of Robinson's nature?

5. a. What does the author mean by "jeune premier"?

   b. From the reference to Robinson as the jeune premier, what may we infer about the other attractive male figure alluded to in this paragraph?

* From *Man and Superman* by George Bernard Shaw. With the permission of The Public Trustee and The Society of Authors.

PART VI

They sat by the fire and filled their mouths with beans and chewed mightily. A few beans slipped out of the side of Lennie's mouth. George gestured with his spoon. "What you gonna say tomorrow when the boss asks you questions?"

Lennie stopped chewing and swallowed. His face was concentrated. "I . . . I ain't gonna . . . say a word."

"Good boy! That's fine, Lennie! Maybe you're gettin' better. When we get the coupla acres I can let you tend the rabbits all right. 'Specially if you remember as good as that."

Lennie choked with pride. "I can remember," he said.

George motioned with his spoon again. "Look, Lennie. I want you to look around here. You can remember this place, can't you? The ranch is about a quarter mile up that way. Just follow the river?"

"Sure," said Lennie. "I can remember this. Di'n't I remember about not gonna say a word?"

"Course you did. Well, look. Lennie—if you jus' happen to get in trouble like you always done before, I want you to come here an' hide in the brush."

"Hide in the brush," said Lennie slowly.

"Hide in the brush till I come for you. Can you remember that?"

"Sure I can, George. Hide in the brush till you come."

"But you ain't gonna get in no trouble, because if you do, I won't let you tend the rabbits." He threw his empty bean can off into the brush.

"I won't get in no trouble, George. I ain't gonna say a word."*

1. What is this passage about?

2. How may we classify it as to type?

3. What is the purpose of this passage?

4. a. What inferences may we draw about Lennie?

   b. About George?

   c. About the relationship between Lennie and George?

5. a. What may we conclude about some of the past experiences of Lennie and George?

   b. What situation does George anticipate?

   c. What plans do George and Lennie have for the future?

* From *Of Mice and Men* by John Steinbeck. Copyright 1937 by John Steinbeck. Reprinted by permission of The Viking Press, Inc.

METHODS OF PARAGRAPH DEVELOPMENT

In earlier sections of this chapter, we have demonstrated how the supporting sentences in a paragraph may reinforce the main thought by: (1) giving evidence to substantiate the topic sentence; (2) providing examples for meaningful generalizations; or (3) enumerating steps for carrying out the central idea. But now that we are ready to study the methods of paragraph development, we must make a closer analysis of supporting sentences and their role in the expansion of the main thought.

Among writers, the methods of developing paragraphs vary. Some have very unorthodox, and sometimes unique, patterns which are handled so skillfully that the reader's comprehension is not adversely affected. Others utilize traditional methods of development or easily recognized variations. These include the use of particulars and details, illustration and example, comparison and contrast, definition, and analogy. Each of these methods will be discussed separately, in order that you may understand its characteristics and the manner in which they affect the thought of the paragraph.

Development by Particulars and Details

This method, used in the majority of expository paragraphs, consists of a main thought accompanied by details which relate to it and to one another; in this fashion, unity of ideas is achieved. For certain kinds of emphasis the writer may give details first and conclude with a statement of the main thought. But regardless of the position of the topic sentence, the use of details and particulars to develop the thought is what characterizes this method.

Narrative and descriptive paragraphs are also developed by particulars and details. But as we have pointed out, in narrative paragraphs the "thought" may be nothing less than the whole incident being related, and in descriptive paragraphs, it is the whole object being pictured.

... and then Peggotty opened a little door and showed me my bedroom. It was the completest and most desirable bedroom ever seen—in the stern of the vessel; with a little window, where the rudder used to go through; a little looking-glass, just the right height for me, nailed against the wall, and framed with oyster-shells; a little bed, which there was just room enough to get into; and a nosegay of seaweed in a blue mug on the table. The walls were whitewashed as white as milk, and the patchwork counterpane made my eyes quite ache with its brightness. One thing I particularly noticed in this delightful house, was the smell of fish; which was so searching, that when I took out my pocket-handkerchief to wipe my nose, I found it smelt exactly as if it had wrapped up a lobster. On my imparting this discovery in confidence to Peggotty, she informed me that her brother dealt in lobsters, crabs, and crawfish; and I afterwards found that a heap of these creatures, in a state of wonderful conglomeration with one another, and never leaving off pinching whatever they laid hold of, were usually to be found in a little wooden outhouse where the pots and kettles were kept.*

MAIN THOUGHT: It was the completest and most desirable bedroom ever seen—in the stern of the vessel.

METHOD OF DEVELOPMENT: Particulars and details
little window
little looking-glass framed with oyster-shells
little bed
blue mug with nosegay of seaweed
whitewashed walls
bright patchwork counterpane
sharp odor of fish
wonderful conglomeration of shellfish in wooden outhouse

Development by Illustration and Example

Often when we make a statement, we provide evidence of its truth by giving an example, or even several examples. Paragraphs which are developed by illustration and example follow this pattern. Such paragraphs consist of a main thought supported by general or specific examples. The paragraph may be brief, presenting only one typical case, or it may be extended to a series of examples, all of which develop the initial thought and prove the conclusion that may be drawn. The appropriateness of the illustration or example will determine how well the thought has been conveyed.

It is often very easy to recognize paragraphs that are developed by this method, for many times the writer introduces his illustration or examples with such transitional phrases as, *to illustrate, for example, for instance, a typical case.* Even when the writer does not use transitional phrases, this method is generally easy to spot if the illustrations and examples are aptly positioned. In the examples which follow, one paragraph has a series of specific examples without a transitional phrase; the other presents a typical case which is introduced by "for instance":

A foolish consistency is the hobgoblin of little minds, adored by little statesmen and philosophers and divines. With consistency a great soul has simply nothing to do. He may as well concern himself with his shadow on the wall. Speak what you think now in hard words and to-morrow speak what to-morrow thinks in hard words again, though it contradict everything you said today.—"Ah, so you shall be sure to be misunderstood."—Is it so

* From *David Copperfield* by Charles Dickens.

bad, then, to be misunderstood? Pythagoras was misunderstood, and Socrates, and Jesus, and Luther, and Copernicus, and Galileo, and Newton, and every pure and wise spirit that ever took flesh. To be great is to be misunderstood.*

MAIN THOUGHT: Whereas small men are concerned with consistency, to great men it is of no importance.

METHOD OF DEVELOPMENT: Examples (specific)
Pythagoras, Socrates, Jesus, Luther, Copernicus, Galileo, Newton

In scientific inquiry it becomes a matter of duty to expose a supposed law to every possible kind of verification, and to take care, moreover, that this is done intentionally, and not left to a mere accident. . . . And in science, as in common life, our confidence in a law is in exact proportion to the absence of variation in the result of our experimental verifications. For instance, if you let go your grasp of an article you may have in your hand, it will immediately fall to the ground. That is a very common verification of one of the best established laws of nature — that of gravitation. The method by which men of science establish the existence of that law is exactly the same as that by which we have established the trivial proposition about the sourness of hard and green apples. But we believe it in such an extensive, thorough, and unhesitating manner because the universal experience of mankind verifies it, and we can verify it ourselves at any time; and that is the strongest possible foundation on which any natural law can rest. †

MAIN THOUGHT: A scientific law is established only after thorough and extensive experimentation yields results that are verifiable.

METHOD OF DEVELOPMENT: Illustration (one typical case)
On releasing an object from one's hand, the article falls to the ground — a common verification of the law of gravity.

Development by Comparison and Contrast

Strictly speaking, when we "compare" two things, we show either how they are alike or how they are different; and when we "contrast" two things, we compare them particularly with an eye to their differences. But for the sake of simplicity we may call the showing of similarities "comparison" and the showing of differences "contrast." A writer may use comparison if he feels the similarities between two things are greater than the differences, or if he wishes to explain an unfamiliar idea or object by showing how it is like a familiar one. On the other hand, if he wants to give evidence of subtle differences between two things which are frequently thought of as having much in common, he sets them

* From "Self-Reliance," by Ralph Waldo Emerson.
† From "The Method of Scientific Investigation," by Thomas Henry Huxley.

in opposition by using contrast. Sometimes the writer may show both similarities and differences in order to give a clearer picture of the relationship between two things.

The methods of comparison and contrast make use of a topic sentence which describes two subjects as being similar or different; the supporting sentences provide specific details for the development of the comparison or the contrast. To present these likenesses or differences a writer may employ a point-by-point basis, relating each item to both subjects at the same time; or he may choose a unit basis whereby he discusses all aspects of one subject before mentioning those of the other. The former method has an advantage when many separate aspects of a problem require collation; an undue burden might be put upon the reader if they were not individually juxtaposed. If the latter method — which encourages development of each idea — is used, a separate section that actually collates the similarities or differences is usually necessary.

Nathaniel Hawthorne and Herman Melville are two of America's most outstanding writers between whom there were strong personal ties as well as a kinship in their literary art. Both of these nineteenth century authors were native New Englanders, neighbors, and friends — who in their leisure Berkshire walks and subsequent letters discussed such topics of common interest as religion, books, and publishers. In Hawthorne's "Rappaccini's Daughter" and Melville's "Benito Cereno" are striking examples of characterization and their concern with the problem of good and evil at work in the universe. Each author presents three key characters whose lives are influenced by the motives and acts of the others. Hawthorne depicts a young and beautiful Italian girl, Beatrice, who is the slave of her selfish, domineering father and his scientific pursuits. Attracted to Beatrice is the daring youth Giovanni whose attempts to free the woman he loves result in his discovery of Rappaccini's evil nature and in his sweetheart's death. In "Benito Cereno" Melville shows a young Spanish ship captain, Don Benito, as a captive of a Negro slave, Babu, who has led the slaves aboard the ship in a successful revolt against their Spanish owner, slain in the mutiny. An American seaman, Captain Delano, believes the vessel to be in distress and boards it. After many enigmatic occurrences he perceives Babu's evil intentions, effects Benito's escape, and takes command of the ship, bound for Lima. Both Hawthorne and Melville describe the consuming qualities of evil; having gone so far in Beatrice and Don Benito, it renders a completely effective rescue impossible. Although Beatrice is no longer exposed to her father's experiments, the antidote that Giovanni intends for her rescue brings about her death. Don Benito, after brooding over the moral wrongs of slavery and his ignominious position, is a man broken in spirit. Though he is physically freed from Babu's control, he seems still to be a captive mentally, and soon after Babu is hanged Don Benito joins him in death.

MAIN THOUGHT: Between Hawthorne and Melville, two of America's outstanding writers, were a personal bond and some similarities of artistic expression

METHOD OF DEVELOPMENT: Comparison (point by point)
I. Background
   A. New Englanders
   B. Common interests (religion, books, writing)
   C. Nineteenth century writers
II. Association
   A. Neighbors
   B. Friends
   C. Correspondents
   D. Walking-companions
III. Similarities in writing
   A. Common theme: problem of good and evil in universe
   B. Parallels between stories
     1. Three key characters
       a. "Rappaccini's Daughter": Rappaccini, Beatrice, and Giovanni
       b. "Benito Cereno": Babu, Benito, Delano
     2. Evil character dominant
       a. Rappaccini's hold over Beatrice
       b. Babu's hold over Don Benito
     3. Consuming quality of evil
       a. Subjugation of human beings
       b. Exploitation of human beings
     4. Partly frustrated rescue
       a. Antidote kills Beatrice
       b. Benito follows Babu in death

Although both Alexander Hamilton and Thomas Jefferson helped mold the political and economic structure of the United States, these two statesmen represent opposite forces in the evolution of our national traditions. Their vital contributions are largely complementary, but fundamentally dissimilar. As one of the leading spokesmen for the Federalist Party, Hamilton urged the establishment of a strong central government of aristocratic character, able to maintain order, protect property rights, and provide the bases of a sound, growing capitalist economy. His *Federalist* papers helped to win ratification of a constitution establishing a federal union instead of a loose confederation of states. He argued eloquently the case for an independent federal judiciary. Once the nation was established, he continued to argue for the maintenance of control by the few able men of property. As first Secretary of the Treasury in the new federal government, he drafted brilliant plans for orderly procedures in government. By laying the foundations for a federal banking system, Hamilton not only aided commerce and industry but helped to place both the government and the economy on a sound footing. Jefferson, as leader of the Republicans, advocated the maintenance of a weak central government of democratic character,

unable to interfere with the personal rights of the individual or to control national life without the consent of strong state governments. He fought the Federalist judges, who tended to value property more than liberty. In economics, he was primarily an equalitarian agrarian, believing that the government and the welfare of society might best be entrusted to the many small land owners whose freedom and equality he sought to protect both from government and from the expansion of commerce and manufacturing. His successful fight against primogeniture and entail in Virginia helped to retard the concentration of property in few hands. By the Louisiana Purchase, he obtained more land for the small farmers of the nation and prevented a war which would probably have brought much suffering to the poor and much added wealth to the rich. By both political and economic means, as party leader, and as president of the country, Jefferson sought to protect the individual landowner's right to "life, liberty, and the pursuit of happiness."

MAIN THOUGHT: The vital contributions of Alexander Hamilton and Thomas Jefferson were fundamentally dissimilar

METHOD OF DEVELOPMENT: Contrast (unit by unit)
I. Alexander Hamilton
   A. Led Federalist Party
   B. Urged establishment of strong central government controlled by aristocratic few
   C. Wrote *Federalist* papers advocating federal union and organization of independent federal judiciary
   D. Served as first Secretary of Treasury in federal government
   E. Drafted plans for orderly government procedures
   F. Laid foundations for federal banking system
   G. Encouraged commerce and industry
II. Thomas Jefferson
   A. Led Republican Party
   B. Advocated maintenance of weak central government, democratic in character and balanced by strong state governments
   C. Fought Federalist judges and their emphasis on property rights
   D. Served as president of nation
   E. Improved prospects for small landholdings
   F. Obtained Louisiana Purchase
   G. Encouraged individual farmer's right to "life, liberty, and pursuit of happiness"

Although the point-by-point basis was used in the comparison, and the unit-by-unit basis in the contrast, they are not perquisites for either method. The writer's choice of comparison or contrast to develop an idea and his decision to use the point-by-point or unit approach will depend on his purpose and topic. Both methods and both approaches may be employed effectively, singly or combined, with or without variations.

Development by Definition

Some paragraphs are about words or ideas whose meanings are not generally understood, or whose connotations are so personal to the writer that he may need to define them in order to convey his thoughts adequately. Or perhaps the word or idea is so vital to the entire composition that a paragraph defining them is a valuable preliminary to the discussion. In either case, the definition may follow a stated question, or it may be an answer to the implied question, "What does this mean?" A writer frequently uses details or examples to clarify his terms. Occasionally, he develops them by the process of elimination — that is, by explaining what something is by first showing what it is not. Regardless of the devices borrowed from other methods, if a writer's purpose is to define, he chooses the method of definition.

A classic is a work which gives pleasure to the minority which is intensely and permanently interested in literature. It lives on because the minority, eager to renew the sensation of pleasure, is eternally curious and is therefore engaged in an eternal process of re-discovery. A classic does not survive for any ethical reason. It does not survive because it conforms to certain canons, or because neglect would not kill it. It survives because it is a source of pleasure, and because the passionate few can no more neglect it than a bee can neglect a flower. The passionate few do not read "the right things" because they are right. That is to put the cart before the horse. "The right things" are the right things solely because the passionate few *like* reading them.*

MAIN THOUGHT: A classic; what it is (A classic is a work of lasting interest to a small but enthusiastic group)

METHOD OF DEVELOPMENT: Definition
    A classic
        is a work
        gives pleasure to an intensely and permanently interested minority
        lives on through their curiosity and re-discovery
        survives as the right thing solely because it brings reading enjoyment to the passionate few

Development by Analogy

Analogy is used to clarify a less familiar idea with a better known one from a different field of experience. Although analogy is a form of comparison, the purpose of it is not to compare the two

* From *Literary Taste* by Arnold Bennett (George H. Doran, 1927).

things themselves, but rather to show a resemblance between their attributes. Many times in conversation we use analogies to add color to our speech, or to aid us in expressing an idea. Thus, when Shakespeare said, "All the world's a stage and all the men and women merely players," he was revealing his idea of life in terms of the theater. He assumed, of course, that we are familiar with the theater and its nomenclature; if we are not, we will probably miss the point of the analogy.

Analogies that use the words *like* or *as* are actually similies; those that do not — such as Shakespeare's comparison of the world to a stage — are more direct, and are called *metaphors*. Often a writer will use specific details to expand and to support the similarities suggested by the initial metaphor or simile. But the test of the effectiveness of an analogy should always be whether it makes the original object or idea clearer, or if it adds imaginative perspective to our understanding. To explain the working of the heart by analogy with pumping stations can be genuinely clarifying; other analogies could be much less so.

In such a day, in September or October, Walden is a perfect forest mirror, set round with stones as precious to my eye as if fewer and rarer. Nothing so fair, so pure, and at the same time so large, as a lake, perchance, lies on the surface of the earth. Sky water. It needs no fence. Nations come and go without defiling it. It is a mirror which no stone can crack. whose quicksilver will never wear off, whose gilding Nature continually repairs; no storms, no dust, can dim its surface ever fresh; — a mirror in which all impurity presented to it sinks, swept and dusted by the sun's hazy brush, — this the light dust-cloth — which retains no breath that is breathed on it, but sends its own to float as cloud high above its surface, and be reflected in its bosom still.†

MAIN THOUGHT: A lake is a perfect and durable mirror

METHOD OF DEVELOPMENT: Analogy
    Unfamiliar idea:
        Qualities of a lake
            Beauty of its frame of stones
            Durability of its surface
            Shining of its surface
            Sun-haze on its surface
            Moisture arising from it
    Familiar idea:
        Qualities of a mirror
            Beauty of its jeweled frame
            Brittleness
            Quicksilver
            Light cloth dusting it
            Breath retained on its surface

Although we are generally familiar with the appearance and mirrorlike reflection of a lake,

† From "The Ponds" in *Walden* by Henry David Thoreau.

Thoreau wishes to point out other qualities of which we probably are not aware. To accomplish this purpose, he uses analogy.

From this example we can understand more clearly the differences between comparison and analogy. Whereas comparison reveals that two ideas or objects *are* alike, analogy indicates that certain aspects of one *suggest* those of another, usually a more familiar object or idea. Thus in this analogy the writer speaks of a lake in terms of a mirror, and suggests that the durability of a lake is like an unbreakable, permanent mirror. Using this procedure, he capitalizes on the reader's knowledge of mirrors, specifically their fragility, to present a lucid and imaginative view of a perfect lake.

Development by Combination of Methods

The methods of paragraph development are not antithetical to one another. In fact, most paragraphs are developed by a combination of the methods we have discussed. Since a writer's major concern is the effectiveness of his ideas, he naturally uses any method or variation he thinks appropriate. But for purposes of classification, we can say that paragraphs with two or more equally prominent methods are developed by combination.

Parasitism is a degenerate condition in which an animal obtains its food at the expense of some other larger animal. It is predatism with the size relations reversed. Some parasites have only very temporary dependence upon a host animal. This is true, for example, of the [female] mosquito which must have a blood meal in order to bring her eggs to a viable condition (the [male] requires only plant juices—the diet otherwise of the [female]—and hence does not bite). Other parasites can get along without a host, but develop more rapidly if a host is available; such are spoken of as *facultative* parasites (from *facultas* = permission, option). Examples are the various leeches, which can operate as predators on snails and insects, or which can derive nourishment faster by sucking blood from a vertebrate. The opposite of a facultative parasite is one that depends entirely on finding the right host—an *obligate* parasite (from the Latin *ob* = about, *ligare* = to bind). Still another distinction can be made between parasites: those that operate while outside the body of the host (ectoparasites), and those that enter to take up an internal position (endoparasites).*

MAIN THOUGHT: Parasitism: what it is and how it operates

METHOD OF DEVELOPMENT: Combination of Methods— Definition and Examples
  I. Definition
     A. Parasitism
     B. Facultative parasites
     C. Obligate parasites
     D. Ectoparasites
     E. Endoparasites
  II. Examples
     A. Female mosquito
     B. Various leeches

In this example, note how the methods of definition and examples have been combined to make the paragraph meaningful. The definitions of parasitism and the kinds of parasites have been clarified by the use of appropriately selected examples.

The following exercise will test your ability to recognize the various methods of paragraph development.

* From *The Biotic World and Man, op cit.*

EXERCISE 9: METHODS OF PARAGRAPH DEVELOPMENT

DIRECTIONS: Answer the questions below each paragraph to check your understanding of its content and your retention of the main ideas in this section.

PART I

Washington has sought the right of self-government in local affairs by the traditional and Constitutional method of petitioning Congress for a redress of its grievances. A Home Rule Committee led by distinguished District citizens has patiently sought to make known to Congress and the country the ills and disadvantages that arise from disfranchisement. Although their hopes have been dashed repeatedly by the Southern clique that controls the House District Committee, they have returned perennially to Congress with cheerful confidence in the ultimate willingness of the American People to extend democracy to all Americans. The granting of statehood to Alaska and Hawaii has fortified that confidence. This seems to be the year for the District of Columbia, the last outcast of American democracy.*

1. a. What is the main thought of this paragraph?

   b. Which sentence best states the thought?

2. What method of development is used?

3. According to the paragraph, what is the traditional way of seeking the right of self-government?

4. What does the author cite as the major obstacle in Washington's bid for self-government in local affairs?

5. What does the author mean when he refers to the District as "the last outcast of American democracy"?

PART II

Reduced to its essence, Dr. Peale's philosphy is this: the mind of man is like an eight-cylinder motor. If it feeds on the "defeat thoughts," it splutters and chokes, like a Cadillac that has been filled with bad gasoline. Weighed down by negative thoughts, man loses his self-confidence and his power to act. Everything in him turns gloomy, somber, sour. The sourer he gets, the more he alienates his friends and associates, thus exacerbating his initial feeling of rejection and insecurity. To escape this vicious cycle, he must cleanse his mind of negative thoughts and inject new positive ones. This will act on his spiritual metabolism like high-octane gasoline on a coughing engine, turning his mind into a "power-producing plant." And how do you go about getting these "positive thoughts"? The answer is simple: by praying (prayer is an essential ritual in the "power-producing process"), by going to church (going to church also ensures a longer life), and above all by dipping into the Bible. †

1. a. What is this paragraph about?

   b. Which sentence best expresses the main thought?

* From "Exiles in the Capitol," by Alan Barth, *The Reporter,* Feb. 4, 1960.
† From "God and Success," by Curtis Cate, *The Atlantic,* April, 1957.

2. What method of development is used?

3. In selecting this method, what basic assumption did the writer make about its importance in conveying the main thought?

4. a. According to the paragraph, what is the result of possessing negative thoughts?

   b. What is the result of possessing positive thoughts?

5. Why does the author use quotation marks with such expressions as "power-producing plant," "defeat thoughts," etc.?

PART III

Hypnosis also is being used in attempts to probe our subconscious to find why we buy or do not buy certain products. Ruthrauff and Ryan, the New York ad agency, has been employing a prominent hypnotist and a panel of psychologists and psychiatrists in its effort to get past our mental blockages, which are so bothersome to probers when we are conscious. The agency has found that hypnosis sharpens our power to recall. We can remember things that we couldn't otherwise remember. One place they've been using it is to try to find why we use the brand of product we do. An official cited the case of a man who under hypnosis told why he preferred a certain make of car and always bought it. This man, under hypnosis, was able to repeat word for word an ad he had read more than twenty years before that had struck his fancy. The agency is vague as to whether it is at this moment using a hypnotist. However, it does uphold the fact that the results to date have been "successful" to the degree that "we believe in years to come it may be employed as a method."*

1. a. What is the main thought of this paragraph?

   b. Which sentence states the thought?

2. What method of development is used?

3. a. According to the paragraph, what is the purpose of the use of hypnosis?

   b. How does hypnosis assist ad agencies in accomplishing this purpose?

4. What does the case cited prove?

5. a. What may we infer about ourselves from the cited case?

   b. What generalizations, if any, can we make from the cited case and our inference?

* From *The Hidden Persuaders* by Vance Packard (David McKay Company, Inc.)

PART IV

If a poem may be said to have an aim, it must be to make the reader see with a new acuteness and feel with a new awareness. To do this the poet may use statement or suggestion; he may try to persuade by careful reason or hypnotize the reader by a frenzied energy of words. He may intoxicate himself and his readers with rhythmical orgies like Swinburne; he may plunge into a flood of free assciations and erupting images like Gerard Manley Hopkins and Hart Crane; he may build a world directly from his backgrounds, like Robert Burns and Robert Frost, or, like Edgar Allan Poe, turn hallucination into an unforgettable otherworld, a misty mid-region of ghoul-haunted palaces, pendulous shadows, and desperate seas.*

1. a. What is the main thought of this paragraph?

   b. Which sentence best expresses the thought?

2. What method of development is used?

3. a. According to the paragraph, what is the probable aim of a poem?

   b. How does Hart Crane attempt to do this?

   c. How does Swinburne attempt this?

4. How do the methods of Robert Frost and Edgar Allan Poe differ?

5. a. Which of the methods mentioned seems most rooted in reality? Why?

   b. Which seems least rooted? Why?

* From "Preface" of *A Treasury of Great Poems, English and American* by Louis Untermeyer. Rev. and enlarged. (Simon and Schuster, Inc., 1955.)

PART V

The American *religionist*—the title is a relatively recent one—has no exact counterpart in any other country. He is not a saint or a holy man, with his staff and his bowl, as we have been brought up to imagine them. There is none of the monk or the mystic about him, though there is quite a touch of the missionary. He is not a man of meditation but an activist; not a man of faith and prayer himself so much as a man who assiduously instructs others in how to acquire faith and how to pray. A religionist does not even need to be a clergyman. His mission is simply to popularize and sell religious health. He is a zealous promoter of psychic comfort, a super-salesman of salvation who has revolutionized the traditional methods of propagating piety by learning to peddle faith with all the *élan* of a Madison Avenue advertiser plugging a new barbiturate.*

1. a. What is this paragraph about?

  b. Which sentence best expresses the thought?

2. What method of development is used?

3. a. According to the paragraph, what is the mission of the American religionist?

  b. What does he advocate?

4. In telling what an American religionist is not, the author constructs an image of what a religionist once was. What is that image?

5. a. What is the author's attitude toward the American religionist?

  b. Which statements most strongly indicate his attitude?

* From "God and Success," *op cit.*

PART VI

Venus and the earth might also be called the twin sisters of the solar system. The orbit of Venus, which the planet travels in 225 days, is nearer to a perfect circle than that of any other planet, and that of the earth is not far behind in this respect. The two planets are approximately of the same size, Venus having a diameter of 7575 miles and the earth having one of 7918 miles, and they are closer together in space than any other major planets.*

1. a. What is this paragraph about?

   b. Which sentence best states the thought?

2. What method of development is used?

3. Which planet is the larger of the two?

4. How long does it take Venus to circle the sun?

5. Which planet may we conclude has the longer year? Why?

---

* From *New Handbook of the Heavens* by Herbert J. Bernard, Dorothy A. Bennett, and H. S. Rice (McGraw-Hill Book Co., Inc., 1941). Used by permission.

PART VII

Visitors from space may have landed on our planet dozens — hundreds — of times during the long, empty ages while Man was still a dream of the distant future. Indeed, they could have landed on 90 per cent of the Earth as recently as two or three hundred years ago — and we would never have heard of it. If one searches through old newspapers and local records, one can find large numbers of curious incidents that could be interpreted as visitations from space. That stimulating if eccentric writer Charles Fort made a collection of such occurrences in his book *Lo!* and one is inclined to give them more weight than any comparable modern reports, for the simple reason that they happened long before anyone had ever thought of space travel. Yet at the same time one cannot take them *too* seriously, because before scientific education was widespread even the commonest celestial phenomena — meteors, comets, auroras, and so on — gave rise to the most incredible stories. As they still do, in fact.*

1. a. What is the main thought of this paragraph?

   b. Which sentence best states it?

2. What method of development is used?

3. a. On what does the author base the possibility that visitors from space may have landed on our planet in the past?

   b. Why is the author disinclined to give much weight to modern reports of visitors from space?

4. Is the author's attitude toward accounts of visitations from space in the past one of belief, disbelief, skepticism or indifference?

5. May we infer that the author believes that there is a possibility that an older civilization than ours may exist on another planet? If so, why?

* From "Where's Everybody?" by Arthur C. Clarke, *Harper's,* Nov., 1957.

PART VIII

Greek mythology is largely made up of stories about gods and goddesses, but it must not be read as a kind of Greek Bible, an account of the Greek religion. According to the most modern idea, a real myth has nothing to do with religion. It is an explanation of something in nature; how, for instance, any and everything in the universe came into existence: men, animals, this or that tree or flower, the sun, the moon, the stars, storms, eruptions, earthquakes, all that is and all that happens. Thunder and lightning are caused when Zeus hurls his thunderbolt. A volcano erupts because a terrible creature is imprisoned in the mountain and every now and then struggles to get free. The Dipper, the constellation called also the Great Bear, does not set below the horizon because a goddess once was angry at it and decreed that it should never sink into the sea. Myths are early science, the result of men's first trying to explain what they saw around them. But there are many so-called myths which explain nothing at all. These tales are pure entertainment, the sort of thing people would tell each other on a long winter's evening. The story of Pygmalion and Galatea is an example; it has no conceivable connection with any event in nature. Neither has the Quest of the Golden Fleece, nor Orpheus and Eurydice, nor many another. This fact is now generally accepted; and we do not have to try to find in every mythological heroine the moon or the dawn and in every hero's life a sun myth. The stories are early literature as well as early science.*

1. a. What is this paragraph about?

   b. Which sentence best states the thought?

2. What method of development is used here?

3. Into what categories does the author divide myths? Cite an example for each category.

4. According to Greek beliefs, what caused:
   (a) volcanic eruptions?

   (b) thunder and lightning?

5. a. What may we infer was the Greek belief concerning the setting of stars and constellations?

   b. Why was The Dipper an exception?

* From *Mythology* by Edith Hamilton (Little, Brown and Co.). Copyright 1940, 1942 by Edith Hamilton.

PART IX

The difference between the satire of [Jonathan] Swift and that of [Richard] Steele and [Joseph] Addison is due mainly to two causes. The first and fundamental cause is the difference between the men in character. Swift's satire was savage because there was savagery in his own nature; whereas Steele was the most genial and kind-hearted of men, and though there may have been some taint of malice in Addison, he was essentially good-natured. The second and subsidiary cause was the difference of the circumstances in which the satires were produced. Swift's great satires were substantive works; and even the shorter occasional papers were for the most part independent of their surroundings. But the papers of Steele and Addison had to conform to the general tone of the periodicals to which they were contributed. . . .*

1. a. What is this paragraph about?

   b. Which sentence best expresses the thought?

2. What method of development is used?

3. a. According to the paragraph, what were the causes of the difference in the satire of the three men?

   b. Which cause does the author feel is most important?

4. a. Which of the three men was most amiable?

   b. On what do you base your judgment?

5. a. What may we infer about the satire of Steele and Addison?

   b. Would we be justified in assuming that Addison's satire might have been more biting if he had been independent of his surroundings as was Swift? If so, why?

* From *English Satire and Satirists, op. cit.*

PART X

Yet, in spite of this midguided Victorian canonization—so alien from the spirit of the father of English history, the Venerable Bede—of the history of the particular country in which one happened to have been born, the unconscious attitude of the Victorian Englishman towards history was that of someone living outside history altogether. He took it for granted—without warrant— that he himself was standing on *terra firma*, secure against being engulfed in that ever-rolling stream in which Time had borne all his less privileged sons away. In his own privileged state of being emancipated, as he supposed, from history, the Victorian Englishman gazed with curiosity, condescension, and a touch of pity, but altogether without apprehension, at the spectacle of less fortunate denizens of other places and periods struggling and foundering in history's flood—in much the same way as, in a mediaeval Italian picture, the saved lean over the balustrade of Heaven to look down complacently at the torments of the damned in Hell. Charles the First—worse luck for him—had been in history, but Sir Robert Walpole, though threatened with impeachment, had just managed to scramble out of the surf, while we ourselves were well beyond high-water mark in a snug coign of vantage where nothing could happen to us. Our more backward contemporaries might, perhaps, still be waist-high in the now receding tide, but what was that to us?*

1. a. What is this paragraph about?

   b. Which sentence best states the thought?

2. What method of development is used?

3. a. According to the paragraph, who was the father of English history?

   b. What "misfortune" befell Charles the First?

   c. What was the attitude of the Victorian Englishman toward history?

4. a. What does the author mean by: "this misguided Victorian canonization . . . of the history of the particular country in which one happened to have been born"?

   b. To whom does the author refer as "our more backward contemporaries"?

5. a. What is the author's attitude toward the Victorian view of history?

   b. By inference, what does he advocate?

   c. Why?

* From *Civilization on Trial* by Arnold Toynbee (Oxford University Press). Copyright 1948.

SUPPLEMENTARY ACTIVITIES

DISCUSSION QUESTIONS: The following questions are based on information given and implied in the paragraphs you have just read in Exercise 9. If necessary, you may reread the paragraphs in order to answer the questions. The Part numbers are given in the parentheses immediately after each question.

1. What points do Dr. Peale's philosophy of "positive thinking" and Cate's definition of the mission of the American "religionist" have in common? (Parts II and V)

2. Many contemporary scientists are convinced that life exists on Venus. What similarities do Venus and Earth share that could be used as argument for the theory that life exists on Venus? (Part VI)

3. How is it possible that visitors from space could have landed on 90 per cent of our planet two or three hundred years ago without our having any knowledge of such landings? (Part VII)

4. Toynbee speaks of the "misguided Victorian canonization" of the history of one's own country. How is a similar canonization of Western Civilization as a whole typical in our American schools today? (Part X)

PARAGRAPH WRITING: Select one of the following topics and write a paragraph using one of the methods of development that we have discussed in this chapter. Below your paragraph, restate the main thought and name the method of development you have used.

1. Why Capital Punishment Should (or Should Not) Be Abolished
2. A Comparative View of Theodore Roosevelt and John F. Kennedy
3. The Republican Party vs. the Democratic Party
4. The Iconoclast Called Progress
5. The Teacher Who Most Influenced My Life

INTERPRETING AN AUTHOR'S TONE

We are all aware that communication through speech involves more than the spoken word. Our attitude on a subject is reflected by our tone of voice. On various occasions we may use the same verbal expressions but with different meanings. Tone qualifies our words and tells the listener whether we are experiencing anger, humor, sarcasm, affection, or any other emotion. In a similar manner, the skillful writer colors his ideas by the tone he uses, and the reader who does not sense this tone often misinterprets the selection or completely misses the point.

Tone is expressed in literature through the artistic handling of words. The writer deliberately chooses terms which evoke emotions such as pathos, anxiety, or exhilaration. The structure and flow of his sentences also aid in communicating the desired feeling. Often, short rather choppy sentences convey action and excitement, whereas long, complicated sentences express slow movement, dejection, or rumination. Metaphors and similes frequently suggest an outlook the writer wishes the reader to assume. In literature, as in conversation, tones are so numerous that it would be unfeasible here to discuss all of them. But the literary tones that are common enough to warrant special attention are the cynical, satirical, sarcastic, humorous or witty, critical, solemn, sentimental, and ironic.

Basic clues for interpreting tone are the writer's subject and purpose. Some subjects lend themselves more naturally to certain tones than others. Mankind, for example, is the prime target of humor, wit, cynicism, satire, and sarcasm. Humor and wit are generally concerned with the ludicrous situations man permits himself to fall into; cynicism and sarcasm are reflected in the weaknesses of man's character and the situations which develop therefrom. In such fields as politics, religion, and education where a change of behavior by man is advocated, satire is prevalent. Irony, like solemn tones, is suitable for these fields and may be chosen in the treatment of other subjects.

The writer's purpose will influence the selection of an appropriate tone. If his primary aim is to amuse his reader, he will choose humor. If he wishes to contrast the expected with the unexpected, the pretentious with the real, he uses wit. If he desires to enlighten his reader on a topic, or to broaden understanding, he will write in a solemn tone. If he wants to show the discrepancies between the way man behaves and the way he should behave, he employs satire. If he decides to criticize, he uses cynicism, sarcasm, or an objectively critical tone, depending upon the type of criticism he wishes to make. If he intends to stir his reader, he sometimes assumes a sentimental, emotional tone. And if he wishes to express his opinions indirectly, but perhaps more dramatically, he selects irony.

As you begin to read critically to interpret the author's tone, you will find that the divisions of subject matter and purpose are not rigidly set. Your best clue is to study the writer's choice and arrangement of the words he selects to convey his ideas.

Cynical Tone

Cynicism is characterized by its pronounced doubt of the goodness of human motives, and of the innate goodness of human action. It has a strong undercurrent that man is basically selfish and corrupt and all that he makes or touches is defiled by this contact. A person who sneers at heroism and attempts to prove that selfish gain motivated the deed is termed a cynic. When this attitude appears in literature, the tone is cynical. The author himself may write from a cynical point of view, so that the entire work is permeated with this doubt of man's nobility. In novels, however, cynicism is often expressed by one character, with the action revolving around his conversion to a more tolerant attitude—or, in some cases, his triumph in proving man's ignominy. The following example illustrates cynicism.

From this arises the question whether it is better to be loved more than feared, or feared more than loved. The reply is, that one ought to be both feared and loved, but as it is difficult for the two to go together, it is much safer to be feared than loved, if one of the two has to be wanting. For it may be said of men in general that they are ungrateful, voluble dissemblers, anxious to avoid danger, and covetous of gain; as long as you benefit them, they are entirely yours; they offer you their blood, their goods, their life, and their children, as I have before said, when the necessity is remote; but when it approaches, they revolt. And the prince who has relied solely on their words, without making other preparations, is ruined; for the friendship which is gained by purchase and not through grandeur and nobility of spirit is bought but not secured, and at a pinch is not to be expended in your service. And men have less scruple in offending one who makes himself loved than one who makes himself feared; for love is held by a chain of obligation which, men being selfish, is broken whenever it serves their purpose; but fear is maintained by a dread of punishment which never fails.*

* From *The Prince and the Discourses* by Niccolò Machiavelli, trans. Luigi Ricci. Revised by E. R. P. Vincent. (Oxford University Press, 1935).

Satirical Tone

By definition, satire is a literary work in which human vices and follies are held up to ridicule or scorn, in order to expose, discredit, and correct them. The tone of such works is termed satirical. Both cynicism and satire deal with the foibles of man; but unlike cynicism, in which the writer's attitude is contemptuous and distrustful of human nature and its motives, satire assumes that man is capable of being noble and good, and attempts to reform him. The satirist is a humanist impatient with humanity. He is concerned with the hiatus between what man is and what he ought to be; he blends this critical attitude with wit and humor, but does not restrict himself to evoking laughter; he may be sarcastic or subtle with innuendoes. Satire differs from other methods of criticism in that it is not as direct, oratorical, or abusive, but instead, is more logical. A satirical tone is best recognized when it uses some kind of comparison which parallels a particular fault with something familiar. For some readers this device obscures the meaning, but for the discerning it makes the censure more striking.

1. Words are like leaves; and where they most abound,
   Much fruit of sense beneath is rarely found.*

COMPARISON: Words and leaves

AREA: Conversation

FAULT: People who talk a great deal, have little of value to say.

2. There is Bryant, as quiet, as cool, and as dignified,
   As a smooth, silent iceberg, that never is ignified
   Save when by reflection 'tis kindled o'nights
   With a semblance of flame by the chill Northern Lights. †

COMPARISON: Byrant with an iceberg

AREA: Poetry

FAULT: William Cullen Bryant's poetry lacks warmth and feeling.

Sarcastic Tone

Sarcasm is similar to cynicism and satire in that it too deals with the follies of human nature. But just as the latter have their specific qualities, a sarcastic tone can also be clearly defined. Cynicism points out faults in order to show the selfishness of man; satire shows them in an effort to reform people or keep them from committing follies; sarcasm strikes out at them because they are foolish, and is not concerned with whether this attack will do good or harm, or whether man can or will change. Sarcasm is more harsh, direct, and personal than satire, expressing anger, spite, or malice, and intentionally wounding feelings. Actually, it is a form of humor and on the surface may seem amusing, but it possesses undertones of contempt not found in other forms of humor or wit. The language of sarcasm is usually bitter, caustic, and stinging. Superficially, the writer seems to be an objective observer, but the anger that is inherent in sarcasm exposes this detachment as a guise and reveals the writer's involvement.

Sometimes, sarcasm is blended into an ironical statement, which is a contradiction between the intended meaning and that which is stated. This is the grim kind of humor often referred to as "tongue in cheek." When irony is used with a sarcastic tone, the result apparently is less harsh, but actually is more biting because of the indirectness.

The following example shows the effect of a sarcastic tone. As you read, note how it gives an impression of a verbal sneer, a characteristic of sarcasm. Later, under *Irony,* you will see an example of sarcasm in an ironical statement.

When we move from Dr. Coué's modest book to those of Dr. Peale we move from a timorous to a confident universe. There is no place here for lily-livered caveats and scruples that are typical of the negative approach to life of Europeans. Dr. Peale's many formulas are altogether positive and guaranteed to work for all sorts of situations, and above all, for hard-pressed business executives down on their luck. Get rid of your negative-thinking friends and learn to have faith, and you will soon be moving mountains of dollars. Invoke God's divine assistance through "deep prayers that have a lot of suction" and you will get what you want in life, or at any rate you will potentially be in a position to get what you want. (This is, fortunately, the only shadow of negative thinking haunting Dr. Peale's books.) ‡

AREA OF CRITICISM: Dr. Peale's formulas for positive thinking.

Humorous and Witty Tones

Humor and wit are frequently associated with each other and are sometimes used synonymously. Although both are meant to arouse keen interest, amusement, or laughter, there are marked differences between the two. Wit is primarily intellectual, depending upon a swift play on words, a facility for clever expression, and a knack for associating ideas or words not usually connected, so as to produce an amusing surprise. Wit thrives on the talent of showing quick perception of the incongruous. It shows great skill in its phraseology, and in its contrasts, comparisons, and paradoxes. On the other hand, humor is more sympathetic in its approach to human values, and good-naturedly

* From "Essay on Criticism, II," by Alexander Pope.
† From *A Fable for Critics* by James Russell Lowell.

‡ From "God and Success," *op. cit.*

exposes the follies and incongruities of human nature. It depicts the ludicrous or comical aspects of life without exhibiting bitterness toward them. Wit is sharp and artistic; humor is gentle and natural. Humor is more apt to provoke laughter, while wit makes us smile and reflect. A witty tone is impressive because of its cleverness. A humorous tone is enjoyable because it laughs, but never scoffs.

1. *Humor*

I have, to be sure, encountered men with complexes. There was, for example, Marvin Belt. He had a complex about airplanes that was quite interesting. He was not afraid of machinery, or of high places, or of crashes. He was simply afraid that the pilot of any plane he got into might lose his mind. "I imagine myself high over Montana," he once said to me, "in a huge, perfectly safe tri-motored plane. Several of the passengers are dozing, others are reading, but I am keeping my eyes glued on the door to the cockpit. Suddenly the pilot steps out of it, a wild light in his eyes, and in a falsetto like that of a little girl he says to me, 'Conductor, will you please let me off at One-Hundred-and-Twenty-fifth Street?'" "But," I said to Belt, "even if the pilot does go crazy, there is still the co-pilot." "No, there isn't," said Belt. "The pilot has hit the co-pilot over the head with something and killed him." Yes, the psychoanalysts can have Marvin Belt. . . .*

2. *Wit*

PRINCE.   Why, thou owest God a death.

FALSTAFF.   'Tis not due yet; I would be loath to pay him before his day. What need I be so forward with him that calls not on me? Well, 'tis no matter; honour pricks me on. Yea, but how if honour prick me off when I come on? how then? Can honour set to a leg? no; or an arm? no; or take away the grief of a wound? no. Honour hath no skill in surgery, then? no. What is honour? a word. What is in that word honour? What is that honour? air. A trim reckoning! Who hath it? he that died o' Wednesday. Doth he feel it? no. Doth he hear it? no. 'Tis insensible, then? Yea, to the dead. But will it not live with the living? no. Why? detraction will not suffer it. Therefore I'll none of it. Honour is a mere scutcheon: and so ends my catechism. †

Take misfortune like a man. Blame it on your wife. ‡

Critical Tone

We have shown that there are various ways of making criticisms. A logical but indirect manner of criticizing man for not being what he should be is

* From "Sex Ex Machina," by James Thurber from *Let Your Mind Alone* (Harper & Row). Copyright © 1937 by James Thurber. Copyright © 1965 by Helen W. Thurber and Rose-Mary Thurber Sauers.

† From *King Henry IV, Part I* by William Shakespeare.

‡ From *The Rest of the Story* by Paul Harvey. By permission of Doubleday & Company, Inc., Publishers.

satire; cynicism is criticism of man for being ignoble and incapable of being otherwise; sarcasm is an attempt—often prompted by anger—to hurt man for being foolish. When a critical tone is employed, the writer looks at the faults of man (individually or collectively), his achievements, or his society openly, objectively, and directly, with an effort to see these faults as they are and to judge them. This type of criticism attempts no subterfuge or camouflage. It prides itself on calling "a spade a spade." It obviously reveals what fault is under attack and precisely what is wrong. This openness of approach is what mainly distinguishes a critical tone from the others.

Concerning the literary works of Hemingway, Faulkner, Dos Passos and Steinbeck:

There is indeed only one question which has not been asked about these four major talents. Why has not any of them produced a fresh or important literary work in the last ten years? Why is the combined output of the group so repetitive of their best earlier work, so empty of any kind of growth or maturity—as though *their* world had stopped moving somewhere in the 1940's? In Hemingway's case one is grateful "The Old Man and the Sea" is as good a tale as it is. But the theme which Hemingway still celebrates is that of solitary suffering in a black Darwinian universe—not too far removed from Jack London's—where one must kill the brothers whom one loves, even one's fish brothers, and where the sharks are the masterpieces of nature. The old man's luck was broken because he went "too far out." This verdict on the tragedy is typical of an artist who has always presented a world of painful consequences and no causes. §

Sentimental Tone

Sentimentality in literature is the antithesis of criticism, particularly of the cynical kind. Instead of doubting the goodness of man, or concentrating on his faults, sentimentality assumes a rather naive faith in human nature. It is characterized by feelings of compassion, sympathy, and tenderness. A sentimental tone is designed to stir the emotions of the reader. In its lowest form it is simply the mood of a "sob story"; at its peak it may possess literary charm and be very powerful in swaying the reader to adopt the attitude of the author. A character in a novel may be presented as sentimental, but this does not constitute a sentimental tone, unless the story is told from his point of view. When the author writes in a sentimental tone, the prevailing impression is that man and his ideals, e.g., truth, honor, virtue, will triumph in the end. Emotionally charged expressions are common in sentimental literature; they play on the sympathies of the

§ From *American Moderns* by Maxwell Geismar (Hill & Wang, Inc.). By permission of the author.

reader and draw him into the battles and victories of the main character. An example of sentimental tone is found in Samuel Richardson's novel *Pamela,* poignantly subtitled *Virtue Rewarded.* The following excerpts show the heroine first in the midst of her tribulations, and secondly, as "virtue triumphs."

1. Excerpts from Pamela's letters to her parents

And distress indeed; for here I am still; and everything has been worse and worse! Oh! the poor unhappy Pamela! —Without any hope left, and ruined in all my contrivances. But, oh! my dear parents, rejoice with me, even in this low plunge of my distress; for your poor Pamela has escaped from an enemy worse than any she ever met with; an enemy she never thought of before, and was hardly able to stand against; I mean the weakness and presumption of her own mind; which had well nigh, had not the Divine Grace interposed, sunk her into the lowest, last abyss of misery and perdition!

2. Later, the triumph

Now, my dear parents; I have but this *one* day, between me and the most solemn rite that can be performed. My heart cannot yet shake off this heavy weight. Sure I am ungrateful to the Divine goodness, and the favour of the best of benefactors! Yet I hope I am not!—For at time, my mind is all exultation, with the prospect of what good tomorrow's happy solemnity may, by the leave of my generous master, put it into my power to do. O how shall I find words to express, as I ought to, my thankfulness, for all the mercies before me!

Solemn Tone

There are many forms of writing which have serious attitudes toward life, ranging from lyrical expressions to definite, prosaic statements. In solemn writing the author states his thoughts formally and ceremoniously. The gravity of expression coupled with the absence of cleverness or humor is the quality which distinguishes this tone from others and makes it recognizable.

But, in a larger sense, we can not dedicate—we can not consecrate—we can not hallow—this ground. The brave men, living and dead, who struggled here have consecrated it, far above our poor power to add or detract. The world will little note, nor long remember what we say here, but it can never forget what they did here. It is for us the living, rather, to be dedicated here to the unfinished work which they who fought here have thus far so nobly advanced. It is rather for us to be here dedicated to the great task remaining before us—that from these honored dead we take increased devotion to that cause for which they gave the last full measure of devotion—that we here highly resolve that these dead shall not have died in vain —that this nation, under God, shall have a new birth of freedom—and that government of the people, by the people, and for the people, shall not perish from the earth.*

* From "The Gettysburg Address," by Abraham Lincoln.

Note how the solemnity of the occasion is reflected in the marked solemnity of tone. But it is not the honoring of the war dead itself that gives this passage gravity. The prose style, you should observe, is formal but not stiff; it repeats the serious words *dedicate* and *devotion;* and there is a measured cadence in the repetition of similar syntactic patterns—*we can not* and the prepositional phrases beginning *of the, by the,* and *for the.*

Ironic Tone

Irony arises from a discrepancy between the outward appearance of a work and its inner meaning. Its outer surface usually appears innocent and is in marked contrast to its inner nature, which possesses depths hidden to and unsuspected by the reader until he begins to probe into the implications of the situation. Since the author creates this outside very deliberately, sometimes ingeniously, but often very simply, to mask the discrepancy, the reader must scrutinize very carefully any material he surmises to be ironical. To get at the real intent of the writer, he must dig into each part of the contrast and study its relationship to the meaning of the whole.

The reader should have at his fingertips a working knowledge of the subtleties and varieties of irony; he must realize that the author may convey a meaning that is opposite to what he actually says, may relate an outcome that runs counter to what is expected, or may cause to emerge from fantasy that which is truth or reality. The reader must be alert to the use of *understatement,* the de-emphasis of an idea by an unpretentious description; to the use of *paradox,* the heightening of an idea by circumstances which seem exactly contradictory.

The oft-used term "irony of fate" refers to the upsetting effects of the unexpected, or the unsuspected, or the unforeseen. In creating this type of irony, often the author's favored *modus operandi* is divine intervention. Generally associated with tragedy, as in *Romeo and Juliet,* the irony of fate is cruel, but mischievously and outrageously, it is often the essence of comedy, as in Shakespeare's *Comedy of Errors.* One does not usually find instances of pure irony: chameleon in character, it blends with and enhances other varieties of tone, especially sarcasm and humor.

Swift's "A Modest Proposal" is one of the most famous ironic essays in English literature. In it—as a way of alerting men to the already tragic conditions in Ireland—he proposes that children be raised for food. Note how genial and helpful the author pretends to be:

I have been assured by a very knowing American of my acquaintance in London, that a young healthy child well nursed is at a year old a most delicious, nourishing, and wholesome food, whether stewed, roasted, baked, or boiled; and I make no doubt that it will equally serve in a fricassee or a ragout.

It is clear that the author cannot be literally serious, and the true meaning of the grotesque image becomes a plea for more humane treatment; the very inhumanity of this passage is intended to reflect less obvious but no less serious inhumanities perpetrated against the Irish at that time. Later, the point is made even more explicit, though Swift maintains his ironic tone.

I grant this food will be somewhat dear, and therefore very *proper for landlords,* who, as they have already devoured most of the parents, seem to have the best title to the children.

Here, the object of Swift's ironic satire—the landlords—becomes clear. And later, still using his ironic method of stating a position opposite to the one he actually endorses, Swift proposes what *will not solve* the Irish problem:

Therefore let no man talk to me of other expedients: *Of taxing our absentees at five shillings a pound: Of using neither clothes, nor household furniture, except what is of our own growth and manufacture: Of utterly rejecting the materials and instruments that promote foreign luxury: Of curing the expensiveness of pride, vanity, idleness, and gaming in women. . . .*

Irony of fate is well demonstrated in de Maupassant's "The Necklace." The loss of a borrowed necklace by Mrs. Loisel and its replacement by one costing thirty-four thousand francs condemn the couple to ten years of grinding work. At the end of the time, when Mrs. Loisel bears no resemblance to her former, pretty self, this incident takes place.

One Sunday, as she was taking a walk in the Champs-Elysées to rid herself of the cares of the week, she suddenly perceived a woman walking with a child. It was Mrs. Forestier, still young, still pretty, still attractive. Mrs. Loisel was affected. Should she speak to her? Yes, certainly. And now that she had paid, she would tell her all. Why not?

She approached her, "Good morning, Jeanne."

Her friend did not recognize her and was astonished to be so familiarly addressed by this common personage. She stammered:

"But, Madame—I do not know—You must be mistaken—"

"No, I am Matilda Loisel."

Her friend uttered a cry of astonishment: "Oh! my poor Matilda! How you have changed—"

"Yes, I have had some hard days since I saw you; and some miserable ones—and all because of you—"

"Because of me? How is that?"

"You recall the diamond necklace that you loaned me to wear to the Commissioner's ball?"

"Yes, very well."

"Well, I lost it."

"How is that, since you returned it to me?"

"I returned another to you exactly like it. And it has taken us ten years to pay for it. You can understand that it was not easy for us who have nothing. But it is finished and I am decently content."

Madame Forestier stopped short. She said:

"You say that you bought a diamond necklace to replace mine?"

"Yes. You did not perceive it then? They were just alike."

And she smiled with a proud and simple joy. Madame Forestier was touched and took both her hands as she replied:

"Oh! my poor Matilda! Mine were false. They were not worth over five hundred francs!"*

Note the sarcastic tone coupled with ironical statement in this passage:

What ample zest! What copious verve! What abundant enthusiasm! What boundless bonhommerie! It's actually hard to imagine that there really was a time when everything wasn't known to be known and everybody didn't know that they knew it. But science says that a time there was; and science is an honorable man. A time there was when even the most omnipotent emperor didn't know that he knew and he never could know that he had B.O.— and can't you imagine his ill-starred consort, mounting her dazzling throne with a hideous case of Morning Mouth? Sure an' 'tis a merciful miracle our mysterious mothers and fabulous fathers got themselves born at all. Hail, hail, the civilization's all here . . . although one rather suspects that something must be not far from wrong when every punk can't automatically become Albert Lincoln or Abraham Einstein, merely by letting a button press itself or (if there must be such a thing as imperfection) by throwing a switch; am I right? Wouldn't a ducky invention like that simplify the whole horrid complicated unemployment problem rather nicely? Answer me, you twenty-five hundred dollar a week apotheosis of cinematographic idiocy. Or (if you prefer) just try to lift those already lifted eyebrows. Hoot, lass, 'tis not a Nude Eel in my sporran either way.†

The American humorist Mark Twain was wonderfully gifted in combining a humorous tone with ironical statement:

Be respectful to your superiors, if you have any, also to strangers, and sometimes to others. If a person offend you, and you are in doubt as to whether it was intentional or not, do not resort to extreme measures; simply watch your chance and hit him with a brick. That will be sufficient. If you shall find that he had not intended any

* From "The Necklace," in *Day and Night Stories* by Guy de Maupassant, trans. Ernest Boyd. Copyright 1924 and renewed 1952 by Alfred A. Knopf. By permission of publisher.

† From "Exit the Boob," by E. E. Cummings, *Esquire,* June, 1935.

offense, come out frankly and confess yourself in the wrong when you struck him; acknowledge it like a man and say you didn't mean to. Yes, always avoid violence; in this age of charity and kindliness, the time has gone by for such things. Leave dynamite to the low and unrefined.*

* From *Mark Twain's Speeches* by Mark Twain (Harper & Bros., 1923).

EXERCISE 10: AUTHOR'S TONE

DIRECTIONS: Below each paragraph are questions about literary tone. Indicate your answer by circling the letter you think is correct.

PART I

I was always embarrassed by the words sacred, glorious, and sacrifice and the expression in vain. We had heard them, sometimes standing in the rain almost out of ear shot, so that only the shouted words came through, and had read them, on proclamations that were slapped up by bill-posters over other proclamations, now for a long time, and I had seen nothing sacred, and the things that were glorious had no glory and the sacrifices were like the stockyards at Chicago if nothing was done with the meat except to bury it. There were many words that you could not stand to hear and finally only the names of places had dignity. . . . Abstract words such as glory, honor, courage, or hallow were obscene beside the concrete names of villages, the number of roads, the names of rivers, the numbers of regiments and the dates.*

1. The tone of the author is:
   - (a) cynical
   - (b) humorous
   - (c) solemn
   - (d) sentimental

2. We may infer that the narrator is:
   - (a) an athlete
   - (b) a college student
   - (c) a salesman
   - (d) a soldier

3. We may also infer that the narrator is talking about:
   - (a) how some people try to escape reality
   - (b) a "pep-talk" by the coach during a football game
   - (c) the emptiness of abstract words in times of war
   - (d) the meanings of abstract words

4. According to the passage, the narrator feels:
   - (a) that such words as _sacred, glorious,_ and _sacrifice_ are inadequate for the reality of war
   - (b) that there are too many proclamations posted on billboards
   - (c) that there is dignity in the use of abstract terms
   - (d) that "pep-talks" have little effect on football players

PART II

It is not a snobbish rich-man's college, devoted to leisurely nonsense. It is the property of the people of the state, and what they want—or what they are told they want—is a mill to turn out men and women who will lead moral lives, play bridge, drive good cars, be enterprising in business, and occasionally mention books, though they are not expected to have time to read them. It is a Ford Motor Factory, and if its products rattle a little, they are beautifully standardized, with perfectly interchangeable parts. Hourly the University of Winnemac grows in numbers and influence, and by 1950 one may expect it to have created an entirely new world-civilization, a civilization larger and brisker and purer. †

* From _A Farewell to Arms_ by Ernest Hemingway (Charles Scribner's Sons).
† From _Arrowsmith_ by Sinclair Lewis. Reprinted by permission of Harcourt, Brace & World, Inc.

1. The author's tone is:
   (a) satirical
   (b) sarcastic
   (c) witty
   (d) cynical

2. It may be inferred that the author is criticizing:
   (a) the automobile industry
   (b) state universities
   (c) social symbols of personal success
   (d) the influence of automation

3. It may also be inferred that the author feels that:
   (a) more colleges like the University of Winnemac are needed
   (b) rich men's colleges are like Ford motor factories
   (c) society needs more men and women who lead moral lives and play bridge
   (d) our civilization places too much importance on conformity

4. According to the passage, the University of Winnemac:
   (a) was founded in 1950
   (b) is a rich-man's college
   (c) is devoted to leisurely nonsense
   (d) is a state university

PART III

It will probably come as a mild shock to no one that there are all of four hundred different kinds of mushrooms. Four hundred and one, really, because when I looked up this fact in the *World Almanac*, I found a new variety growing out of Page 29. Now, what are mushrooms? Nothing more or less than toadstools, though why they are called toadstools is beyond me; I have yet to see a toad sitting on a stool, although I have combed all the books dealing with the subject. Of course I haven't had a chance to study the books yet—all I've been able to do is comb them, but still, it seems a peculiar name to give an unoffending mushroom, doesn't it? It was probably made up by someone who hated mushrooms and thought he could get even. But why should anyone hate mushrooms? The little fellow goes about his business quietly; once in a while he kills a family of twenty or thirty people, but then, what right has anyone to have a family of twenty or thirty people? I was wrapping up some laundry in a newspaper recently and saw a note about a man who had thirty children. This sort of thing can't go on indefinitely, no matter what the man says.*

1. The tone of the author is:
   (a) cynical
   (b) satirical
   (c) humorous
   (d) sarcastic

2. According to the passage, mushrooms:
   (a) come in 29 varieties
   (b) are occasionally poisonous
   (c) were found growing out of a newspaper
   (d) were discovered by a man with thirty children

3. The passage strongly implies that:
   (a) the author likes mushrooms
   (b) the *World Almanac* names 401 varieties of mushrooms
   (c) mushrooms look like toadstools
   (d) the author discovered a variety of toadstools

* From *The Best of S. J. Perelman* by S. J. Perelman (Random House, Inc., 1947).

4. It may be inferred that:
   (a) some varieties of mushrooms are homes of toads
   (b) some people cannot distinguish between the poisonous and harmless varieties of mushrooms
   (c) few people are aware that there are many varieties of mushrooms
   (d) very little is known about mushrooms

PART IV

Man, at his best, remains a sort of one-lunged animal, never completely rounded and perfect, as a cockroach, say, is perfect. If he shows one valuable quality, it is almost unheard of for him to show any other. Give him a head, and he lacks a heart. Give him a heart of a gallon capacity, and his head holds scarcely a pint. The artist, nine times out of ten, is a dead-beat and given to the debauching of virgins, so-called. The patriot is a bigot, and, more often than not, a bounder and a poltroon. The man of physical bravery is often on a level, intellectually, with a Baptist clergyman. The intellectual giant has bad kidneys and cannot thread a needle. In all my years of search in this world, from the Golden Gate in the West to the Vistula in the East, and from the Orkney Islands in the North to the Spanish Main in the South, I have never met a thoroughly moral man who was honorable.*

1. The author's tone is:
   (a) cynical
   (b) satirical
   (c) sarcastic
   (d) sentimental

2. We may infer from the passage that the author feels that:
   (a) even the cockroach is imperfect
   (b) many of Nature's creatures are more perfect than man
   (c) a moral man is the most perfect animal
   (d) having bad kidneys is a sign of intelligence

3. We may also infer that the author feels that:
   (a) the artist is the least perfect man
   (b) the intellectual giant is the most nearly perfect man
   (c) a Baptist clergyman is intellectually inferior
   (d) the man of physical bravery is intellectually superior

4. We may conclude from the author's opinions the perfect man is:
   (a) like a cockroach
   (b) a completely rounded one-lunged animal
   (c) one who has a valuable quality
   (d) moral, brave, kind, and intelligent

* From "The Good Man," by H. L. Mencken in *The Vintage Mencken,* gathered by Alistair Cooke. Copyright 1924 by Alfred A. Knopf, Inc., and renewed 1952 by H. L. Mencken. By permission of publisher.

PART V

Isobel's spirit, tangling through the dense thickets of inarticulate, useless suffering, would go on. "Behold, I kept all Thy Commandments," she cried, bewildered and betrayed, betrayed by all she held to, her very goodness, service to others, the virtues so strongly kept that they had festered within her. Isobel had ripened to her ruin, and all of them were guilty, each one, subtle or crude, had pushed her farther into disaster. Unni, merely by *being* Unni, the sensual sure male, making love to other women but refusing Isobel; Fred, throwing her back to loneliness, unwilling to share, refusing companionship on his walks; Anne, most brutal, taking Isobel's gift, the golden room, and using it for her own purposes—perhaps it was destiny, but at this moment it looked very much like cold-blooded ruthlessness; and finally John, the least to blame, striking a pose and thus bludgeoning Isobel into her final catastrophe . . . all, all had contrived to Isobel's undoing. Lost in the maze of righteousness was the vibrant woman, madness holding dominion over the proud spirit, now useless. Such loss, such waste, such desolation, and to what purpose? Oh better, far better be Rukmini. Rukmini had felt her ecstasy and lived her death. Rukmini, of the shining hour and the quick oblivion. To her was not dealt out this long lingering, this insentient waiting for nothing at all.*

1. The tone of this paragraph is:
   (a) satirical
   (b) solemn
   (c) sentimental
   (d) sarcastic

2. According to the paragraph, Isobel envied:
   (a) Unni
   (b) Anne
   (c) Rukmini
   (d) John

3. Apparently the author's purpose is to:
   (a) ridicule Isobel
   (b) condemn Isobel
   (c) commiserate with Isobel
   (d) scorn man for his weaknesses

4. We may conclude from the paragraph that Isobel has:
   (a) gone mad
   (b) committed suicide
   (c) killed Rukmini
   (d) triumphed over the evils that befell her

PART VI

To parents who wish to lead a quiet life I would say: Tell your children that they are very naughty—much naughtier than most children. Point to the young people of some acquaintances as models of perfection and impress your own children with a deep sense of their own inferiority. You carry so many more guns than they do that they cannot fight you. This is called moral influence, and it will enable you to bounce them as much as you please. They think you know and they will not have yet caught you lying often enough to suspect that you are not the unworldly and scrupulously truthful person which you represent yourself to be; nor yet will they know how great a coward you are, nor how soon you will run away, if they fight you with persistency and judgment. You keep the dice and throw them both for your children and yourself.†

* From *The Mountain is Young* by Han Suyin (Putnam's & Coward-McCann). Copyright 1958 by the author.
† From *The Way of All Flesh* by Samuel Butler (E.P. Dutton & Co., 1916, and Jonathan Cape Ltd.). By permission of The Executors of the Samuel Butler Estate.

1. The tone of the author is:
   (a) cynical
   (b) witty
   (c) solemn
   (d) ironical

2. According to the author, the best defense children have against their parents is:
   (a) deceitfulness
   (b) emulation
   (c) apathy
   (d) determination

3. Moral influence is described in the paragraph as:
   (a) being unworldly and scrupulously truthful with your children
   (b) persistency and fairness in judgment
   (c) not being caught lying too often
   (d) using your size to frighten children into obedience

4. We may conclude that the author:
   (a) sympathizes with children
   (b) is disdainful of family relations
   (c) believes that fathers and mothers should be honored
   (d) believes in permissiveness with children

PART VII

I had hitherto seen only one side of the Academy, the other being appropriated to the advancers of speculative learning, of whom I shall say something when I have mentioned one illustrious person more, who is called among them *the universal artist.* He told us he had been thirty years employing his thoughts for the improvement of human life. He had two large rooms full of wonderful curiosities, and fifty men at work. Some were condensing air into a dry tangible substance, by extracting the nitre, and letting the aqueous or fluid particles percolate; others softening marble for pillows and pin-cushions; others petrifying the hoofs of a living horse to preserve them from foundering. The artist himself was at that time busy upon two great designs; the first, to sow land with chaff, wherein he affirmed the true seminal virtue to be contained, as he demonstrated by several experiments which I was not skillful enough to comprehend. The other was, by a certain composition of gums, minerals, and vegetables outwardly applied, to prevent the growth of wool upon two young lambs; and he hoped in a reasonable time to propagate the breed of naked sheep all over the kingdom.*

1. The author's tone is:
   (a) sarcastic
   (b) cynical
   (c) satirical
   (d) critical

* From *Gulliver's Travels* by Jonathan Swift.

2. We may infer that the author is talking about:
   (a) abstract artists
   (b) scientists
   (c) college professors
   (d) political leaders

3. We may also infer that the author feels:
   (a) there is a definite need for a universal artist
   (b) scientists often spend time on discoveries that are meaningless for humanity
   (c) more college professors should be involved in speculative learning
   (d) political leaders devise devious schemes to extort taxpayers' money

4. We may conclude that the author advocates:
   (a) financial and scholastic aid for universal artists
   (b) re-dedication by scientists to causes that will be of more tangible benefit to humanity
   (c) the placement of more emphasis on speculative learning in colleges and universities
   (d) an investigation of governmental and political spendings

PART VIII

   I learned to smoke, first, cornsilk wrapped in newspaper. I can taste it to this day. We never had the patience to let the cornsilk really dry. I don't imagine kids do that very much any more, mostly because they've never heard of it. What you do is take the cornsilk, spread it out in the sun until it is brown, like the little beard you find in the husk. Wrap it in a spill of newspaper—it'll look more like a very small ice-cream cone than anything else—set fire to the end, being careful not to torch off your eyebrows. My recollection is that it bore no relationship to tobacco, but it wasn't bad at all. It had one big virtue. When caught, you had not committed a sin, as you did later when you smoked real cigarettes. Real cigarettes stunted your growth, we knew that. What that meant to us was that your growth stopped, right there. It was not impeded. You just plain stopped growing, as if you were frozen. You would be three feet tall when you were sixty years old. It was in no way contradictory that we never saw a grownup three feet tall. They had never smoked as children, and certainly the ones who had were not going to walk around in the daylight letting everybody know what *they* had done.*

1. The tone of the author is:
   (a) sentimental
   (b) sarcastic
   (c) humorous
   (d) critical

2. The author's purpose is to:
   (a) warn parents about their children's smoking attempts
   (b) warn children about the evils of smoking
   (c) dispel the fallacy of stunted growth
   (d) reminisce about the days when he was a kid

3. Apparently the author as a child believed that smoking cornsilk:
   (a) was a delightful sin
   (b) stunted your growth
   (c) was more fun than smoking real cigarettes
   (d) did not affect your growth

4. We may conclude that the theory of stunted growth:
   (a) was started by the children themselves
   (b) did not deter children from smoking cigarettes later
   (c) was successful in preventing children from smoking
   (d) was not accepted by the children

PART IX

Huck's relationship with his father [in Mark Twain's *Huckleberry Finn*] is melodrama. So is the shooting of Boggs, or the tar and feathering of the Duke and King. A proof of their being melodrama is the ease with which one moves from a scene of violence to a humorous dialogue. For example, the encounter of Huck and Jim with the thieves and murderers aboard the *Walter Scott* is followed by the minstrel show, end-men sort of humor of "Was Solomon Wise?" Verisimilitude offers no problem when reality merges with unreality or horror dissolves innocently into comedy, but sometimes Twain's sense of proper distance, the degree and nature of the stylization he is employing, fails him and the action becomes gruesomely real. An instance of this is Huck's telling of the murders in "Why Harney Rode Away for His Hat." The starkness is too unrelieved. The scene does not respect the premises nor the general tone of the novel, and, even though it might work in another novel, it does not work here.*

1. The author's tone is:
   (a) solemn
   (b) critical
   (c) sarcastic
   (d) cynical

2. The author's purpose is to:
   (a) ridicule Mark Twain as a writer
   (b) point out the merits of *The Adventures of Huckleberry Finn*
   (c) criticize *The Adventures of Huckleberry Finn*
   (d) criticize Huckleberry Finn as a character

3. We may infer that the author feels that melodrama:
   (a) is one of the virtues of *Huckleberry Finn*
   (b) helps to provide smooth movement in the novel
   (c) adds to the humor of the novel
   (d) is the source of some of the flaws in *Huckleberry Finn*

4. We may conclude that, in the author's view, *Huckleberry Finn:*
   (a) is a great novel in spite of its flaws
   (b) has been greatly overrated
   (c) proves that Mark Twain was a great novelist
   (d) has been unjustly attacked by critics

* From "Why *Huckleberry Finn* is Not the Great American Novel," by William Van O'Connor, *College English*, Oct., 1955. Reprinted with the permission of the National Council of Teachers of English and William Van O'Connor.

PART X

Who bends not his ear to any bell, which upon any occasion rings? but who can remove it from that bell which is passing a piece of himself out of this world? No man is an island, entire of itself; every man is a piece of the continent, a part of the main; if a clod be washed away by the sea, Europe is the less, as well as if a promontory were, as well as if a manor of thy friend's or of thine own were; any man's death diminishes me, because I am involved in mankind; and therefore never send to know for whom the bell tolls; it tolls for thee.*

1. The tone of the author is:
    (a) solemn
    (b) critical
    (c) satirical
    (d) sentimental

2. The author is concerned in this paragraph with:
    (a) the finality of death
    (b) man's relationship to mankind
    (c) the selfishness of man
    (d) the immortality of man

3. The purpose of the metaphor involving the island and the continent is to:
    (a) demonstrate man's isolation
    (b) stress the inadequacies of man's means of communication
    (c) show man's connection with all men
    (d) prove man's dominion over the earth

4. We may conclude that the author feels:
    (a) mankind is greater and more important than any one man
    (b) no man is indispensable
    (c) mankind shares the suffering and death of each man
    (d) each man meets his fate alone

* From "Meditation XVII," by John Donne in *Devotions Upon Emergent Occasions* (University of Michigan Press, 1959).

SUPPLEMENTARY ACTIVITIES

DISCUSSION QUESTIONS: Answer the following questions which are based on the contents of the paragraphs you have just read in Exercise 10. If necessary, reread the paragraph. After each question, the Part number is indicated in parentheses.

1. Hemingway, in *A Farewell to Arms,* states: "the sacrifices [in war] were like the stockyards at Chicago if nothing were done with the meat except to bury it." What is the meaning of this statement? (Part I)

2. American society is filled with symbols of social status. What are some of the present symbols of social and personal success? (Part II)

3. Some of the examples Swift used for his satirical barbs in the eighteenth century are not so far-fetched in the twentieth century. What practical purposes can our modern scientists find for condensed air? (Part VII)

4. When Donne wrote "no man is an island," he was thinking of an individual's relationship to the rest of humanity. How is his meaning applicable to any political or social problem of today? (Part X)

PARAGRAPH WRITING: Choose one of the following tones and write a paragraph that illustrates the characteristics of that tone. For guidance, first reread the discussion on the tone you select.

1. humorous
2. cynical
3. sarcastic
4. critical
5. sentimental
6. ironic

REVIEW EXERCISE

DIRECTIONS: In the exercises you are to apply all of the principles we have emphasized in this chapter. Read each paragraph and write answers to the following questions:

1. What is the main thought?
2. How may it be classified as to type?
3. What is the method of development?
4. What is the tone?
5. Now, circle the letter of your choice.

PART I

As western heroes go, [television's] Maverick is singularly unheroic. He abhors gunplay, because as he himself once observed, "Half the population of this town is faster on the draw than I am." On the rare occasions when he is forced to stand up and shoot it out with the villain, he survives only through skulduggery or dumb luck. In the face of danger, Maverick quite sensibly tries to sneak away. There are only five things that can persuade him to come to the aid of a damsel in distress: greed, libido, curiosity, anger or self-preservation. "There are times," he has said, "when a man must rise above principle."*

1.

2.

3.

4.

5. We may infer from the paragraph that Maverick's principles:
   (a) are typical of western heroes
   (b) are derived through skulduggery and dumb luck
   (c) are greed, libido, curiosity, anger, and self-preservation
   (d) are also unconventional

PART II

Let me tell you about the very rich. They are different from you and me. They possess and enjoy early, and it does something to them, makes them soft where we are hard, and cynical where we are trustful, in a way that, unless you were born rich, it is very difficult to understand. They think deep in their hearts, that they are better than we are because we had to discover the compensations and refuges of life for ourselves. Even when they enter deep into our world or sink below us, they still think that they are better than we are. They are different. The only way I can describe young Anson Hunter is to approach him as if he were a foreigner and cling stubbornly to my point of view. If I accept his for a moment I am lost—I have nothing to show but a preposterous movie.†

1.

* From "This is a Television Cowboy?" by Marion Hargrove, *Life* Magazine, Jan. 19, 1959. © 1959 Time Inc.
† From "The Rich Boy," by F. Scott Fitzgerald in *Stories by F. Scott Fitzgerald*, ed. Malcom Cowley (Charles Scribner's Sons).

2.

3.

4.

5. We may conclude from the paragraph that the author:
   (a) is among the very rich
   (b) is contemptuous of the very rich
   (c) feels the very rich are superior to others
   (d) thinks Anson Hunter is not typical of the very rich

PART III

All mankind is of one author, and is one volume; when one man dies, one chapter is not torn out of the book, but translated into a better language; and every chapter must be so translated; God employs several translators; some pieces are translated by age, some by sickness, some by war, some by justice; but God's hand is in every translation, and his hand shall bind up all our scattered leaves again, for that library where every book shall lie open to one another.*

1.

2.

3.

4.

5. We may infer that the author believes:
   (a) that wars are the instruments of the devil
   (b) sickness is man's payment for wrongdoings
   (c) there is a life after death
   (d) all of the above

PART IV

For a moment it may seem possible to defend the poem ["Trees" by Joyce Kilmer] by appealing to the title, "Trees," pointing out that no over-all consistency is called for: one tree is like the babe nursing at its mother's breast; another tree is a girl lifting her arms to pray, and so on. But this defense is probably more damaging than the charge it seeks to meet; for the poem provides no real basis for seeing one tree as babe and another as a devout young woman.†

1.

2.

* From "Meditation XVII," *op. cit.*
† From *Understanding Poetry,* Third Ed., by Cleanth Brooks and Robert Penn Warren (Holt, Rinehart, and Winston, Inc., 1960).

3.

4.

5. We may conclude that the authors believe:
   (a) the poet should have dealt with only one tree
   (b) the poet should maintain a consistent development of imagery
   (c) poets should avoid the use of analogies and images
   (d) there is no basis for comparison between a tree and a babe

PART V

The association of Lincoln and Twain may seem appropriate at first glance — but only at first glance. Presumably [William Dean] Howells meant that both men discovered their need for comedy in the pathos and tragedy of the human condition, that both men were sons of a frontier society. To a degree, then, the comparison holds. But to allow for a detailed comparison, Lincoln should have to have written novels, or Twain to have been a politician, statesman, or writer of speeches. Insofar as Lincoln the writer and Twain the writer can be compared, Lincoln is the greater. Lincoln's wit, also in a vernacular idiom, is frequently more subtle than Twain's and may be expected to be more lasting. Lincoln's ability in writing an analytical prose, flexible and closely reasoned, and his ability in writing a serious and, when the occasion required, solemn rhetoric were also greater than Twain's. The seriousness and solemnity in Twain are of innocence betrayed, as in the concluding paragraph of *The Mysterious Stranger*. Lincoln's seriousness is that of a man dealing with the world, in its own terms when forced to, but also above it, urging it to create its destiny in ways that make for the fullest sense of achievement and dignity. If Lincoln had written novels, he would, without doubt, have been a greater novelist than Twain. His virtues include Twain's and surpass them.*

1.

2.

3.

4.

5. The author implies that Lincoln and Twain:
   (a) are not at all alike
   (b) are very much alike
   (c) were concerned with the same problems
   (d) were engaged in different kinds of writing

* From "Why *Huckleberry Finn* is Not the Great American Novel," *op. cit.*

PROGRESS TEST

PART I

DIRECTIONS: Check your understanding and retention of the principles of paragraph analysis by answering the following questions. Do not refer to the discussion in the text.

1. Define the following terms and explain their relationship to a paragraph.
   (a) main thought

   (b) topic sentence

   (c) key words

   (d) supporting details

2. List the types of paragraphs and describe the characteristics of each.

3. Explain the functions in a paragraph of:
   (a) unity

   (b) coherence

   (c) emphasis

4. List five methods of paragraph development and describe the characteristics of each.

5. Name five types of literary tones and discuss the distinguishing characteristics of each.

PART II

DIRECTIONS: Read the following paragraph and answer the questions without looking back to the explanations in the chapter.

A remarkable but little noted fact has just occurred to me, a fact that I can no more understand than the poetry of T. S. Eliot. Why is it that all geniuses look like the Devil? I mean, of course, literally. Voltaire and Shakespeare, Anatole France and Henry Van Dyke, Pulitzer and Shaw—all of them have features like Mephistopheles. Shaw especially is satanic. He would resent being told this—not because of any moral associations he may have, but because he considers himself incomparably superior intellectually to the Devil. But this is by the way, for we are speaking of appearances alone. In the first place, Shaw has a satanic beard (I am not sure that I should not say the Devil has a Shavian beard). It is a beard as long as his prologues, and as pointed as his mephitic doctrines. The beard and the bushy eyebrows—large as moustaches—give Shaw an appearance not unlike an Airedale. Which recalls that Shaw is a one-man man. He once said, "I and Anatole France are two wise men in a world of fools,"—and now only he is left. His eyes are two chips of flint on which his ideas strike fire. At the outer edge of each eye three wrinkles shoot out like prongs in a pitchfork and mark him for the cynical devil that he is. I cannot remember ever seeing a nose in any of his pictures, but I imagine that, if there really is one, it is a fine, sharp, shriveled affair, acidulated from sour paradoxes. His face is widest at his eyes; then it grows gradually narrower until it finally disappears under a thin coating of grayish-blond hair spiraled up at the sides so that he seems to have two horns.

The Devil!*

1. What is the main thought?

2. Is the topic sentence stated or implied? Explain answer.

3. What are the key words of the topic sentence?

4. How do the specific details of the paragraph support the topic sentence?

5. Are there any sentences which could be deleted without destroying the unity of the paragraph? If so, which ones?

6. How is coherence achieved?

* From "An Impression of G.B.S. (by one who has never seen him)," by Robert L. Zetler and W. George Crouch in *Advanced Writing*. Copyright 1951 The Ronald Press Company.

7. Where has the emphasis been placed in the paragraph?

8. How may the paragraph be classified as to type?

9. What is the method of development?

10. What is the tone?

11. What may be inferred about Shaw's personality?

12. What may be concluded about the writer's attitude toward Shaw?

READING THE WORK AS A WHOLE

INTRODUCTION

The annoyance, humiliation, or outrage which follows the realization that one needs to improve his reading is best dispersed by a vigorous search for help. Although such help can be self-administered, our own analysis of our defects is often too severe or too lenient. Experienced guidance serves our purposes best. This section offers aid in reading selections longer than the single paragraph. Though the advantages of reading more efficiently are manifold, certainly the primary one is to be able to read with speed and with discernment material which is of substantial length and challenging content. To this end Chapter III is devoted.

The combination of principles that was operative in Chapter I (Sentence Analysis) and Chapter II (Paragraph Analysis) also provides the procedure for reading the work as a whole: determining the elements of sentences to discover their meaning and the relationships of ideas; grasping denotations and connotations of words to understand their contextual meanings; discovering the main idea of paragraphs and the details which define, illustrate, or in some way clarify that main idea; becoming aware of explicit and implicit information; observing the interrelationships of ideas as revealed by transitional devices and emphasis; noting the tone of the writing. Because these principles involve the main substance of critical reading, few new factors will have to be introduced in this chapter. Analysis of the long selection, assuming facility gained from Chapters I and II, consists chiefly of a shift in point of view—a shift necessitated by the extended length of the selection to be read.

Following the essays and excerpts from nonfiction (prose fiction, poetry, and drama are dealt with separately in Chapter IV) are six types of exercises: (1) general questions on the structure of the selection; (2) comprehensive questions on content; (3) critical questions designed to develop the ability to evaluate what is read; (4) discussion questions and/or composition topics; (5) lists of allusive or figurative expressions, the understanding of which requires either a special knowledge or a general "feel" for language; (6) vocabulary lists of words kept in their original phrases to allow connotative interpretations and to develop a "sense" of usage.

The following essay by Bertrand Russell will acquaint the reader with preliminary steps in a satisfactory pattern of analysis. At the end of the essay is a discussion of how it should be read and analyzed. The reader should first examine the essay carefully, then follow the sample analysis step by step.

JOSEPH CONRAD*

Bertrand Russell

I made the acquaintance of Joseph Conrad in September 1913, through our common friend Lady Ottoline Morrell. I had been for many years an admirer of his books, but should not have ventured to seek acquaintance without an introduction. I traveled down to his house near Ashford in Kent in a state of somewhat anxious expectation. My first impression was one of surprise. He spoke English with a very strong foreign accent, and nothing in his demeanor in any way suggested the sea. He was an aristocratic Polish gentleman to his fingertips. His feeling for the sea, and for England, was one of romantic love—love from a certain distance, sufficient to leave the romance untarnished. His love for the sea began at a very early age. When he told his parents that he wished for a career as a sailor, they urged him to go into the Austrian navy, but he wanted adventure and tropical seas and strange rivers surrounded by dark forests; and the Austrian navy offered him no scope for these desires. His family were horrified at his seeking a career in the English merchant marine, but his determination was inflexible.

He was, as anyone may see from his books, a very rigid moralist and politically far from sympathetic with revolutionaries. He and I were in most of our opinions by no means in agreement, but in something very fundamental we were extraordinarily at one.

My relation to Joseph Conrad was unlike any other that I have ever had. I saw him seldom, and not over a long period of years. In the outworks of our lives, we were almost strangers, but we shared a certain outlook on human life and human destiny, which, from the very first, made a bond of extreme strength. I may perhaps be pardoned for quoting a sentence from a letter that he wrote to me very soon after we had become acquainted. I should feel that modesty forbids the quotation except for the fact that it expresses so exactly what I felt about him. What he expresses and I equally felt was, in his words, "A deep admiring affection which, if you were never to see me again and forgot my existence tomorrow, would be unalterably yours *usque ad finem."*

Of all that he had written I admired most the terrible story called *The Heart of Darkness,* in which a rather weak idealist is driven mad by horror of the tropical forest and loneliness among savages. This story expresses, I think, most completely his philosophy of life. I felt, though I do not know whether he would have accepted such an image, that he thought of civilized and morally tolerable human life as a dangerous walk on a thin crust of barely cooled lava which at any moment might break and let the unwary sink into fiery depths. He was very conscious of the various forms of passionate madness to which men are prone, and it was this that gave him such a profound belief in the importance of discipline. His point of view, one might perhaps say, was the antithesis of Rousseau's: "Man is born in chains, but he can become free." He becomes free, so I believe Conrad would have said, not by letting loose his impulses, not by being casual and uncontrolled, but by subduing wayward impulse to a dominant purpose.

He was not much interested in political systems, though he had some strong political *feelings.* The strongest of these were love of England and hatred of Russia, of which both are expressed in *The Secret Agent:* and the hatred of Russia, both Czarist and revolutionary, is set forth with great power in *Under Western Eyes.* His dislike of Russia was that which was traditional in Poland. It went so far that he would not allow merit to either Tolstoy or Dostoievsky. Turgeniev, he told me once, was the only Russian novelist he admired.

Except for love of England and hatred of Russia, politics did not much concern him. What interested him was the individual human soul faced with the indifference of nature, and often with the hostility of man, and subject to inner struggles with passions both good and bad that led toward destruction. Tragedies of loneliness occupied a great part of his thought and feeling. One of his most typical stories is *Typhoon.* In this story the captain, who is a simple soul, pulls his ship through by unshakable courage and grim determination. When the storm is over, he writes a long letter to his wife telling about it. In his account his own part is, to him, perfectly simple. He has merely performed his captain's duty as, of course, anyone would expect. But the reader, through his narrative, becomes aware of all that he has done and dared and endured. The letter, before he sends it off, is read surreptitiously by his steward, but is never read by anyone else at all because his wife finds it boring and throws it away unread.

The two things that seem most to occupy Conrad's imagination are loneliness and fear of what is strange. *An Outcast of the Islands* like *The Heart of Darkness* is concerned with fear of what is strange. Both come together in the extraordinarily moving story called *Amy Foster.* In this story a South-Slav peasant, on his way to America, is the sole survivor of the wreck of his ship, and is cast away in a Kentish village. All the village fears and ill treats him, except Amy Foster, a dull, plain girl who brings him bread when he is starving and finally marries him. But she, too, when, in fever, her husband reverts to his native language, is seized with a fear of his strangeness, snatches up their child and abandons him. He dies alone and hopeless. I have wondered at times how much of this man's loneliness Conrad had felt among the English and had suppressed by a stern effort of will.

Conrad's point of view was far from modern. In the modern world there are two philosophies: the one, which stems from Rousseau, and sweeps aside discipline as unnecessary; the other, which finds its fullest expression in totalitarianism, which thinks of discipline as essentially imposed from without. Conrad adhered to the older tradition, that discipline should come from within. He despised indiscipline, and hated discipline that was merely external.

In all this I found myself closely in agreement with him. At our very first meeting, we talked with continually increasing intimacy. We seemed to sink through layer after layer of what was superficial, till gradually both reached the central fire. It was an experience unlike any other that I have known. We looked into each other's eyes, half appalled and half intoxicated to find ourselves together in such a region. The emotion was as intense as passionate love, and at the same time all-embracing. I came away bewildered, and hardly able to find my way among ordinary affairs.

I saw nothing of Conrad during the war or after it until my return from China in 1921. When my first son was born in that year I wished Conrad to be as nearly his godfather as was possible without a formal ceremony. I wrote to Conrad saying: "I wish, with your permission, to call my son John Conrad . . . Conrad is a name in which I see merits." He accepted the position and duly presented my son with the cup which is usual on such occasions. . . . I never again saw him to speak to. Once I saw him across the street, in earnest conversation with a man I did not know, standing outside the door of what had been my grandmother's house. . . . I did not like to interrupt what seemed a serious conversation, and I went away. When he died, shortly afterwards, I was sorry I had not been bolder. The house is gone, demolished by Hitler. Conrad, I suppose, is in process of being forgotten. But his intense and passionate nobility shines in my memory like a star seen from the bottom of a well. I wish I could make his light shine for others as it shone for me.

Sample Analysis of JOSEPH CONRAD

The most satisfactory pattern of analysis requires first a survey of broad and general characteristics and then the investigation of specific details, since this is the normal order in which certain aspects of discourse become apparent. Here, then, we must first discover Russell's *approach* to his subject — *how* he describes, relates, or explains it.

An author's approach will be objective or subjective, depending on how impersonally or personally he shapes his material. Objective writing entails a serious attempt to exclude any personal references, opinions, prejudices, or statements colored by isolated and unverifiable impressions; in other words, the writer wishes only to analyze or report the facts. One should not be misled, however, into thinking that this approach is necessarily more accurate than the subjective; such an inference is erroneous. The subjective approach is deliberately personal, and the display of inner emotions and private impressions, the reporting of ideas and opinions based solely on the author's limited, but often revealing, observation can produce a picture more "true" and more "accurate" than a very empirical and objective account.

The obvious question, then, is — How do we identify these approaches? First, we must answer more specific questions.

1. Does the author make reference to himself?
2. Is the author interested in his own private impressions or responses, or is he more concerned with facts?
3. Does the author treat all aspects of the subject or only one?
4. Does the author solicit the reader's agreement?

Certain statements in the above selection readily yield the answers we require. Lord Russell *does* make references to himself ("I made the acquaintance of . . ."); he *is* primarily concerned with his own impression of Joseph Conrad ("My first impression was one of surprise. . . . He and I were in most of our opinions by no means in agreement. . . . My relation to Joseph Conrad was unlike any other that I have ever had. . . ."). We notice also that Russell discusses only *his* impressions, and although he does not appear to be unduly anxious for the reader to agree with him, the answers to the first three questions are sufficient to tell us that Russell's approach is quite personal: the selection is clearly subjective.

Having established this broad classification, we can proceed to narrower concerns. What type of selection is "Joseph Conrad"? By asking this question, we can best discover the purpose of the selection — what it was written for, and what it is supposed to do. Here is a list of possible purposes:

1. To tell a story
2. To explain a theory or practice
3. To describe something
4. To persuade or influence us to believe something
5. To defend something
6. To attack something
7. To amuse us
8. To excite us

With some exceptions, the above purposes usually belong to the following types of writing:

1. To tell a story — Narration: the presentation of events or action in chronological or causal order
2. To explain a theory or practice — Exposition: the explanation or clarification or definition of an issue
3. To describe something — Description
4. To persuade or influence } Argument: an attempt to
5. To defend something } change or alter
6. To attack something } belief or action
7. To amuse } any of the above types of writing
8. To excite }

The purpose of the article on Joseph Conrad can be identified by the process of elimination. Russell is certainly not trying to excite or amuse us; nor is he defending or attacking anything. He does not seem interested here in influencing our beliefs, nor is he simply telling a story. Although the information given about the subject, Conrad, may help to clarify some aspects of his life and work, it is not designed specifically to define or explain him. Rather, Russell is presenting a vivid portrait. Thus, the selection can be classified as Description, and, because it is about a person, Biographical Description.

We are ready now to consider the theme; this will lead us into the heart of analysis.

How do we determine the theme of a given written work? Consider first the meaning of the title, then note whatever devices there may be, such as the use of italics and leading phrases, which emphasize the main idea. Often an author will plunge immediately into his subject, stating the topic, or asking a question the answer to which *is* the theme or main idea. The theme may be implied, however, and not specifically stated. In "Joseph Conrad" the title and first sentence explicitly establish the main concern of the selection. In other works this will not be as obvious.

The next and more difficult step is to discover in what way the theme or main idea is limited or defined. *All* aspects of a theme can scarcely be discussed in one article; we must thus discover the particular focus, the special limitations Russell has imposed on his discussion of Conrad. The question now is: *What* does he say about Conrad? Such limitation and focus are often subtle, or even elusive. Of the many things to say about Conrad, we know from the first two sentences that Russell will treat him as a personal acquaintance. "I made the acquaintance of Joseph Conrad in September 1913, through our common friend Lady Ottoline Morrell. I had been for many years an admirer of his books, but should not have ventured to seek acquaintance without an introduction."

This matter-of-fact tone gradually changes. Each subsequent reference Russell makes to their friendship—not to Conrad's thoughts and works—records the rarity and depth of the mutual regard, the extraordinarily strong bond of their common beliefs, its endurance despite infrequent encounters.

The crescendo of this affection comes toward the end in the emotionally charged revelation of the effect of Conrad upon the author. His final tributes to Conrad—perpetuating his name, feeling too awed to interrupt a conversation, desiring to share his inspiration with others—further attest to his devotion.

We also know that he is concentrating on the man, not his books. Conrad as a person—not an author—is revealed by such remarks as "He spoke English with a very strong foreign accent. . . . He was an aristocratic Polish gentleman to his fingertips." The references to Conrad's books are made only to delineate further the character of the man: "*The Heart of Darkness* . . . expresses, I think, most completely his philosophy of life."

Closer examination provides us with even more specific information about the theme. What is Russell saying about Conrad, the man? What were his impressions of the man? In this case even a cursory reading of the article (reading the first few sentences of each paragraph) is enough to give us a lead. The observations made about Conrad are of a general nature: "He was . . . a very rigid moralist. . . . He was not much interested in political systems. . . . The two things that seem most to occupy Conrad's imagination are . . ." We know that Russell sees the character of Joseph Conrad as it is revealed in the latter's philosophy of life, his attitude toward politics, and the principal elements of his imagination.

It is to our advantage, at this point, to note the development of the theme. How is it put together? Knowing exactly and specifically what the selection is about, we can be sure of retaining this information if we know the structure of the article, since it is the structure which shows the relationship of ideas and the subordination of some ideas to others.

Here is a list of possible methods of development, several of which are often combined in a work.

1. *Illustration:* One example is given to describe or support the theme
2. *Detail:* A series of examples, facts, or impressions is given to describe or support the theme
3. *Comparison:* The similarities of two or more ideas, things, or persons are shown
4. *Contrast:* The dissimilarities in ideas, things, or persons are shown
5. *Causes:* The reasons why a problem or situation exists are given
6. *Effects:* The results or effects of a situation or problem are given

We have already noted that the purpose of the selection is to describe and that the three principal statements about Conrad (his philosophy of life, his political beliefs, and his imaginative force) compose the specific theme. Obviously this selection contains "a series of examples, factors, or impressions" given "to describe" the theme. The overall method of development is by detail.

We may now begin a detailed analysis of the content and give our attention to the finer points. In order to understand fully the content of a selection, we should:

1. Ask questions *as we read*
2. Look for key words and phrases that emphasize important ideas (*it is important to remember . . . the first reason is . . . finally . . . in conclusion . . . a comparison exists . . . one possible answer is . . .*)
3. Note any italicized words and any enumeration or lettering of a series of points
4. Keep a good dictionary close by and look up definitions of words not completely understood, but try to understand the words in context
5. Understand the function of transitional words (*but, and, however, nevertheless, yet, instead,* etc.)
6. Discover the meanings of idiomatic expressions
7. Know the meanings of allusions and references
8. Know the connotations of words

The questions that follow each piece in the "Selections for Analysis" are designed for such a penetrating study, and it is hoped that their constant use will make comprehensive reading and good analysis habitual.

The outline below is, briefly, the suggested method of reading a long selection.

   I. Determine the author's approach to his subject

UNITY, COHERENCE, AND EMPHASIS IN THE WHOLE WORK

A reading selection, like any product of intelligence, is more than the sum of its parts. Just as variously colored pigments applied to a canvas do not make a work of art, neither do words, sentences, and paragraphs automatically make, when put together, prose—at least not *good* prose. Obviously, the *way* in which the artist applies his paints to canvas and the way he establishes a relationship of colors and/or shapes to each other determine the painting's excellence. In like manner, it is the *way* in which a writer puts his sentences and paragraphs together and the *way* they relate to each other that make the material comprehensible and impressive. Comprehensibleness and impressiveness are obtained by devices which assure unity, coherence, and emphasis in the work. It is to these three terms, already discussed with reference to smaller units of prose, that we are directing your attention now in the whole work.

Read the following essay, "Homestead and Fort," and see if you can discover, on your own, these aspects of good prose. Then, note the explanation which identifies and clarifies these terms.

HOMESTEAD AND FORT*

Alan Gowan

[1] Well into the 19th century, travelers through older-settled regions of the United States were struck by their differing characteristics. From one region to the next, changes in the shapes of fields and fences, the kinds of crops grown and trees planted, were plain. Even more obvious were differences in types of buildings—barns and forts, churches, houses, and the furniture in them; for it is in what he builds that man always has put his most distinctive stamp on the landscape.

[2] And still today, despite all that development builders and urban renewalists have done to wipe out old landmarks, plenty of survivors from the colonial epoch and descendants in their traditions remain. You can find them everywhere: in the shadow of superhighways and skyscrapers; on the back streets of villages and ancient farms; buried deep in slums. And you can find them in every kind of condition; as no more than gaunt walls and chimney stacks rising out of a tumble of foundation stones, honeysuckle, briar roses and wild apple trees; as conglomerates of the additions and remodelings of half a dozen generations; as meticulous period restorations serving as museums of furniture. Through them, much of the American landscape is still colored today by the diversity of early American civilization.

[3] Colonial America was a land of diverse peoples, all trying, in the manner of migrants from time immemorial, to perpetuate in their New World their culture from the Old; and their buildings showed it. Distinctive and consistent preferences for certain materials and dispositions; for characteristic proportions of height to width, roof to wall, solid to void; for peculiar structural and decorative details—all unmistakably reveal the various parts of the Old World from which their original builders had come. Originally, their differences were great enough—not merely as between New Spain and New Netherlands, but even between New England and Virginia—that the various New World colonies seemed to be quite distinct, with separate lives and histories; and historically they still are, to the extent that we can hardly understand 17th-century American art without considering it in terms of nationalistic cultural expression, as we shall in chapters following.

[4] But at the same time we can see in retrospect that all these peoples responded to their new surroundings in a fundamentally similar way. However great their differences in building or furniture detail may be, in retrospect it seems clear that essentially the same principles appear throughout—principles which, surpassing national traditions, manifest in common the characteristics of that universal phase in social evolution we call folk art.

[5] After the pioneer's cabin and plank bench built for a day's shelter or a year's convenience, come the family homestead, the local church, the community fort—folk architecture, with folk furniture in them, made by local craftsmen to last generations. They mark that last stage in the growth of civilization when a land has been explored and claimed, and society begins to settle into more stable and organized patterns of life. Still anonymous products of community life, their straightforward construction and direct use of materials still reminiscent of earlier bitter struggles with raw nature, they have much in common with Stone and Iron Age forms. But essentially they are very different. In them is expressed a new and much more favorable relationship between man and nature. The primitive builder was dominated by the materials he used, and the axeman still left them raw; but these are the work of men with enough time and resources and experience behind them to develop specialized skills in masonry, carpentry, joinery, to be perfectly familiar with their materials and manage them with ease. And now too more specialized kinds of buildings and furniture can appear; no longer having to worship in houses, use chests for chairs or churches for forts, settlements can begin to provide themselves with something like the precise forms they want. Now builders are able to go beyond mere stability or convenience and begin to make their work

* From *Images of American Living*. Copyright © 1964 by Alan Gowan. Published by J. B. Lippincott Company.

suit their tastes; in a word, to consider matters of fitness, design, or beauty.

This selection was chosen for its unity, coherence, and emphasis: these can be broken down into their component parts. First, the author has taken as his thesis for the entire development of the paragraphs the fundamental folk art underlying the apparent differences in early America. Each topic sentence, generally the first, for each paragraph is easily identified, and supports a new idea for the entire pattern: physical characteristics, paragraph 1; survivals attesting to these differences, paragraph 2; diversity of ancestry reflected in the culture transplanted to the New World, paragraph 3; the common principle of folk art, paragraph 4; and the evolvement of this art from the utilitarian to the artistic, paragraph 5.

The ample illustrations for each new idea alert the reader to the truth of the author's observations. Maintaining the oneness or unity of idea essential to the well-cast paragraph, each sentence grows out of the other by a natural sequence of ideas, helpful transitions, and synonymous phrases. A detailed examination will clarify this point.

The idea in the first sentence of "differing characteristics" in "older-settled regions" of the country continues in the second sentence with the synonymous words, "changes in the shapes of fields," etc., which occur "from one region to the next." The third sentence uses as developmental words "differences in types of buildings" which occur as man's changes "on the landscape." These three sentences are more closely knit by the modification of the "characteristics" in sentence 1 to supporting details of *fields, fences, crops, trees* in sentence 2, to more supporting details of "barns, forts,

churches, houses, furniture" in sentence 3. For this latter group in sentence 3, "barns, forts, churches, houses, furniture," the writer provides virtually a second appositive construction, "what he builds."

In the second paragraph "plenty of survivors" receives the focus of attention in sentence 1. The next reference is to their being "everywhere," then to their being "in every kind of condition." And the pronoun "them" in the last sentence is the summarizing word tying in words and sentences and ideas.

This historical analysis progresses with unifying, transitional phrases of *time* from paragraph to paragraph: "well into the 19th century" in paragraph 1; "and still today" in paragraph 2; "Colonial America," "originally," "historically," "still" in paragraph 3. In the last paragraph are "After . . . come," "that last stage in the growth of civilization," "Still," "new and much more favorable relationship," and "now."

Thus the selection gains unity from the presentation of its ideas, first, through logical sequence: their careful development one after the other in both sentences and paragraphs, aided by a variety of value judgments on the quality and quantity of the types of material selected for illustration. Coherence is achieved by the use of synonyms, appositives, adverbial phrases, and other supporting details, especially of comparison and contrast. Order and emphasis are answered by the historical evolution, formally organized in time from Colonial America to contemporary America (there is even a reference to the Stone and Iron Ages), and formally organized in terms of the origins and artisanship of the American peoples; note how emphatically these references to time occur at the beginnings of paragraphs.

SELECTIONS FOR ANALYSIS

THE SILENT GENERATION*

Thornton Wilder

A younger generation has been calling attention to itself again. These crises in the public appraisal of the young used to occur at longer intervals; now, with the acceleration of social changes, they appear with increasing frequency. Some of us remember the Jazz Age; this was followed by the Lost Generation; now we are in a state of alarm about the Silent Generation.

I have been given an article on "The Younger Generation" which appeared in *Time* magazine on November 5, 1951, and have been asked to comment on it. There I read that these young people "do not issue manifestoes, make speeches, or carry posters . . . do not want to go into the Army. . . . Their ambitions have shrunk. . . . They want a good secure job . . . either through fear, passivity, or conviction, they are ready to conform. . . . They are looking for a faith."

All this I recognize. I propose that we read the manifestations differently.

The Jazz Age preceded and accompanied the first world war. There was a breaking of windows and great scandal. It made evident to all that the American home or the patriarchal pattern had come to an end. The young people won the latchkey. Then the young men went off to the war. That made them heroes. As heroes they acquired more liberties than they had seized as rebellious bad boys. The Lost Generation was the generation that did not know what to do with its new liberties. The younger generation of today is facing the too-long delayed task of consolidating its liberty and of impressing upon it a design, a meaning, and a focus. No wonder they strike us as silent.

An even greater task rests on their shoulders. They are fashioning the Twentieth Century Man. They are called upon to illustrate what the Germans call a "life-style" for our times. This work is usually done by men and women of middle age, but in the accelerated tempo of these war-punctuated years a man or woman of forty-five is out of date. He does not respect or despise the same institutions as an intelligent person in the middle twenties, does not read the same books, admire the same art, nor agree on the same social or cultural premises. The Silent Generation (loquacious enough among its contemporaries) holds its tongue because it cannot both explore itself and explain itself.

The first charge against these young people is apathy. They do not fling themselves into causes; they are not easily moved to enthusiasm; the expression on their faces is impassive, is "dead pan."

But I know where they learned this impassivity. They

learned it at home, as adolescents, guarding themselves against their parents. Guardedness is not apathy. In all my reading I have discovered no age in which there was so great a gulf between parent and child. A seismic disturbance has taken place in the home. Within forty years America has ceased to be a patriarchy; it is moving toward a matriarchy but has not yet recognized and confirmed it. There is nothing wrong with a matriarchy; it does not connote any emasculation of men; it is merely a shift of balance. What is woeful for all parties is the time of transition. These young people grew up in the fluctuating tides of indeterminate authority. A father was no longer held to be, *ex officio,* wise and unanswerable. The mother had not yet learned the rules of supporting and circumscribing her new authority. Father, mother, and children have had daily to improvise their roles. This led to a constant emotional racket in the air. The child either learned a silent self-containment or fell into neurosis.

The second charge is that they "aim low"—they want a good secure job. The article in *Time* says that, as far as their domestic life is concerned, they look forward to a "suburban idyll."

What they want, at all cost, is not to find themselves in "false situations." Life is full of false situations, especially American life today. The most frequent and glaring of them is incompetence in high places. My generation saw a great deal of this in government, in the Army, in culture, and in education. We exercised our wit upon it, but we were ourselves (not yet free of patriarchal influence) still vaguely respectful of rank, office and status. This generation is not impressed by any vested authority whatever. And their freedom to judge authority is accompanied by their willingness to be judged. Their caution reposes upon their unwillingness to exercise any authority or responsibility for which they do not feel themselves to be solidly prepared and adequate. They hate the false and they shrink from those conspicuous roles which all but inevitably require a certain amount of it. I find this trait very promising. Plato was the first to say that high place is best in the hands of those who are reluctant to assume it.

I have said that the Silent Generation is fashioning the Twentieth Century Man. It is not only suffering and bearing forward a time of transition, it is figuring forth a new mentality.

In the first place, these young people will be the first truly international men and women. At last it has ceased to be a mere phrase that the world is one. Compared to them my generation was parochial. Their experience and their reading—their newspapers as well as their textbooks—have impressed upon them that the things which all men hold in common are more important and more productive than the things which separate them. In the Twenties and Thirties one felt oneself to be one among millions; these young people feel themselves to be one among billions. They know it not as a fact learned, but as a self-evident condition; they know it in their bones. On the one hand the individual has shrunk; on the other, the individual has been driven to probe more deeply within himself to find the basis for a legitimate assertion of the claim of self. This conviction is new and its consequences

---

* First appeared in the 75th Anniversary issue of *The Yale Daily News,* New Haven, Connecticut, 1953, the copyright holder. Reprinted here by Special Permission of the author and the publisher.

are far-reaching — in international relations, in religion, in social reform, in art, and in the personal life.

For instance, we went to war against and among "foreigners" and "enemies." That attitude was narrow; henceforward all wars are civil wars. This generation goes forward not to punish and destroy, but to liberate oppressed and misguided brothers. The Army authorities go into anxious huddles over the unabashed candor with which young men can be heard exploring ways of avoiding military service. The Army — like the church, like the university — is an echoing gallery of outdated attitudes and sentiments. It still thinks soldiers can be coerced and it still thinks that the primary qualifications of a soldier are courage and obedience. In a machine warfare, the soldier is a king of engineers; his primary virtue is technical skill and his function is co-operation, not obedience.

Most of us were Protestants; the beliefs held by others were the objects of our all but condescending anthropological curiosity. Today these young people are interested in the nature of belief itself. Some of us in the previous generations hurled ourselves into social reform and social revolution; we did it with a personal passion that left little room for deliberation and long time planning. To correct one abuse we were ready to upset many a benefit. It was of such crusaders that the Sidney Webbs were finally driven to say, "We hate moral indignation." The emerging International Man will move less feverishly in his enlarged thought-world. This generation is silent because these changes call not for argument but for rumination. The mistakes of the previous generations are writ large over the public prints.

These young people are setting new patterns for the relation of the individual to the society about him. The condition of being unimpressed by authorities and elders has thrown them back more resolutely on themselves. They are similarly unimpressed by time-honored conventions. For instance, young married couples today make few concessions to the more superficial aspects of social life. In my generation young brides suffered if their street address was not "right" and if their table silver was not distinguished. Young men were very conscious of influential connections, commissions in the Army, membership in good clubs. Members of this generation exhibit a similar insistence on wishing to be appraised for themselves alone. How often I have known them to conceal sedulously the fact that they come of privileged family. This insistence on being accepted as an individual produces an unprecedented candor. A college girl said to me: "You know I've always been an awful liar. I'm trying to get over it." A veteran, in the presence of his stricken parents, informed a mixed company that he had been a "psycho" for six months after the war. Such expressions reveal the consolidations of a liberty — the liberty of belonging to oneself and not to a social fiction.

These paragraphs have been part description, part explanation, part testimony of faith. Faith is in constant correspondence with doubt. It may be that these young people have been injured by the forces which have been sweeping across the world in their formative years. It may be that what I have called their self-containment is rather a cautious withdrawal from the demands of life. It may be that they lack passion and the constructive imagination. My faith returns, however, with each new encounter. I have just crossed the ocean with a boatload of choice young "Fulbrights" (all hail to the Senator!). The traits I have been describing reappear constantly. They have two orientations well in hand, to themselves and to the larger ranges of experience. It is toward those middle relationships that they are indifferent — current opinion and social usage and the imperatives of traditional religion, patriotism, and morality. Their parents wring their hands over them; their professors find them lukewarm or cool; the Army grows anxious; we older friends are often exasperated. These impatiences are provoked by the fact that they wish to live correctly by their lights and not by ours. In proportion as we are free we must accord them that.

Questions on THE SILENT GENERATION

A. General questions on structure

   1. Is the point of view objective or subjective? What phrases or sentences determine the point of view?

   2. Classify the selection according to type (description, exposition, argument, narration).

   3. Where do you discover the central idea?

   4. For what purpose is the article written? Where do you find this answer?

   5. Select a portion of the article that is developed by cause; by effect; by contrast.

B. Questions on content

   1. What is Mr. Wilder's attitude toward the statements made in the *Time* magazine article? Does he believe they are true?

   2. Does he justify, attack, or re-interpret the statements made in the *Time* article?

   3. What first comparison is made between the "Lost Generation" and the "Silent Generation"?

   4. Why is the Silent Generation silent?

5. What two charges does Mr. Wilder cite as the principal ones lodged against the Silent Generation?

6. What is Mr. Wilder's answer to the first charge? The second?

7. What is the responsibility of the Silent Generation to the future?

8. What are the characteristics of the "Twentieth Century Man"?

C. Questions for critical analysis

1. Is there any evidence of bias? How old do you think Thornton Wilder was when he wrote this? Why? Does this have any bearing on his point of view? Would you expect him to take this stand? What makes his views significant?

2. Are the author's personal experiences sufficient to justify his attitude toward the younger generation?

3. What attitude does the author seem to strike in the first sentence? Is it sustained?

4. What is the tone of the last paragraph? Why do you suppose this tone was selected?

5. Is the information in the selection timely, dated, or timeless? Explain your answer.

D. Discussion and/or composition topics

    1. Have adults in America failed the younger generation? In what ways?

    2. Do you agree with Mr. Wilder's explanations? Why do you oppose or share his sympathies?

    3. Why might changes in the authority structure of society contribute to the growth of a Silent Generation?

    4. What personal evidence can you find to support or to contradict Wilder's assertions?

    5. What novels written in the fifties and sixties contain images of the Silent Generation?

E. Explain the following expressions and sentences

    1. "they know it in their bones"

    2. [the Silent Generation] "cannot both explore itself and explain itself"

    3. "they 'aim low'"

    4. "Life is full of false situations"

    5. "high place is best in the hands of those who are reluctant to assume it"

F. Explain the following allusions

    1. the Lost Generation

    2. the Jazz Age

    3. the Sidney Webbs

    4. Fulbrights

G. Define the italicized words, explaining in each case the contextual meaning

1. "the *acceleration* of social changes"

2. "issue *manifestoes*"

3. "through fear, *passivity,* or conviction"

4. "they are ready to *conform*"

5. "the *patriarchal* pattern"

6. "Guardedness is not *apathy*"

7. "*loquacious* enough"

8. "[their] expression . . . is *impassive*"

9. "A *seismic* disturbance"

10. "toward a *matriarchy*"

11. "*emasculation* of men"

12. "the *fluctuating* times"

13. "*indeterminate* authority"

14. "*circumscribing* her new authority"

15. "to *improvise* their rules"

16. "silent *self-containment*"

17. "*incompetence* in high places"

18. "caution *reposes*"

19. "*conspicuous* roles"

20. "my generation was *parochial*"

21. "a legitimate *assertion*"

22. "the *unabashed candor*"

23. "can be *coerced*"

24. "*condescending anthropological* curiosity"

25. "call . . . for *rumination*"

26. "to conceal *sedulously*"

27. "the *imperatives* of traditional religion"

28. "often *exasperated*"

29. "we must *accord* them that"

THE WITCHCRAFT DELUSION IN COLONIAL CONNECTICUT*

John M. Taylor

Witchcraft in its generic sense is as old as human history. It has written its name in the oldest of human records. In all ages and among all peoples it has taken firm hold on the fears, convictions and consciences of men. Anchored in credulity and superstition, in the dread and love of mystery, in the hard and fast theologic doctrines and teachings of diabolism, and under the ban of the law from its beginning, it has borne a baleful fruitage in the lives of the learned and the unlearned, the wise and the simple.

King and prophet, prelate and priest, jurist and lawmaker, prince and peasant, scholars and men of affairs have felt and dreaded its subtle power, and sought relief in code and commandment, bull and anathema, decree and statute—entailing even the penalty of death—and all in vain until in the march of the races to a higher civilization, the centuries enthroned faith in the place of fear, wisdom in the place of ignorance, and sanity in the seat of delusion.

In its earlier historic conception witchcraft and its demonstrations centered in the claim of power to produce certain effects, "things beyond the course of nature," from supernatural causes, and under this general term all its occult manifestations were classified with magic and sorcery, until the time came when the Devil was identified and acknowledged both in church and state as the originator and sponsor of the mystery, sin and crime—the sole father of the Satanic compacts with men and women, and the law both canonical and civil took cognizance of his malevolent activities.

In the Acropolis mound at Susa in ancient Elam, in the winter of 1901–02, there was brought to light by the French expedition in charge of the eminent savant, M. de Morgan, one of the most remarkable memorials of early civilization ever recovered from the buried cities of the Orient.

It is a monolith—a stele of black diorite—bearing in bas-relief a likeness of Hammurabi (the Amrephel of the Old Testament; Genesis XIV, i), and the sixth king of the first Babylonian dynasty, who reigned about 2250 B.C.; and there is also carved upon it, in archaic script in black letter cuneiform—used long after the cursive writing was invented—the oldest body of laws in existence and the basis of historical jurisprudence.

It is a remarkable code quickly made available through translation and transliteration by the Assyrian scholars, and justly named, from its royal compiler, Hammurabi's Code. He was an imperialist in purpose and action, and in the last of his reign of fifty-five years he annexed or assimilated the suzerainty of Elam, or Southern Persia, with Assyria to the north, and also Syria and Palestine, to the Mediterranean Sea.

This record in stone originally contained nineteen columns of inscriptions of four thousand three hundred and fourteen lines, arranged in two hundred and eighty sections, covering about two hundred separate decisions or edicts. There is substantial evidence that many of the laws were of greater antiquity than the code itself, which is a thousand years older than the Mosaic code, and there are many striking resemblances and parallels between its provisions, and the law of the covenant, and the deuteronomy laws of the Hebrews.

The code was based on personal responsibility. It protects the sanctity of an oath before God, provides among many other things for written evidence in legal matters, and is wonderfully comprehensive and rich in rules for the conduct of commercial, civic, financial, social, economic, and domestic affairs.

These sections are notably illustrative:

"If a man, in a case (pending judgment), utters threats against the witnesses (or), does not establish the testimony that he has given, if that case be a case involving life, that man shall be put to death.

"If a judge pronounces a judgment, renders a decision, delivers a verdict duly signed and sealed and afterwards alters his judgment, they shall call that judge to account for the alteration of the judgment which he had pronounced, and he shall pay twelvefold the penalty which was in the said judgment, and, in the assembly, they shall expel him from his seat of judgment, and he shall not return, and with the judges in a case he shall not take his seat.

"If a man practices brigandage and is captured, that man shall be put to death.

"If a woman hates her husband, and says: 'thou shalt not have me,' they shall inquire into her antecedents for her defects; and if she has been a careful mistress and is without reproach and her husband has been going about and greatly belittling her, that woman has no blame. She shall receive her presents and shall go to her father's house.

"If she has not been a careful mistress, has gadded about, has neglected her house and has belittled her husband, they shall throw that woman into the water.

"If a physician operates on a man for a severe wound with a bronze lancet and causes the man's death, or opens an abscess (in the eye) of a man with a bronze lancet and destroys the man's eye, they shall cut off his fingers.

"If a builder builds a house for a man and does not make its construction firm and the house, which he has built, collapses and causes the death of the owner of the house, that builder shall be put to death."

It is, however, with only one of King Hammurabi's wise laws that this inquiry has to do, and it is this:

"If a man has placed an enchantment upon a man, and has not justified himself, he upon whom the enchantment is placed to the Holy River (Euphrates) shall go; into the Holy River he shall plunge. If the Holy River holds (drowns) him he who enchanted him shall take his house. If on the contrary, the man

* Monograph, New York, 1908.

is safe and thus innocent, the wizard loses his life, and his house."

There can be no more convincing evidence of the presence and power of the great witchcraft superstition among the primitive races than this earliest law; and it is to be especially noted that it prescribes one of the very tests of guilt—the proof by water—which was used in another form centuries later, on the continent, in England and New England, at Wurzburg and Bonn, at Rouen, in Suffolk, Essex and Devon, and at Salem and Hartford and Fairfield, when, "the Devil starteth himself up in the pulpit, like a meikle black man, and calling the row (roll) everyone answered, Here!"

Witchcraft's reign in many lands and among many peoples is also attested in its remarkable nomenclature. Consider its range in ancient, medieval and modern thought as shown in some of its definitions: Magic, sorcery, soothsaying, necromancy, astrology, wizardry, mysticism, occultism, and conjuring, of the early and middle ages; compacts with Satan, consorting with evil spirits, and familiarity with the Devil, of later times; all at last ripening into an epidemic demonopathy with its countless victims of fanaticism and error, malevolence and terror, of persecution and ruthless sacrifices.

It is still most potent in its evil, grotesque, and barbaric forms, in Fetichism, Voodooism, Bundooism, Obeahism, and Kahunaism, in the devil and animal ghost worship of the black races, completely exemplified in the arts of the Fetich wizard on the Congo; in the "Uchawi" of the Wasequhha mentioned by Stanley; in the marriage customs of the Soudan devil worshippers; in the practices of the Obeah men and women in the Caribbees—notably their power in matters of love and business, religion and war—in Jamaica; in the incantations of the kahuna in Hawaii; and in the devices of the voodoo or conjure doctor in the southern states; in the fiendish rites and ceremonies of the red men,—the Hoch-e-ayum of the Plains Indians, the medicine dances of the Cheyennes and Arapahoes, the fire dance of the Navajos, the snake dance of the Moquis, the sun dance of the Sioux, in the myths and tales of the Cherokees; and it rings in many tribal chants and songs of the East and West.

It lives as well, and thrives luxuriantly, ripe for the full vintage, in the minds of many people to whom this or that trivial incident or accident of life is an omen of good or evil fortune with a mysterious parentage. Its roots strike deep in that strange element in human nature which dreads whatsoever is weird and uncanny in common experiences and sees strange portents and dire chimeras in all that is unexplainable to the senses. It is made most virile in the desire for knowledge of the invisible and intangible, that must ever elude the keenest inquiry, a phase of thought always to be reckoned with when imagination runs riot, and potent in its effect, though evanescent as a vision the brain sometimes retains of a dream, and as senseless in the cold light of reason as Monna Sidonia's invocation at the Witches' Sabbath:
(*Romance of Leonardo da Vinci*, p. 97, Merejkowski.)

> "Emen Hetan, Emen Hetan, Palu, Baalberi,
> Astaroth help us Agora, Agora, Patrisa,
> Come and help us.
> Garr-r: Garr-r, up: Don't knock
> Your head: We fly: We fly:"

And who may count himself altogether free from the subtle power of the old mystery with its fantastic imageries, when the spirit of unrest is abroad? Who is not moved by it in the awesome stillness of night on the plains, or in the silence of the mountains or of the somber forest aisles; in wild winter nights when old tales are told; in fireside visions as tender memories come and go? And who, when listening to the echoes of the chambers of the restless sea when deep calleth unto deep, does not hear amid them some weird and haunting refrain like Leland's sea song?

> "I saw three witches as the wind blew cold
> In a red light to the lee;
> Bold they were and overbold
> As they sailed over the sea;
> Calling for One Two Three;
> Calling for One Two Three;
> And I think I can hear
> It a ringing in my ear,
> A-calling for the One, Two, Three."

Questions on THE WITCHCRAFT DELUSION IN COLONIAL CONNECTICUT

A. General questions on structure

  1. Is this a subjective or objective account?

  2. Are any attempts made to influence the reader, or is the selection candidly informative?

  3. What is the purpose of the selection?

B. Questions on content

  1. According to the first paragraph, what is the source of beliefs in witchcraft?

  2. How was witchcraft once defined and what created a change in this definition?

  3. What was the nature of the discovery made at Susa by the French expedition?

  4. According to this discovery, what legal provision was made for the Elamites concerning witchcraft?

  5. According to the author, what does this discovery prove?

  6. What evidence does the author give for the wide reign of witchcraft?

  7. Is witchcraft out of date? If not, what evidence can you cite of its survival?

  8. What provides for the growth of beliefs in witchcraft?

C. Questions for critical analysis

  1. What is the function of the quotation by Merejkowski? Of the Leland sea song?

  2. What effect is created by the questions in the last paragraph?

3. Is the author's attitude toward witchcraft one of awe, disgust, or indifference? Explain your answer.

4. Does the author appear to have sufficient evidence for his claims? Does it seem as though he is familiar with his subject as a scholar, or is this a pastime of his?

5. Analyze this author's style of writing. Is it plain or elaborate, quiet or ostentatious? What patterns does he use? How effective is his style, and how well suited is it to its subject? Does the author "popularize" witchcraft?

D. Discussion and/or composition topics

1. Why have even the leading men of earlier periods dreaded witchcraft? What is its "subtle power"?

2. What things displace or destroy a belief in witches?

3. Are superstitions ever useful?

4. What is extrasensory perception?

5. Try to explain how and why several specific aspects of witchcraft might have begun.

E. Vocabulary: Define the italicized words, explaining in each case their contextual meaning

1. "its *generic* sense"

2. "Anchored in *credulity*"

3. "*theologic* doctrines"

4. "teachings of *diabolism*"

5. "the *ban* of the law"

6. *"baleful fruitage"*

7. "bull and *anathema*"

8. "seat of *delusion*"

9. *"occult* manifestations"

10. "Satanic *compacts*"

11. "both *canonical* and civil"

12. "took *cognizance*"

13. *"malevolent* activities"

14. "eminent *savant*"

15. "separate . . . *edicts*"

16. "is also *attested*"

17. "remarkable *nomenclature*"

18. "epidemic *demonopathy*"

19. *"dire chimeras"*

20. "*evanescent* as a vision"

from COLLEGE ALGEBRA*

M. Richardson

A BRIEF LESSON IN LOGIC

Mathematics is logical in nature, and mathematical writing is precise, compact, and logical in style. Therefore a brief review of certain elementary but fundamental logical concepts and terms is given here.

When two statements are so related that the second *must* be true *if* the first is true, we say that the second *follows from* the first, or the second is a *logical consequence* of the first, or the first implies the second. The first statement is called the *hypothesis* and the second is called the *conclusion.*

Example 1. Hypothesis x = 2 and y = 5
Conclusion x + y = 7

If the conclusion of an argument really follows inescapably from the hypothesis, the argument is called *valid.* The process of drawing inescapable conclusions from given hypotheses is called *deduction* or *deductive reasoning.*

The proposition of example 1 may be written as: (a) If x = 2 and y = 5, then x + y = 7; or (b) "x = 2 and y = 5" implies "x + y = 7."

In a statement of the form "If A is true, then B is true," or "A implies B," A is the *hypothesis* and B is the *conclusion.* This statement does not assert that A is true or that B is true. It asserts merely that *If A were true, then B would have to be true.* That is, *in a valid argument, the truth of the hypothesis guarantees the truth of the conclusion.*

Example 2. "If today were Election day[1] then tomorrow would be Wednesday" is a valid argument even if today is neither Election Day nor any other Tuesday.

Note that the conclusion may be true even if the hypothesis is false. Thus, in example 2, the conclusion would be true if today were any Tuesday in the year.

Therefore, *in a valid argument, the truth of the conclusion does not guarantee the truth of the hypothesis. But the falsity of the conclusion does guarantee the falsity of the hypothesis.*

[1] We assume that Election Day in the U.S.A. is, by definition, the Tuesday after the first Monday of November.

Questions on COLLEGE ALGEBRA

A. General questions on structure

1. How do you know that this selection is objective?

2. Can an author write subjectively about this subject? Is there room for interpretation? Why, or why not?

3. What is the purpose of the selection?

4. Why does the author italicize certain words or groups of words?

5. What words best describe the style used? Is this the style best suited to the subject? Does the author follow his criteria for "mathematical writing"?

B. Questions on content

1. What is the difference between "elementary" and "fundamental" concepts?

2. What is an hypothesis?

3. What determines a valid argument?

4. What is deduction?

5. Complete each of the following statements with one of these phrases:
   "must be true"   "must be false"   "may be true or false"
   a. If the hypothesis is true, then the conclusion _____
   b. If the hypothesis is false, then the conclusion _____
   c. If the conclusion is true, then the hypothesis _____
   d. If the conclusion is false, then the hypothesis _____

C. Discussion and/or composition topics

1. How important is mathematics in everyday living? Give specific examples.

2. If you never have the need or occasion to use algebra, would there be any advantage at all to studying and understanding it?

3. What application can be made of logical reasoning in business, daily life, law? Give specific examples.

D. Vocabulary: Define the italicized words, explaining in each case their contextual meanings.

1. "*inescapable* conclusions"

2. "'x = 2 and y = 5' *implies* 'x + y = 7'"

3. "This statement does not *assert*"

4. "the hypothesis *guarantees*"

5. "the *falsity* of the conclusion"

THE COMING OF MEN LIKE OURSELVES*

H. G. Wells

The Neanderthal type of man prevailed in Europe at least for tens of thousands of years. For ages that make all history seem a thing of yesterday, these nearly human creatures prevailed. If the Heidelberg jaw was that of a Neanderthaler, and if there is no error in the estimate of the age of that jaw, then the Neanderthal race lasted out for more than 200,000 years! Finally, between 40,000 and 25,000 years ago, as the Fourth Glacial Age softened towards more temperate conditions, a different human type came upon the European scene, and it would seem, exterminated *Homo Neanderthalensis.*

This new type was probably developed in South Asia or Africa, or in lands now submerged in the Mediterranean basins, and as more remains are collected and evidence accumulates, men will learn more of their early stages. At present we can only guess where and how, through the slow ages, parallel with the Neanderthal cousin, these first *true men* arose out of some more ape-like progenitor. For hundreds of centuries they were acquiring skill of hand and limb, and power and bulk of brain, in that still unknown environment. They were already far above the Neanderthal level of achievement and intelligence when first they came into our ken, and they had already split into two or more very distinctive races.

These newcomers did not migrate into Europe in the strict sense of the word, but rather, as century by century the climate ameliorated, they followed the food and plants to which they were accustomed, as these spread into the new realms that opened to them. The ice was receding, vegetation was increasing, big game of all sorts was becoming more abundant. Steppe-like conditions, conditions of pasture and shrub, were bringing with them vast herds of wild horse. Ethnologists (students of race) class these new human races in the same species as ourselves, and with all human races subsequent to them, under one common specific name of *Homo sapiens.* They had quite human brain-cases and hands. Their teeth and their necks were anatomically as ours are.

We know of two distinct sorts of skeletal remains in this period, the first of these known as the Cro-Magnon race, and the second the Grimaldi race; but the great bulk of the human traces and appliances we find are either without human bones or with insufficient bones for us to define their associated physical type. There may have been many more distinct races than those two. There may have been intermediate types. In the grotto of Cro-Magnon it was that complete skeletons of one main type of these newer Palaeolithic men, these true men, were first found, and so it is that they are spoken of as Cro-Magnards.

These Cro-Magnards were a tall people with very broad faces, prominent noses, and, all things considered, astonishingly big brains. The brain capacity of the woman

* From *The Outline of History* by H.G. Wells (A.P. Watt & Son). Copyright 1920 Herbert George Wells © G. P. Wells 1956. With the permission of the Executors.

in the Cro-Magnon cave exceeded that of the average male today. Her head had been smashed by a heavy blow. There were also in the same cave with her the complete skeleton of an older man, nearly six feet high, the fragments of a child's skeleton and the skeletons of two young men. There were also flint implements and perforated sea-shells, used, no doubt, as ornaments. Such is one sample of the earliest true men. But at the Grimaldi cave near Mentone were discovered two skeletons also of the later Palaeolithic Period but of a widely contrasted type, with negroid characteristics that point rather to the negroid type. They reach in type towards the Boskop race of South Africa of which we have already told. There can be no doubt that we have to deal in this period with at least two, and probably more, highly divergent races of true men. They may have overlapped in time, or Cro-Magnards may have followed the Grimaldi race, and either or both may have been contemporary with the late Neanderthal men. Various authorities have very strong opinions upon these points, but they are, at most, opinions.

The appearance of these truly human postglacial Palaeolithic peoples was certainly an enormous leap forward in the history of mankind. Both of these main races had a human fore-brain, a human hand, an intelligence very like our own. They dispossessed *Homo Neanderthalensis* from his caverns and his stone quarries. And they agreed with modern ethnologists, it would seem, in regarding him as a different species. Unlike most savage conquerors, who take the women of the defeated side for their own and interbreed with them, it would seem that the true men would have nothing to do with the Neanderthal race, women or men. There is no trace of any intermixture between the races, in spite of the fact that the newcomers, being also flint users, were establishing themselves in the very same spots that their predecessors had occupied.

We know nothing of the appearance of the Neanderthal man, but this absence of intermixture seems to suggest an extreme hairiness, an ugliness, or a repulsive strangeness in his appearance over and above his low forehead, his beetle brows, his ape neck, and his inferior stature. Or he—and she—may have been too fierce to tame. Says Sir Harry Johnston, in a survey of the rise of modern man in his *Views and Reviews:* "The dim racial remembrance of such gorilla-like monsters, with cunning brains, shambling gait, hairy bodies, strong teeth, and possibly cannibalistic tendencies, may be the germ of the ogre in folklore . . . ."

These true men of the Palaeolithic Age, who replaced the Neanderthalers, were coming into a milder climate, and although they used the caves and shelters of their predecessors, they lived largely in the open. They were hunting peoples, and some or all of them appear to have hunted the mammoth and the wild horse as well as the reindeer, bison, and aurochs. They ate much horse. At a great open-air camp at Solutre, where they seem to have had annual gatherings for many centuries, it is estimated that there are the bones of 100,000 horses, besides reindeer, mammoth, and bison bones. They probably followed herds of horses, the little bearded ponies of that age, as these moved after pasture. They hung about on the flanks of the herd, and became very wise about its habits and dispositions. A large part of these men's lives must have been spent in watching animals.

Whether they tamed and domesticated the horse is still an open question. Perhaps they learnt to do so by degrees as the centuries passed. At any rate, we find late Palaeolithic drawings of horses with marks about the heads that are strongly suggestive of bridles, and there exists a carving of a horse's head showing what is perhaps a rope of twisted skin or tendon. But even if they tamed the horse, it is still more doubtful whether they rode it or had much use for it when it was tamed. The horse they knew was a wild pony with a beard under its chin, not up to carrying a man for any distance. It is improbable that these men had yet learnt the rather unnatural use of animal's milk as food. If they tamed the horse at last, it was the only animal they seem to have tamed. They had no dogs, and they had little to do with any sort of domesticated sheep or cattle.

It greatly aids us to realize their common humanity that these earliest true men could draw. Indeed they drew astonishingly well. They were by all standards savages, but they were artistic savages. They drew better than any of their successors down to the beginnings of history. They drew and painted on the cliffs and walls of the caves they had wrested from the Neanderthal men. And the surviving drawings come to the ethnologist, puzzling over bones and scraps, with the effect of a plain message shining through guesswork and darkness. They drew on bones and antlers; they carved little figures.

These later Palaeolithic people not only drew remarkably well for our information, and with an increasing skill as the centuries passed, but they have also left us other information about their lives in their graves. They buried. They buried their dead, often with ornaments, weapons, and food; they used a lot of colour in the burial, and evidently painted the body. From that one may infer that they painted their bodies during life. Paint was a big fact in their lives. They were inveterate painters; they used black, brown, red, yellow, and white pigments, and the pigments they used endure to this day in the caves and on the cliff surfaces of France and Spain. Of all modern races, none has shown so pictorial a disposition; the nearest approach to it has been among the American Indians.

These drawings and paintings of the later Palaeolithic people went on through a long period of time, and present wide fluctuations in artistic merit. In its early stages the drawing is often primitive like the drawing of clever children; quadrupeds are usually drawn with one hind-leg and one fore-leg, as children draw them to this day; the legs on the other side were too much for the artists' technique. Possibly the first drawings began as children's drawings begin, out of idle scratchings. The savage scratched with a flint on a smooth rock surface, and was reminded of some line or gesture. But their solid carvings are at least as old as their first pictures. The earlier drawings betray a complete incapacity to group animals.

As the centuries progressed, more skilful artists appeared. The representations of beasts became at last astonishingly vivid and live. But even at the crest of their artistic time they still drew in profile as children do; perspective and the fore-shortening needed for back and front views were too much for them. The mammoth and the horse are among the commonest themes. In the caves of the north of Spain there are no drawings of men, only of animals; but in eastern Spain there are many paintings dating from the later divisions of this period in which human figures are displayed. Some of the people also made little ivory and soapstone statuettes, and among these are some very fat female figures. They are like Bushmen women. The human sculpture of the earlier times inclined to caricature, and generally such human figures as they represent are far below the animal studies in vigour and veracity.

Later on there was more grace and less coarseness in the human representations. One small ivory head discovered is that of a girl with an elaborate coiffure. These people at a later stage also scratched and engraved designs on ivory and bone. Some of the most interesting groups of figures are carved very curiously round bone, and especially round rods of deer bone, so that it is impossible to see the entire design all together. Figures have also been found modelled in clay, although no Palaeolithic people made any use of pottery.

Many of the paintings are found in the depths of unlit caves. They are often difficult of access. The artists must have employed lamps to do their work, and shallow soapstone lamps in which fat could have been burnt have been found. Whether the seeing of these cavern paintings was in some way ceremonial or under what circumstances they were seen, we are now altogether at a loss to imagine. In the south and east of Spain, however, the drawings are not in caves, but upon overhung rock shelters in a good light.

Archaeologists distinguish at present three chief stages in the history of these newer Palaeolithic men, these true men, in Europe, and we must name these stages here. But it may be as well to note at the same time that it is a matter of the utmost difficulty to distinguish which of two deposits in different places is the older or newer. We may very well be dealing with the work of more or less contemporary and different races when we think we are dealing with successive ones. We are dealing, the reader must bear in mind, with little disconnected patches of material, a few score altogether.

The earliest stage usually distinguished by the experts is the *Aurignacian* (from the grotto of Aurignac); it is characterized by very well-made flint implements, and by a rapid development of art and more particularly of statuettes and wall paintings. The most esteemed of the painted caves is ascribed to the latter part of this, the first of the three subdivisions of the newer Palaeolithic. The second subdivision of this period is called the *Solutrian* (from Solutre), and is distinguished particularly by the quality and beauty of its stone implements; some of its razor-like blades are only equalled and not surpassed by the very best of the Neolithic work. They are of course unpolished, but the best specimens are as thin as steel blades and almost as sharp. Finally, it would seem, came the *Magdalenian* (from La Madeleine) stage, in which the horse and reindeer were dwindling in numbers and the red deer coming into Europe. The stone implements are smaller, and there is a great quantity of bone harpoons, spearheads, needles, and the like.

The hunters of the third and last stage of the later Palaeolithic Age appear to have supplemented a diminishing food supply by fishing. The characteristic art of the period consists of deep reliefs done upon bone and line engraving upon bone. It is to this period that the designs drawn round bones belong, and it has been suggested that these designs upon round bones were used to print coloured designs upon leather. Some of the workmanship on bone was extraordinarily fine. Parkyn quotes from de Mortillet about the Reindeer Age (Magdalenian) bone needles, that they "are much superior to those of later, even historical, times, down to the Renaissance. The Romans, for example, never had needles comparable to those of the Magdalenian epoch."

It is quite impossible at present to guess at the relative lengths of these ages. We are not even positive about their relative relationship. Each lasted perhaps for four or five or more thousand years, more than double the time from the Christian era to our own day. Moreover, these divisions are based mainly upon the remains found in France and the north of Spain. As we go into the south of Spain and Italy and North Africa, their characteristics are no longer traceable. There was a different type of life to the south, different food and different equipment.

At last it would seem that circumstances began to turn altogether against these hunting newer Palaeolithic people who had flourished for so long in Europe. They disappeared. New kinds of men appeared from the south and east, replacing them. These latter seem to have brought in bow and arrows; they had domesticated animals and cultivated the soil. A new way of living, the Neolithic way of living, spread over the European area; and the life of the Reindeer Age and of the later Palaeolithic men, after a reign vastly greater than the time between ourselves and the very earliest beginnings of recorded history, passed off the European stage.

There is, perhaps, a disposition on the part of some writers to exaggerate the intellectual and physical qualities of these later Palaeolithic men and make a wonder of them. Collectively considered, these people had remarkable gifts, but a little reflection will show they had almost as remarkable deficiencies. The tremendous advance they display upon their Neanderthal predecessors and their special artistic gift must not blind us to their very obvious limitations. For all the quantity of their brains, the quality was narrow and special. They had vivid perceptions, an acute sense of animal form, they had the real artist's impulse to render; so far they were fully grown human beings. But that disposition to paint and draw is shown to-day by the Bushmen, by Californian Indians, and by Australian black fellows; it is not a mark of all-round high intellectual quality.

Questions on THE COMING OF MEN LIKE OURSELVES

A. General questions on structure

   1. What is the purpose of this selection?

   2. What type of selection is it?

   3. Is the author objective? Why does he account for views other than his own?

B. Questions on content

   1. What evidence is given by some ethnologists supporting the theory that the Neanderthal man and the Cro-Magnon man intermixed? Why does the author reject this theory? How valid is his reasoning?

   2. What geographic area was probably the birthplace of the "true man"?

   3. What were the physical differences between the Neanderthal and the Cro-Magnon man? Between the Cro-Magnon man and the Grimaldi man?

   4. What probably caused the movement of the "true man" north?

   5. From where do the names Cro-Magnon and Grimaldi come?

   6. Why do ethnologists believe that Cro-Magnons painted their bodies in life?

   7. What evidence is there that these "true men" ate horses?

   8. How do the horses of the Paleolithic Age differ from the modern horse?

C. Discussion and/or composition topics

   1. Self-awareness in early man as seen in the subject of his drawings
   2. The origin of the ogre in folklore
   3. Tools and weapons of Paleolithic men—what they were and why they must have been developed

D. Vocabulary: Define the italicized words, explaining in each case their contextual meanings.

1. "*temperate* conditions"

2. "ape-like *progenitor*"

3. "did not *migrate*"

4. "the climate *ameliorated*"

5. "*Steppe-like* conditions"

6. "*intermediate* types"

7. "In the *grotto*"

8. "*perforated* sea-shells"

9. "the *pigments* they used"

DOWN WITH DREAMS!*

The highly quotable Dr. Samuel Johnson wrote to Mrs. Thrale from Skye: "The use of travelling is to regulate imagination by reality, and, instead of thinking how things may be, to see them as they are."

A commendable notion, we think. We learned long ago that rose-colored glasses have no place in the securities business, that it is absolutely necessary to see things as they are instead of as they may be. That's why we have a large Research Department—to view the stock market in realistic, down-to-earth fashion and pass its observations along to our customers.

We think investors should always trust facts, not fancies—and that's where we come in. Our Research Department is prepared to help you regulate imagination by reality on request. All you have to do is write a letter telling us how much money you would like to invest or what securities you own at present and indicating your major investment objective. The information you supply will be held in strictest confidence, and you'll receive an objective, conscientious, well-informed reply.

Address—

Joseph C. Quinn, Department SB–105
Merrill Lynch, Pierce, Fenner & Smith
Incorporated

Questions on DOWN WITH DREAMS!

A. General questions on structure

1. Is the point of view objective or subjective? What does the use of the pronoun "we" suggest about the point of view?

2. Is the reader being encouraged or persuaded to do something? If so, what? Is this the *purpose* of the text?

3. The answer to question 2 suggests the type of writing this is—what is that type?

B. Questions on content

1. The quotation from Samuel Johnson suggests an appeal to what class of people?

2. Is the quotation aptly used or is its meaning forced to apply to the purpose of the selection?

3. The selection does not explain "Mrs. Thrale" or "Skye." What assumptions does the article make about the reader's background? How important is it for a reader to be able to identify these names?

4. This is advertising copy. Is the tone that which is generally used in such material? Explain your answer.

* With the permission of Merrill Lynch, Pierce, Fenner & Smith, Inc.

5. Is the corporation "selling" its services or are they "offering" a service? Is there in this case a difference?

6. What is the relationship between the title and the service the firm has to offer?

C. Discussion questions

1. The Merrill Lynch, Pierce, Fenner & Smith corporation uses a literary reference as a springboard into the world of money-making. Discuss the relationship. Is it absurd? Natural?
2. From the style of the advertisement, what opinion can be formed about the corporation?
3. Successful advertising copy is supposed to encourage business. How successful do you think this is?

D. Vocabulary: Give synonyms for the italicized words or phrases.

1. "A *commendable* notion"

2. "*rose-colored glasses*"

3. "*securities business*"

4. "trust facts, not *fancies*"

5. "*regulate imagination*"

6. "*investment objective*"

THE OWL WHO WAS GOD*

James Thurber

Once upon a starless midnight there was an owl who sat on the branch of an oak tree. Two ground moles tried to slip quietly by, unnoticed. "You!" said the owl. "Who?" they quavered, in fear and astonishment, for they could not believe it was possible for anyone to see them in that thick darkness. "You two!" said the owl. The moles hurried away and told the other creatures of the field and forest that the owl was the greatest and wisest of all animals because he could see in the dark and because he could answer any question. "I'll see about that," said a secretary bird, and he called on the owl one night when it was again very dark. "How many claws am I holding up?" said the secretary bird. "Two," said the owl, and that was right. "Can you give me another expression for 'that is to say' or 'namely'?" asked the secretary bird. "To wit," said the owl. "Why does a lover call on his love?" asked the secretary bird. "To woo," said the owl.

The secretary bird hastened back to the other creatures and reported that the owl was indeed the greatest and wisest animal in the world because he could see in the dark and because he could answer any question. "Can he see in the daytime, too?" asked a red fox. "Yes," echoed a dormouse and a French poodle. "Can he see in the daytime, too?" All the other creatures laughed loudly at this silly question, and they set upon the red fox and his friends and drove them out of the region. Then they sent a messenger to the owl and asked him to be their leader.

When the owl appeared among the animals it was high noon and the sun was shining brightly. He walked very slowly, which gave him an appearance of great dignity, and he peered about him with large, staring eyes, which gave him an air of tremendous importance. "He's God!" screamed a Plymouth Rock hen. And the others took up the cry "He's God!" So they followed him wherever he went and when he began to bump into things they began to bump into things, too. Finally he came to a concrete highway and he started up the middle of it and all the other creatures followed him. Presently a hawk, who was acting as outrider, observed a truck coming toward them at fifty miles an hour, and he reported to the secretary bird and the secretary bird reported to the owl. "There's danger ahead," said the secretary bird. "To wit?" said the owl. The secretary bird told him. "Aren't you afraid?" he asked. "Who?" said the owl calmly, for he could not see the truck. "He's God!" cried all the creatures again, and they were still crying "He's God!" when the truck hit them and ran them down. Some of the animals were merely injured, but most of them, including the owl, were killed.

Moral: You can fool too many of the people too much of the time.

Questions on THE OWL WHO WAS GOD

A. General questions on structure

1. What type of selection is this—descriptive, narrative, argumentative or expository? Do the first two words give you a clue?

2. In this type of selection, where do you expect to find the central idea—near the beginning or the end? Why?

B. Questions on content

1. Why do the animals laugh at the question of whether the owl can see in the daylight? Can he?

2. What are the implications of having the declaration of the owl's divinity put into the mouth of a Plymouth Rock hen?

3. Why do the animals "bump into things" when the owl does?

* From *The New Yorker,* April 29, 1939. Reprinted by permission. Copyright © 1939 The New Yorker Magazine, Inc.

4. Are the questions which the secretary bird puts to the owl deliberately or accidentally those which the owl could answer?

5. What implications about "heresy" lie in the expulsion of the red fox, dormouse, and French poodle from the region?

C. Questions for critical analysis

1. What knowledge of the sound of an owl's call need you have to make his "answers" plausible?

2. What image does the secretary bird invoke?

3. What other fable—concerning a group of animals following another animal blindly—does this remind you of? Is there any thematic relationship?

4. Is the author serious, playful, or both?

5. Explain the "moral"—what famous quotation is it reminiscent of?

D. Discussion and/or composition topics
   1. What is being said about the nature of Belief?
   2. Does man create his gods?

E. Vocabulary: Define the following terms.

   1. *quavered*

   2. *peered*

   3. *outrider*

THE MATTER OF BEING INTERESTING*

Louis Kronenberger

In spite, or maybe because, of all that has been written on how to acquire friends, exude personality and dazzle dinner parties, America today boasts pathetically few interesting people. By interesting one means, of course, quite the reverse of "interesting"—quite the reverse of travelers who give memorably minute accounts of their trips to the interior of Kenya; or people who have the ear, or hold the hand, or scratch the back, of the great and celebrated. One means people—it seems sad to have to say what one means—who because of their brains, charm, liveliness, responsiveness, wit are a pleasure to be with. And a pleasure whether one chooses to talk sense or nonsense, since the test of interesting people is that subject matter doesn't matter.

So few are such people that American life is chiefly conducted on the principle that human beings are dull. In general, American social life constitutes an evasion of talking to people. Most Americans don't, in any vital sense, get together; they only do things together. They meet by day to shop, play golf or tennis or canasta or bridge, go to football or baseball games, to matinees and movies. By night they gather—whether before or after feeding—to play cards or look at television, or they go to night games or movies or shows, or night clubs and bars. Though the servant problem has had something to do with the growing custom of dining out, people also dine out so that they can dance as well, or listen to music, or stare at the people around them. Such conversation as occurs tends to narrow down in subject matter and flatten out in style. Americans generally—Americans of all income groups—aren't interested in any great number of subjects, nor very bright or vivacious about such as they are. There are the people (and they make up the vast majority) whose chief delight, whose only alternative to bridge or baseball, the office or the household, is gossip. There are, again, the people (and they are rather more numerous than one might suppose) whose passion is for the "worth-while." The sad thing is that the first group can't make their gossiping sprightly, nor the second their earnestness stimulating. Gossip is, of course, the very life of conversation—if by gossip one means the all-too-human side of people, and if by people one means Einstein or Shelley as well as the members of the country club. Gossip—however intolerable when pursued with the sheer malice of the rocking-chair brigade—is the very watering can of conversation when indulged in with any tact. But just because it can be so spiteful, it needs to be handled with a certain real lightness, a certain sense of something left unsaid: the test, I would think, is that someone who gossips well has a reputation for being good company or even a wit, never for being a gossip.

Immemorial target for satire though it is, the pursuit of the worth-while must yet be touched on, since the plain

* From *Company Manners,* copyright 1951, 1953, 1954 by Louis Kronenberger, reprinted by permission of the publishers, The Bobbs-Merrill Company, Inc.

sad point is that it can't possibly be laughed out of existence. There is no need to go after it at its worst, among women's-club discussion groups, or people with social-worker minds. But very near kin to them, particularly in social life, are people who are both informed and intelligent, who may well possess opinions both sound and their own. Nor need such people, in order to strangle enjoyment, be opinionated or dogmatic: they may be really estimable people to meet, they may provide a stimulating exchange of views and meeting of minds. But that is all one *does* meet; as people they are ciphers, they lack temperament, they lack personality, they lack grace: *they* are not interesting. Even while they are flooding the conversation with light, they are draining it of color; even where they help restore one's faith in human nature, they help kill one's taste for social intercourse. And most of the time they are by no means so lacking in ego or assertiveness as I have permitted them to be; they all too often crush conversation by their need to hold the floor, or spoil it by their ability to suggest the classroom. . . .

The fascinating necessarily tends to call a certain attention to itself; the interesting need not. An evening spent with a fascinating person leaves vivid memories; one spent with interesting people has merely a sort of bouquet. One conceivable test of talk with a really interesting person is that you can't remember a single thing he said. I have already been didactic past my bedtime, and I won't try further to define what makes a man interesting, or to what extent it is inborn and to what extent acquired; but I doubt whether it can be acquired through anything you send for, enroll in or read up on.

But I would stress that an interesting person is far more than the reverse of a bore. There are plenty of people lively or intelligent enough to be agreeable company, or individual enough to have, as it were, documentary interest, or who have a flibbertigibbet charm that keeps them from being dull, or are so high-powered or downright appalling as to make "bore" the very last word that one would apply to them. Yet all these people, the likable no less than the offensive, do, I think, fail to interest us in the end: they remain pleasant to be with, but that is something else. The really interesting human being, like the really interesting writer, combines something personal with something artistic: both not only have manner enough to carry off what they do, but have an instinct about what is worth doing, and in just what degree, and with just how much gusto; and they never speak one's language so well as by not speaking at all. Plainly, the whole basis of sound social intercourse is knowing when not to finish a sentence. But of course such procedure penalizes people who are well informed, people who tend professionally to debate, discuss, diagnose, analyze, instruct and advise; and since most intellectuals today earn both their livings and their reputations by doing several of these things, most intellectuals today are not, in the perhaps peculiar sense that I use the word, interesting. . . .

The whole matter involves the difference between the salon at its brightest and the schoolroom at its worst, the difference between holding the table and holding the floor. I don't know that on any basis of self-interest one need any longer go to much trouble, because, plainly, being interesting is no longer enough. It is better, and I dare say no harder, to be impressive. And besides, this is no age when people fold their legs; this is an age when people are on the run; when, no longer even furtively, they are always glancing at their wrist watches; when business keeps them rushing from one place to another; and they escape boredom by staying nowhere long enough to be bored. I would guess that the few people who are interesting in society less and less form any part of it. After all, they are among the few people left who are also not bored with themselves.

Questions on THE MATTER OF BEING INTERESTING

A. General questions on structure

   1. According to the title, what word is about to be defined or described?

   2. How does Mr. Kronenberger limit the central idea expressed in the title in the very first paragraph?

   3. The subject matter requires a subjective approach. Why?

   4. Which of the eight purposes listed in the Introduction to this chapter is applicable here?

B. Questions on content

   1. How is "gossip" to be handled if it is to function as "the watering can of conversation"?

   2. When is gossip intolerable?

   3. When do seekers of the "worth-while," even when they are both informed and intelligent, fail to be genuinely interesting people?

   4. What evidence is given for the assumption that "American life is chiefly conducted on the principle that human beings are dull"? How convincing is this evidence?

   5. How is it possible that the opposite of a bore is not necessarily an interesting person?

C. Questions for critical analysis

   1. What phrases in the first paragraph indicate that the selection will contain sharply satirical comments?

   2. Where do you suppose Mr. Kronenberger places himself? Does he imply that he is that rare person, the interesting man? Is there any suggestion of personal bitterness or is the tone one of playfulness with an edge to it?

3. What is there about a social worker that might make Mr. Kronenberger use the expression "people with social-worker minds" with such obvious disdain?

4. One cannot help being impressed by the author's cleverness with language. Is he ever too "clever"? Does he, by his bright and calculatedly fetching language, ever become, himself, one of the *fascinating* rather than one of the *interesting?*

D. Discussion and/or composition topics

1. The Anatomy of a Bore
2. Do Americans Know How to Live?
3. Gossip vs. Wit
4. A "Fascinating" Man vs. an "Interesting" Man

E. Explain the following expressions and sentences.

1. "while they are flooding the conversation with light, they are draining it of color. . . ."

2. "this is no age when people fold their legs. . . ."

3. "the whole basis of sound social intercourse is knowing when not to finish a sentence. . . ."

F. Vocabulary

1. Note whether the following pairs of words taken from the selection are synonymous or not, depending upon their context. Explain the difference, when they are not.

a. *liveliness — responsiveness*

b. *great — celebrated*

c. *get together — do things together*

d. *In spite of — because of*

e. *bright — vivacious*

f. *a good gossip — a wit*

g. *informed — intelligent*

h. *opinionated — dogmatic*

i. *ego — assertiveness*

2. What contextual meaning have the following words?
   a. *"Interesting"* and *interesting* (paragraph 1)

   b. *ciphers* (paragraph 3)

   c. *flibbertigibbet charm* (paragraph 5)

   d. *impressive* and *interesting* (paragraph 6)

   e. *fascinating* and *interesting* (paragraph 4)

UNITY AND LIBERTY*

Denis W. Brogan

The word "school" in America covers every type of educational institution. Being "at school" may mean being at a kindergarten or at Harvard. School, too, has kept much of its Greek meaning. It is a system of organization and training for leisure as well as work. And it has become more and more adjusted to its environment, undertaking to do more than it can (which is very American) and doing much more than it seems to do (which is also very American).

The social and political role of American education cannot be understood if it is thought of as being primarily a means of formal instruction. If it is so thought of, it will be overrated and underrated. It will be overrated because the figures of two million college students, of seven million high-school students will dazzle the visitor used to seeing opportunities for higher education doled out (except in Soviet Russia) on a combined class-and-intellectual basis. It will be underrated if, at any stage below the highest (that is, below the great universities), the academic standards are compared with those of a good English, French, or pre-Hitler German school. If these millions of boys and girls are to be judged by their academic accomplishment, they will be judged harshly. But they are not to be so judged, for their schools are doing far more than instruct them: they are letting them instruct each other in how to live in America.

Of those millions, a large section will be the children of immigrants to whom English is still largely a foreign tongue. Of these millions, a very large proportion will be the children of migrants from different parts of the United States. Others will be the children of rural-bred parents, forced to adjust themselves to the new urban world. They have to learn a common language, common habits, common tolerances, a common political and national faith. And they do. It is this aim and this success that justify the lavish buildings of the local high school; not merely the classrooms and the laboratories, but the gymnasium, the field-house where basketball can be played in comfort in the depth of the bitter winter, the swimming pools in which the summer heat can be endured.

It is true that the teachers are relatively badly paid and have an inferior social as well as economic standing, insecure tenure and politics making their condition worse. More money spent on men might get better results than more money spent on buildings. But it is easier to get the materials for buildings than the materials for teachers. As long as American society remains individualistic, competitive, confident that the answers to the present are in the future, not in the past, it is going to take more than money to seduce the right men and women in adequate numbers away from the life of action. And, a point too seldom remembered, the necessity for

providing teachers for the two million college students hampers recruiting for high schools. In many cases, the colleges are doing what is really high-school work and it matters comparatively little where the good teachers are, as long as they are teaching.

The political function of the schools is to teach Americanism, meaning not merely political and patriotic dogma, but the habits necessary to American life. This justifies the most extravagant items in the curriculum. Since the ability to play bridge is one of the marks of Americanism in a suburb, it is reasonable that there should be bridge clubs in schools. The main political achievement of the high schools and grammar schools is to bring together the young of all classes and all origins, to provide, artificially, the common background that in an old, rural society is provided by tradition, by the necessary collaboration of village life. The elementary schools —the "grade" schools—do this, too, but as far as an American town is broken up into racial blocs, the Ethan Allen Public School may have mainly Polish pupils, the Zachary Chandler mainly Welsh. Only in the Warren G. Harding High School is a big enough common pool formed in which Americans can be made.

Some of that Americanization is, of course, done deliberately and formally. Mr. Carlton Hayes pointed out long ago that the ritual of flag-worship and oath-taking in an American school is a religious observance. Little boys and girls, in a school from which religion in the old sense is barred, solemnly rising each morning and reciting together the "American's Creed" are performing a religious exercise as truly as if they began the day with "I believe in God the Father Almighty" or asserted that "There is no God but God."

And that these daily rituals are religious has been at last affirmed by the Supreme Court in a series of cases in which the children of a fanatical sect, Jehovah's Witnesses, had been excluded from schools for refusing to give to the flag honors that, so their parents had taught them, were due to God alone. In 1940, all the Court except Chief Justice Stone held that flag-worship was among the things that were Caesar's. Since that year, however, by a majority they decided that the religious rights of the children were being infringed. What is significant in the cases is not the Court's reversal of itself but the reality of the issue presented to it. For to the Court, and to the overwhelming majority of the American people, the objections of the Witnesses were as unintelligible as the objections of the Christians to making a formal sacrifice to the Divine Emperor were to Trajan and Pliny. The school board of Minersville, Pennsylvania, was faced with a real problem when it was asked to admit that children refusing to take part in the most sacred rite of the day should be allowed to associate with the believing children of the formally unestablished national church of the United States. So, too, was the state of Oregon when it found Catholic and Lutheran children refusing to go to the schools it provided. But in both cases the Supreme Court held, finally, that compulsory Americanism was not Americanism at all, that coerced belief was not what the American people needed to stay united. This was not Germany or

Russia but the country of Jefferson and Justice Holmes.

The flag-worship of the American school and the American nation was brought home in war time to the British public in an episode that, if funny, was also very revealing. For the London makers of ladies' underwear who adorned their garments with American flags were innocent of any insulting or even frivolous intention. At the same time, a revue chorus in London was attired in Union Jack handkerchiefs and nothing else — to the public indifference. But the flag, in America, is more than a mere symbol among many others. It is the regimental color of a regiment in which all Americans are enrolled. Its thirteen stripes and forty-eight stars are symbols far better understood than the complicated heraldry of crosses of Saint George, Saint Andrew, and Saint Patrick imposed on each other in a way that only experts understand. It was Lincoln's task to see that the number of stars in the flag was not diminished by eleven during his term of office. It was the discovery that the flag still flew over Fort McHenry, despite the British fleet, that moved Francis Scott Key to write:

> "Oh, say, can you see by the dawn's early light,
> What so proudly we hailed at the twilight's
>   last gleaming;
> Whose broad stripes and bright stars, thro'
>   the perilous fight,
> O'er the ramparts we watched were so gal-
>   lantly streaming?"

What he wrote in 1814, tens of millions of Americans have since sung or tried to sing. And when Barbara Frietchie in Whittier's poem rebuked Stonewall Jackson with:

> "Shoot if you must this old gray head,
> But spare your country's flag," she said,

she was speaking for all Americans for whom the Stars and Stripes was still their country's flag as it had been, till recently, that of General Jackson.

Thus Americanism by ritual is an important and necessary part of the function of the American school. And because it is best carried out in schools, it matters little that the high school curriculum has been so widened that it no longer means a great deal that this boy or that girl has graduated from it — if we are looking for proof of academic achievement. But graduation from high school is reasonable proof that a great deal has been learned about American ways of life, that lessons in practical politics, in organization, in social ease have been learned that could not have been learned in factory or office.

And if the high school seems to devote too much time and money to social life, penalizing the poor boy or girl more than a theoretically less democratic educational system might do, it is thus early impressing an awkward truth on the boy or girl who is both mediocre and poor. It also penalizes the really able boy or girl who is not kept in good enough intellectual training. And if the main business of the school, is, in fact, the Americanization of the children of newcomers, the parents of "old American stock" have a good reason (to add to less good ones) for not sending their children to learn what they know already, at the cost of diminishing their chance of learning what they do not know. If English is native to your children and to their home, it is not merely undemocratic to object to having their progress held up and their accent debased by the tone of a high school largely immigrant in composition.

The task of an American school in many regions is to teach the American language, to enable it to compete with Spanish, with French, with Yiddish, with Polish, with German, with Swedish. Another task is to give, through the language and the literature of the language, a common vocabulary and a common fund of allusion, fable, and sentiment. With a fluid population this has not been easy. And the countless teachers who have labored pedantically, formally, with complete and erroneous conviction that there were correct standards, have been heroes as important in the mass as was William McGuffey, whose *Eclectic Readers* sold over one hundred and twenty million copies and helped to make the Union. The teachers were heroes because, although English won against all its rivals, it was itself going through important changes, in vocabulary, in grammar, in sound, becoming the new tongue we are beginning to call American. The teachers who stuck by the rules, who worshipped at the New England shrines in Concord, were bound to lose, but their struggle was not pure waste. For the common tongue, hammered out by millions of immigrants, would have been poor in vocabulary and structure but for the people Mr. Mencken calls the dominies and who call themselves schoolmen. The creation of general literacy and a common written and spoken tongue, intelligible everywhere except possibly in the deep South, is an achievement as remarkable as the creation of Mandarin Chinese or Low Latin, or Hellenistic Greek, and this tongue is certain to be the new *lingua franca* of the world.

The making of American has been mixed-up in English minds with the making of American slang. Slang, as we should know, is one of the great sources of language. French is improved Latin slang. And slang has contributed a good deal to American. It is a generation since Mr. Dooley said that when his countrymen had finished with the English language it would look as if it had been run over by a musical comedy. Since then it has been run over by *Hellzapoppin*. But it is possible, indeed very easy, to overestimate the role of slang. It is more and more the creation of professional artists, "makers." The Hollywood prose masters provide a current and often short-lived jargon; the boys and girls, men and women, who wish to be on the beam or in the groove, may murmur with admiration, "I wish I had said that," And Whistler's classical answer to Wilde is certainly appropriate: "You will, Oscar — you will!" But not for long. Some slang will enter the language; some words will lose their meaning or acquire new ones; syntax will be loosened up. But formal speech as taught in schools will still be very important. The high-school English teacher, for all her pedantry, is as much a maker of the American language as Messrs. Runyon and O'Hara. Two streams of language may run roughly parallel, but in time they will merge; they will provide American with many interesting variations, do for American what its dual Germanic and Latin character does for English. That time has not yet come, but it is on the way. And the future character of this truly national tongue is foreshadowed in the drawing by Mr. Peter Arno in which an indignant citizen tells another: "I consider your conduct unethical and lousy."

Most American parents do not want, or are not able, to send their children to anything but public high schools, and the life in such a school is a training in life for America. It may be and often is a training in life *against* Europe. For Europe is the background from which many of the children are reacting and from which they must be delivered if they are to be Americanized. For nearly all immigrants, America is promotion, and this promotion is more clearly felt by their children. The old people may hanker after the old country, but the children—whatever sentimental feelings for their ancestral homes they may have, especially when provoked—are, above all else, anxious to be Americans.

Necessarily something is lost here. The least-common-denominator, Americanism of the schools, is not a complete substitute for a native culture. What the first-generation American children learn to despise may include elements in their moral diet that are not replaced. A new American whose pride in that promotion involves mere contempt for the habits, what Americans call the "folkways" or "mores," of his parents is not necessarily a good American. So attempts are made to instill pride in the ancestral cultures of the European lands from which the immigrants come. The University of Pittsburgh, located in one of the main melting pots of America, has a set of rooms illustrating the culture of various European countries. In the case of the Greeks, the room may instill adequate pride; in the case of the Scots (if any such need is felt) a shrine of Robert Burns may serve. But, for many of the peasant immigrants, the old country is backward though beloved, while for their children it is merely backward.

Americanization comes not from preservation of Slovak or Italian peasant culture, but from speedy assimilation to "American" culture. And that assimilation may take the form of distinction in anything that the American world obviously values. In the narrow sense of culture, there may even be a temptation to go for those courses that have no immigrant stigma on them. Thus I have been told by an eminent Scandinavian-American that it is difficult to get good students of Scandinavian literature and language at the University of Minnesota, although most of the students have fairly recent Scandinavian connections. They will study French but not Swedish, for "French is not a servant's language." Latin, emblem of functionless "culture," plays something of the same role; it is a symbol of liberation.

Study is not the only way up to Americanization, to acceptance. Sport is another—and one that does the job more dramatically for the newcomers gifted with what it takes to excel in competitive contests, with what is needed to win personal and community and institutional glory.

When Fanny Ellsler, the ballet dancer, came to Boston, her performance was solemnly inspected from the highest motives by Emerson and Margaret Fuller. "The dance began; both sat serenely silent; at last Emerson spoke. 'Margaret,' he said, 'this is poetry.' 'No, Waldo,' replied Margaret; 'it is not poetry, it is religion.'" And the great football games of today are religious ceremonies in this sense. It is significant that the graduating classes in Muncie High School a generation ago took such mottoes as "Deo duce" and today take mottoes stressing the "Bearcat Spirit," the "Bearcats" being the school basketball team. But a Greek would know where he was at a basketball game uniting boys and girls, parents and civic leaders, in a common passion for competitive achievement. It may be hard on the academic work of the school. It may even slightly annoy a schoolboy, who like Mr. Burton Rascoe combines excellence in gymnastics and music (as the Greeks put it), to find that his views on literature are less interesting to the other sex than his prowess at football. But sport, school sport, college sport, does unite the parents, the children, and the community. And sport is rigorously democratic. The sons of Czechs and Poles can score there, can break through the barriers that stand in the way of the children of "Bohunks" and "Polacks." And although Harvard may secretly rejoice when it can put a winning team on to Soldier's Field whose names suggest the *Mayflower*, it would rather put on a team that can beat Yale, even though it is not a "Yankee" team, than go down to defeat with the descendants of generations of Brahmins. And in the Middle West, sport is a real means of promotion. The Ohio high school that produced the great Negro runner, Jesse Owens, was prouder of him than if he had made Phi Beta Kappa at Ohio State; and Hitler would have made a less serious mistake if he had snubbed a great American scholar whose race he didn't like than he did by sulking at the Olympic Games when the Herrenvolk were beaten by a Negro. It is a frontier tradition; Lincoln's great strength gave him a prestige that helped him as a lawyer and politician. The great athlete performing for the glory of the school, college, state, or nation, is a less egoistic figure than the great scholar pursuing his own studies with an undemocratic concentration. And the Negroes, whose greatest hero is Joe Louis, not Paul Robeson, are not substantially wrong so far. In American society as it is, a Negro heavy-weight champion, like a Negro tap-dancer, is a better adjusted figure than a great Negro artist—or America is a less maladjusted society for them. Of course, this will not and should not last. The Irish were rising when their great hero became Governor Al Smith, rather than a successor of John L. Sullivan, the "Boston strong boy." But to get assent to a Negro's *right* to be heavy-weight champion is something—as those will agree who remember the frenzied search round 1910 for a "white hope" to save the heavy-weight championship from the indignity of being held by Jack Johnson. Great Indian athletes like Jim Thorpe, great Negro football heroes like Paul Robeson in his earlier days, the polyglot teams put on the field by the great Swedish coach Knute Rockne for the "Irish" of Notre Dame—these become "All American" figures in a wider and deeper sense than that in which the Yale of Walter Camp understood the term.

The cheer leaders, the new "jongleurs de Notre

Dame," the "majorettes," shapely women more or less involved with musical instruments, the massed cheering sections of the students, the massed yelling sections of the alumni — these are the equivalent of the crowds at the great Hellenic festivals in which barbarians were not allowed to compete. The Rose Bowl, the Cotton Bowl, the other intersectional games — these are instruments of national unity, and the provision of such instruments is no mean duty of colleges and universities. It is a religious exercise of a kind a Greek would have understood, however remote it may be from the university as understood by Abelard or Saint Thomas Aquinas or John Harvard.

The university, as these men understood it, exists all the same and exists to play a great national part, for the level of academic learning in America is perhaps the only branch of American life where the promise of rapid progress upward has been consistently kept. It is not as easy to define the nature of that progress as it is to affirm its existence.

Questions on UNITY AND LIBERTY

A. General questions on structure and content

1. The title of this selection is quite broad. What possible subject areas could such a title encompass?

2. The first sentence tells you how the general subject, the American character, is to be limited. What is the specific subject? Could the selection be an excerpt from a book? Why?

3. Can American schools be fairly judged by applying the standards of European schools? By what criteria should American schools be judged?

4. Why do American schools emphasize the "materials for buildings" rather than the "materials for teaching"?

5. What is the purpose of American language teaching in the schools?

6. How does the worship of the flag symbol affect the attitude of the majority of Americans toward Jehovah's Witnesses' children who refuse to salute the flag?

7. Why is sport "rigorously democratic"?

B. Questions for critical analysis

1. Is Mr. Brogan antagonistic toward American schools, or impartial?

2. What is unique about American education?

3. What facets of the American character does the selection explain?

4. What disadvantages might the third-generation children of immigrant families suffer as the consequence of being Americanized?

C. Discussion and/or composition topics

1. Does education along democratic lines necessarily result in inferior education and a reduction of academic standards, or can that be avoided?

2. How meaningful is an American high school diploma? College diploma? Compare with European concepts of education.

3. Are we better citizens as a result of being Americanized in our public schools? What are the possible dangers of "Americanizing" young students?

4. Is there any regional emphasis or glorification taught in public schools? Does this contradict Mr. Brogan's thesis?

D. Vocabulary

1. Define each italicized term according to its context in the phrase.

a. "the necessary *collaboration* of village life"

b. "a *fanatical* sect"

c. "that *coerced* belief"

d. "the complicated *heraldry* of crosses of Saint George, Saint Andrew, and Saint Patrick"

e. "*penalizing* the poor boy or girl"

f. "With a *fluid* population"

g. "a complete and *erroneous* conviction"

h. "a current and often short-lived *jargon*"

i. "the . . . English teacher, for all her *pedantry*"

j. "Lincoln's great strength gave him a *prestige*"

2. Explain the italicized term according to its context in the phrase.

a. "In 1940, all the *Court* except Chief Justice Stone held that flag-worship was among the *things that were Caesar's.*"

b. "For to the Court . . . the objections of the [Jehovah's] Witnesses were as unintelligible as the objections of the *Christians* to making a formal sacrifice to the *Divine Emperor* were to Trajan and Pliny."

c. "This was not Germany or Russia but the country of *Jefferson* and *Justice Holmes.*"

d. "The . . . English teacher . . . is as much a maker of the American language as *Messrs. Runyon and O'Hara.*"

e. "And although Harvard may secretly rejoice when it can put a winning team on to *Soldier's Field* whose names suggest the *Mayflower,* it would rather put on a team that can beat Yale . . . than go down to defeat with the descendants of generations of *Brahmins.*"

from GENESIS*

In the beginning God created the heavens and the earth. 2. The earth was without form and void, and darkness was upon the face of the deep; and the Spirit of God was moving over the face of the waters.

3. And God said, "Let there be light"; and there was light. 4. And God saw that the light was good; and God separated the light from the darkness. 5. God called the light Day, and the darkness he called Night. And there was evening and there was morning, one day.

6. And God said; "Let there be a firmament in the midst of the waters, and let it separate the waters from the waters." 7. And God made the firmament and separated the waters which were under the firmament from the waters which were above the firmament. And it was so. 8. And God called the firmament Heaven. And there was evening and there was morning, a second day.

9. And God said, "Let the waters under the heavens be gathered together into one place, and let the dry land appear." And it was so. 10. God called the dry land Earth, and the waters that were gathered together he called Seas. And God saw that it was good. 11. And God said, "Let the earth put forth vegetation, plants yielding seed, and fruit trees bearing fruit in which is their seed, each according to its kind, upon the earth." And it was so. 12. The earth brought forth vegetation, plants yielding seed according to their own kinds, and trees bearing fruit in which is their seed, each according to its kind. And God saw that it was good. 13. And there was evening and there was morning, a third day.

14. And God said, "Let there be lights in the firmament of the heavens to separate the day from the night; and let them be for signs and for seasons and for days and years, 15. and let them be lights in the firmament of the heavens to give light upon the earth." And it was so. 16. And God made the two great lights, the greater light to rule the day, and the lesser light to rule the night; he made the stars also. 17. And God set them in the firma-ment of the heavens to give light upon the earth, 18. to rule over the day and over the night, and to separate the light from the darkness. And God saw that it was good. 19. And there was evening and there was morning, a fourth day.

20. And God said, "Let the waters bring forth swarms of living creatures, and let birds fly above the earth across the firmament of the heavens." 21. So God created the great sea monsters and every living creature that moves, with which the waters swarm, according to their kinds, and every winged bird according to its kind. And God saw that it was good. 22. And God blessed them, saying, "Be fruitful and multiply and fill the waters in the seas, and let birds multiply on the earth." 23. And there was evening and there was morning, a fifth day.

24. And God said, "Let the earth bring forth living creatures according to their kinds: cattle and creeping things and beasts of the earth according to their kinds." And it was so. 25. And God made the beasts of the earth according to their kinds and the cattle according to their kinds, and everything that creeps upon the ground according to its kind. And God saw that it was good.

26. Then God said, "Let us make man in our image, after our likeness; and let them have dominion over the fish of the sea, and over the birds of the air, and over the cattle, and over all the earth, and over every creeping thing that creeps upon the earth." 27. So God created man in his own image, in the image of God he created him; male and female he created them. 28. And God blessed them, and God said to them, "Be fruitful and multiply, and fill the earth and subdue it; and have dominion over the fish of the sea and over the birds of the air and over every living thing that moves upon the earth." 29. And God said, "Behold, I have given you every plant yielding seed which is upon the face of all the earth, and every tree with seed in its fruit; you shall have them for food. 30. And to every beast of the earth, and to every bird of the air, and to everything that creeps on the earth, everything that has the breath of life, I have given every green plant for food." And it was so. 31. And God saw everything that he had made, and behold, it was very good. And there was evening and there was morning, a sixth day.

Thus the heavens and the earth were finished, and all the host of them.

---

* From the *Revised Standard Version of the Bible*, Copyrighted 1946 and 1952.

Questions on GENESIS

A. General questions on structure

   1. Would you classify this selection as objective or subjective? Give reasons for your answer.

   2. Since the title of the selection should be familiar to you, you can anticipate the subject matter.

     a. Look up the word "genesis" in a dictionary.

     b. Note the relationship of the title to the first three words in the selection.

   3. What effect does the constant use of the word *and* have? Is it annoying or soothing? How does the effect of *and* differ from that of *but, therefore, thus,* etc., where a causal or logical relationship exists?

   4. Is the selection argumentative, narrative, or descriptive? On what elements do you base your answer?

B. Question on content

   How is the creation of things effected?

     a. Does God "make" or "build" the earth and all its parts?
     b. Or does He call the appearance of things into being?
     c. Is there a *logos* or logic to the order in which the various aspects of the world are created?

C. Discussion topic

   Compare Genesis with the Gospel of John. How do these "beginnings" differ?

D. Vocabulary (varies according to version of Holy Bible used)

1. *genesis*

2. *firmament*

3. *vegetation*

4. *swarm*

5. *dominion*

SOCIALISM AND CHILDREN*

George Bernard Shaw

In the case of young children we have gone far in our interference with the old Roman rights of parents. For nine mortal years the child is taken out of its parents' hands for most of the day, and thus made a State school child instead of a private family child. The records of the Society for the Prevention of Cruelty to Children are still sickening enough to show how necessary it is to protect children against their parents; but the bad cases are scarce, and show that it is now difficult for the worst sort of parent to evade for long the school attendance officer, the teacher, and the police. Unfortunately the proceedings lead to nothing but punishment of the parents: when they come out of prison the children are still in their hands. When we have beaten the cat for cruelty we give it back its mouse. We have now, however, taken a step in the right direction by passing an Act of Parliament by which adoptive parents have all the rights of real parents. You can now adopt a child with complete security against the parents coming to claim the child back again whenever it suits them. All their rights pass to you by the adoption. Bad natural parents can be completely superseded by adoptive ones: it remains only to make the operation compulsory where it is imperative. Compulsory adoption is already an old established institution in the case of our Poor Law Guardians. Oliver Twist was a compulsory adopted child. His natural parents were replaced by very unnatural ones. Mr. Bumble is being happily abolished; but there must still be somebody to adopt Oliver. When equality of income makes an end of his social disadvantages there will be no lack of childless volunteers.

Our eyes are being opened more and more to the fact that in our school system education is only the pretext under which parents get rid of the trouble of their children by bundling them off into a prison or child farm which is politely called a school. We also know, or ought to know, that institutional treatment of children is murderous for infants and bad for all children. Homeless infants can be saved from that by adoption; but the elder children are forcing us to face the problem of organizing child life as such, giving children constitutional rights just as we have had to give them to women, and ceasing to shirk that duty either by bundling the children off to Bastilles called schools or by making the child the property of its father (in the case of an illegitimate child, of its mother) as we have ceased to shirk women's rights by making the woman the property of her husband. The beginnings of such organization are already visible in the Girl Guides and the Boy Scouts. But the limits to liberty which the State has to set and the obligations which it has to impose on adults are as imperative for children as for adults. The Girl Guide cannot be always guiding nor the Boy Scout always scouting. They must qualify themselves for adult citizenship by certain acquirements whether they

like it or not. This is our excuse for school: they must be educated.

Education is a word that in our mouths covers a good many things. At present we are only extricating ourselves slowly and, as usual, reluctantly and ill humoredly, from our grossest stupidities about it. One of them is that it means learning lessons, and that learning lessons is for children, and ceases when they come of age. I, being a septuagenarian, can assure you confidently that we never cease learning to the extent of our capacity for learning until our faculties fail us. As to what we have been taught in school and college, I should say roughly that as it takes us all our lives to find out the meaning of the small part of it that is true and the error of the large part that is false, it is not surprising that those who have been "educated" least know most. It is gravely injurious to both children and adults to be forced to study any subjects for which they have no natural aptitude unless some ulterior object which they have at heart gives them a factitious keenness to master it. Mental disablement caused in this way is common in the modern examination-passing classes. Dickens's Mr. Toots is not a mere figure of fun: he is an authentic instance of a sort of imbecility that is dangerously prevalent in our public school and university products. Toots is no joke.

Even when a natural aptitude exists it may be overcome by the repulsion created by coercive teaching. If a girl is unmusical, any attempt to force her to learn to play Beethoven's sonatas is torture to herself and to her teachers, to say nothing of the agonies of her audiences when her parents order her to display her accomplishment to visitors. But unmusical girls are as exceptional as deaf girls. The common case of a rooted loathing for music, and a vindictive hope that Beethoven may be expiating a malevolent life in eternal torment, is that of the normally musical girl who, before she had ever heard a sonata or any other piece of music played well enough to seem beautiful to her, has been set to practise scales in a cold room, rapped over the knuckles when she struck a wrong note, and had the Pathetic Sonata rapped and scolded and bullied into her bar by bar until she could finger it out without a mistake. That is still what school-taught music means to many unfortunate young ladies whose parents desire them to have accomplishments, and accordingly pay somebody who has been handled in the same way to knock this particular accomplishment into them. If these unhappy victims thought that Socialism meant compulsory music they would die in the last ditch fighting against it; and they would be right.

If I were writing a book for men I should not speak of music: I should speak of verses written in literary Latin (meaning a sort of Latin that nobody ever spoke), of Greek, and of algebra. Many an unhappy lad who would have voluntarily picked up enough Latin and Greek to read Virgil, Horace, and Homer, or to whom Descartes, Newton, and Einstein would be heroes such as Handel, Mozart, Beethoven, and Wagner are to unspoilt musicians, loathes every printed page except in a newspaper detective story, and shrinks from an algebraic symbol or a diagram of the parallelogram of forces as a criminal from a prison. This is the result of our educational mania.

* From *The Intelligent Woman's Guide to Socialism and Capitalism*, 1928. Reprinted by permission of the Public Trustee and The Society of Authors.

When Eton was founded, the idea was that the boys should be roused at six in the morning and kept hard at their Latin without a moment's play until they went to bed. And now that the tendency is to keep them hard at play instead, without a moment for free work, their condition is hardly more promising. Either way an intelligent woman, remembering her own childhood, must stand aghast at the utter disregard of the children's ordinary human rights, and the classing of them partly as animals to be tamed and broken in, for which, provided the methods are not those of the trainer of performing animals, there is something to be said, and partly as inanimate sacks into which learning is to be poured *ad libitum,* for which there is nothing to be said except what can be said for the water torture of the Inquisition, in which the fluid was poured down the victims' throats until they were bloated to death. But there was some method in this madness. I have already hinted to you what you must have known very well, that children, unless they are forced into a quiet, sedentary, silent, motionless, and totally unnatural association with adults, are so troublesome at home that humane parents who would submit to live in a bear-garden, or a monkey-house rather than be cruelly repressive, are only too glad to hand them over to anyone who will profess to educate them, whilst the desperate struggle of the genteel dis-endowed younger son and unmarried daughter class to find some means of livelihood produces a number of persons who are willing to make a profession of child farming under the same highly plausible pretext.

Socialism would abolish this class by providing its members with less hateful and equally respectable employment. Nobody who had not a genuine vocation for teaching would adopt teaching as a profession. Sadists, female and male, who now get children into their power so as to be able to torture them with impunity, and child fanciers (who are sometimes the same people) of the kind that now start amateur orphanages because they have the same craze for children that some people have for horses and dogs, although they often treat them abominably, would be checkmated if the children had any refuge from them except the homes from which they had been practically turned out, and from which they would be promptly returned to their tyrants with the assurance that if they were punished it served them right for being naughty. Within a few days of writing this I have read as part of the day's news of a case in which a mother summoned a schoolmaster because he had first caned her boy for hiccuping, which is not a voluntary action, and then, because the boy made light of the punishment, fell on him in a fury and thrashed him until he raised wheals on him that were visible eight days afterwards. Magistrates are usually as lenient in dealing with these assaults as with similar assaults by husbands on their wives (assaults by wives are laughed out of court): indeed they usually dismiss the case with a rebuke to the victim for being an unmanly little coward and not taking his licking in good part; but this time they admitted that the punishment, as they called it, was too severe; and the schoolmaster had to pay the mother's costs, though nobody hinted at any unfitness on his part for the duties he

had assumed. And, in fairness, it did not follow that the man was a savage or a Sadist, any more than it follows that married people who commit furious assaults on one another have murderous natural dispositions. The truth is that just as married life in a one-room tenement is more than human nature can bear even when there are no children to complicate it, life in the sort of prison we call a school, where the teacher who hates her work is shut in with a crowd of unwilling, hostile, restless children, sets up a strain and hatred that explodes from time to time in onslaughts with the cane, not only for hiccuping, but for talking, whispering, looking out of the window (inattention), and even moving. Modern psychological research, even in its rather grotesque Freudian beginnings, is forcing us to recognize how serious is the permanent harm that comes of this atmosphere of irritation on the one side and suppression, terror, and reactionary naughtiness on the other. Even those who do not study psychology are beginning to notice that chaining dogs makes them dangerous, and is a cruel practice. They will presently have misgivings about chained children too, and begin to wonder whether thrashing and muzzling them is the proper remedy.

As a general result we find that what we call education is a failure. The poor woman's child is imprisoned for nine years under pretext of teaching it to read, write, and speak its own language: a year's work at the outside. And at the end of the nine years the prisoner can do none of these things presentably. In 1896, after twenty-six years of compulsory general education, the secretary of the Union of Mathematical Instrument Makers told me that most of his members signed with a mark. Rich male children are kept in three successive prisons, the preparatory school, the public school (meaning a very exclusive private school malversating public endowments), and the university, the period of imprisonment being from twelve to fourteen years, and the subjects taught including classical languages and higher mathematics. Rich female children, formerly imprisoned in the family dungeon under a wardress called a governess, are now sent out like their brothers. The result is a slightly greater facility in reading and writing, the habits and speech of the rich idle classes, and a moral and intellectual imbecility which leaves them politically at the mercy of every bumptious adventurer and fluent charlatan who has picked up their ways and escaped their education, and morally on the level of medieval robber barons and early capitalist buccaneers. When they are energetic and courageous, in spite of their taming, they are public dangers: when they are mere sheep, doing whatever their class expects them to do, they will follow any enterprising bell-wether to the destruction of themselves and the whole community. Fortunately humanity is so recuperative that no system of suppression and perversion can quite abort it; but as far as our standard lady's and gentleman's education goes the very least that can be said against it is that most of its victims would be better without it.

It is, however, incidentally advantageous. The university student who is determined not to study, gains from the communal life of the place a social standing that is painfully lacking in the people who have been brought up in a brick box in ill mannered intercourse with too many older people and three or four younger ones, all keeping what they call their company manners (meaning an affectation which has no desirable quality except bare civility) for the few similarly reared outsiders who are neither too poor to be invited in nor too rich to condescend to enter the box. Nobody can deny that these middle class families which cannot afford the university for their sons, and must send them out as workers at fifteen or so, appear utterly unpresentable vulgarians compared to our university products. The woman from the brick box maintains her social position by being offensive to the immense number of people whom she considers her inferiors, reserving her civility for the very few who are clinging to her own little ledge on the social precipice; for inequality of income takes the broad, safe, and fertile plain of human society and stands it on edge so that everyone has to cling desperately to her foothold and kick off as many others as she can. She would cringe to her superiors if they could be persuaded to give her the chance, whereas at a university she would have to meet hundreds of other young women on equal terms, and to be at least commonly civil to everybody. It is true that university manners are not the best manners, and that there is plenty of foundation for the statement that Oxford and Cambridge are hotbeds of exclusiveness, university snobs being perhaps the most incorrigible of all snobs. For all that, university snobbery is not so disabling as brick box snobbery. The university woman can get on without friction or awkwardness with all sorts of people, high or low, with whom the brick box woman simply does not know how to associate. But the university curriculum has nothing to do with this. On the contrary, it is the devoted scholar who misses it, and the university butterfly, barely squeezing through her examinations, who acquires it to perfection. Also, it can now be acquired and greatly improved on by young people who break loose from the brick box into the wider social life of clubs and unofficial cultural associations of all kinds. The manners of the garden city and the summer school are already as far superior to the manners of the university college as these are to the manners of the brick box. There is no word that has more sinister and terrible connotations in our snobbish society than the word promiscuity; but if you exclude its special and absurd use to indicate an imaginary condition of sexual disorder in which every petticoat and every coat and trousers fall into one another's embraces at sight, you will see that social promiscuity is the secret of good manners, and that it is precisely because the university is more promiscuous than the brick box, and the Theosophical or Socialist summer school more promiscuous than the college, that it is also the better mannered.

Socialism involves complete social promiscuity. It has already gone very far. When the great Duke of Wellington fell ill, he said, "Send for the apothecary," just as he would have said, "Send for the barber"; and the apothecary no doubt "your Graced" him in a very abject manner: indeed I can myself remember famous old physicians, even titled ones, who took your fee exactly as a butler used to take your tip. In the seventeenth century a nobleman would sometimes admit an actor to an intimate friendship; but when he wrote to him he began his letter, not "My dear So and So," but "To Betterton the player." Nowadays a duke who went on like that would be ridiculed as a Pooh Bah. Everybody can now travel third class in England without being physically disgusted by their fellow-travelers. I remember when second class carriages, now extinct, were middle class necessities.

The same process that has levelled the social intercourse between dukes and doctors or actors can level it between duchesses and dairymaids, or, what seems far less credible, between doctors' wives and dairymaids. But whilst Socialism makes for this sort of promiscuity it will also make for privacy and exclusiveness. At present the difference between a dairymaid and any decent sort of duchess is marked, not by a wounding difference between the duchess's address to the dairymaid and her address to another duchess, but by a very marked difference between the address of a dairymaid to the duchess and her address to another dairymaid. The decent duchess's civility is promiscuous; but her intimate friendship and society is not. Civility is one thing, familiarity quite another. The duchess's grievance at present is that she is obliged by her social and political position to admit to her house and table a great many people whose tastes and intellectual interests are so different from her own that they bore her dreadfully, whilst her income cuts her off from familiar intercourse with many poor people whose society would be delightful to her, but who could not afford her expensive habits. Equality would bring to the duchess the blessing of being able to choose her familiars as far as they were willing to respond. She would no longer have to be bored by men who could talk about nothing but fox hunting or party politics when she wanted to talk about science or literature, dressmaking or gardening, or, if her tastes were more curious, the morbidities of psycho-analysis. Socialism, by steamrollering our class distinctions (really income distinctions) would break us up into sets, cliques, and solitaries. The duchess would play golf (if people could still find no more interesting employment for their leisure) with any charwoman, and lunch with her after; but the intimate circle of the duchess and the charwoman would be more exclusive and highly selected than it can possibly be now. Socialism thus offers the utmost attainable society and the utmost attainable privacy. We should be at the same time much less ceremonious in our public relations and much more delicate about intruding on one another in our private ones.

You may say, what has all this to do with education? Have we not wandered pretty far from it? By no means: a great part of our education comes from our social intercourse. We educate one another; and we cannot do this if half of us consider the other half not good enough to talk to. But enough of that side of the subject. Let us leave the social qualifications which children, like adults, pick up from their surroundings and from the company they keep, and return to the acquirements which the State must impose on them compulsorily, providing the teachers and schools and apparatus; testing the success of the teaching; and giving qualifying certificates to those who have passed the tests.

It is now evident in all civilized States that there are certain things which people must know in order to play their part as citizens. There are technical things that must be learned, and intellectual conceptions that must be understood. For instance, you are not fit for life in a modern city unless you know the multiplication table, and agree that you must not take the law into your own hands. That much technical and liberal education is indispensable, because a woman who could not pay fares and count change, and who flew at people with whom she disagreed and tried to kill them or scratch their eyes out, would be as incapable of civilized life as a wild cat. In our huge cities reading is necessary, as people have to proceed by written directions. In a village or a small country town you can get along by accosting the police officer, or the railway porter or station-master, or the post-mistress, and asking them what to do and where to go; but in London five minutes of that would bring business and locomotion to a standstill; the police and railway officials, hard put to it as it is answering the questions of foreigners and visitors from the country, would be driven mad if they had to tell everybody everything. The newspapers, the postal and other official guides, the innumerable notice boards and direction posts, do for the London citizen what the police constable or the nearest shop-keeper rather enjoys doing for the villager, as a word with a stranger seems an almost exciting event in a place where hardly anything else happens except the motion of the earth.

In the days when even the biggest cities were no bigger than our country towns, and all civilized life was conducted on what we should call village lines, "clergy," or the ability to read and write, was not a necessity; it was a means of extending the mental culture of the individual for the individual's own sake, and was quite exceptional. This notion still sticks in our minds. When we force a girl to learn to read, and make that an excuse for imprisoning her in a school, we pretend that the object of it is to cultivate her as an individual, and open to her the treasures of literature. That is why we do it so badly and take so long over it. But our right to cultivate a girl in any particular way against her will is not clear, even if we could claim that sitting indoors on a hard seat and being forbidden to talk or fidget or attend to anything but the teacher cultivated a girl more highly than the free activities from which this process cuts her off. The only valid reason for forcing her at all costs to acquire the technique or reading, writing, and arithmetic enough for ordinary buying and selling is that modern civilized life is impossible without them. She may be said to have a natural right to be taught them just as she has a natural right to be nursed and weaned and taught to walk.

So far the matter is beyond argument. It is true that in teaching her how to write you are also teaching her how to forge cheques and write spiteful anonymous letters, and that in teaching her to read you are opening her mind to foul and silly books, and putting into her hands those greatest wasters of time in the world, the novels that are not worth reading (say ninety-nine out of every hundred).

All such objections go down before the inexorable necessity for the accomplishments that make modern life possible: you might as well object to teaching her how to use a knife to cut her food on the ground that you are also teaching her how to cut the baby's throat. Every technical qualification for doing good is a technical qualification for doing evil as well; but it is not possible to leave our citizens without any technical qualifications for the art of modern living on that account.

But this does not justify us in giving our children technical education and damning the consequences. The consequences would damn us. If we teach a girl to shoot without teaching her also that thou shalt not kill, she may send a bullet through us the first time she loses her temper; and if we proceed to hang her, she may say, as so many women now say when they are in trouble, "Why did nobody tell me?" This is why compulsory education cannot be confined to technical education. There are parts of liberal education which are as necessary in modern social life as reading and writing; and it is this that makes it so difficult to draw the line beyond which the State has no right to meddle with the child's mind or body without its free consent. Later on we may make conditions: for instance, we may say that a surveyor must learn trigonometry, a sea captain navigation, and a surgeon at least as much dexterity in the handling of saws and knives on bones and tissues as a butcher acquires. But that is not the same thing as forcing everybody to be a qualified surveyor, navigator, or surgeon. What we are now considering is how much the State must force everyone to learn as the minimum qualification for life in a civilized city. If the Government forces a woman to acquire the art of composing Latin verses, it is forcing on her an accomplishment which she can never need to exercise, and which she can acquire for herself in a few months if she should nevertheless be cranky enough to want to exercise it. There is the same objection to forcing her to learn the calculus. Yet somewhere between forcing her to learn to read and put two and two together accurately, and forcing her to write sham Horace or learn the calculus, the line must be drawn. The question is, where to draw it.

On the liberal side of education it is clear that a certain minimum of law, constitutional history, and economics is indispensable as a qualification for a voter even if ethics are left entirely to the inner light. In the case of young children, dogmatic commandments against murder, theft, and the more obvious possibilities of untutored social intercourse, are imperative; and it is here that we must expect fierce controversy. I need not repeat all that we have already been through as to the impossibility of ignoring this part of education and calling our neglect Secular Education. If on the ground that the subject is a controversial one you leave a child to find out for itself whether the earth is round or flat, it will find out that it is flat, and, after blundering into many mistakes and superstitions, be so angry with you for not teaching it that it is round, that when it becomes an adult voter it will insist on its own children having uncompromising positive guidance on the point.

What will not work in physics will not work in metaphysics either. No Government, Socialist or anti-Socialist or neutral, could possibly govern and administer a highly artificial modern State unless every citizen had a highly artificial modern conscience: that is, a creed or body of beliefs which would never occur to a primitive woman, and a body of disbeliefs, or negative creed, which would strike a primitive woman as fantastic blasphemies that must bring down on her tribe the wrath of the unseen powers. Modern governments must therefore inculcate these beliefs and disbeliefs, or at least see that they are inculcated somehow; or they cannot carry on. And the reason we are in such a mess at present is that our governments are trying to carry on with a set of beliefs and disbeliefs that belong to bygone phases of science and extinct civilizations. Imagine going to Moses or Mahomet for a code to regulate the modern money market!

If we all had the same beliefs and disbeliefs, we could go smoothly on, whether to our destruction or the millennium. But the conflicts between contradictory beliefs, and the progressive repudiations of beliefs which must continue as long as we have different patterns of mankind in different phases of evolution, will necessarily produce conflicts of opinion as to what should be taught in the public schools under the head of religious dogma and liberal education. At the present moment there are many people who hold that it is absolutely necessary to a child's salvation from an eternity of grotesque and frightful torment in a lake of burning brimstone that it should be baptized with water, as it is born under a divine curse and is a child of wrath and sin, and that as it grows into a condition of responsibility it must be impressed with this belief, with the addition that all its sins were atoned for by the sacrifice of Christ, the Son of God, on the cross, this atonement being effectual only for those who believe in it. Failing such belief the efficacy of the baptism is annulled, and the doom of eternal damnation reincurred. This is the official and State-endowed religion in our country today; and there is still on the statute book a law decreeing heavy punishments for anyone who denies its validity, which no Cabinet dares repeal.

Now it is not probable that a fully developed Socialist State will either impress these beliefs on children or permit any private person to do so until the child has reached what is called in another connection the age of consent. The State has to protect the souls of the children as well as their bodies; and modern psychology confirms common experience in teaching that to horrify a young child with stories of brimstone hells, and make it believe that it is a little devil who can only escape from that hell by maintaining a sinless virtue to which no saint or heroine has ever pretended, is to injure it for life more cruelly than by any act of bodily violence that even the most brutal taskmaster would dare to prescribe or justify. To put it quite frankly and flatly, the Socialist State, as far as I can guess, will teach the child the multiplication table, but will not only not teach it the Church Catechism, but if the State teachers find that the child's parents have been teaching it the Catechism otherwise than as a curious historical document, the parents will be warned that if they persist the child will be taken out of their hands and handed over to the Lord Chancellor, exactly as the children of Shelley were when their maternal grandfather denounced his son-in-law as an atheist.

Further, a Socialist State will not allow its children to be taught that polygamy, slaughter of prisoners of war, and blood sacrifices, including human sacrifices, are divinely appointed institutions; and this means that it will not allow the Bible to be introduced in schools otherwise than as a collection of old chronicles, poems, oracles, and political fulminations, on the same footing as the travels of Marco Polo, Goethe's *Faust,* Carlyle's *Past and Present* and *Sartor Resartus,* and Ruskin's *Ethics of the Dust.* Also the doctrine that our life in this world is only a brief preliminary episode in preparation for an all-important life to come, and that it does not matter how poor or miserable or plague ridden we are in this world, as we shall be gloriously compensated in the next if we suffer patiently. will be prosecuted as seditious and blasphemous.

Such a change would not be so great as some of us fear, though it would be a cataclysm if our present toleration and teaching of these doctrines were sincere. Fortunately it is not. The people who take them seriously, or even attach any definite meaning to the words in which they are formulated, are so exceptional that they are mostly marked off into little sects which are popularly regarded as not quite sane. It may be questioned whether as much as one per cent of the people who describe themselves as members of the Church of England, sending their children to its baptismal fonts, confirmation rite, and schools, and regularly attending its services, either know or care what they are committed to by its dogmas or articles, or read and believe them as they read and believe the morning paper. Possibly the percentage of Nonconformists who know the Westminster Confession and accept it may be slightly larger, because Nonconformity includes the extreme sects; but as these sects play the most fantastic variations on the doctrine of the Catechism, Nonconformity covers views which have been violently persecuted by the Church as blasphemous and atheistic. I am quite sure that unless you have made a special study of the subject you have no suspicion of the variety and incompatibility of the British religions that come under the general heading of Christian. No Government could possibly please them all. Queen Elizabeth, who tried to do it by drawing up thirty-nine articles alternately asserting and denying the disputed doctrines, so that every woman could find her own creed affirmed there and the other woman's creed denounced, has been a complete failure except as a means of keeping tender consciences and scrupulous intellects out of the Church. Ordinary clergymen subscribe them under duress because they cannot otherwise obtain ordination. Nobody pretends that they are all credible by the same person at the same moment; and few people even know what they are or what they mean. They could all be dropped silently without any shock to the real beliefs of most of us.

A Capitalist Government must inculcate whatever doctrine is best calculated to make the common people docile wage slaves; and a Socialist Government must equally inculcate whatever doctrine will make the sovereign people good Socialists. No Government, whatever its policy may be, can be indifferent to the formation of the inculcated common creed of the nation. Society is impossible unless the individuals who compose it have the same beliefs as to what is right and wrong in commonplace conduct. They must have a common creed antecedent to the Apostles' creed, the Nicene creed, the Athanasian creed, and all the other religious manifestoes. Queen Mary Tudor and Queen Elizabeth, King James the Second and King William the Third, could not agree about the Real Presence; but they all agreed that it was wrong to rob, murder, or set fire to the house of your neighbor. The sentry at the gate of Buckingham Palace may disagree with the Royal Family on many points, ranging from the imperial policy of the Cabinet, or the revision of the Prayer Book, to which horse to back for the Derby; but unless there were perfect harmony between them as to the proper limits to the use of his rifle and bayonet their social relation could not be maintained: there could be neither king nor sentry. We all deprecate prejudice; but if all of us were not animated sacks of prejudices, and at least nine-tenths of them were not the same prejudices so deeply rooted that we never think of them as prejudices but call them common sense, we could no more form a community than so many snakes.

This common sense is not all inborn. Some of it is: for instance, a woman knows without being told that she must not eat her baby, and that she must feed it and rear it at all hazards. But she has not the same feeling about paying her rates and taxes, although this is as necessary to the life of society as the rearing of infants to the life of humanity. A friend of mine who was a highly educated woman, the head of a famous college in the north of London, fiercely disputed the right of the local authority to have the drainage of the college examined by a public sanitary inspector. Her creed was that of a jealously private lady brought up in a private house; and it seemed an outrage to her that a man with whom she was not on visiting terms should be legally privileged to walk into the most private apartments of her college otherwise than at her invitation. Yet the health of the community depends on a general belief that this privilege is salutary and reasonable. The enlargement of the social creed to that extent is the only way to get rid of cholera epidemics. But this very able and highly instructed lady, though still in the prime of life, was too old to learn.

The social creed must be imposed on us when we are children; for it is like riding, or reading music at sight: it can never become a second nature to those who try to learn it as adults; and the social creed, to be really effective, must be a second nature to us. It is quite easy to give people a second nature, however unnatural, if you catch them early enough. There is no belief, however grotesque and even villainous, that cannot be made a part of human nature if it is inculcated in childhood and not contradicted in the child's hearing. Now that you are grown up, nothing could persuade you that it is right to lame every woman for life by binding her feet painfully in childhood on the ground that it is not ladylike to move about freely like an animal. If you are the wife of a general or admiral nothing could persuade you that when the King dies you and your husband are bound in honor to commit suicide so as to accompany your sovereign into the next world. Nothing could persuade you that it is every widow's duty to be cremated alive with the dead body of her husband. But if you had been caught early enough you could have been made to believe and do all these things exactly as Chinese, Japanese, and Indian women have believed and done them. You may say that these were heathen Eastern women, and that you are a Christian Western. But I can remember when your grandmother, also a Christian Western, believed that she would be disgraced forever if she let anyone see her ankles in the street, or (if she was "a real lady") walk there alone. The spectacle she made of herself when, as a married woman, she put on a cap to announce to the world that she must no longer be attractive to men, and the amazing figure she cut as a widow in crepe robes symbolic of her utter desolation and woe, would, if you could see or even conceive them, convince you that it was purely her luck and not any superiority of western to eastern womanhood that saved her from the bound feet, the suttee, and the hara-kiri. If you still doubt it, look at the way in which men go to war and commit frightful atrocities because they believe it is their duty, and also because the women would spit in their faces if they refused, all because this has been inculcated upon them from their childhood, thus creating the public opinion which enables the Government not only to raise enthusiastic volunteer armies, but to enforce military service by heavy penalties on the few people who, thinking for themselves, cannot accept wholesale murder and ruin as patriotic virtues.

It is clear that if all female children are to have their minds formed as the mind of Queen Victoria was formed in her infancy, a Socialist State will be impossible. Therefore it may be taken as certain that after the conquest of Parliament by the proletariat, the formation of a child's mind on that model will be prevented by every means within the power of the Government. Children will not be taught to ask God to bless the squire and his relations and keep us in our proper stations, nor will they be brought up in such a way that it will seem natural to them to praise God because he makes them eat whilst others starve, and sing while others do lament. If teachers are caught inculcating that attitude they will be sacked: if nurses, their certificates will be cancelled, and jobs found for them that do not involve intercourse with young children. Victorian parents will share the fate of Shelley. Adults must think what they please subject to their being locked up as lunatics if they think too unsocially; but on points that are structural in the social edifice, constitutional points as we call them, no quarter will be given in infant schools. The child's up-to-date second nature will be an official second nature, just as the obsolete second nature inculcated at our public schools and universities is at present.

When the child has learnt its social creed and catechism, and can read, write, reckon, and use its hands: in short, when it is qualified to make its way about in modern cities and do ordinary useful work, it had better be left to find out for itself what is good for it in the direction of higher cultivation. If it is a Newton or a Shakespeare it will learn the calculus or the art of the theatre without having them shoved down its throat: all that is necessary is that it should have access to books, teachers, and theatres. If its mind does not want to be highly cultivated, its mind should be let alone on the ground that its mind knows best what is good for it. Mentally, fallow is as important as seedtime. Even bodies can be exhausted by overcultivation. Trying to make people champion athletes indiscriminately is as idiotic as trying to make them Ireland Scholars indiscriminately. There is no reason to expect that Socialist rule will be more idiotic than the rule which has produced Eton and Harrow, Oxford and Cambridge, and Squeers.

Questions on SOCIALISM AND CHILDREN

A. General questions on structure

   1. What clues in the first two or three sentences suggest strong bias and subjectivity on the part of the author?

   2. The title of the selection is quite general. In the light of Shaw's reputation as a writer, what assumptions can be made from the title about the content of this essay?

   3. What "aspect" of children is the focal point of the selection? What part does socialism play in that connection?

   4. Answers to 1. and 2. should make it obvious that this essay is argumentative. What is the proposition, i.e., the idea the author is trying to persuade us to accept?

   5. Select six instances of emotional language and/or invective in the paragraph that begins: "As a general result we find that what we call education. . . ."

   6. Is the author ill-humored, satiric, humorous, or grave? Explain your answer.

   7. Does the tone of the article complement the subjective or detract from it? Are there any variations in tone?

   8. What principles govern the organization of the selection?

B. Questions on content

   1. What does Shaw say are our real reasons for sending our children to school?

   2. Why is he in favor of the then recently approved adoptive laws?

   3. What are the flaws in the education of the upper classes? Which of these flaws would socialism eradicate, and how?

4. What should be the real nature and purpose of education? Be specific.

5. What attacks are levied against the middle class? How would socialism ameliorate the "outrages" of this class?

6. Why is an exclusively technical education dangerous? What should supplement it?

7. Why would Shaw remove all Christian or other religious dogma from schools? What devices does he employ to show school catechism absurd?

8. Would the socialist regime be devoid of learned dogma? Explain.

C. Discussion and/or composition topics

1. What does Shaw do with the specific references to laws, schools, organizations, etc., which make the selection appear opinionated?
2. Does the author appear to have a particular attitude toward women? (Note the title of the book from which this selection comes.)
3. In spite of Shaw's aggressiveness, what truths about education has he pointed out?
4. Comment on the following statement: "College education unfits us for eighty per cent of the useful, productive work being done."
5. Of the several social classes, Shaw is vitriolic in his attacks on the middle class. Is this justifiable? Explain.

D. Vocabulary: Define, in context, the italicized words, and note touches of satire, irony, and invective.

1. "is only the *pretext*"

2. "ceasing to *shirk*"

3. "being a *septuagenarian*"

4. "educational *mania*"

5. "*ad libitum*"

6. *"sedentary"*

7. *"genteel disendowed* younger son"

8. "highly *plausible"*

9. "torture them with *impunity"*

10. "he raised *wheals"*

11. "a savage or a *Sadist"*

12. *"grotesque* Freudian beginnings"

13. "fluent *charlatan"*

14. "the most *incorrigible* of all"

15. "social *promiscuity"*

16. "much *dexterity"*

17. *"inculcate* these beliefs"

18. "or the *millennium"*

19. "prosecuted as *seditious* and *blasphemous"*

MAN AGAINST DARKNESS*

W. T. Stace

This selection is particularly challenging and stimulating. If you apply efficiently the reading skills that you have been exposed to in Chapters I, II, and III, you should be able to read this essay with ease. No questions follow the selection. You are to read it on your own and try to get from it, without direction or prompting, as much significance as you can. Once you have completed it, your satisfaction at having fully comprehended the selection will be an indication of how well you have achieved the goals of the preceding chapters.

I

The Catholic bishops of America recently issued a statement in which they said that the chaotic and bewildered state of the modern world is due to man's loss of faith, his abandonment of God and religion. For my part I believe in no religion at all. Yet I entirely agree with the bishops. It is no doubt an oversimplification to speak of *the* cause of so complex a state of affairs as the tortured condition of the world today. Its causes are doubtless multitudinous. Yet allowing for some element of oversimplification, I say that the bishops' assertion is substantially true.

M. Jean-Paul Sartre, the French existentialist philosopher, labels himself an atheist. Yet his views seem to me plainly to support the statement of the bishops. So long as there was believed to be a God in the sky, he says, men could regard him as the source of their moral ideals. The universe, created and governed by a fatherly God, was a friendly habitation for man. We could be sure that, however great the evil in the world, good in the end would triumph and the forces of evil would be routed. With the disappearance of God from the sky all this has changed. Since the world is not ruled by a spiritual being, but rather by blind force, there cannot be any ideals, moral or otherwise, in the universe outside us. Our ideals, therefore, must proceed only from our own minds; they are our own inventions. Thus the world which surrounds us is nothing but an immense spiritual emptiness. It is a dead universe. We do not live in a universe which is on the side of our values. It is completely indifferent to them.

Years ago Mr. Bertrand Russell, in his essay, "A Free Man's Worship," said much the same thing.

"Such in outline, but even more purposeless, more void of meaning, is the world which Science presents for our belief. Amid such a world, if anywhere, our ideals henceforward must find a home. . . . Blind to good and evil, reckless of destruction, omnipotent matter rolls on its relentless way; for man, condemned today to lose his dearest, tomorrow himself to pass through the gate of darkness, it remains only to cherish, ere yet the blow falls, the lofty thoughts that ennoble his little day; . . . to worship at the shrine his own hands have built; . . . to sustain alone, a weary but unyielding Atlas, the world that his own ideals have fashioned despite the trampling march of unconscious power."

It is quite true that Mr. Russell's personal attitude to the disappearance of religion is quite different from either that of M. Sartre or the bishops or myself. The bishops think it a calamity. So do I. M. Sartre finds it "very distressing." And he berates as shallow the attitude of those who think that without God the world can go on just the same as before, as if nothing had happened. This creates for mankind, he thinks, a terrible crisis. And in this I agree with him. Mr. Russell, on the other hand, seems to believe that religion has done more harm than good in the world, and that its disappearance will be a blessing. But his picture of the world, and of the modern mind, is the same as that of M. Sartre. He stresses the *purposelessness* of the universe, the fact that man's ideals are his own creations, that the universe outside him in no way supports them, that man is alone and friendless in the world.

Mr. Russell notes that it is science which has produced this situation. There is no doubt that this is correct. But the way in which it has come about is not generally understood. There is a popular belief that some particular scientific discoveries or theories, such as the Darwinian theory of evolution, or the views of geologists about the age of the earth, or a series of such discoveries have done the damage. It would be foolish to deny that these discoveries have had a great effect in undermining religious dogmas. But this account does not at all go to the root of the matter. Religion can probably outlive any scientific discoveries which could be made. It can accommodate itself to them. The root cause of the decay of faith has not been any particular discovery of science, but rather the general spirit of science and certain basic assumptions upon which modern science, from the seventeenth century onwards, has proceeded.

II

It was Galileo and Newton—notwithstanding that Newton himself was a deeply religious man—who destroyed the old comfortable picture of a friendly universe governed by spiritual values. And this was effected, not by Newton's discovery of the law of gravitation nor by any of Galileo's brilliant investigations, but by the general picture of the world which these men and others of their time made the basis of the science, not only of their own day, but of all succeeding generations down to the present. That is why the century immediately following Newton, the eighteenth century, was notoriously an age of religious skepticism. Skepticism did not have to wait for the discoveries of Darwin and the geologists in the nineteenth century. It flooded the world immediately after the age of the rise of science.

Neither the Copernican hypothesis nor any of Newton's or Galileo's particular discoveries were the real causes. Religious faith might well have accommodated

* From *The Atlantic*, Sept., 1948.

itself to the new astronomy. The real turning point between the medieval age of faith and the modern age of unfaith came when the scientists of the seventeenth century turned their backs upon what used to be called "final causes." The final cause of a thing or event meant the purpose which it was supposed to serve in the universe, its cosmic purpose. What lay back of this was the presupposition that there is a cosmic order or plan and that everything which exists could in the last analysis be explained in terms of its place in this cosmic plan, that is, in terms of its purpose.

Plato and Aristotle believed this, and so did the whole medieval Christian world. For instance, if it were true that the sun and the moon were created and exist for the purpose of giving light to man, then this fact would explain why the sun and moon exist. We might not be able to discover the purpose of everything, but everything must have a purpose. Belief in final causes thus amounted to a belief that the world is governed by purposes, presumably the purposes of some overruling mind. This belief was not the invention of Christianity. It was basic to the whole of Western civilization, whether in the ancient pagan world or in Christendom, from the time of Socrates to the rise of science in the seventeenth century.

The founders of modern science—for instance, Galileo, Kepler, and Newton—were mostly pious men who did not doubt God's purpose. Nevertheless they took the revolutionary step of consciously and deliberately expelling the idea of purpose as controlling nature from their new science of nature. They did this on the ground that inquiry into purposes is useless for what science aims at: namely, the prediction and control of events. To predict an eclipse, what you have to know is not its purpose but its causes. Hence science from the seventeenth century onwards became exclusively an inquiry into causes. The conception of purpose in the world was ignored and frowned on. This, though silent and almost unnoticed, was the greatest revolution in human history, far outweighing in importance any of the political revolutions whose thunder has reverberated through the world.

For it came about in this way that for the past three hundred years there has been growing up in men's minds, dominated as they are by science, a new imaginative picture of the world. The world, according to this new picture, is purposeless, senseless, meaningless. Nature is nothing but matter in motion. The motions of matter are governed, not by any purpose, but by blind forces and laws. Nature in this view, says Whitehead—to whose writings I am indebted in this part of my paper—is "merely the hurrying of material, endlessly, meaninglessly." You can draw a sharp line across the history of Europe dividing it into two epochs of very unequal length. The line passes through the lifetime of Galileo. European man before Galileo—whether ancient pagan or more recent Christian—thought of the world as controlled by plan and purpose. After Galileo European man thinks of it as utterly purposeless. This is the great revolution of which I spoke.

It is this which has killed religion. Religion could survive the discoveries that the sun, not the earth, is the center; that men are descended from simian ancestors;

that the earth is hundreds of millions of years old. These discoveries may render out of date some of the details of older theological dogmas, may force their restatement in new intellectual frameworks. But they do not touch the essence of the religious vision itself, which is the faith that there is plan and purpose in the world, that the world is a moral order, that in the end all things are for the best. This faith may express itself through many different intellectual dogmas, those of Christianity, of Hinduism, of Islam. All and any of these intellectual dogmas may be destroyed without destroying the essential religious spirit. But that spirit cannot survive destruction of belief in a plan and purpose of the world, for that is the very heart of it. Religion can get on with any sort of astronomy, geology, biology, physics. But it cannot get on with a purposeless and meaningless universe.

If the scheme of things is purposeless and meaningless, then the life of man is purposeless and meaningless too. Everything is futile, all effort is in the end worthless. A man may, of course, still pursue disconnected ends, money, fame, art, science, and may gain pleasure from them. But his life is hollow at the center. Hence the dissatisfied, disillusioned, restless, spirit of modern man.

The picture of a meaningless world, and a meaningless human life, is, I think, the basic theme of much modern art and literature. Certainly it is the basic theme of modern philosophy. According to the most characteristic philosophies of the modern period from Hume in the eighteenth century to the so-called positivists of today, the world is just what it is, and that is the end of all inquiry. There is no reason for its being what it is. Everything might just as well have been quite different, and there would have been no reason for that either. When you have stated what things are, what things the world contains, there is nothing more which could be said, even by an omniscient being. To ask any question about *why* things are thus, or what purpose their being so serves, is to ask a senseless question, because they serve no purpose at all. For instance, there is for modern philosophy no such thing as the ancient problem of evil. For this once famous question presupposes that pain and misery, though they seem so inexplicable and irrational to us, must ultimately subserve some rational purpose, must have their places in the cosmic plan. But this is nonsense. There is no such overruling rationality in the universe. Belief in the ultimate irrationality of everything is the quintessence of what is called the modern mind.

It is true that, parallel with these philosophies which are typical of the modern mind, preaching the meaninglessness of the world, there has run a line of idealistic philosophies whose contention is that the world is after all spiritual in nature and that moral ideals and values are inherent in its structure. But most of these idealisms were simply philosophical expressions of romanticism, which was itself no more than an unsuccessful counterattack of the religious against the scientific view of things. They perished, along with romanticism in literature and art, about the beginning of the present century, though of course they still have a few adherents.

At the bottom these idealistic systems of thought were rationalizations of man's wishful thinking. They were born of the refusal of men to admit the cosmic darkness. They were comforting illusions within the warm glow of which the more tender-minded intellectuals sought to shelter themselves from the icy winds of the universe. They lasted a little while. But they are shattered now, and we return once more to the vision of a purposeless world.

III

Along with the ruin of the religious vision there went the ruin of moral principles and indeed of all values. If there is a cosmic purpose, if there is in the nature of things a drive towards goodness, then our moral systems will derive their validity from this. But if our moral rules do not proceed from something outside us in the nature of the universe—whether we say it is God or simply the universe itself—then they must be our own inventions. Thus it came to be believed that moral rules must be merely an expression of our own likes and dislikes. But likes and dislikes are notoriously variable. What pleases one man, people, or culture displeases another. Therefore morals are wholly relative.

This obvious conclusion from the idea of a purposeless world made its appearance in Europe immediately after the rise of science, for instance in the philosophy of Hobbes. Hobbes saw at once that if there is no purpose in the world there are no values either. "Good and evil," he writes, "are names that signify our appetites and aversions; which in different tempers, customs, and doctrines of men are different. . . . Every man calleth that which pleaseth him, good; and that which displeaseth him, evil."

This doctrine of the relativity of morals, though it has recently received an impetus from the studies of anthropologists, was thus really implicit in the whole scientific mentality. It is disastrous for morals because it destroys their entire traditional foundation. That is why philosophers who see the danger signals, from the time at least of Kant, have been trying to give to morals a new foundation, that is, a secular or nonreligious foundation. This attempt may very well be intellectually successful. Such a foundation, independent of the religious view of the world, might well be found. But the question is whether it can ever be a *practical* success, that is, whether apart from its logical validity and its influence with intellectuals, it can ever replace among the masses of men the lost religious foundation. On that question hangs perhaps the future of civilization. But meanwhile disaster is overtaking us.

The widespread belief in "ethical relativity" among philosophers, psychologists, ethnologists, and sociologists is the theoretical counterpart of the repudiation of principle which we see all around us, especially in international affairs, the field in which morals have always had the weakest foothold. No one any longer effectively believes in moral principles except as the private prejudices either of individual men or of nations or cultures. This is the inevitable consequence of the doctrine of ethical relativity, which in turn is the inevitable consequence of believing in a purposeless world.

Another characteristic of our spiritual state is loss of belief in the freedom of the will. This also is a fruit of the scientific spirit, though not of any particular scientific discovery. Science has been built up on the basis of determinism, which is the belief that every event is completely determined by a chain of causes and is therefore theoretically predictable beforehand. It is true that recent physics seems to challenge this. But so far as its practical consequences are concerned, the damage has long ago been done. A man's actions, it was argued, are as much events in the natural world as is an eclipse of the sun. It follows that men's actions are as theoretically predictable as an eclipse. But if it is certain now that John Smith will murder Joseph Jones at 2:15 P.M. on January 1, 1963, what possible meaning can it have to say that when that time comes John Smith will be *free* to choose whether he will commit the murder or not? And if he is not free, how can he be held responsible?

It is true that the whole of this argument can be shown by a competent philosopher to be a tissue of fallacies—or at least I claim that it can. But the point is that the analysis required to show this is much too subtle to be understood by the average entirely unphilosophical man. Because of this, the argument against free will is generally swallowed whole by the unphilosophical. Hence the thought that man is not free, that he is the helpless plaything of forces over which he has no control, has deeply penetrated the modern mind. We hear of economic determinism, cultural determinism, historical determinism. We are not responsible for what we do because our glands control us, or because we are the products of environment or heredity. Not moral self-control, but the doctor, the psychiatrist, the educationist, must save us from doing evil. Pills and injections in the future are to do what Christ and the prophets have failed to do. Of course I do not mean to deny that doctors and educationists can and must help. And I do not mean in any way to belittle their efforts. But I do wish to draw attention to the weakening of moral controls, the greater or less repudiation, of personal responsibility which, in the popular thinking of the day, result from these tendencies of thought.

IV

What then, is to be done? Where are we to look for salvation from the evils of our time? All the remedies I have seen suggested so far are, in my opinion, useless. Let us look at some of them.

Philosophers and intellectuals generally can, I believe, genuinely do something to help. But it is extremely little. What philosophers can do is to show that neither the relativity of morals nor the denial of free will really follows from the grounds which have been supposed to support them. They can also try to discover a genuine secular basis for morals to replace the religious basis which has disappeared. Some of us are trying to do these things. But in the first place philosophers unfortunately are not agreed about these matters, and their disputes are utterly confusing to non-philosophers. And in the second place their influence is practically negligible because their analyses necessarily take place on a level on which the masses are totally unable to follow them.

The bishops, of course, propose as remedy a return to belief in God and in the doctrines of the Christian religion. Others think that a new religion is what is needed. Those who make these proposals fail to realize that the crisis in man's spiritual condition is something unique in history for which there is no sort of analogy in the past. They are thinking perhaps of the collapse of the ancient Greek and Roman religions. The vacuum then created was easily filled by Christianity, and it might have been filled by Mithraism if Christianity had not appeared. By analogy they think that Christianity might now be replaced by a new religion, or even that Christianity itself, if revivified, might bring back health to men's lives.

But I believe that there is no analogy at all between our present state and that of the European peoples at the time of the fall of paganism. Men had at that time lost their belief only in particular dogmas, particular embodiments of the religious view of the world. It had no doubt become incredible that Zeus and the other gods were living on the top of Mount Olympus. You could go to the top and find no trace of them. But the imaginative picture of a world governed by purpose, a world driving towards the good — which is the inner spirit of religion — had at that time received no serious shock. It had merely to re-embody itself in new dogmas, those of Christianity or some other religion. Religion itself was not dead in the world, only a particular form of it.

But now the situation is quite different. It is not merely that particular dogmas, like that of the virgin birth, are unacceptable to the modern mind. That is true, but it constitutes a very superficial diagnosis of the present situation of religion. Modern skepticism is of a wholly different order from that of the intellectuals of the ancient world. It has attacked and destroyed not merely the outward forms of the religious spirit, its particularized dogmas, but the very essence of that spirit itself, belief in a meaningful and purposeful world. For the founding of a new religion a new Jesus Christ or Buddha would have to appear, in itself a most unlikely event and one for which in any case we cannot afford to sit and wait. But even if a new prophet and a new religion did appear, we may predict that they would fail in the modern world. No one for long would believe in them, for modern men have lost the vision, basic to all religion, of an ordered plan and purpose of the world. They have before their minds the picture of a purposeless universe, and such a world-picture must be fatal to any religion at all, not merely to Christianity.

We must not be misled by occasional appearances of a revival of the religious spirit. Men, we are told, in their disgust and disillusionment at the emptiness of their lives, are turning once more to religion, or are searching for a new message. It may be so. We expect such wistful yearnings of the spirit. We must expect men to wish back again the light that is gone, and to try to bring it back. But however they may wish and try, the light will not shine again — not at least in the civilization to which we belong.

Another remedy commonly proposed is that we should turn to science itself, or the scientific spirit, for our salvation. Mr. Russell and Professor Dewey both make this proposal, though in somewhat different ways. Professor Dewey seems to believe that discoveries in sociology, the application of scientific method to social and political problems, will rescue us. This seems to me to be utterly naïve. It is not likely that science, which is basically the cause of our spiritual troubles, is likely also to produce the cure for them. Also it lies in the nature of science that, though it can teach us the best means for achieving our ends, it can never tell us what ends to pursue. It cannot give us any ideals. And our trouble is about ideals and ends, not about the means for reaching them.

V

No civilization can live without ideals, or to put it in another way, without a firm faith in moral ideas. Our ideals and moral ideas have in the past been rooted in religion. But the religious basis of our ideals has been undermined, and the superstructure of ideals is plainly tottering. None of the commonly suggested remedies on examination seems likely to succeed. It would therefore look as if the early death of our civilization were inevitable.

Of course we know that it is perfectly possible for individual men, very highly educated men, philosophers, scientists, intellectuals in general, to live moral lives without any religious convictions. But the question is whether a whole civilization, a whole family of peoples, composed almost entirely of relatively uneducated men and women, can do this.

If follows, of course, that if we could make the vast majority of men as highly educated as the very few are now, we might save the situation. And we are already moving slowly in that direction through the techniques of mass education. But the critical question seems to concern the time-lag. Perhaps in a few hundred years most of the population will, at the present rate, be sufficiently highly educated and civilized to combine high ideals with an absence of religion. But long before we reach any such stage, the collapse of our civilization may have come about. How are we to live through the intervening period?

I am sure that the first thing we have to do is to face the truth, however bleak it may be, and then next we have to learn to live with it. Let me say a word about each of these two points. What I am urging as regards the first is complete honesty. Those who wish to resurrect Christian dogmas are not, of course, consciously dishonest. But they have that kind of unconscious dishonesty which consists in lulling oneself with opiates and dreams. Those who talk of a new religion are merely hoping for a new opiate. Both alike refuse to face the truth that there is, in the universe outside man, no spirituality, no regard for values, no friend in the sky, no help or comfort for man of any sort. To be perfectly honest in the admission of this fact, not to seek shelter in new or old illusions, not to indulge in wishful dreams about this matter, this is the first thing we shall have to do.

I do not urge this course out of any special regard for the sanctity of truth in the abstract. It is not self-evident to me that truth is the supreme value to which all else must be sacrificed. Might not the discoverer of a truth which would be fatal to mankind be justified in suppressing it, even in teaching men a falsehood? Is truth more valuable than goodness and beauty and happiness? To think so is to invent yet another absolute, another religious delusion in which Truth with a capital T is substituted for God. The reason why we must now boldly and honestly face the truth that the universe is non-spiritual and indifferent to goodness, beauty, happiness, or truth is not that it would be wicked to suppress it, but simply that it is too late to do so, so that in the end we cannot do anything else but face it. Yet we stand on the brink, dreading the icy plunge. We need courage. We need honesty.

Now about the other point, the necessity of learning to live with the truth. This means learning to live virtuously and happily, or at least contentedly, without illusions. And this is going to be extremely difficult because what we have now begun dimly to perceive is that human life in the past, or at least human happiness, has almost wholly depended upon illusions. It has been said that man lives by truth, and that the truth will make us free. Nearly the opposite seems to me to be the case. Mankind has managed to live only by means of lies, and the truth may very well destroy us. If one were a Bergsonian one might believe that nature deliberately puts illusions into our souls in order to induce us to go on living.

The illusions by which men have lived seem to be of two kinds. First, there is what one may perhaps call the Great Illusion—I mean the religious illusion that the universe is moral and good, that it follows a wise and noble plan, that it is gradually generating some supreme value, that goodness is bound to triumph in it. Secondly, there is a whole host of minor illusions on which human happiness nourishes itself. How much of human happiness notoriously comes from the illusions of the lover about his beloved? Then again we work and strive because of the illusions connected with fame, glory, power, or money. Banners of all kinds, flags, emblems, insignia, ceremonials, and rituals are invariably symbols of some illusion or other. The British Empire, the connection between mother country and dominions, is partly kept going by illusions surrounding the notion of kingship. Or think of the vast amount of human happiness which is derived from the illusion of supposing that if some non-

sense syllable, such as "sir" or "count" or "lord," is pronounced in conjunction with our names, we belong to a superior order of people.

There is plenty of evidence that human happiness is almost wholly based upon illusions of one kind or another. But the scientific spirit, or the spirit of truth, is the enemy of illusions and therefore the enemy of human happiness. That is why it is going to be so difficult to live with the truth.

There is no reason why we should have to give up the host of minor illusions which render life supportable. There is no reason why the lover should be scientific about the loved one. Even the illusions of fame and glory may persist. But without the Great Illusion, the illusion of a good, kindly, and purposeful universe, we shall *have* to learn to live. And to ask this is really no more than to ask that we become genuinely civilized beings and not merely sham civilized beings.

I can best explain the difference by a reminiscence. I remember a fellow student in my college days, an ardent Christian, who told me that if he did not believe in a future life, in heaven and hell, he would rape, murder, steal, and be a drunkard. That is what I call being a sham civilized being. On the other hand, not only could a Huxley, a John Stuart Mill, a David Hume, live great and fine lives without any religion, but a great many others of us, quite obscure persons, can at least live decent lives without it.

To be genuinely civilized means to be able to walk straightly and to live honorably without the props and crutches of one or another of the childish dreams which have so far supported men. That such a life is likely to be ecstatically happy I will not claim. But that it can be lived in quiet content, accepting resignedly what cannot be helped, not expecting the impossible, and thankful for small mercies, this I would maintain. That it will be difficult for men in general to learn this lesson I do not deny. But that it will be impossible I would not admit since so many have learned it already.

Man has not yet grown up. He is not adult. Like a child he cries for the moon and lives in a world of fantasies. And the race as a whole has perhaps reached the great crisis of its life. Can it grow up as a race in the same sense as individual men grow up? Can man put away childish things and adolescent dreams? Can he grasp the real world as it actually is, stark and bleak, without its romantic or religious halo, and still retain his ideals, striving for great ends and noble achievements? If he can, all may yet be well. If he cannot, he will probably sink back into the savagery and brutality from which he came, taking a humble place once more among the lower animals.

Part **2**

Skills for Reading

Chapter IV

READING FOR RECREATION

INTRODUCTION

Your reading until now has been primarily in expository prose. Here, however, you will read a sampling of literary works—prose fiction, poetry, and drama—and since this type of writing often differs so radically in its methods and purposes, it is well to begin with the broad question, "What is literature?"

Joseph Conrad has said, in "The Condition of Art," that literature "is an attempt to find in its forms, in its colors, in its light, in its shadows, in the aspects of matter and the facts of life, what of each is fundamental, what is enduring and essential—the very truth of their existence." Literature, thus, should not wear with age, but should—with minor topical explanations—provide delight and wisdom to all generations. Conrad affirms further that his task as a literary artist is, by the "power of the written word," "to make us hear, to make us feel, and to make us see." Faulkner, as you read in Chapter I, stresses the need for literature to register the "problems of the human heart in conflict with itself," and the need for literature to concern itself with "the old universal truths . . . love and honor and pity and pride and compassion and sacrifice." Literature, then, will not primarily be an analysis of life, but a presentation of it; it will attempt to catch in their turns the paradox, the irony, the hope, the frustration, the complexity, the dreaming, the terror, the joy, the tragedy, the pathos, and the comedy that compose the human experience. It will attempt to uncover inner values by creating real people and real experiences. The first task of the literary work is to insist that you "hear," "feel," and "see" its story and image. To do this, it will often resort to more richly connotative or suggestive language than expository prose normally employs: it will use ambiguity, symbol, vivid image, figures of speech, sound patterns, and subtle tone to engage its readers; sometimes its language will *seem* to reproduce the patterns and phrases of everyday speech, but even then it will be a highly selective diction, aptly chosen from much that is dross—it will be a measured, tightened, shrewdly constructed language. W. B. Yeats, the great Irish poet, implies that though a line may well take an author hours of "stitching and unstitching," the final test of a work's achievement will be that it "seem a moment's thought." Alexander Pope implies that literature will say "What oft was thought, but ne'er so well expressed." It may hold a slightly slanted mirror to our own lives so that perhaps for the first time we "see ourselves"; or it may offer a glimpse of that which we have not yet even dreamed existed, and thus expand broadly the ken of our experiences and hopes. Literature is an art form and also a form of entertainment; its brand of wisdom is unique and subtly imparted.

The following books provide extensive definitions and discussions of the various forms of literature: Meyer E. Abrams, editor of revised edition of Daniel S. Norton and Peters Rushton, *Glossary of Literary Terms* (New York: Holt, Rinehart & Winston, 1957); Cleanth Brooks and Robert B. Heilman, *Understanding Drama: Twelve Plays* (New York: Holt, 1948); Cleanth Brooks and Robert Penn Warren, *Understanding Fiction* (New York: Appleton-Century-Crofts, 1959); and Cleanth Brooks and Robert Penn Warren, *Understanding Poetry* (New York: Holt, Rinehart & Winston, 1960).

THE SHORT STORY

A short story usually attempts, within the limitation of its length, to depict a whole action and to make a particular revelation about one or more of its central characters. Since it is short, the story usually has but a few incidents, and a limited canon of characters. Its characters must be developed rapidly, and there is usually a single climax to the action. There will probably be a single plot (the sequence of related and motivated events), and a single central conflict (elements or forces that clash).

A story will be told from a particular perspective, or point of view: if it is told in the first person by a character involved with the action, it will thus be subjective, the details colored by the narrator's character; it may be told from the third person, but manifest special focus on or sympathy for one character; or it may be told by an omniscient author who tries for a balanced, objective view of the whole action. The setting of a story is the locale or background against which the action takes place; it should be aptly suited to the action. Poe, for instance, frequently writes about despair, isolation, and terror, and thus appropriately sets his stories in gloomy, depressing backgrounds—haunted houses, catacombs, etc. The theme—which should be distinguished from a message—emerges from the interaction of plot, characters, and setting; the theme will help disclose the meaning of a story.

You should pay particular attention to the way Poe and de Maupassant create character. Notice how our total understanding of a character is de-pendent not only upon how well the author has directly described the person, but also on what the character says, how he acts (and reacts), and what others say and think about him. Since the short story is so brief, virtually every word should contribute to the effect the author wishes to convey. You should especially note the climactic portions of sentences, paragraphs, and the story itself for keys to meanings. Always be careful to ascertain the author's tone and attitude—whether he is sympathetic, ironic, or satiric. Remember that an author has an infinite number of choices he can make when writing a story: the exact order of progression and the smallest detail should receive your closest scrutiny. The meaning of the story will be a complex of every particular it contains.

Close explication of a work of literature, contrary to the judgment of many beginning students, does not "dry out" or destroy the pleasure of reading it: such scrutiny can only make your appreciation of literature a much richer experience.

A STRANGE FANCY*

Guy de Maupassant

It was at the end of the dinner opening the hunting season, at the house of Marquis de Bertrans. Eleven hunters, eight young women, and the doctor of the neighborhood were seated around the great illuminated table covered with fruits and flowers.

They came to speak of love, and a great discussion arose, the eternal discussion, as to whether one could love truly but once or many times. They cited examples of people who had never had but one serious love; they also cited other examples of others who had loved often, violently. The men, generally, pretended that the passion, like a malady, could strike the same person many times, and strike to kill if an obstacle appeared in its path. Although the point of view was not contestable, the women, whose opinion depended upon poesy more than on observation, affirmed that love, true love, the great love, could only fall once upon a mortal; that it was like a thunderbolt, this love, and that a heart touched by it remained ever after so vacant, ravaged, and burned out that no other powerful sentiment, even a dream, could again take root.

The marquis, having loved much, combated this belief in lively fashion:

"I will tell you that one can love many times with all his strength and all his soul. You cite to me people who have killed themselves for love as proof of the impossibility of a second passion. I answer that if they had not been guilty of this foolishness of suicide, which removed them from all chance of another fall, they would have been healed; and they would have recommenced, again and again, until their natural death. It is with lovers as it is with drunkards. He who has drunk will drink—he who has loved will love. It is simply a matter of temperament."

They chose the doctor as arbitrator, an old Paris physician retired to the country, and begged him to give his opinion.

To be exact, he had none. As the marquis had said, "it is an affair of temperament."

"As for myself," he continued, "I have known of one passion which lasted fifty-five years without a day of respite, and which was terminated only by death."

The marquis clapped his hands.

"This is beautiful," said a lady. "And what a dream to be so loved! What happiness to live fifty-five years enveloped in a deep, living affection! How happy and benign must be the life of one who is adored like that!"

The doctor laughed:

"In fact, madame," said he, "you are deceived on that point, because the one loved was a man. You know him, it is M. Chouquet, the village pharmacist. And as for the woman, you knew her, too; it is the old woman who put cane seats in chairs, and came every year to this house. But how can I make you comprehend the matter?"

The enthusiasm of the women fell. On their faces a look of disgust said: "Pooh!" as if love could only strike

* From *Complete Short Stories of Guy de Maupassant.* Intro. by Artin Artinian. Hanover House, 1955.

those fine and distinguished creatures who were worthy of the interest of fashionable people.

The doctor continued:

"I was called three months ago, to the bedside of this old woman. She was dying. She had come here in the old carriage that served her for a house, drawn by the nag that you have often seen, and accompanied by her two great black dogs, her friends and guard. The curate was already there. She made us the executors of her will, and in order to unveil the meaning of her testament, she related the story of her life. I have never heard anything more singular or more affecting.

"Her father made chair seats and so did her mother. She had never known a home in any one place upon the earth. As a little girl she went around ragged and dirty. They would stop beside the road at the entrance to towns, unharness the horse and let him browse; the dog would go to sleep with his nose in his paws; the little one would play in the grass while the father and mother, under the shade of the elms bordering the roadside, would reseat all the old chairs in the neighborhood.

"No one ever talked in this ambulance dwelling. After the necessary words to decide who should make the tour of the houses and who should call out the well-known 'Chairs to mend!' they would sit down to plait the straw, face to face or side by side.

"When the child went too far away or struck up an acquaintance with some urchin in the village the angry voice of the father would call her: 'You come back here, you brat!' And these were the only words of tenderness she ever heard.

"When she grew larger they sent her around to collect the worn-out chairs to be rebottomed. Then she made some acquaintances from place to place among the street children. Then it would be the parents of her new friends who would call brutally to their children: 'Will you come here, you scamp! Let me catch you talking to that barefoot again!'

"Often the boys would throw stones at her. Sometimes ladies would give her a few pennies and look at her closely.

"One day—she was then eleven years old—as they were passing through this place, she met the little Chouquet behind the cemetery, weeping because some comrade had stolen two sous from him. The tears of this little well-to-do citizen, one of those fortunate ones from whom in her queer noddle she had imagined herself cut off, one of those beings always content and joyous, quite upset her. She went up to him, and when she learned the cause of his trouble, she poured into his hands all her savings, seven sous, which he took quite naturally, drying his tears. Then, mad with joy, she had the audacity to embrace him. As he was counting the money attentively, he allowed her to do it. Seeing that she was not repulsed nor beaten, she did the same thing again. She embraced him with arms and heart. Then she ran away.

"What could have taken place in her miserable head after that? Did she attach herself to this booby because she had sacrificed for him her vagabond fortune or because she had given to him her first tender kiss? The mystery is the same for the small as for the great.

"For months she dreamed of this corner of the cemetery and of this boy. In the hope of seeing him again, she robbed her parents, keeping back a sou here and there, either from a chair seat or upon the provisions which she was sent to buy.

"When she returned here she had two francs in her pocket, but she only saw the little druggist very properly behind the big colored bottle of his father's shop, between a red decanter and a tapeworm. She loved him there still more, charmed, aroused to ecstasy by this glory of colored water, this apotheosis of shining crystal.

"This picture became an ineffaceable memory, and when she saw him the following year playing marbles near the school with his comrades, she threw herself upon him, seized him in her arms and kissed him with such violence that he began to howl with fear. Then in order to appease him, she gave him all her money — seventy cents, a real treasure which he looked at with bulging eyes.

"He took it and let her caress him as much as she wished.

"During the next four years she turned into his hand all her surplus, which he pocketed with a clear conscience, in exchange for permitted kisses. There was sometimes fifteen cents, sometimes forty and once only five and one-half — and she wept with pain and humiliation at this, but it had been a bad year. The last time there was a five-franc piece, a great round piece which made him laugh with content.

"She thought of nothing but him; and he waited her return with a certain impatience, running to meet her, which made the heart of the girl leap with joy.

"Then he disappeared. They sent him away to college. She found it out by skillful questioning. Then she used her diplomacy to change her parents' itinerary and make them pass through there in vacation. She succeeded but for one year; then for two years she did not see him; then she scarcely recognized him, so much was he changed; he was so large and handsome in his coat with the brass buttons and so imposing. He feigned not to see her and passed proudly by near her.

"She wept over it for two days, and after that she suffered without ceasing.

"Every year she returned here, passing him without daring to bow, and without his deigning to raise his eyes to her. She loved him passionately. She said to me: 'Doctor, he is the only man I have seen on earth; I have not known that there are others existing.'

"Her parents died. She continued their trade but took with her two dogs instead of one, two terrible dogs that no one would dare encounter.

"One day in entering this village, where her heart still remained, she perceived a young woman coming out of the Chouquet shop on the arm of her well-beloved. It was his wife. He was married.

"That evening she threw herself into the pond on the mayor's estate. A drunken man got her out and took her to the pharmacy. Chouquet, the son, came down in his dressing-gown to care for her and, without appearing to recognize her, loosed her clothing and rubbed her, then said in a hard voice: 'My, but you are foolish! It is not necessary to make a beast of yourself like this!'

"That was sufficient to cure her. He had spoken to her! She was happy for a long time.

"He wanted no remuneration for his services, but she insisted upon paying him well. And all her life was spent like this. She made chair seats and thought of Chouquet. Every year she saw him behind his large windows. She had the habit of buying from him all her medical needs. In this way she could see him near to and speak to him and still give him a little money.

"As I told you in the beginning, she died this spring. After having related her sad history, she begged me to give to him whom she had so patiently loved all the savings of her life, because she had worked only for him, she said, fasting, even, in order to put aside and to be sure that he would think of her at least once after she was dead.

"She then gave me two thousand three hundred and twenty-seven francs. I allowed the curate twenty-seven for burial and carried off the rest when she had drawn her last breath.

"The next day I took myself to the house of the Chouquets. They had just finished breakfast, sitting opposite each other, large and red, smelling of their pharmaceutical products, important and satisfied.

"They made me be seated; they offered me a kirsch, which I accepted; then I commenced my discourse in an emotional voice, persuaded that they were going to weep.

"When they understood that he had been loved by this vagabond, this chair mender, this rover, Chouquet bounced with indignation, as if she had robbed him of his reputation, of the esteem of honest people, of his honor, of something of that delicacy that was dearer to him than life.

"His wife, also exasperated, kept repeating: 'The beggar! The beggar!' without being able to find any other word.

"He got up and walked around the table with long strides, his Greek cap tipped over his ear. He muttered: 'Think of it, Doctor! This is a horrible thing to happen to a man! What is to be done? Oh, if I had known this while she was alive I would have had her arrested and shut up in prison. And she wouldn't have got out, I can tell you!'

"I was stupefied at the result of my pious proceedings. I neither knew what to say nor what to do. But I had to complete my mission. I said: 'She has charged me to give you all her savings, which amount to two thousand three hundred francs. As what I have told you seems to be so very disagreeable to you, perhaps it would be better to give this money to the poor.'

"They looked at me, the man and the woman, impotent from shock. I drew the money from my pocket, miserable money from all the country and of every mark, gold and sous mixed. Then I asked: 'What do you decide?'

"Mme. Chouquet spoke first. She said: 'But since it was the last wish of this woman — it seems to me that it would be difficult to refuse it.'

"The husband, somewhat confused, answered: 'We could always buy with that money something for our children.'

"I remarked, dryly: 'As you wish!'

"He continued: 'Yes, give it to us, since she has put it in your charge. We can always find means of using it in some good work.'

"I laid down the money, bowed and went out.

"The next day Chouquet came to me and said brusquely: 'She must have left a wagon here, that—that woman. What are you going to do with this wagon?'

"'Nothing,' I said. 'Take it if you wish.'

"'Exactly. Just what I want. I will make a lean-to of it for my kitchen stove.'

"He was going, but I recalled him. 'She also left an old horse and her two dogs. Do you want them?'

"He stopped, surprised: 'Ah no,' he answered, 'what could I do with them? Dispose of them as you wish.'

"Then he laughed and extended his hand which I took. What else could I do? In our country a medical man and a druggist should not be enemies.

"I have kept the dogs at my house. The curate, who has a large yard, took the horse. The wagon serves Chouquet as a cabin, and he has bought five railroad bonds with the money.

"This is the only profound love that I have met in my life."

The doctor was silent. Then the marquis, with tears in his eyes, sighed: "Decidedly, it is only women who know how to love."

Guide Questions on A STRANGE FANCY

1. From the first paragraph what can you tell of the characters and the society in which they live?

2. What would account for the differences in opinion of the men and women about love? Differences in experiences? A natural sexual antagonism? A difference in sentimentalism?

3. From paragraph 9 of the story, one may infer that a great love brings great joy. Does the story support such an implication?

4. How did the childhood of the chairmender contribute to her great weakness for Chouquet?

5. Do the character traits which Chouquet manifested in his early acceptance of her love continue unchanged into his adult life? Justify your answer with supporting details.

6. Although the red decanter of the apothecary has a literal meaning, what is its figurative meaning?

7. For purposes of comparison, can you think of any other story which treats the idea of fidelity or total commitment to the loved one? You might wish to refer to Somerset Maugham's novel *Of Human Bondage.*

8. The outstanding characteristic of the short story is its compactness (singleness of impression, economy of dialogue so that every word counts; deft but brief presentation of character). In what way does this story illustrate this characteristic?

9. The short story or the novel may emphasize any one of the following elements: plot (emphasis is on what happens), character (emphasis is on a person or persons involved), atmosphere (emphasis is on setting, mood, or tone), theme (emphasis is on some idea or observation concerning life). What is the emphasis in "A Strange Fancy"?

THE CASK OF AMONTILLADO

Edgar Allan Poe

The thousand injuries of Fortunato I had borne as I best could; but when he ventured upon insult, I vowed revenge. You, who so well know the nature of my soul, will not suppose, however, that I gave utterance to a threat. At length I would be avenged; this was a point definitely settled; but the very definitiveness with which it was resolved precluded the idea of risk. I must not only punish, but punish with impunity. A wrong is unredressed when the avenger fails to make himself felt as such to him who has done the wrong.

It must be understood that neither by word nor deed had I given Fortunato cause to doubt my good-will. I continued, as was my wont, to smile in his face, and he did not perceive that my smile now was at the thought of his immolation.

He had a weak point, this Fortunato, although in other regards he was a man to be respected and even feared. He prided himself on his connoisseurship in wine. Few Italians have the true virtuoso spirit. For the most part their enthusiasm is adopted to suit the time and opportunity, to practise imposture upon the British and Austrian millionaires. In painting and gemmary Fortunato, like his countrymen, was a quack; but in the matter of old wines he was sincere. In this respect I did not differ from him materially: I was skillful in the Italian vintages myself, and bought largely whenever I could.

It was about dusk one evening, during the supreme madness of the carnival season, that I encountered my friend. He accosted me with excessive warmth, for he had been drinking much. The man wore motley. He had on a tight-fitting parti-striped dress, and his head was surmounted by the conical cap and bells. I was so pleased to see him that I thought I should never have done wringing his hand.

I said to him: "My dear Fortunato, you are luckily met. How remarkably well you are looking to-day! But I have received a pipe of what passes for Amontillado, and I have my doubts."

"How?" said he. "Amontillado? A pipe? Impossible! And in the middle of the carnival!"

"I have my doubts," I replied; "and I was silly enough to pay the full Amontillado price without consulting you in the matter. You were not to be found, and I was fearful of losing a bargain."

"Amontillado!"

"I have my doubts."

"Amontillado!"

"And I must satisfy them."

"Amontillado!"

"As you are engaged, I am on my way to Luchesi. If any one has a critical turn, it is he. He will tell me—"

"Luchesi cannot tell Amontillado from sherry."

"And yet some fools will have it that his taste is a match for your own."

"Come, let us go."

"Whither?"

"To your vaults."

"My friend, no; I will not impose upon your good nature. I perceive you have an engagement. Luchesi—"

"I have no engagement; come."

"My friend, no. It is not the engagement, but the severe cold with which I perceive you are afflicted. The vaults are insufferably damp. They are encrusted with nitre."

"Let us go, nevertheless. The cold is merely nothing. Amontillado! You have been imposed upon. And as for Luchesi, he cannot distinguish sherry from Amontillado."

Thus speaking, Fortunato possessed himself of my arm. Putting on a mask of black silk, and drawing a *roquelaire* closely about my person, I suffered him to hurry me to my palazzo.

There were no attendants at home; they had absconded to make merry in honor of the time. I had told them that I should not return until the morning, and had given them explicit orders not to stir from the house. These orders were sufficient, I well knew, to insure their immediate disappearance, one and all, as soon as my back was turned.

I took from their sconces two flambeaux, and, giving one to Fortunato, bowed him through several suites of rooms to the archway that led into the vaults. I passed down a long and winding staircase, requesting him to be cautious as he followed. We came at length to the foot of the descent, and stood together on the damp ground of the catacombs of the Montresors.

The gait of my friend was unsteady, and the bells upon his cap jingled as he strode.

"The pipe?" said he.

"It is farther on," said I; "but observe the white web-work which gleams from these cavern walls."

He turned toward me, and looked into my eyes with two filmy orbs that distilled the rheum of intoxication.

"Nitre?" he asked at length.

"Nitre," I replied. "How long have you had that cough?"

"Ugh! ugh! ugh!—ugh! ugh! ugh!—ugh! ugh! ugh!—ugh! ugh! ugh!—ugh! ugh! ugh!"

My poor friend found it impossible to reply for many minutes.

"It is nothing," he said, at last.

"Come," I said, with decision, "we will go back; your health is precious. You are rich, respected, admired, beloved; you are happy, as once I was. You are a man to be missed. For me it is no matter. We will go back; you will be ill, and I cannot be responsible. Besides, there is Luchesi—"

"Enough," he said; "the cough is a mere nothing; it will not kill me. I shall not die of a cough."

"True—true," I replied; "and, indeed, I had no intention of alarming you unnecessarily; but you should use all proper caution. A draught of this Medoc will defend us from the damps."

Here I knocked off the neck of a bottle which I drew from a long row of its fellows that lay upon the mould.

"Drink," I said, presenting him the wine.

He raised it to his lips with a leer. He paused and nodded to me familiarly, while his bells jingled.

"I drink," he said, "to the buried that repose around us."

"And I to your long life."

He again took my arm and we proceeded.

"These vaults," he said, "are extensive."

"The Montresors," I replied, "were a great and numerous family."

"I forget your arms."

"A huge human foot d'or, in a field azure; the foot crushes a serpent rampant whose fangs are imbedded in the heel."

"And the motto?"

"Nemo me impune lacessit."

"Good!" he said.

The wine sparkled in his eyes and the bells jingled. My own fancy grew warm with the Medoc. We had passed through walls of piled bones, with casks and puncheons intermingling, into the inmost recesses of the catacombs. I paused again, and this time I made bold to seize Fortunato by an arm above the elbow.

"The nitre!" I said; "see, it increases. It hangs like moss upon the vaults. We are below the river's bed. The drops of moisture trickle among the bones. Come, we will go back ere it is too late. Your cough—"

"It is nothing," he said; "let us go on. But first, another draught of the Medoc."

I broke and reached him a flagon of De Grâve. He emptied it at a breath. His eyes flashed with a fierce light. He laughed and threw the bottle upward with a gesticulation I did not understand.

I looked at him in surprise. He repeated the movement —a grotesque one.

"You do not comprehend?" he said.

"Not I," I replied.

"Then you are not of the brotherhood."

"How?"

"You are not of the masons."

"Yes, yes," I said; "yes, yes."

"You? Impossible! A mason?"

"A mason," I replied.

"A sign," he said.

"It is this," I answered, producing a trowel from beneath the folds of my *roquelaire.*

"You jest!" he exclaimed, recoiling a few paces. "But let us proceed to the Amontillado."

"Be it so," I said, replacing the tool beneath the cloak, and again offering him my arm. He leaned upon it heavily. We continued our route in search of the Amontillado. We passed through a range of low arches, descended, passed on, and, descending again, arrived at a deep crypt, in which the foulness of the air caused our flambeaux rather to glow than flame.

At the most remote end of the crypt there appeared another less spacious. Its walls had been lined with human remains, piled to the vault overhead, in the fashion of the great catacombs of Paris. Three sides of this interior crypt were still ornamented in this manner. From the fourth the bones had been thrown down, and lay promiscuously upon the earth, forming at one point a mound of some size. Within the wall thus exposed by the displacing of the bones we perceived a still interior recess, in depth about four feet, in width three, in height

six or seven. It seemed to have been constructed for no especial use within itself, but formed merely the interval between two of the colossal supports of the roof of the catacombs, and was backed by one of their circumscribing walls of solid granite.

It was in vain that Fortunato, uplifting his dull torch, endeavored to pry into the depth of the recess. Its termination the feeble light did not enable us to see.

"Proceed," I said; "herein is the Amontillado. As for Luchesi—"

"He is an ignoramus," interrupted my friend, as he stepped unsteadily forward, while I followed immediately at his heels. In an instant he had reached the extremity of the niche, and, finding his progress arrested by the rock, stood stupidly bewildered. A moment more and I had fettered him to the granite. In its surface were two iron staples, distant from each other about two feet, horizontally. From one of these depended a short chain, from the other a padlock. Throwing the links about his waist, it was but the work of a few seconds to secure it. He was too much astounded to resist. Withdrawing the key I stepped back from the recess.

"Pass your hand," I said, "over the wall; you cannot help feeling the nitre. Indeed it is very damp. Once more let me implore you to return. No? Then I must positively leave you. But I must first render you all the little attentions in my power."

"The Amontillado!" ejaculated my friend, not yet recovered from his astonishment.

"True," I replied; "the Amontillado."

As I said these words I busied myself among the pile of bones of which I have before spoken. Throwing them aside, I soon uncovered a quantity of building stone and mortar. With these materials and with the aid of my trowel, I began vigorously to wall up the entrance of the niche.

I had scarcely laid the first tier of the masonry when I discovered that the intoxication of Fortunato had in a great measure worn off. The earliest indication I had of this was a low, moaning cry from the depth of the recess. It was not the cry of a drunken man. There was then a long and obstinate silence. I laid the second tier, and the third, and the fourth; and then I heard the furious vibrations of the chain. The noise lasted for several minutes, during which, that I might hearken to it with the more satisfaction, I ceased my labors and sat down upon the bones. When at last the clanking subsided, I resumed the trowel, and finished without interruption the fifth, the sixth, and the seventh tier. The wall was now nearly upon a level with my breast. I again paused, and, holding the flambeaux over the masonwork, threw a few feeble rays upon the figure within.

A succession of loud and shrill screams, bursting suddenly from the throat of the chained form, seemed to thrust me violently back. For a brief moment I hesitated, I trembled. Unsheathing my rapier, I began to grope with it about the recess; but the thought of an instant reassured me. I placed my hand upon the solid fabric of the catacombs and felt satisfied. I reapproached the wall. I replied to the yells of him who clamored.

I re-echoed, I aided, I surpassed them in volume and in strength. I did this, and the clamorer grew still.

It was now midnight, and my task was drawing to a close. I had completed the eighth, the ninth, and the tenth tier. I had finished a portion of the last and the eleventh; there remained but a single stone to be fitted and plastered in. I struggled with its weight; I placed it partially in its destined position. But now there came from out the niche a low laugh that erected the hairs upon my head. It was succeeded by a sad voice, which I had difficulty in recognizing as that of the noble Fortunato. The voice said:

"Ha! ha! Ha!—he! he!—a very good joke indeed, an excellent jest. We will have many a rich laugh about it at the palazzo—he! he! he!—over our wine—he! he! he!"

"The Amontillado!" I said.

"He! he! he!—he! he! he!—yes, the Amontillado. But is it not getting late? Will not they be awaiting us at the palazzo,—the Lady Fortunato and the rest? Let us be gone."

"Yes," I said, "let us be gone."

"For the love of God, Montresor!"

"Yes," I said, "for the love of God!"

But to these words I hearkened in vain for a reply. I grew impatient. I called aloud:

"Fortunato!"

No answer. I called again.

"Fortunato!"

No answer still. I thrust a torch through the remaining aperture and let it fall within. There came forth in return only a jingling of bells. My heart grew sick—on account of the dampness of the catacombs. I hastened to make an end of my labor. I forced the last stone into its position; I plastered it up. Against the new masonry I re-erected the old rampart of bones. For the half of a century no mortal has disturbed them. *In pace requiescat!*

Guide Questions on THE CASK OF AMONTILLADO

1. This story is written in the first person. What is the effect of this choice? How does it help to reveal the character of Montresor?

2. In the first sentence the narrator refers to certain wrongs he has suffered at the hand of Fortunato. Are these "injuries" and "insults" ever made explicit? Why has Poe so referred to them?

3. Why does Poe set the story "during the supreme madness of the carnival season"? Note the effective use of the catacombs.

4. In what ways does Montresor play upon Fortunato's pride? Why is this so important to his plan?

5. What evidence do you find of irony in the story? Explain how the presence of so much irony is appropriate to this story.

6. Certain details—the cap and bells, the nitre, Luchesi, and the Amontillado wine—are repeated frequently throughout the story. Explain their use and Poe's repetition of them. Do they serve any structural purpose?

7. Toward the end of the story Fortunato makes a series of exclamations that the narrator repeats verbatim. Explain the psychological effect of these repetitions.

8. Study the last paragraph closely. Has Montresor accomplished his revenge according to the criteria he established in the first paragraph? Of what importance is the revelation that the action of the story took place fifty years prior to the narration? Why do we learn this so late?

POETRY

The most frequent quarrel beginning students of poetry have is epitomized in the question: "But why didn't he just say what he meant?" The poet does say what he means, and could not have said the same thing in any other words; the surest way to see this is by attempting to paraphrase a first-rate poem. Invariably the result will be much longer, totally lacking in the "music" of the poem, and not nearly so suggestive. Poetry is at first difficult to understand because it is the most compressed or compact form of literary expression; the poet has intensified human experience in his exacting choice and patterning of words to appeal both to the intellect and emotions of the reader.

Part of the *meaning* of a poem will be contained in the very sound of its words. Note in the following passage from Alexander Pope's "Essay on Criticism" how the sound of the lines actually does "seem an echo to the sense" and in fact becomes a part of the *sense* of the line.

True ease in writing comes from Art, not Chance,
As those move easiest who have learn'd to dance.
'Tis not enough no harshness gives offence;
The sound must seem an echo to the sense.
Soft is the strain when zephyr gently blows,
And the smooth stream in smoother numbers flows;
But when loud surges lash the sounding shore,
The hoarse rough verse should like the torrent roar.
When Ajax strives some rock's vast weight to throw,
The line, too, labours, and the words move slow:
Not so when swift Camilla scours the plain,
Flies o'er th' unbending corn, and skims along the main.

Notice in the eighth line, for example, how the words are deliberately chosen to suggest the harsh, cacophonous, and monotonous pounding of the waves. Say the phrase "hoarse rough verse" aloud. Though the three words only contain a total of three syllables, their length or duration is much greater than, say, "skims along"; the repetition of harsh consonants—*r* and the *rs* combination—contributes to the slowness and difficulty of pronouncing the phrase, and so does the fact that each syllable is accented. Study the other lines in this passage and try to see how in each Pope is exemplifying the principle that the "sound must seem an echo to the sense."

To describe what a poet has done to create a particular effect, it will be helpful to know the three basic meters of poetry, and a few basic terms of prosody. Iambic meter is the most common in English poetry because it most closely parallels the normal rhythm of speech. It is an unaccented followed by an accented syllable. In the following line from John Milton's famous sonnet on his blindness, each foot is iambic.

When I / consi / der how / my light / is spent

Trochaic meter is the reverse of iambic—or, an accented then an unaccented syllable. The beginning of William Blake's "The Tyger" is a good example of this meter, which is often used for songs or for dramatic emphasis.

Tyger! / Tyger! / burning /

The spondaic meter is composed of two accented syllables placed together. In the phrase "The hoarse rough verse," the first foot is iambic, the second spondaic. This foot slows down a poem considerably, and may be used to suggest duration, melancholy, or heaviness.

Poetry frequently employs metaphors, similes, symbols, and paradoxes—all highly suggestive forms of expression—to make an image or idea clearer or more evocative or more poignant. Metaphors and similes are comparisons, the difference lying in the fact that the latter states the comparison by using a "like" or "as." "He is a cow" is a metaphor; note how much more direct and effective it is than "He is like a cow." In certain poems, like "On First Looking into Chapman's Homer," by John Keats, a metaphor or simile will be extended for several lines. Symbolism also implies likeness between an idea and an image: the lamb is a common symbol for gentleness and, by historical reference, for Christ. Paradox is an apparent contradiction of terms; in "Holy Sonnet X," John Donne paradoxically implies that when we die we actually "wake eternally."

Since poetry tries to capture the essence of things, its difficulty often emerges from the fact that it omits so much that is unessential to meaning but common in everyday speech. The line "Dull sublunary lovers' love" from a poem by John Donne is a highly compressed version of something like, "The love of those lovers who are mundane and earthy is dull." Poetry also attempts to suggest much more than it actually states; that is why poems of even short length warrant so much discussion and meditation: they will not disclose all that they are so easily that their interest is rapidly exhausted.

But the difficulty in understanding poetry is quickly compensated for. There are lines of poetry which you will hear once and never forget because they so poignantly capture an idea or feeling you have had and could not define; or they may compellingly force you to recognize a truth you did not before know existed. Read poems much more slowly than you read passages of prose; learn the meanings of every word and every phrase; and try to observe how the order of progression could not be changed.

SONNET EIGHTEEN

William Shakespeare

Shall I compare thee to a summer's day?
Thou art more lovely and more temperate:
Rough winds do shake the darling buds of May,
And summer's lease hath all too short a date:
Sometime too hot the eye of heaven shines,
And often is his cold complexion dimm'd;
And every fair from fair sometime declines,
By chance, or nature's changing course, untrimm'd:
But thy eternal summer shall not fade,
Nor lose possession of that fair thou ow'st;
Nor shall Death brag thou wander'st in his shade,
When in eternal lines to time thou grow'st:
    So long as men can breathe, or eyes can see,
    So long lives this, and this gives life to thee.

Guide Questions

1. a. The first eight lines of an English sonnet present the situation or problem or the illustration of the main idea; the last six lines resolve the conflict. Apply this division to this poem.

   b. Even if you did not know the traditional division of the sonnet, what conjunction would signal beyond a doubt the change in thought?

2. What objection does the poet raise to each of nature's wonders?

3. What are the different meanings of "fair" in line 7?

4. a. Is the unchanged beauty of the beloved existent in the eye of the beholder only?

   b. How is it possible for one to grow more and more lovely with the passage of time?

5. How effective are the words "temperate," "thy eternal summer"?

6. The poetic device of attributing human qualities to inanimate or natural objects is beautifully illustrated here. Comment on some of these illustrations.

7. What is the poet's gift of immortality to his beloved?

8. To which of the five senses does this poem primarily appeal? Explain your answer.

9. Gerard Manley Hopkins says that "Poetry is speech framed for contemplation of the mind by the way of hearing, or speech framed to be heard for its own sake and interest even over and above its interest of meaning." Do you agree with this statement? Explain your answer.

HOLY SONNET X

John Donne

Death be not proud, though some have called thee
Mighty and dreadful, for thou art not so,
For those, whom thou think'st thou dost overthrow,
Die not, poor Death, nor yet canst thou kill me.
From rest and sleep, which but thy pictures be,
Much pleasure, then from thee much more must flow,
And soonest our best men with thee do go,
Rest of their bones and soul's delivery.
Thou art slave to Fate, Chance, kings, and desperate men,
And dost with poison, war, and sickness dwell,
And poppy or charms can make us sleep as well,
And better than thy stroke; why swell'st thou then?
One short sleep past, we wake eternally,
And death shall be no more; Death, thou shalt die.

Guide Questions

1. To whom is the poem addressed? What other approaches might Donne have used? Comment on the effectiveness of his choice.

2. What attitude does the author take toward death? In what ways does this differ from the common attitude? What evidence does Donne use to support his "argument"? What is the dramatic effect of Donne's attitude?

3. Explain why Donne can say that Death cannot kill him.

4. In what way are "rest" and "sleep" but the pictures of Death? What is the effect of this comparison?

5. Why does Donne say that Death is a "slave"? Why are "Fate, Chance, kings, and desperate men" chosen as its masters?

6. Explain the words "poppy" and "charms."

7. By what logic can Donne say Death will die?

VIRTUE

George Herbert

Sweet day, so cool, so calm, so bright,
  The bridal of the earth and sky;
The dew shall weep thy fall to night,
    For thou must die.

Sweet rose, whose hue angry and brave
  Bids the rash gazer wipe his eye;
Thy root is ever in its grave,
    And thou must die.

Sweet spring, full of sweet days and roses,
  A box where sweets compacted lie;
My music shows ye have your closes,
    And all must die.

Only a sweet and virtuous soul,
  Like seasoned timber, never gives;
But though the whole world turn to coal,
    Then chiefly lives.

Guide Questions

1. "Virtue" has particularly brilliant architectonics. Analyze its structure and explain the particular ordering of the four stanzas. Might the order of the first three be changed? What is their logic of progression?

2. Study the repetition of the word "sweet" in the poem. Is it overused? What criteria would you use for judging this? Does the word increment or increase in meaning as the poem progresses?

3. Study the last line of each stanza. Comment on the length and effectiveness of this line.

4. How appropriate is the personification of the dew? Of the rose?

5. By what logic is the rose called "angry and brave"?

6. Explain the meaning of the line, "Thy root is ever in its grave."

7. How effective is the comparison of the spring to a box of chocolates? Is this image far-fetched in itself or in the poem? Why, or why not?

8. Note the dramatic reversal in the last stanza. How effective is the comparison of a "sweet and virtuous soul" to "seasoned timber"?

9. Compare the theme of "Virtue" with that of John Donne's "Holy Sonnet X."

from ESSAY ON MAN
Epistle II

Alexander Pope

Know then thyself, presume not God to scan;
The proper study of Mankind is Man.
Placed on this isthmus of a middle state,
A Being darkly wise, and rudely great:
With too much knowledge for the Sceptic side,
With too much weakness for the Stoic's pride,
He hangs between; in doubt to act, or rest;
In doubt to deem himself a God, or Beast;
In doubt his Mind or Body to prefer;
Born but to die, and reas'ning but to err;
Alike in ignorance, his reason such,
Whether he thinks too little, or too much:
Chaos of Thought and Passion, all confused;
Still by himself abused, or disabused;
Created half to rise, and half to fall;
Great lord of all things, yet a prey to all;
Sole judge of Truth, in endless Error hurled:
The glory, jest, and riddle of the world!

Guide Questions

1. Note the continual use of paradox throughout this passage. In what way does its use reflect Pope's theme?

2. Analyze the structure of individual lines and pairs of lines. Describe Pope's pattern of stating the nature of man.

3. Explain the third line.

4. Why does Pope call man "darkly wise" and "rudely great"? Explain how man might have too much knowledge to be a *sceptic,* and too much weakness to be a *stoic.* Define the italicized terms.

5. Analyze the last line of this passage. How does it reflect the paradoxical condition of man, according to Pope? Need Pope's view of man necessarily be negative or nihilistic?

THE TYGER

William Blake

Tyger! Tyger! burning bright
In the forests of the night,
What immortal hand or eye
Could frame thy fearful symmetry?

In what distant deeps or skies
Burnt the fire of thine eyes?
On what wings dare he aspire?
What the hand dare seize the fire?

And what shoulder, and what art,
Could twist the sinews of thy heart?
And when thy heart began to beat,
What dread hand? and what dread feet?

What the hammer? what the chain?
In what furnace was thy brain?
What the anvil? what dread grasp
Dare its deadly terrors clasp?

When the stars threw down their spears,
And water'd heaven with their tears,
Did He smile his work to see?
Did He who made the Lamb make thee?

Tyger! Tyger! burning bright
In the forests of the night,
What immortal hand or eye
Dare frame thy fearful symmetry?

Guide Questions

1. First read the poem through closely to determine its tone. What is the effect of so many questions? What are the dominant images in the poem?

2. Study the meter and the rhyme scheme. Do they in any way contribute to the tone?

3. Is this poem about a real tiger? What lines support your interpretation? If the Tyger is a symbol, what might it symbolize?

4. Note the implied comparison of the Tyger to the Lamb in the last line of stanza five. What religious connotations has this comparison? What might the Lamb symbolize?

5. Do you find any evidence of irony in the poem?

6. Do the lines "When the stars threw down their spears, / And water'd heaven with their tears," make reference to a particular event?

7. Why does the last stanza repeat the first? What change has been made? Why?

COMPOSED UPON WESTMINSTER BRIDGE

William Wordsworth

Earth has not anything to show more fair:
Dull would be he of soul who could pass by
A sight so touching in its majesty:
This city now doth, like a garment, wear
The beauty of the morning; silent, bare,
Ships, towers, domes, theatres, and temples lie
Open unto the fields, and to the sky;
All bright and glittering in the smokeless air.
Never did sun more beautifully steep
In his first splendour, valley, rock, or hill;
Ne'er saw I, never felt, a calm so deep!
The river glideth at his own sweet will:
Dear God! the very houses seem asleep;
And all that mighty heart is lying still.

Guide Questions

1. It is helpful to know before beginning this poem that Wordsworth wrote chiefly in praise of the natural world. What is being compared throughout this poem? (Westminster Bridge spans the Thames River in London.) What is the purpose of the comparison? Is it maintained throughout the poem?

2. Why does Wordsworth use the image of a "garment" in the fourth line?

3. What is implied by the phrase "smokeless air"?

4. What effect has the personification (attributing human qualities to inanimate things) of the houses and the city in the last two lines?

5. At what time of day does the poet write this poem? Is his appreciation of the city dependent upon this?

6. Fully describe the feelings of the poet at the time he wrote this poem. How accurately does he communicate them?

ON FIRST LOOKING INTO CHAPMAN'S HOMER

John Keats

Much have I travell'd in the realms of gold,
　　And many goodly states and kingdoms seen;
　　Round many western islands have I been
Which bards in fealty to Apollo hold.
Oft of one wide expanse had I been told
　　That deep-brow'd Homer ruled as his demesne;
　　Yet did I never breathe its pure serene
Till I heard Chapman speak out loud and bold:
Then felt I like some watcher of the skies
　　When a new planet swims into his ken;
Or like stout Cortez when with eagle eyes
　　He star'd at the Pacific — and all his men
Looked at each other with a wild surmise —
　　Silent, upon a peak in Darien.

Guide Questions

1. Keats wrote this sonnet one night after reading the translation of Homer's *Iliad* and *Odyssey* by George Chapman (1559–1634). It is important to note that Keats had read Alexander Pope's translations from Homer earlier, and that thus Homer's "world" was already familiar to him. How does the last fact help to explain the first line of the poem? Would it be possible to know of Keats's prior reading of Homer without such information?

2. This poem is particularly rich in figures of speech. What is being compared in lines 1–4? What figure of speech is this extended image? Explain the phrases "realms of gold" and "western islands."

3. Each word in a poem must be thoroughly understood if you are to understand its meaning. What are the meanings of each of the following words, and how are they used in the poem: "bards," "fealty," "demesne," "ken," "Apollo," and "surmise"?

4. How appropriate is the simile in which Keats compares himself to an astronomer?

5. How appropriate is the comparison to an explorer? Does it injure your appreciation of the poem to learn that Keats mistook Cortez for Balboa?

6. How would you describe the reaction of the men upon discovering the Pacific? Explain the phrase "wild surmise."

7. What is the theme of "On First Looking into Chapman's Homer"?

MY LAST DUCHESS

Robert Browning

Ferrara

That's my last Duchess painted on the wall,
Looking as if she were alive. I call
That piece a wonder, now: Frà Pandolf's hands
Worked busily a day, and there she stands.
Will't please you sit and look at her? I said
"Frà Pandolf" by design, for never read
Strangers like you that pictured countenance,
The depth and passion of its earnest glance,
But to myself they turned (since none puts by
The curtain I have drawn for you, but I)
And seemed as they would ask me, if they durst,
How such a glance came there; so, not the first
Are you to turn and ask thus. Sir, 'twas not
Her husband's presence only, called that spot
Of joy into the Duchess' cheek: perhaps
Frà Pandolf chanced to say, "Her mantle laps
Over my lady's wrist too much," or "Paint
Must never hope to reproduce the faint
Half-flush that dies along her throat": such stuff
Was courtesy, she thought, and cause enough
For calling up that spot of joy. She had
A heart—how shall I say?—too soon made glad.
Too easily impressed: she liked whate'er
She looked on, and her looks went everywhere.
Sir, 'twas all one! My favour at her breast,
The dropping of the daylight in the West,
The bough of cherries some officious fool
Broke in the orchard for her, the white mule
She rode with round the terrace—all and each
Would draw from her alike the approving speech,
Or blush, at least. She thanked men,—good! but thanked
Somehow—I know not how—as if she ranked
My gift of a nine-hundred-years-old name
With anybody's gift. Who'd stoop to blame
This sort of trifling? Even had you skill
In speech—(which I have not)—to make your will
Quite clear to such an one, and say, "Just this
Or that in you disgusts me; here you miss,
Or there exceed the mark"—and if she let
Herself be lessoned so, nor plainly set
Her wits to yours, forsooth, and made excuse,
—E'en then would be some stooping, and I choose
Never to stoop. Oh Sir, she smiled, no doubt,
Whene'er I passed her; but who passed without
Much the same smile? This grew; I gave commands;
Then all smiles stopped together. There she stands
As if alive. Will't please you rise? We'll meet
The company below, then. I repeat,
The Count your master's known munificence
Is ample warrant that no just pretence
Of mine for dowry will be disallowed;
Though his fair daughter's self, as I avowed
At starting, is my object. Nay, we'll go
Together down, sir! Notice Neptune, though,
Taming a sea-horse, thought a rarity,
Which Claus of Innsbruck cast in bronze for me!

Guide Questions

1. This poem is a dramatic monologue. It is not delivered by the poet himself but by a character whom he has created. Through his monologue this person will reveal his own character and incidents which previously took place. Who is the speaker? To whom is he speaking? Which lines tell you this?

2. With what tone does the narrator speak? Does this tone differ from the author's?

3. Why does the speaker repeat that the figure in the painting looks so much as if she were alive?

4. What is revealed by the fact that only the speaker can draw the curtain which usually covers the painting? How does this hint at his character?

5. What was the character of the woman whose portrait is being observed? Be careful: the description and the interpretation of her character are not given by Browning but by the speaker; his may not be an objective view. Analyze the lady's actions carefully. Was she a flirt? Was she an innocent young girl? Was she in any way indiscreet?

6. What has happened to her? How do you know?

7. Why does the speaker disclose so much information about himself and the woman whose portrait he is speaking about?

8. Compare the technique of this poem to that in "Ulysses." In which poem is the emphasis on character? In which on ideas?

ULYSSES

Alfred, Lord Tennyson

It little profits that an idle king,
By this still hearth, among these barren crags,
Match'd with an aged wife, I mete and dole
Unequal laws unto a savage race,
That hoard, and sleep, and feed, and know not me.
I cannot rest from travel: I will drink
Life to the lees: all times I have enjoy'd
Greatly, have suffer'd greatly, both with those
That loved me, and alone; on shore, and when
Thro' scudding drifts the rainy Hyades
Vext the dim sea: I am become a name;
For always roaming with a hungry heart
Much have I seen and known,—cities of men
And manners, climates, councils, governments,
Myself not least, but honour'd of them all,—
And drunk delight of battle with my peers,
Far on the ringing plains of windy Troy.
I am a part of all that I have met;
Yet all experience is an arch wherethro'
Gleams that untravell'd world, whose margin fades
For ever and for ever when I move.
How dull it is to pause, to make an end,
To rust unburnish'd, not to shine in use!
As tho' to breathe were life. Life piled on life
Were all too little, and of one to me
Little remains: but every hour is saved
From that eternal silence, something more,
A bringer of new things; and vile it were
For some three suns to store and hoard myself,
And this gray spirit yearning in desire
To follow knowledge like a sinking star,
Beyond the utmost bound of human thought.
    This is my son, mine own Telemachus,
To whom I leave the sceptre and the isle,—
Well-loved of me, discerning to fulfil

This labour, by slow prudence to make mild
A rugged people, and thro' soft degrees
Subdue them to the useful and the good.
Most blameless is he, centred in the sphere
Of common duties, decent not to fail
In offices of tenderness, and pay
Meet adoration to my household gods,
When I am gone. He works his work, I mine.
    There lies the port; the vessel puffs her sail:
There gloom the dark, broad seas. My mariners,
Souls that have toil'd, and wrought, and thought with me,—
That ever with a frolic welcome took
The thunder and the sunshine, and opposed
Free hearts, free foreheads,—you and I are old;
Old age hath yet his honour and his toil;
Death closes all: but something ere the end,
Some work of noble note, may yet be done,
Not unbecoming men that strove with Gods.
The lights begin to twinkle from the rocks;
The long day wanes; the slow moon climbs; the deep
Moans round with many voices. Come, my friends,
'Tis not too late to seek a newer world.
Push off, and sitting well in order smite
The sounding furrows; for my purpose holds
To sail beyond the sunset, and the baths
Of all the western stars, until I die.
It may be that the gulfs will wash us down:
It may be we shall touch the Happy Isles,
And see the great Achilles, whom we knew.
Tho' much is taken, much abides; and tho'
We are not now that strength which in old days
Moved earth and heaven, that which we are, we are,—
One equal temper of heroic hearts,
Made weak by time and fate, but strong in will
To strive, to seek, to find, and not to yield.

Guide Questions

1. Look up the legend of Ulysses in the library and place this poem in its setting after the hero's adventures and return home.

2. To what is the present condition of frustration due, as revealed by Ulysses in the opening lines? What is the greater contributor to his unrest: his home life or his ambition?

3. a. What to Ulysses is the essence of life?

   b. What is his attitude toward sailors?

   c. How is the life of Telemachus in marked contrast to that which Ulysses desires? Consider other contrasts in the poem (for example, words like "dim" and "gleams").

   d. Do such contrasts aid you in coming to terms with the total effect of the poem?

4. Though the world has changed much since Ulysses' time, is this poem contemporary? Does it have any application to modern life?

5. What is Ulysses' view of death?

6. What is the emotional effect of this poem on the reader? Does it prompt you to meditate upon your life to this point, to see its joys, sorrows, its unfilled ideals? Do you gain strength from reading this poem?

7. The first three lines of this poem reveal that an old man is speaking. In fact the poem is the reflection of the aged Ulysses upon his past life. Compare in terms of attitude, setting, and language three other poems whose points of view are those of old men. Suggested poems are the Old English "The Seafarer," T. S. Eliot's "Gerontion," and William Butler Yeats' "Among School Children."

8. In *The Poem: A Critical Anthology,* Josephine Miles comments that "Poetry is the art of language by line." Does this quotation apply to "Ulysses"?

BECAUSE I COULD NOT STOP
FOR DEATH*

Emily Dickinson

Because I could not stop for Death —
He kindly stopped for me —
The Carriage held but just Ourselves —
And Immortality.

We slowly drove — He knew no haste
And I had put away
My labor and my leisure too,
For His Civility —

We passed the School, where Children strove
At Recess — in the Ring —
We passed the Fields of Gazing Grain —
We passed the Setting Sun —

Or rather — He passed Us —
The Dews drew quivering and chill —
For only Gossamer, my Gown —
My Tippet — only Tulle —

We paused before a House that seemed
A Swelling of the Ground —
The Roof was scarcely visible —
The Cornice — in the Ground —

Since then — 'tis Centuries — and yet
Feels shorter than the Day
I first surmised the Horses Heads
Were toward Eternity —

Guide Questions

1. How does the poet envision Death? What is different about this view? What is its effect on the reader?

2. Time and timelessness are important elements in this poem. Specifically discuss their significance to the poet's meaning.

3. What does the "House" represent? How does its introduction in the poem affect the meaning?

4. Do you see any relationship between the visual image "Horses Heads" in the last stanza and that of the "Carriage" in the first? Relate to poet's choice of word "surmised."

* From *The Poems of Emily Dickinson,* ed. Thomas H. Johnson (The Belknap Press of Harvard University Press). Copyright 1951, 1955 by The President and Fellows of Harvard College. By permission of the publishers.

5. The diction in this poem is simple, unaffected, and concise. Explain how it contributes to making the poem a personal and universal statement of human experience.

6. What are the dramatic qualities of the poem?

7. This poem often appears in anthologies of poetry under the title "The Chariot." Relate the symbolism of this title to the poet's handling of the subject.

8. Explain the meaning of the third stanza.

9. Explain the reference to "Gossamer" and "Tulle." What do they add to the poem?

10. Compare this poem with Shakespeare's "Sonnet Eighteen."

11. Allen Tate calls this poem "one of the most perfect in the English language," but Yvor Winters disagrees. What is your reaction to the poem?

RICHARD CORY*

Edwin Arlington Robinson

Whenever Richard Cory went down town,
We people on the pavement looked at him;
He was a gentleman from sole to crown,
Clean favored, and imperially slim.

And he was always quietly arrayed,
And he was always human when he talked;
But still he fluttered pulses when he said,
"Good-morning," and he glittered when he walked.

And he was rich—yes, richer than a king—
And admirably schooled in every grace:
In fine, we thought that he was everything
To make us wish that we were in his place.

So on we worked, and waited for the light,
And went without the meat, and cursed the bread;
And Richard Cory, one calm summer night,
Went home and put a bullet through his head.

Guide Questions

1. Notice the tense of the verb throughout the poem. Does this aspect of the poem foreshadow the death of Richard Cory?

2. There are three suggestions of Cory's regal qualities. What are they?

3. Explain the contrast between "he was always quietly arrayed" and "he glittered when he walked."

4. a. How do we recognize Richard Cory as a man of taste and inner sensitivity?

   b. Does his suicide indicate the difficulty of such a man to adjust to twentieth-century life as you know it?

5. Does the poem leave you with the feeling that the "light" of the last stanza will ever come for the poor laborers?

* Reprinted with the permission of Charles Scribner's Sons from *The Children of the Night* by Edward Arlington Robinson, 1897.

6. Although this poem is close to prose in its narrative technique, rendering it or paraphrasing it in prose changes it. How would a newspaper account of Cory's death contrast with the lyrical version?

7. The genius of Robinson as a poet lies in his insight into the paradoxes of life and his ability to express them in precise language. How does the poem support this statement?

MUSÉE DES BEAUX ARTS*

W. H. Auden

About suffering they were never wrong,
The Old Masters: how well they understood
Its human position; how it takes place
While someone else is eating or opening a window or just
    walking dully along;
How, when the aged are reverently, passionately waiting
For the miraculous birth, there always must be
Children who did not specially want it to happen, skating
On a pond at the edge of the wood:
They never forgot
That even the dreadful martyrdom must run its course
Anyhow in a corner, some untidy spot
Where the dogs go on with their doggy life and the torturer's horse
Scratches its innocent behind on a tree.

In Brueghel's *Icarus,* for instance: how everything turns
    away
Quite leisurely from the disaster; the ploughman may
Have heard the splash, the forsaken cry,
But for him it was not an important failure; the sun shone
As it had to on the white legs disappearing into the green
Water; and the expensive delicate ship that must have
    seen
Something amazing, a boy falling out of the sky,
Had somewhere to get to and sailed calmly on.

Guide Questions

1. Explain the title of the poem.

2. Who are the "Old Masters" referred to in the second line? Who is Brueghel? What is the mythological story of Icarus? Before you do research on Brueghel and Icarus, what art form would you assume — from the last image of the poem — is referred to?

3. Analyze the diction and imagery of the poem. Is it appropriate? In what ways might "doggy life" and "innocent behind" — images that seem unpoetic — be fitting here?

4. What is the "it" referred to twice in the third line? Does this work take on more meanings as the poem progresses? What is the importance of the fact that "it" takes place "while someone else is eating or opening a window or just walking dully along"?

5. Explain "miraculous birth." Why was the image stated in these terms?

6. In what way, and for what purpose, does Auden contrast the aged with children?

7. Explain the image of the "torturer's horse."

8. How does the description of Brueghel's *Icarus* coincide with the previous images in this poem, and how does it finally reveal the theme?

DESERT PLACES*

Robert Frost

Snow falling and night falling fast, oh, fast
In a field I looked into going past,
And the ground almost covered smooth in snow,
But a few weeds and stubble showing last.

The woods around it have it — it is theirs,
All animals are smothered in their lairs.
I am too absent-spirited to count:
The loneliness includes me unawares.

And lonely as it is, that loneliness
Will be more lonely ere it will be less,
A blanker whiteness of benighted snow,
With no expression — nothing to express.

They cannot scare me with their empty spaces
Between stars — on stars void of human races.
I have it in me so much nearer home
To scare myself with my own desert places.

Guide Questions

1. Describe the circumstances of this poem and their relationship to the speaker.

2. What is the meaning of the line "that loneliness will be more lonely ere it will be less"?

3. Explain the double reference to the snow as "benighted" and relate to the meaning of the poem.

4. What is the comparison the observer makes between one's inner self and one's outer world? Relate to title.

5. Who is "They" in the fourth stanza?

6. Compare modern scientific theories with the poet's "on stars void of human races."

7. How does the last stanza influence the reader with its abrupt change of mood?

8. Note the repetition of the words in the poem. What effect does the poet achieve?

9. Comment on the repetition of the word "scare."

10. What would happen to the meaning of the poem if a stanza were omitted?

IN JUST-SPRING*

E. E. Cummings

in Just-
spring   when the world is mud-
luscious the little
lame balloonman

whistles   far   and wee

and eddieandbill come
running from marbles and
piracies and it's
spring

when the world is puddle-wonderful

the queer
old balloonman whistles
far   and   wee
and bettyandisbel come dancing

from hop-scotch and jump-rope and

it's
spring
and
   the

          goat-footed

    balloonMan   whistles
far
and
wee

Guide Questions

1. Comment on the poet's juxtaposition of unusual word images with hyphens like "puddle-wonderful," "mud-luscious," "goat-footed."

2. a. Explain the "wee" in the poem, its unexpectedness at the end of its line.

    b. What word would we normally expect to complete "far and _____"?

    c. What is the effect of the "wee" hanging in the air at the very end?

3. The pictures of spring are simple: the theme is easily understood. Yet there is here the freshness and lyricism of delightful poetry. What are the ingredients of this freshness?

4. How do the eccentricities of the typography enhance the effect of the poem: the world as seen through the eyes of a child?

5. The poem is built up in virtually three groups of almost parallel constructions beginning with the phrase about spring. What is the function of this arrangement or structure?

6. It might be interesting for you to conceive of a poem that Cummings might write based on the coming of spring in the life of an adult. What details might he set forth in contrast to those of a child?

7. Much medieval and modern poetry uses symbolic reference, that is, the naming of some object of sense which stands for something less definable either by convention or content. Could "the balloonman" of this poem be symbolic?

THIS RENASCENT TIME*

Lewis H. Fenderson

There will be a sentient time
When blind rub eyes and see;
The century-quieted mute, slowly at first
As war young in an alien land,
Will touch stiff tongues to lips, dampen,
Speak small words mellifluous as music.
Delirious time!
The unheeding deaf
No longer haunting faces for a sign
Will hear all awesome sounds,
Birds chirp, the din of joy.
For the restrained,
Time of silenced invective, wrist links freed;
Faltering steps transmuting fear to courage
Will strengthen at a festival of new experience —
Blurred, whirling time!
Canticle time for cripples will it be;
The blemished, spastic, agonized,
Renewed will creep from hiding, seemly then,
Extend a virgin hand to fraternize,
A chastening time.
There will the horde wait, each an entity
Whole as the first man in the pristine clime
Nor wiser nor more spiritual, only rapturous
This renascent time.

Guide Questions

1. a. Name at least five groups who will be rejuvenated with the coming of this time.

   b. Is this a utopian time or an actual one?

2. How does the poet regard experiences we take for granted?

3. Who is "the first man in the pristine clime"?

4. Select the phrases parallel with "This renascent time." Point out the fitness of each phrase for the group described.

* From the *Howard University Magazine*, Jan., 1964.

5. The poet is careful in his choice of words: "*sentient* time," "*small* words *mellifluous* as music," "the *din* of joy," "a *festival* of new experience," "*Canticle* time for cripples." Define each italicized word.

6. a. Is the mood of the poem a depressing or a joyous one?

   b. Point out phrases to characterize the mood.

7. How does the poet create, by words, sympathy for the handicapped of the earth?

8. Although the poet might not wish this work to be described as a "poem of spring," would it be appropriate to designate it as such? On what grounds?

DRAMA

The major difference between the drama and all other forms of literature is that it is written to be enacted upon the stage and is governed by the laws of dramatic presentation. All other differences will stem from this one. A play may be written in poetry, as are most of Shakespeare's plays, or in prose, as are Ibsen's and most others in the modern period; but the final test of its success must always be how it appears on the stage.

The lyric poet does not necessarily create character, and when he does, it need not be through dialogue; the prose writer will resort to frequent description or narration. The dramatist, though, must rely almost wholly upon dialogue and direct action to evoke his response. The drama exists only in the present: it is "happening" as you see it. Though some modern playwrights—like Arthur Miller in *Death of a Salesman*—employ the flashback, the action remains immediate to the viewer. The poet, novelist, or short story writer usually writes as if the action has already occurred; he uses the past tense or the historical present.

But though the play is written to be seen, it can be read—with the aid of stage directions and a projection of the reader via his imagination into the theatre—with great delight. Drama has perhaps more immediacy than the other forms of literature: its success is not to be found solely or separately in the beauty of its language, its capacity to render a mood, or in its vivid character portrayal, but in the dramatic confrontations of characters in action.

ILE*

Eugene O'Neill

CHARACTERS

BEN, the cabin boy
THE STEWARD
CAPTAIN KEENEY
SLOCUM, second mate
MRS. KEENEY
JOE, a harpooner
Members of the crew of the
steam whaler *Atlantic Queen*

Scene. Captain Keeney's cabin on board the steam whaling ship *Atlantic Queen*—a small, square compartment about eight feet high with a skylight in the center looking out on the poop deck. On the left (the stern of the ship) a long bench

* From *The Long Voyage Home: Seven Plays of the Sea* by Eugene O'Neill. Copyright 1919 and renewed 1946 by Eugene O'Neill. Reprinted by permission of Random House, Inc.

with rough cushions is built in against the wall. In front of the bench, a table. Over the bench, several curtained portholes.

In the rear, left, a door leading to the Captain's sleeping quarters. To the right of the door a small organ, looking as if it were brand new, is placed against the wall.

On the right, to the rear, a marble-topped sideboard. On the sideboard, a woman's sewing basket. Farther forward, a doorway leading to the companionway; and past the officers' quarters to the main deck.

In the center of the room, a stove. From the middle of the ceiling a hanging lamp is suspended. The walls of the cabin are painted white.

There is no rolling of the ship, and the light which comes through the skylight is sickly and faint, indicating one of those gray days of calm when ocean and sky are alike dead. The silence is unbroken except for the measured tread of someone walking up and down on the poop deck overhead.

It is nearing two bells—one o'clock—in the afternoon of a day in the year 1895.

At the rise of the curtain there is a moment of intense silence. Then the Steward enters and commences to clear the table of the few dishes which still remain on it after the Captain's dinner. He is an old, grizzled man dressed in dungaree pants, a sweater, and a woolen cap with earflaps. His manner is sullen and angry. He stops stacking up the plates and casts a quick glance upward at the skylight; then tiptoes over to the closed door in rear and listens with his ear pressed to the crack. What he hears makes his face darken and he mutters a furious curse. There is a noise from the doorway on the right and he darts back to the table.

Ben enters. He is an overgrown, gawky boy with a long, pinched face. He is dressed in sweater, fur cap, etc. His teeth are chattering with the cold and he hurries to the stove, where he stands for a moment shivering, blowing on his hands, slapping them against his sides, on the verge of crying.

THE STEWARD: (*In relieved tones—seeing who it is*) Oh, 'tis you, is it? What're ye shiverin' 'bout? Stay by the stove where ye belong and ye'll find no need of chatterin'.

BEN: It's c-c-cold. (*Trying to control his chattering teeth—derisively*) Who d'ye think it were—the Old Man?

THE STEWARD: (*Makes a threatening move—Ben shrinks away*) None o' your lip, young un, or I'll learn ye. (*More kindly*) Where was it ye've been all o' the time—the fo'c's'tle?

BEN: Yes.

THE STEWARD: Let the Old Man see ye up for'ard monkeyshinin' with the hands and ye'll get a hidin' ye'll not forget in a hurry.

BEN: Aw, he don't see nothin'. (*A trace of awe in his tones—he glances upward*) He just walks up and down like he didn't notice nobody—and stares at the ice to the no'the'ard.

THE STEWARD: (*The same tone of awe creeping into his voice*) He's always starin' at the ice. (*In a sudden rage, shaking his fist at the skylight*) Ice, ice, ice! Damn him and damn the ice! Holdin' us in for nigh on a year—nothin' to see but ice—stuck in it like a fly in molasses!

BEN: (*Apprehensively*) Ssshh! He'll hear ye.

THE STEWARD: (*Raging*) Aye, damn him, and damn the Arctic seas, and damn this stinkin' whalin' ship of his, and damn me for a fool to ever ship on it! (*Subsiding as if realizing the uselessness of this outburst—shaking his head—slowly, with deep conviction*) He's a hard man—as hard a man as ever sailed the seas.

BEN: (*Solemnly*) Aye.

THE STEWARD: The two years we all signed up for are done this day. Blessed Christ! Two years o' this dog's life, and no luck in the fishin', and the hands half starved with the food runnin' low, rotten as it is; and not a sign of him turnin' back for home! (*Bitterly*) Home! I begin to doubt if ever I'll set foot on land again. (*Excitedly*) What is it he thinks he's goin' to do? Keep us all up here after our time is worked out till the last man of us is starved to death or frozen? We've grub enough hardly to last out the voyage back if we started now. What are the men goin' to do 'bout it? Did ye hear any talk in the fo'c's'tle?

BEN: (*Going over to him—in a half-whisper*) They said if he don't put back south for home today they're goin' to mutiny.

THE STEWARD: (*With grim satisfaction*) Mutiny? Aye, 'tis the only thing they can do; and serve him right after the manner he's treated them—'s if they weren't no better nor dogs.

BEN: The ice is all broke up to s'uth'ard. They's clear water's far 's you can see.

He ain't got no excuse for not turnin' back for home, the men says.

THE STEWARD: (*Bitterly*) He won't look nowheres but no'the'ard where they's only the ice to see. He don't want to see no clear water. All he thinks on is gittin' the ile—'s if it was our fault he ain't had good luck with the whales. (*Shaking his head*) I think the man's mighty nigh losin' his senses.

BEN: (*Awed*) D'you really think he's crazy?

THE STEWARD: Aye, it's the punishment o' God on him. Did ye ever hear of a man who wasn't crazy do the things he does? (*Pointing to the door in rear*) Who but a man that's mad would take his woman—and as sweet a woman as ever was—on a stinkin' whalin' ship to the Arctic seas to be locked in by the rotten ice for nigh on a year, and maybe lose her senses forever—for it's sure she'll never be the same again.

BEN: (*Sadly*) She useter be awful nice to me before—(*His eyes grow wide and frightened*)—she got—like she is.

THE STEWARD: Aye, she was good to all of us. 'Twould have been hell on board without her; for he's a hard man—a hard, hard man—a driver if there ever was one. (*With a grim laugh*) I hope he's satisfied now—drivin' her on till she's near lost her mind. And who could blame her? 'Tis a God's wonder we're not a ship full of crazed people—with the damned ice all the time, and the quiet so thick you're afraid to hear your own voice.

BEN: (*With a frightened glance toward the door on right*) She don't never speak to me no more—jest looks at me 's if she didn't know me.

THE STEWARD: She don't know no one—but him. She talks to him—when she does talk—right enough.

BEN: She does nothin' all day long now but sit and sew—and then she cries to herself without makin' no noise. I've seen her.

THE STEWARD: Aye, I could hear her through the door a while back.

BEN: (*Tiptoes over to the door and listens*) She's cryin' now.

THE STEWARD: (*Furiously—shaking his fist*) God send his soul to hell for the devil he is! (*There *is the noise of some one coming slowly down the companionway stairs. The Steward hurries to his stacked-up dishes. He is so nervous from fright that he knocks off the top one, which falls and breaks on the floor. He stands aghast, trembling with dread. Ben is violently rubbing off the organ with a piece of cloth which he has snatched from his pocket. Captain Keeney appears in the doorway on right and comes into the cabin, removing his fur cap as he does so. He is a man of about forty, around five-ten in height but looking much shorter on account of the enormous proportions of his shoulders and chest. His face is massive and deeply lined, with gray-blue eyes of a bleak hardness, and a tightly clenched, thin-lipped mouth. His thick hair is long and gray. He is dressed in a heavy blue jacket and blue pants stuffed into his sea-boots. He is followed into the cabin by the Second Mate, a rangy six-footer with a lean weather-beaten face. The Mate is dressed about the same as the Captain. He is a man of thirty or so.)*

KEENEY: *(Comes toward the Steward—with a stern look on his face. The Steward is visibly frightened and the stack of dishes rattles in his trembling hands. Keeney draws back his fist and the Steward shrinks away. The fist is gradually lowered and Keeney speaks slowly.)* 'Twould be like hitting a worm. It is nigh on two bells, Mr. Steward, and this truck not cleared yet.

THE STEWARD: *(Stammering)* Y-y-yes, sir.

KEENEY: Instead of doin' your rightful work ye've been below here gossipin' old woman's talk with that boy. *(To Ben, fiercely)* Get out o' this, you! Clean up the chart room. *(Ben darts past the Mate to the open doorway.)* Pick up that dish, Mr. Steward!

THE STEWARD: *(Doing so with difficulty)* Yes, sir.

KEENEY: The next dish you break, Mr. Steward, you take a bath in the Bering Sea at the end of a rope.

THE STEWARD: *(Tremblingly)* Yes, sir. *(He hurries out. The Second Mate walks slowly over to Captain.)*

MATE: I warn't 'specially anxious the man at the wheel should catch what I wanted to say to you, sir. That's why I asked you to come below.

KEENEY: *(Impatiently)* Speak your say, Mr. Slocum.

MATE: *(Unconsciously lowering his voice)* I'm afeared there'll be trouble with the hands by the look o' things. They'll likely turn ugly, every blessed one o' them, if you don't put back. The two years they signed up for is up to-day.

KEENEY: And d'you think you're tellin' me somethin' new, Mr. Slocum? I've felt it in the air this long time past. D'you think I've not seen their ugly looks and the grudgin' way they worked? *(The door in rear is opened and Mrs. Keeney stands in the doorway. She is a slight, sweet-faced little woman primly dressed in black. Her eyes are red from weeping and her face drawn and pale. She takes in the cabin with a frightened glance and stands as if fixed to the spot by some nameless dread, clasping and unclasping her hands nervously. The two men turn and look at her.)*

KEENEY: *(With rough tenderness)* Well, Annie?

MRS. KEENEY: *(As if awakening from a dream)* David, I— *(She is silent. The Mate starts for the doorway.)*

KEENEY: *(Turning to him—sharply)* Wait!

MATE: Yes, sir.

KEENEY: D'you want anything, Annie?

MRS. KEENEY: *(After a pause, during which she seems to be endeavoring to collect her thoughts)* I thought maybe—I'd go up on deck, David, to get a breath of fresh air. *(She stands humbly awaiting his permission. He and the Mate exchange a significant glance)*

KEENEY: It's too cold, Annie. You'd best stay below to-day. There's nothing to look at on deck—but ice.

MRS. KEENEY: *(Monotonously)* I know—ice, ice, ice! But there's nothing to see down here but these walls. *(She makes a gesture of loathing)*

KEENEY: You can play the organ, Annie.

MRS. KEENEY: *(Dully)* I hate the organ. It puts me in mind of home.

KEENEY: *(A touch of resentment in his voice)* I got it just for you.

MRS. KEENEY: *(Dully)* I know. *(She turns away from them and walks slowly to the bench on left. She lifts up one of the curtains and looks through a porthole; then utters an exclamation of joy)* Ah, water! Clear water! As far as I can see! How good it looks after all these months of ice! *(She turns round to them, her face transfigured with joy)* Ah, now I must go up on deck and look at it, David.

KEENEY: *(Frowning)* Best not to-day, Annie. Best wait for a day when the sun shines.

MRS. KEENEY: *(Desperately)* But the sun never shines in this terrible place.

KEENEY: *(A tone of command in his voice)* Best not to-day, Annie.

MRS. KEENEY: *(Crumbling before this command—abjectly)* Very well, David. *(She stands there staring straight before her as if in a daze. The two men look at her uneasily)*

KEENEY: *(Sharply)* Annie!

MRS. KEENEY: *(Dully)* Yes, David.

KEENEY: Me and Mr. Slocum has business to talk about—ship's business.

MRS. KEENEY: Very well, David. *(She goes slowly out, rear, and leaves the door three-quarters shut behind her)*

KEENEY: Best not have her on deck if they's goin' to be any trouble.

MATE: Yes, sir.

KEENEY: And trouble they's going to be. I feel it in my bones. *(Takes a revolver from the pocket of his coat and examines it)* Got your'n?

MATE: Yes, sir.

KEENEY: Not that we'll have to use 'em—not if I know their breed of dog—jest to frighten 'em up a bit. *(Grimly)* I ain't never been forced to use one yit; and trouble I've had by land and by sea 's long as I ken remember, and will have till my dyin' day, I reckon.

MATE: *(Hesitatingly)* Then you ain't goin'—to turn back?

KEENEY: Turn back! Mr. Slocum, did you ever hear o' me pointin' s'uth for home with only a measly four hundred barrel of ile in the hold?

MATE: *(Hastily)* No, sir—but the grub's gettin' low.

KEENEY: They's enough to last a long time yit, if they're careful with it; and they's plenty o' water.

MATE: They say it's not fit to eat—what's left; and the two years they signed on fur is up to-day. They might make trouble for you in the courts when we git home.

KEENEY: To hell with 'em! Let them make what law trouble they kin. I don't give a damn 'bout the money. I've got to git the ile! *(Glancing sharply at the Mate)* You ain't turnin' no damned sea lawyer, be you, Mr. Slocum?

MATE: *(Flushing)* Not by a hell of a sight, sir.

KEENEY: What do the fools want to go home fur now? Their share o' the four hundred barrel wouldn't keep 'em in chewin' terbacco.

MATE: *(Slowly)* They wants to git back to their folks an' things, I s'pose.

KEENEY: *(Looking at him searchingly)* 'N you want to turn back, too. *(The Mate looks down confusedly before his sharp gaze)* Don't lie, Mr. Slocum. It's writ down plain in your eyes. *(With grim sarcasm)* I hope, Mr. Slocum, you ain't agoin' to jine the men agin me.

MATE: *(Indignantly)* That ain't fair, sir, to say sich things.

KEENEY: *(With satisfaction)* I warn't much afeard o' that, Tom. You been with me nigh on ten year and I've learned ye whalin'. No man kin say I ain't a good master, if I be a hard one.

MATE: I warn't thinkin' of myself, sir—'bout turnin' home, I mean. *(Desperately)* But Mrs. Keeney, sir—seems like she ain't jest satisfied up here, ailin' like—what with the cold an' bad luck an' the ice an' all.

KEENEY: *(His face clouding—rebukingly but not severely)* That's my business, Mr. Slocum. I'll thank you to steer a clear course o' that. *(A pause)* The ice'll break up soon to no'th'ard. I could see it startin' to-day. And when it goes and we git some sun, Annie'll perk up. *(Another pause—then he bursts forth)* It ain't the damned money what's keepin' me up in the Northern seas, Tom. But I can't go back to Homeport with a measly four hundred barrel of ile. I'd die fust. I ain't never come back home in all my days without a full ship. Ain't that truth?

MATE: Yes, sir, but this voyage you been ice-bound, an'—

KEENEY: *(Scornfully)* And d'you s'pose any of 'em would believe that—any o' them skippers I've beaten voyage after voyage? Can't you hear 'em laughin' and sneerin'—Tibbots 'n' Harris 'n' Simms and the rest—and all o' Homeport makin' fun o' me? "Dave Keeney what boasts he's the best whalin' skipper out o' Homeport comin' back with a measly four hundred barrel of ile?" *(The thought of this drives him into a frenzy, and he smashes his fist down on the marble top of the sideboard)* Hell! I got to git the ile, I tell you. How could I figger on this ice? It's never been so bad before in the thirty year I been acomin' here. And now it's breakin' up. In a couple o' days it'll be all gone. And they's whale here, plenty of 'em. I know they is and I ain't never gone wrong yit. I got to git the ile! I got to git it in spite of all hell, and by God, I ain't agoin' home till I do git it! *(There is the sound of subdued sobbing from the door in rear. The two men stand silent for a moment, listening. Then Keeney goes over to the door and looks in. He hesitates for a moment as if he were going to enter—then closes the door softly. Joe, the harpooner, an enormous six-footer with a battered, ugly face, enters from right and stands waiting for the Captain to notice him)*

KEENEY: *(Turning and seeing him)* Don't be standin' there like a gawk, Harpooner, speak up!

JOE: *(Confusedly)* We want—the men, sir— they wants to send a depitation aft to have a word with you.

KEENEY: *(Furiously)* Tell 'em to go to— *(Checks himself and continues grimly)* Tell 'em to come. I'll see 'em.

JOE: Aye, Aye, sir. *(He goes out)*

KEENEY: *(With a grim smile)* Here it comes, the trouble you spoke of, Mr. Slocum, and we'll make short shift of it. It's better to crush such things at the start than let them make headway.

MATE: *(Worriedly)* Shall I wake up the First and Fourth, sir? We might need their help.

KEENEY: No, let them sleep. I'm well able to handle this alone, Mr. Slocum. *(There is the shuffling of footsteps from outside and five of the crew crowd into the cabin, led by Joe. All are dressed alike— sweaters, sea-boots, etc. They glance uneasily at the Captain, twirling their fur caps in their hands)*

KEENEY: *(After a pause)* Well? Who's to speak fur ye?

JOE: *(Stepping forward with an air of bravado)* I be.

KEENEY: *(Eyeing him up and down coldly)* So you be. Then speak your say and be quick about it.

JOE: *(Trying not to wilt before the Captain's glance and avoiding his eyes)* The time we signed up for is done to-day.

KEENEY: *(Icily)* You're tellin' me nothin' I don't know.

JOE: You ain't pintin' fur home yit, far's we kin see.

KEENEY: No, and I ain't agoin' to till this ship is full of ile.

JOE: You can't go no further no'the with the ice afore ye.

KEENEY: The ice is breaking up.

JOE: *(After a slight pause during which the others mumble angrily to one another)* The grub we're gittin' now is rotten.

KEENEY: It's good enough fur ye. Better men than ye are have eaten worse. *(There is a chorus of angry exclamations from the crowd)*

JOE: *(Encouraged by this support)* We ain't agoin' to work no more less you puts back for home.

KEENEY: *(Fiercely)* You ain't, ain't you?

JOE: No; and the law courts'll say we was right.

KEENEY: To hell with your law courts! We're at sea now and I'm the law on this ship. *(Edging up toward the harpooner)* And every mother's son of you what don't obey orders goes in irons. *(There are more angry exclamations from the crew. Mrs. Keeney appears in the doorway in rear and looks on with startled eyes. None of the men notice her)*

JOE: *(With bravado)* Then we're a-goin to mutiny and take the old hooker home ourselves. Ain't we, boys? *(As he turns his head to look at the others, Keeney's fist shoots out to the side of his jaw. Joe goes down in a heap and lies there. Mrs. Keeney gives a shriek and hides her face in her hands. The men pull out their sheath knives and start a rush, but stop when they find themselves confronted by the revolvers of Keeney and the Mate)*

KEENEY: *(His eyes and voice snapping)* Hold still! *(The men stand huddled together in a sullen silence. Keeney's voice is full of mockery)* You've found out it ain't safe to mutiny on this ship, ain't you? And now git for'ard where ye belong, and— *(He gives Joe's body a contemptuous kick)* Drag him with you. And remember the first man of ye I see shirkin' I'll shoot dead as sure as there's a sea under us, and you can tell the rest the same. Git for'ard now! Quick! *(The men leave in cowed silence, carrying Joe with them. Keeney turns to the Mate with a short laugh and puts his revolver back in his pocket)* Best get up on deck, Mr. Slocum, and see to it they don't try none of their skulkin' tricks. We'll have to keep an eye peeled from now on. I know 'em.

MATE: Yes, sir. *(He goes out, right. Keeney hears his wife's hysterical weeping and turns around in surprise—then walks slowly to her side)*

KEENEY: *(Putting an arm around her shoulder— with gruff tenderness)* There, there, Annie. Don't be afeard. It's all past and gone.

MRS. KEENEY: *(Shrinking away from him)* Oh, I can't bear it! I can't bear it any longer!

KEENEY: *(Gently)* Can't bear what, Annie?

MRS. KEENEY: *(Hysterically)* All this horrible brutality, and these brutes of men, and this terrible ship, and this prison cell of a room, and the ice all around, and the silence. *(After this outburst she calms down and wipes her eyes with her handkerchief)*

KEENEY: *(After a pause during which he looks down at her with a puzzled frown)* Remember, I warn't hankerin' to have you come on this voyage, Annie.

MRS. KEENEY: I wanted to be with you, David, don't you see? I didn't want to wait back there in the house all alone as I've been doing these last six years since we were married—waiting, and watching, and fearing—with nothing to keep my mind occupied—not able to go back teaching school on account of being Dave Keeney's wife. I used to dream of sailing on the great, wide, glorious ocean. I wanted to be by your side in the danger and vigorous life of it all. I wanted to see you the hero they make you out to be in Homeport. And instead— *(Her voice grows tremulous)* All I find is ice and cold—and brutality! *(Her voice breaks)*

KEENEY: I warned you what it'd be, Annie. "Whalin' ain't no ladies' tea-party," I says to you, and "you better stay to home where you've got all your woman's comforts." *(Shaking his head)* But you was so set on it.

MRS. KEENEY: *(Wearily)* Oh, I know it isn't your fault, David. You see, I didn't believe you. I guess I was dreaming about the old Vikings in the storybooks and I thought you were one of them.

KEENEY: *(Protestingly)* I done my best to make it as cozy and comfortable as could be. *(Mrs. Keeney looks around her in wild scorn)* I even sent to the city for the organ for ye, thinkin' it might be soothin' to ye to be playin' it times when they was calms and things was dull like.

MRS. KEENEY: *(Wearily)* Yes, you were very kind, David. I know that. *(She goes to left and lifts the curtains from the porthole and looks out—then suddenly bursts forth:)* I won't stand it—I can't stand it —pent up by these walls like a prisoner. *(She runs over to him and throws her arms around him, weeping. He puts his arm protectingly over her shoulders)*

Take me away from here, David! If I don't get away from here, out of this terrible ship, I'll go mad! Take me home, David! I can't think any more. I feel as if the cold and the silence were crushing down on my brain. I'm afraid. Take me home!

KEENEY: *(Holds her at arm's length and looks at her face anxiously)* Best go to bed, Annie. You ain't yourself. You got fever. Your eyes look so strange like. I ain't never seen you look this way before.

MRS. KEENEY: *(Laughing hysterically)* It's the ice and the cold and the silence—they'd make anyone look strange.

KEENEY: *(Soothingly)* In a month or two, with good luck, three at the most, I'll have her filled with ile and then we'll give her everything she'll stand and pint for home.

MRS. KEENEY: But we can't wait for that—I can't wait. I want to get home. And the men won't wait. They want to get home. It's cruel, it's brutal for you to keep them. You must sail back. You've got no excuse. There's clear water to the south now. If you've a heart at all you've got to turn back.

KEENEY: *(Harshly)* I can't, Annie.

MRS. KEENEY: Why can't you?

KEENEY: A woman couldn't rightly understand my reason.

MRS. KEENEY: *(Wildly)* Because it's a stupid, stubborn reason. Oh, I heard you talking with the Second Mate. You're afraid the other captains will sneer at you because you didn't come back with a full ship. You want to live up to your silly reputation even if you have to beat and starve men and drive me mad to do it.

KEENEY: *(His jaw set stubbornly)* It ain't that, Annie. Them skippers would never dare sneer to my face. It ain't so much what anyone'd say—but— *(He hesitates, struggling to express his meaning)* You see—I've always done it—since my first voyage as skipper. I always come back—with a full ship—and—it don't seem right not to—somehow. I been always first whalin' skipper out

o' Homeport, and— Don't you see my meanin', Annie? *(He glances at her. She is not looking at him but staring dully in front of her, not hearing a word he is saying)* Annie! *(She comes to herself with a start)* Best turn in, Annie, there's a good woman. You ain't well.

MRS. KEENEY: *(Resisting his attempts to guide her to the door in rear)* David! won't you please turn back?

KEENEY: *(Gently)* I can't, Annie—not yet awhile. You don't see my meanin'. I got to git the ile.

MRS. KEENEY: It'd be different if you needed the money, but you don't. You've got more than plenty.

KEENEY: *(Impatiently)* It ain't the money I'm thinkin' of. D'you think I'm as mean as that?

MRS. KEENEY: *(Dully)* No—I don't know—I can't understand— *(Intensely)* Oh, I want to be home in the old house once more and see my own kitchen again, and hear a woman's voice talking to me and be able to talk to her. Two years! It seems so long ago—as if I'd been dead and could never go back.

KEENEY: *(Worried by her strange tone and the far-away look in her eyes)* Best go to bed, Annie. You ain't well.

MRS. KEENEY: *(Not appearing to hear him)* I used to be lonely when you were away. I used to think Homeport was a stupid, monotonous place. Then I used to go down on the beach, especially when it was windy and the breakers were rolling in, and I'd dream of the fine free life you must be leading. *(She gives a laugh which is half a sob)* I used to love the sea then. *(She pauses; then continues with slow intensity)* But now—I don't ever want to see the sea again.

KEENEY: *(Thinking to humor her)* 'Tis no fit place for a woman, that's sure. I was a fool to bring ye.

MRS. KEENEY: *(After a pause—passing her hand over her eyes with a gesture of pathetic weariness)* How long would it take us to reach home—if we started now?

KEENEY: *(Frowning)* 'Bout two months, I reckon, Annie, with fair luck.

MRS. KEENEY: (*Counts on her fingers—then murmurs with a rapt smile*) That would be August, the latter part of August, wouldn't it? It was on the twenty-fifth of August we were married, David, wasn't it?

KEENEY: (*Trying to conceal the fact that her memories have moved him—gruffly*) Don't *you* remember?

MRS. KEENEY: (*Vaguely—again passes her hand over her eyes*) My memory is leaving me—up here in the ice. It was so long ago. (*A pause—then she smiles dreamily*) It's June now. The lilacs will be all in bloom in the front yard—and the climbing roses on the trellis to the side of the house—they're budding. (*She suddenly covers her face with her hands and commences to sob*)

KEENEY: (*Disturbed*) Go in and rest, Annie. You're all wore out cryin' over what can't be helped.

MRS. KEENEY: (*Suddenly throwing her arms around his neck and clinging to him*) You love me, don't you, David?

KEENEY: (*In amazed embarrassment at this outburst*) Love you? Why d'you ask me such a question, Annie?

MRS. KEENEY: (*Shaking him—fiercely*) .But you do, don't you, David? Tell me!

KEENEY: I'm your husband, Annie, and you're my wife. Could there be aught but love between us after all these years?

MRS. KEENEY: (*Shaking him again—still more fiercely*) Then you do love me. Say it!

KEENEY: (*Simply*) I do, Annie!

MRS. KEENEY: (*Gives a sigh of relief—her hands drop to her sides. Keeney regards her anxiously. She passes her hand across her eyes and murmurs half to herself*) I sometimes think if we could only have had a child. (*Keeney turns away from her, deeply moved. She grabs his arm and turns him around to face her—intensely*) And I've always been a good wife to you, haven't I, David?

KEENEY: (*His voice betraying his emotion*) No man has ever had a better, Annie.

MRS. KEENEY: And I've never asked for much from you, have I, David? Have I?

KEENEY: You know you could have all I got the power to give ye, Annie.

MRS. KEENEY: (*Wildly*) Then do this this once for my sake, for God's sake—take me home! It's killing me, this life—the brutality and cold and horror of it. I'm going mad. I can feel the threat in the air. I can hear the silence threatening me—day after gray day and every day the same. I can't bear it. (*Sobbing*) I'll go mad, I know I will. Take me home, David, if you love me as you say. I'm afraid. For the love of God, take me home! (*She throws her arms around him, weeping against his shoulder. His face betrays the tremendous struggle going on within him. He holds her out at arm's length, his expression softening. For a moment his shoulders sag, he becomes old, his iron spirit weakens as he looks at her tear-stained face*)

KEENEY: (*Dragging out the words with an effort*) I'll do it, Annie—for your sake—if you say it's needful for ye.

MRS. KEENEY: (*With wild joy—kissing him*) God bless you for that, David! (*He turns away from her silently and walks toward the companionway. Just at that moment there is a clatter of footsteps on the stairs and the Second Mate enters the cabin*)

MATE: (*Excitedly*) The ice is breakin' up to no'the'ard, sir. There's a clear passage through the floe, and clear water beyond, the lookout says. (*Keeney straightens himself like a man coming out of a trance. Mrs. Keeney looks at the Mate with terrified eyes*)

KEENEY: (*Dazedly—trying to collect his thoughts*) A clear passage? To no'the'ard?

MATE: Yes, sir.

KEENEY: (*His voice suddenly grim with determination*) Then get her ready and we'll drive her through.

MATE: Aye, aye, sir.

MRS. KEENEY: (*Appealingly*) David!

KEENEY: (*Not heeding her*) Will the men turn to willin' or must we drag 'em out?

MATE: They'll turn to willin' enough. You put the fear o' God into 'em, sir. They're meek as lambs.

KEENEY: Then drive 'em—both watches. (*With grim determination*) They's whale t'other side o' this floe and we're going to git 'em.

MATE: Aye, aye, sir. (*He goes out hurriedly. A moment later there is the sound of scuffling feet from the deck outside and the Mate's voice shouting orders*)

KEENEY: (*Speaking aloud to himself—derisively*) And I was agoin' home like a yaller dog!

MRS. KEENEY: (*Imploringly*) David!

KEENEY: (*Sternly*) Woman, you ain't adoin' right when you meddle in men's business and weaken 'em. You can't know my feelin's. I got to prove a man to be a good husband for ye to take pride in. I got to git the ile, I tell ye.

MRS. KEENEY: (*Supplicatingly*) David! Aren't you going home?

KEENEY: (*Ignoring this question—commandingly*) You ain't well. Go and lay down a mite. (*He starts for the door*) I got to git on deck.

MRS. KEENEY: (*He goes out. She cries after him in anguish*) David! (*A pause. She passes her hand across her eyes—then commences to laugh hysterically and goes to the organ. She sits down and starts to play wildly an old hymn. Keeney re-enters from the doorway to the deck and stands looking at her angrily. He comes over and grabs her roughly by the shoulder*)

KEENEY: Woman, what foolish mockin' is this? (*She laughs wildly and he starts back from her in alarm*) Annie! What is it? (*She doesn't answer him. Keeney's voice trembles*) Don't you know me, Annie? (*He puts both hands on her shoulders and turns her around so that he can look into her eyes. She stares up at him with a stupid expression, a vague smile on her lips. He stumbles away from her, and she commences softly to play the organ again*)

KEENEY: (*Swallowing hard—in a hoarse whisper, as if he had difficulty in speaking*) You said—you was agoin' mad—God! (*A long wail is heard from the deck above*)

Ah Bl-o-o-o-ow! (*A moment later the Mate's face appears through the sky-light. He cannot see Mrs. Keeney*)

MATE: (*In great excitement*) Whales, sir—a whole school of 'em—off the starb'd quarter 'bout five miles away—big ones!

KEENEY: (*Galvanized into action*) Are you lowerin' the boats?

MATE: Yes, sir.

KEENEY: (*With grim decision*) I'm a-comin' with ye.

MATE: Aye, aye, sir. (*Jubilantly*) You'll git the ile now right enough, sir. (*His head is withdrawn and he can be heard shouting orders*)

KEENEY: (*Turning to his wife*) Annie! Did you hear him? I'll git the ile. (*She doesn't answer or seem to know he is there. He gives a hard laugh, which is almost a groan*) I know you're foolin' me, Annie. You ain't out of your mind—(*Anxiously*)—be you? I'll git the ile now right enough—jest a little while longer, Annie—then we'll turn hom'ard. I can't turn back now, you see that, don't ye? I've got to git the ile. (*In sudden terror*) Answer me! You ain't mad, be you? (*She keeps on playing the organ, but makes no reply. The Mate's face appears again through the skylight*)

MATE: All ready, sir. (*Keeney turns his back on his wife and strides to the doorway, where he stands for a moment and looks back at her in anguish, fighting to control his feelings*)

MATE: Comin', sir?

KEENEY: (*His face suddenly grown hard with determination*) Aye. (*He turns abruptly and goes out. Mrs. Keeney does not appear to notice his departure. Her whole attention seems centered in the organ. She sits with half-closed eyes, her body swaying a little from side to side to the rhythm of the hymn. Her fingers move faster and faster and she is playing wildly and discordantly as* THE CURTAIN FALLS)

Guide Questions on ILE

1. How does the Steward establish immediately the character of the Captain and the mood of the crew toward the leader?

2. a. Do you think the crew would be any more sympathetic to him if they knew his reason for delaying the return?   b. Is this really a good reason for delaying the voyage home?

3. Do you think a stronger woman than Mrs. Keeney would have succumbed to the situation?

4. How does Captain Keeney's physical appearance reaffirm his bulk, his ruthlessness, his ambition?

5. Despite Keeney's hardness, we catch a glimpse of his tenderness for his wife. Yet in his treatment of her, what signs does he give that he can't or won't comprehend her plight?

6. Captain Keeney does handle his men well in terms of recognizing their mood and of crushing their rebellion. Why does he have such contempt for them? For the law?

7. Was Mrs. Keeney an incurable romantic or a wife genuinely unwilling to be separated from her husband?

8. Do you think the Captain worked hard enough to discourage his wife from taking the trip, or did he undervalue the hardship she would endure?

9. What do you think is the true condition of Mrs. Keeney at the end—a temporary condition of madness or a permanent one?

10. Despite the Captain's hardness, do you feel pity or sympathy for his frustration, his desire to be a good husband, his putting oil before all else?

11. a. Which scene or scenes are the most dramatically constructed?

    b. Which could be most forcefully presented by the actors?

12. Do the stage directions help to establish an atmosphere which allows you to enter into the mood or feeling of the play? Explain.

13. a. Explain the differences in the levels of speech used by the characters.

    b. Does this difference indicate anything more about the characters?

14. In what ways is the play as a form different from the other forms of literature to which you have been exposed?

Chapter V

SPEED READING

INTRODUCTION

The selections presented on the following pages have been chosen for you to read as timed exercises. Of varying lengths (the shorter passages are first), these excerpts lend themselves to a quick perusal by the reader whose purpose is to understand the incident that is narrated.

Before you begin the practice readings, have available a clock which you can use for timing your reading of each selection. Pace yourself by following these suggestions:

1. Concentrate on picking out only the key words of each sentence. Group them as you move along a line of print.
2. Read to get the main idea of each passage.
3. Try to glean the meanings of unfamiliar words from their context.
4. Do not reread a sentence or pause to reflect until you have completed the entire selection.
5. Compete with yourself. Start each new exercise with the determination to read it at a faster rate than the preceding one.

After you finish reading each selection, jot down your reading time in the space provided at the end of the passage. Next, answer the comprehension and vocabulary questions without referring again to the text. Determine your rate of comprehension from the Table on pages 341–42. On the Performance Chart on pages 343–44, record your rate and, after your papers are returned, record your comprehension and vocabulary scores.

To encourage further progress, supplement your reading diet with this schedule: For thirty minutes each day, read a newspaper, magazine, or your favorite book of nonfiction as rapidly as you can. Follow the suggestions in the preceding paragraphs. Remember in your selection of speed-reading materials that wide spacing between lines, division of words into columns or short lines, and large letters or boldface print expedite the reading of both familiar and unfamiliar subjects. Do not sacrifice comprehension for speed, but try gradually to increase both. Adjust your rate according to your purpose and the type of material you have selected to read.

SPEED READING SELECTIONS

from THE LIFE OF SAMUEL JOHNSON

James Boswell

(596 Words)

AT night, Mr. Johnson and I supped in a private room at the Turk's Head coffee-house, in the Strand. "I encourage this house (said he,) for the mistress of it is a good civil woman, and has not much business."

"Sir, I love the acquaintance of young people; because, in the first place, I don't like to think myself growing old. In the next place, young acquaintances must last longest, if they do last; and then, Sir, young men have more virtue than old men; they have more generous sentiments in every respect. I love the young dogs of this age: they have more wit and humour and knowledge of life than we had; but then the dogs are not so good scholars. Sir, in my early years I read very hard. It is a sad reflection but a true one, that I knew almost as much at eighteen as I do now. My judgement, to be sure, was not so good; but I had all the facts. I remember very well, when I was at Oxford, an old gentleman said to me, 'Young man, ply your book diligently now, and acquire a stock of knowledge; for when years come upon you, you will find that poring upon books will be but an irksome task.'"

* * *

I spoke of Sir James Macdonald as a young man of most distinguished merit, who united the highest reputation at Eton and Oxford, with the patriarchal spirit of a great Highland Chieftain. I mentioned that Sir James had said to me, that he had never seen Mr. Johnson, but he had a great respect for him, though at the same time it was mixed with some degree of terrour. JOHNSON. "Sir, if he were to be acquainted with me, it might lessen both. . . ."

He maintained that a boy at school was the happiest of human beings. I supported a different opinion, from which I have never yet varied, that a man is happier; and I enlarged upon the anxiety and sufferings which are endured at school. JOHNSON. "Ah! Sir, a boy's being flogged is not so severe as a man's having the hiss of the world against him. Men have a solicitude about fame; and the greater share they have of it, the more afraid they are of losing it. . . ."

We talked of the education of children; and I asked him what he thought was best to teach them first. JOHNSON. "Sir, it is no matter what you teach them first, any more that what leg you shall put into your breeches first. Sir, you may stand disputing which is best to put in first, but in the meantime your breech is bare. Sir, while you are considering which of two things you should teach your child first, another boy has learnt them both. . . ."

* * *

On Saturday, July 30, Dr. Johnson and I took a sculler at the Temple-stairs, and set out for Greenwich. I asked him if he really thought a knowledge of the Greek and Latin languages an essential requisite to a good education. JOHNSON. "Most certainly, Sir; for those who know them have a very great advantage over those who do not. Nay, Sir, it is wonderful what a difference learning makes upon people even in the common intercourse of life, which does not appear to be connected with it." "And yet, (said I) people go through the world very well, and carry on the business of life to good advantage, without learning." JOHNSON. "Why, Sir, that may be true in cases where learning cannot possibly be of any use; for instance, this boy rows us as well without learning, as if he could sing the song of Orpheus to the Argonauts, who were the first sailors." He then called to the boy, "What would you give, my lad, to know about the Argonauts?" "Sir, (said the boy,) I would give what I have." Johnson was much pleased with his answer, and we gave him a double fare. Dr. Johnson then turning to me, "Sir, (said he,) a desire of knowledge is the natural feeling of mankind; and every human being, whose mind is not debauched, will be willing to give all that he has, to get knowledge."

Time: _____

Comprehension Test on THE LIFE OF SAMUEL JOHNSON

PART I

DIRECTIONS: Circle the most appropriate answer.

1. Dr. Johnson loves young people, especially young scholars, because:

   (a) they offer no challenge to old scholars
   (b) what they lack in knowledge they make up in judgment
   (c) they possess more virtue than old men

2. The advice of the old gentleman at Oxford was:

   (a) to stay perpetually young
   (b) to gain knowledge in one's youth
   (c) to put one's knowledge to good use

3. The joys of education to Dr. Johnson included:

   (a) acquiring judgment as well as facts
   (b) acquiring fame and keeping it
   (c) the differences it makes in one's everyday life

4. Dr. Johnson advises immediate training of the young so that:

   (a) they can begin to learn as soon as they begin to don long pants
   (b) they can be prepared to meet the competition of their peers
   (c) they will know how to pay attention to their appearance

5. Dr. Johnson favored learning classical languages, for they:

   (a) provided every person with some degree of comfort
   (b) gave their possessor a means of knowing the glories of the past
   (c) bestowed upon their owner a great advantage over the nonlinguist

PART II

DIRECTIONS: Define the following words according to their use in the context.

1. "*ply* your book diligently"

2. "with the *patriarchal* spirit of a great Highland *Chieftain*"

3. "in the meantime your *breech* is bare"

4. "Dr. Johnson and I took a *sculler*"

5. "every human being, whose mind is not *debauched*"

PART III

DIRECTIONS: Answer these questions briefly.

1. Dr. Johnson's appreciation and love of people was deeply rooted in his character. Give at least three examples of his sympathy for persons in different walks of life.

2. Why is the term "dogs" used to describe young men?

3. (a) Do you agree with Dr. Johnson that at eighteen one has learned almost as much as he can at a later age?

   (b) Is a boy at school happier than a man in the world? Explain your answer.

4. Why was Sir James Macdonald an excellent representative of Dr. Johnson's idea of a young man?

5. Is Dr. Johnson correct in believing that "a desire of knowledge is the natural feeling of mankind" and that "every human being, whose mind is not debauched, will be willing to give all that he has, to get knowledge"?

from DRY SEPTEMBER*

William Faulkner

(729 Words)

She was thirty-eight or thirty-nine. She lived in a small frame house with her invalid mother and a thin, sallow, unflagging aunt, where each morning between ten and eleven she would appear on the porch in a lace-trimmed boudoir cap, to sit swinging in the porch swing until noon. After dinner she lay down for a while, until the afternoon began to cool. Then, in one of the three or four new voile dresses which she had each summer, she would go downtown to spend the afternoon in the stores with the other ladies, where they would handle the goods and haggle over the prices in cold, immediate voices, without any intention of buying.

She was of comfortable people—not the best in Jefferson, but good people enough—and she was still on the slender side of ordinary looking, with a bright, faintly haggard manner and dress. When she was young she had had a slender, nervous body and a sort of hard vivacity which had enabled her for a time to ride upon the crest of the town's social life as exemplified by the high school party and church social period of her contemporaries while still children enough to be unclassconscious.

She was the last to realize that she was losing ground; that those among whom she had been a little brighter and louder flame than any other were beginning to learn the pleasure of snobbery—male—and retaliation—female. That was when her face began to wear that bright, haggard look. She still carried it to parties on shadowy porticoes and summer lawns, like a mask or a flag, with that bafflement of furious repudiation of truth in her eyes. One evening at a party she heard a boy and two girls, all schoolmates, talking. She never accepted another invitation.

She watched the girls with whom she had grown up as they married and got homes and children, but no man

ever called on her steadily until the children of the other girls had been calling her "aunty" for several years, the while their mothers told them in bright voices about how popular Aunt Minnie had been as a girl. Then the town began to see her driving on Sunday afternoons with the cashier in the bank. He was a widower of about forty—a high-colored man, smelling always faintly of the barber shop or of whisky. He owned the first automobile in town, a red runabout; Minnie had the first motoring bonnet and veil the town ever saw. Then the town began to say: "Poor Minnie." "But she is old enough to take care of herself," others said. That was when she began to ask her old schoolmates that their children call her "cousin" instead of "aunty."

It was twelve years now since she had been relegated into adultery by public opinion, and eight years since the cashier had gone to a Memphis bank, returning for one day each Christmas, which he spent at an annual bachelors' party at a hunting club on the river. From behind their curtains the neighbors would see the party pass, and during the over-the-way Christmas day visiting they would tell her about him, about how well he looked, and how they heard that he was prospering in the city, watching with bright, secret eyes her haggard, bright face. Usually by that hour there would be the scent of whisky on her breath. It was supplied her by a youth, a clerk at the soda fountain: "Sure; I buy it for the old gal. I reckon she's entitled to a little fun."

Her mother kept to her room altogether now; the gaunt aunt ran the house. Against that background Minnie's bright dresses, her idle and empty days, had a quality of furious unreality. She went out in the evenings only with women now, neighbors, to the moving pictures. Each afternoon she dressed in one of the new dresses and went downtown alone, where her young "cousins" were already strolling in the late afternoons with their delicate, silken heads and thin, awkward arms and conscious hips, clinging to one another or shrieking and giggling with paired boys in the soda fountain when she passed and went on along the serried store fronts, in the doors of which the sitting and lounging men did not even follow her with their eyes any more.

Time: _____

Comprehension Test on DRY SEPTEMBER

PART I

DIRECTIONS: Circle the most appropriate answer.

1. Her chief source of social contacts was:

    (a) her immediate family of her mother and aunt
    (b) her "cousins," children of her schoolmates
    (c) her women neighbors

2. Her social status in the community was:

    (a) one of inherited and assured permanence
    (b) one of continued vivacious leadership
    (c) a steadily deteriorating one

3. Her acceptance of invitations to parties ceased when she:

    (a) realized that she would never marry
    (b) felt she was too shy to attract a suitor
    (c) overheard the conversation of three former schoolmates

4. Like a true gentlewoman, Minnie faithfully maintained the traditions of:

    (a) personal shopping almost to the point of self-indulgence
    (b) a daily ritual of leisurely activities to fill in her nonworking hours
    (c) faithful service in the church

5. The tragedy of Minnie's existence was:

    (a) the circumscribed life she had to lead in a small town
    (b) her failure to perceive in time that life was passing her by
    (c) her attraction to men beneath her status

PART II

DIRECTIONS: Define the following words according to their use in the context.

1. "a thin, *sallow, unflagging* aunt"

2. "*haggle* over the prices in cold, *immediate* voices"

3. "the pleasure of . . . *retaliation* . . . female"

4. "on shadowy *porticoes* and summer lawns"

5. "she had been *relegated* into adultery"

6. "along the *serried* store fronts"

PART III

DIRECTIONS: Answer these questions briefly.

1. From the author's description of her, was Minnie the sort of person you would consider "attractive"? Consider such factors as age, personal appearance, vivaciousness, self-esteem.

2. Close reading of the words used to describe Minnie shows several examples of the word "bright" which are worth exploring for connotative differences. Consider use in "a *bright,* faintly haggard manner and dress," "a little *brighter* and louder flame," "*bright,* secret eyes," "*bright* dresses."

3. Trace the change in her social life from its crest to its state at the conclusion of the selection. Would you surmise a strong possibility of any more changes?

4. The judgment of the townspeople toward her becomes colder and harsher as time passes. Give examples of their gradual hostility.

5. Though it never materialized, do you think a match between Minnie and the widower would have had good chances for success? Why?

from CRESS DELAHANTY*

Jessamyn West

(775 Words)

She was as happy as a snail that expels the last grain of sand which has separated its sensitive, fluid body from its shell. Now she flowed back against the walls of her house in pure contentment. She stood stock still and shut her eyes and listened to the house sounds: first the dry, gusty breathing of the wind and the shingle's tap, then the lessening hiss of the tea kettle as the breakfast fire died, and the soft, animal pad of the rug as a slackening air current let it fall.

She opened her eyes. In the dining room the curtains lifted and fell with a summer movement in the autumn wind. She felt this to be perfect happiness: to stand in one room and watch in another the rise and fall of curtains. The egg-rimmed dishes still stood on the uncleared breakfast table. She regarded the disorder happily. "Oh," she whispered, "it's like being the only survivor on an abandoned ship."

Stealthily she ran to lower all the blinds so that the room was left in yellow, dusty twilight. Then she made herself a fire of the petroleum-soaked refuse from the oil fields that they used for wood. When the oil began to bubble and seethe, and the flames darted up, black and red, she started her work.

She cleared the fumed oak library table and ranged her books and papers precisely before her. Now her day began. Now she inhabited two worlds at once, and slid amphibian-like from one to the other, and had in each the best. Mist-like she moved in Shelley's world of luminous mist, and emerged to hold her hand to the fire and to listen to the bone-dry sound of the wind in the palm trees.

She laid her hand across her open book feeling that the words there were so strong and beautiful that they would enter her veins through her palms and so flow to her heart. She listened to the wind and saw all the objects that bent before it: she saw the stately movement of dark tree tops, the long ripple of bleached, hair-like grass, the sprayed sea water, the blown manes of horses in open pasture, the lonely sway of electric signs along dusty main streets. "Far across the steppes," she said, "and the prairie lands, the high mesas and the grass-

covered pampas." She watched the oil bubble stickily out of the wood and wondered what it was like to feel again after these thousands of years the touch of the wind.

But this was dreaming, not doing her work. She opened her notebook to a half-filled page, headed: "Beautiful, Lilting Phrases from Shelley." The list slid across her tongue like honey: "Rainbow locks, bright shadows, riven waves, spangled sky, aery rocks, sanguine sunrise, upward sky, viewless gale." She felt the texture of the words on her fingers as she copied them. The shingle tapped, the wind blew grittily across the pane, the fire seethed.

She finished Shelley and started on her own word list. She was through with the o's, ready to begin on the p's. She opened her old, red dictionary. What words would she find here? Beautiful, strange ones? She looked ahead—*pamero:* a cold wind that sweeps over the pampas; *parsalene:* a mock moon; *panada:* bread crumbs boiled in milk; *picaroon:* a rogue; *pilgarlic:* a bald-headed man; *plangent:* resounding like a wave. Her eyes narrowed regarding this rich store.

She rolled her bobby socks up and down, back and forth over across her ankles and copied words and definitions. When she finished the q's she put her word notebook away and took out one called "The Poems of Crescent Delahanty, Volume III." Each Sunday she copied one poem from her week's output into her poem book. Her poems were nothing like Shelley's. Shelley was beautiful, but he was not a modern. Cress was a modern, and when she wrote poetry she scorned the pretty and euphonious. This week's poem was called, "You Do Not Have to Wipe the Noses of Your Dreams," and Cress thought it as stark and brutal as anything she had ever done. Slowly she copied it:

> *I was lithe and had dreams;*
> *Now I am fat and have children.*
> *Dreams are evanescent*
> *Dreams fade.*
> *Children do not.*
> *But then you do not have to*
> *Wipe the noses of your dreams.*

"Yes," she said to her father, having remembered the poems, hers and Shelley's, the long list of words, "I finished my studying all right."

"Did anyone come while we were gone?" Mother asked.

"Mrs. Beal knocked, but she left before I got to the door."

Time: _____

Comprehension Test on CRESS DELAHANTY

PART I

DIRECTIONS: Circle the most appropriate answer.

1. Cress feels the ebb and flow of air in the house and compares it to:

   (a) a snail's excreting sand from the body
   (b) the movement of a ghostly dwelling
   (c) the material of pure poetry

2. Her two worlds encompass:

   (a) the poetic and the physical
   (b) the routine and the exciting
   (c) the world of the imagination and the world of harsh reality

3. Her dreams take her roving, among other places, over:

   (a) the Sahara Desert
   (b) the steppes of Russia
   (c) Mount Olympus

4. One feels that Cress, when grown, will be known as:

   (a) a poet
   (b) a precocious young girl
   (c) a good mother

5. In contrast to Cress' fancifulness, her father and mother seem:

   (a) normal parents
   (b) impatient and lacking in understanding of her moods
   (c) unaware of her childishness

PART II

DIRECTIONS: Define the following words according to their use in the context.

1. "She stood *stock* still"

2. "*fumed* oak library table"

3. "slid *amphibian-like*"

4. "grass-covered *pampas*"

5. "the pretty and *euphonious*"

6. "Dreams are *evanescent*"

PART III

DIRECTIONS: Answer these questions briefly.

1. Why is this episode so typically adolescent (Cress is twelve years old)?

2. Is this amphibian-like transition from one world to another apt to last with her? With the average adult?

3. How does the author overwhelm you with the sensory impressions that Cress evokes and calls forth in her imagination?

4. Despite her bent toward fantasy, Cress is orderly in her approach to her work and in her reactions to solitude. Is this at variance with your impression of her?

5. Despite the objectivity with which the author discusses Cress, do you feel that she might be in sympathy with her youthful ardor?

from THE ADVENTURES OF HUCKLEBERRY FINN

Mark Twain

(822 Words)

They swarmed up towards Sherburn's house, a-whooping and raging like Injuns, and everything had to clear the way or get run over and tromped to mush, and it was awful to see. Children was heeling it ahead of the mob, screaming and trying to get out of the way; and every window along the road was full of women's heads, and there was nigger boys in every tree, and bucks and wenches looking over every fence; and as soon as the mob would get nearly to them they would break and skaddle back out of reach. Lots of the women and girls was crying and taking on, scared most to death.

They swarmed up in front of Sherburn's palings as thick as they could jam together, and you couldn't hear yourself think for the noise. It was a little twenty-foot yard. Some sung out "Tear down the fence! tear down the fence!" Then there was a racket of ripping and tearing and smashing, and down she goes, and the front wall of the crowd begins to roll in like a wave.

Just then Sherburn steps out onto the roof of his little front porch, with a double-barrel gun in his hand, and takes his stand, perfectly ca'm and deliberate, not saying a word. The racket stopped, and the wave sucked back.

Sherburn never said a word—just stood there, looking down. The stillness was awful creepy and uncomfortable. Sherburn run his eye slow along the crowd; and wherever it struck the people tried a little to outgaze him, but they couldn't; they dropped their eyes and looked sneaky. Then pretty soon Sherburn sort of laughed; not the pleasant kind, but the kind that makes you feel like when you are eating bread that's got sand in it.

Then he says, slow and scornful:

"The idea of *you* lynching anybody! It's amusing. The idea of you thinking you had pluck enough to lynch a *man!* Because you're brave enough to tar and feather poor friendless cast-out women that come along here, did that make you think you had grit enough to lay your hands on a *man?* Why, a *man's* safe in the hands of ten thousand of your kind—as long as it's daytime and you're not behind him.

"Do I know you? I know you clear through. I was born and raised in the South, and I've lived in the North; So I know the average all around. The average man's a coward. In the North he lets anybody walk over him that wants to, and goes home and prays for a humble spirit to bear it. In the South one man, all by himself, has stopped a stage full of men in the daytime, and robbed the lot. Your newspapers call you a brave people so much that you think you *are* braver than any other people—whereas you're just *as* brave, and no braver. Why don't your juries hang murderers? Because they're afraid the man's friends will shoot them in the back, in the dark—and it's just what they *would* do.

"So they always acquit; and then a *man* goes in the night, with a hundred masked cowards at his back, and lynches the rascal. Your mistake is, that you didn't bring a man with you; that's one mistake, and the other is that you didn't come in the dark and fetch your masks. You brought *part* of a man—Buck Harkness, there—and if you hadn't had him to start you, you'd 'a' taken it out in blowing.

"You didn't want to come. The average man don't like trouble and danger. *You* don't like trouble and danger. But if only *half* a man—like Buck Harkness, there—shouts 'Lynch him! lynch him!' you're afraid to back down—afraid you'll be found out to be what you are—*cowards*—and so you raise a yell, and hang yourselves onto that half-a-man's coat-tail, and come raging up here, swearing what big things you're going to do. The pitifulest thing out is a mob; that's what an army is—a mob; they don't fight with courage that's born in them, but with courage that's borrowed from their mass, and from their officers. But a mob without any *man* at the head of it is *beneath* pitifulness. Now the thing for *you* to do is to droop your tails and go home and crawl in a hole. If any real lynching's going to be done it will be done in the dark, Southern fashion; and when they come they'll bring their masks, and fetch a *man* along. Now *leave*—and take your half-a-man with you"—tossing his gun up across his left arm and cocking it when he says this.

The crowd washed back sudden, and then broke all apart, and went tearing off every which way, and Buck Harkness he heeled it after them, looking tolerable cheap. I could 'a' stayed if I wanted to, but I didn't want to.

Time: _____

Comprehension Test on THE ADVENTURES OF HUCKLEBERRY FINN

PART I

DIRECTIONS: Circle the most appropriate answer.

1. Early in the selection, the actions of the mob are compared to:

   (a) the rolling motion of a wave
   (b) the semi-formal order of a military division
   (c) the wantonness of children at play

2. Sherburn's decisive action stopped them because of:

   (a) his loaded shotgun
   (b) his scornful survey of the crowd
   (c) his slashing indictment of their courage

3. Sherburn said that they were "courageous" because of:

   (a) their birth in the South
   (b) their tarring and feathering of women
   (c) their leaders' control over them

4. Sherburn says a lynching, Southern fashion, takes place:

   (a) after a jury acquittal
   (b) in broad daylight
   (c) after the publication of a laudatory newspaper account

5. After the episode, Buck Harkness:

   (a) lost his effectiveness as the leader
   (b) decided to let Sherburn alone
   (c) relinquished the idea of carrying out the lynching

PART II

DIRECTIONS: Define the following words according to their use in the context.

1. "*bucks* and *wenches* looking over every fence"

2. "in front of Sherburn's *palings*"

3. "*tolerable* cheap"

4. "thinking you had *pluck* enough"

5. "you had *grit* enough"

6. "The crowd *washed* back sudden"

PART III

DIRECTIONS: Answer these questions briefly.

1. The dialect of the story contributes a distinctive quality to the writing. Point out at least five examples of regional speech that is, nevertheless, graphic.

2. Except for Sherburn, the participants in the story are described in derogatory words or terms. Point out at least five examples of such scornful references. How does their use affect the reader's response?

3. The excerpt is full of references to the visual and auditory senses. Point out carefully and precisely the interrelationship of the two senses on the action.

4. Is the average man, as Sherburn says, a coward? He describes the "bravery" of the Southerner in contrast to that of the Northerner. What evidence for this contrast does he give? Is it genuine evidence? What evidence can you give to support or refute the statement?

5. One of the marks of true literature is its universality. In the light of contemporary struggle for human dignity and liberty, how appropriate and valuable for reading and discussion is this selection?

THE POISONING OF KING JAMES I*

Hugh Ross Williamson

(881 Words)

On March 5, 1625, King James I, who was at his favourite country residence at Theobalds, was taken ill of a tertian ague. It was not considered serious and on March 11, he was well enough to sign and dispatch a safe-conduct for the Conde de Gondomar, the former Spanish ambassador who was then in Spain, to return to England. Among other things, Gondomar was bound to bring an adverse report on the Duke of Buckingham's recent conduct in Spain, and the gossip at court was that he was returning at the King's invitation "to put a flea in the Duke's ear." Nobody, least of all Buckingham, doubted that the Spaniard's coming would "mean the Duke's discredit." The day after the safe-conduct was signed, James was sufficiently strong to contemplate being moved to Hampton Court and Buckingham, who had been going to and fro between Theobalds and his own residence, Wallingford House, in London, arranged with his mother to send to Dunmow for a special plaster made by a doctor there.

The Countess of Buckingham applied the plaster to the King's wrists, in defiance of protests from his doctors; and James grew rapidly worse. As soon as the plasters were taken off and normal medical treatment restored, the King once more improved. On March 21 the plasters were again applied and the King grew so very much worse that one of the doctors, Craig, used such strong language that he was ordered to leave Court, while another, Hayes, was called out of bed to take the plasters off.

Buckingham then had prepared by his own servant, Baker, a special julep which he took to James with his own hand. James drank twice but refused the third time. This was on March 22.

On March 23, all hope of the King's life was abandoned. The Bishop in attendance on him told him that his end was near and the next day he received Holy Communion in company with all his attendants except Buckingham, who excused himself on the grounds that he had stomach-ache.

On March 27, James died. Immediately afterwards a paper was brought to the doctors to sign "that the ingredients of the julep and the plasters were safe," but, even knowing what the displeasure of the now all-powerful Buckingham meant, they refused. (Their conduct in this matter was sworn on oath by the physicians themselves before a select Committee in 1627.)

* From *Enigmas of History*. Reprinted with permission of The Macmillan Company and Michael Joseph Ltd. Copyright © 1957 by Hugh R. Williamson

When, in 1626, Buckingham was impeached by the House of Commons, the thirteenth article of the charge referred to these events, though the specific accusation of poison was avoided. To save the Duke, Charles I dissolved Parliament.

For over two hundred years after James' death, the theory that Buckingham poisoned him was never seriously called in question. The only problem which engaged the attention of historians was whether or not King Charles I was privy to it; or at least implicated in the sense in which the accusation was put by Milton: "To omit other evidences, he that would not suffer a Duke that was accused of it to come to his trial must needs have been guilty of it himself."

When, in 1653, Bulstrode Whitelock was the English ambassador to Sweden, he found Queen Christina interested in the subject. She asked him the details of the matter. He had been in the 1626 Parliament, and as a lawyer and the son of a judge, had weighed the evidence carefully. After his recital of the facts of the case, Queen Christina replied: "Certainly he was poisoned" and thus endorsed the general contemporary verdict.

The reversal of this verdict to such an extent that the mere asking of the question nowadays is held "unworthy of a serious historian" is due entirely to S. R. Gardiner, who is accepted, without any attempt at verification, by academic historians. In the fifth volume of his *History of England,* published in 1883, Gardiner assumed that the medical evidence for poisoning is worthless. This conclusion, he bases on a pamphlet written in 1862 and published in Calcutta by Dr. Norman Chevers, Principal of the Calcutta Medical College: *Did James the First of England die from the Effects of Poison?* Gardiner dismisses the weighty circumstantial evidence as worthless because, he says: "the only ground for supposing it to have any value is cut away once it is understood that Buckingham had no object in poisoning the King." As Gardiner's own reconstruction of that background is one of his own more obvious inaccuracies and his treatment of the event is marked by his usual technique of suppressing awkward facts, his opinion is of little value. It has not even the merit of making a real case; for Dr. Chevers admits that the administration of the julep, even if it were quite harmless, would aggravate the illness and pronounces that "nothing could have been less appropriate," citing as an example "a Superintendent's Surgeon in the Bengal Medical Service who died in 1856, whose fatal attack was excited by a draught of beer shortly followed by one of milk." Thus, if the question is put in the form: "Did Buckingham kill the King?" ignoring the question of poison, Dr. Chevers's pamphlet is not on S. R. Gardiner's side.

One may therefore pose the question as an unsolved historical mystery.

Time: _____

Comprehension Test on THE POISONING OF KING JAMES I

PART I

DIRECTIONS: Circle the appropriate answer.

1. General contemporary verdict at the time of the death of King James I and at the present time holds that:

    (a) the death of King James I was due to poisoning
    (b) the person responsible is not known
    (c) his successor, Charles I, was innocent of any knowledge of the mystery

2. The political overtones of the crime lie primarily in the:

    (a) recall of the former Ambassador to Spain
    (b) maintenance of good diplomatic relations between England and Sweden
    (c) plotting of Charles I to gain the throne from King James

3. The suspicion of the King's death by design arises from the evidence that:

    (a) when the plasters were removed, his condition improved
    (b) at the beginning of the sickness he apparently recovered, an unexpected change in a victim of poisoning
    (c) Queen Christina added the weight of her judgment to this view

4. That the Duke of Buckingham gained immediate power is evident from:

    (a) his absence from the final meeting of the King with his attendants
    (b) the court physicians' full awareness of the consequences of his displeasure
    (c) the dissolution of Parliament by Charles I for his protection

5. The evidence of S. R. Gardiner does not refute the evidence of the King's death by poisoning because:

    (a) any drink may be potentially fatal to a person who cannot tolerate it
    (b) he is accepted by scholars
    (c) he assumes the medical evidence is worthless

PART II

DIRECTIONS: Define the following words according to their use in the context.

1. "taken ill of a _tertian ague_"

2. "Buckingham was _impeached_ by the House of Commons"

3. "whether or not King Charles I was _privy_ to it; or at least _implicated_"

4. "without any attempt at _verification_"

5. "Gardiner dismisses the _weighty circumstantial_ evidence"

PART III

DIRECTIONS: Answer these questions briefly.

1. How do you account for the continuing interest in the problem of the poisoning of King James I even though its classification by the author as an "enigma" of history indicates its insolubility?

2. This nonfiction excerpt, like much nonfiction, holds much interest for the attentive reader, for it possesses many characteristics of drama or fiction. Substantiate such characteristics as the interplay of characters, the element of suspense, a discernible plot, ruling passions like ambition and greed for power, by reference to this historical mystery.

3. The story would lend itself admirably to being made into a play or historical novel. Can you think of any plays or fictionalized history accounts based similarly on British royalty?

4. There is in this account a striking example for you of the academic problems of the weighing of all types of evidence, controversy among scholars, and methods of historical research. Discuss each problem both with reference to the story and to any other examples you may have met in your academic studies.

5. The interested reader wonders about the Duke of Buckingham's "recent conduct in Spain," the kind of king James I was, the effect of plasters on an ailment like tertian ague, the subsequent histories of Charles I and the Duke of Buckingham. You might be so intrigued by one or several of these questions that you will seek further information on your own. Do any other questions occur to you? About what questions above would you like to know more?

from THE LITTLE WORLD OF DON CAMILLO*

Giovanni Guareschi

(889 Words)

Don Camillo had let himself go a bit in the course of a little sermon. He had made some rather pointed allusions to *"certain people,"* and so on the following evening when he seized the ropes of the church bells all hell broke loose. Some damned soul had tied firecrackers to the clappers of the bells. No harm done of course, but there was a din of explosions shattering enough to give the ringer heart failure.

Don Camillo said nothing. He celebrated the evening service in perfect composure before a crowded congregation. Peppone was in the front row, and every countenance was a picture of fervor. It was enough to infuriate a saint, but Don Camillo was no novice in self-control and his audience went home disappointed.

As soon as the big doors of the church were closed, Don Camillo snatched up an overcoat and on his way out made a hasty genuflection before the altar.

"Don Camillo," said Christ, "put it down."

"I don't understand," protested Don Camillo.

"Put it down!"

Don Camillo drew a heavy stick out from under his coat and laid it in front of the altar.

"Not a pleasant sight, Don Camillo."

"But, Lord! It isn't even oak; it's only poplar, light and supple," Don Camillo pleaded.

"Go to bed, Don Camillo, and forget about Peppone."

Don Camillo threw up his hands and went to bed with a temperature. But on the following evening when Peppone's wife came to the rectory, he leaped to his feet as though a firecracker had gone off under his chair.

"Don Camillo," began the woman, who was obviously upset. But Don Camillo interrupted her.

"Get out of my sight, sacrilegious creature!"

"Don Camillo, never mind about that foolishness. At Castellino there is that poor devil who tried to support Peppone. They have driven him out of the village!"

Don Camillo counted to ten and lit a cigar. "Well, what of it, comrade? Why should you bother about it?"

The woman started to shout. "I'm bothering because they came to tell Peppone, and he has gone rushing off to Castellino like a lunatic. And he has taken his Tommy gun with him!"

"I see, then you have got concealed arms, have you?"

"Don Camillo, never mind about politics! Can't you understand that Peppone is out to kill? Unless you help me, my husband is done for!"

Don Camillo laughed unpleasantly. "Which will teach him to tie firecrackers to my bells. I shall be pleased to watch him die in jail! You get out of my house!"

Ten minutes later, Don Camillo, with his skirts tucked up almost to his neck, was pedaling like a lunatic along the road to Castellino on a racing bike that belonged to the son of his assistant.

There was a splendid moon and when he was within a few miles of Castellino, Don Camillo saw by its light a man sitting on the wall of the little bridge that spans the river. He slowed down, since it is always best to be prudent when one travels by night, and stopped some ten yards from the bridge, holding in his hand a small object that he happened to have had in his pocket.

"Have you seen a big man go by on a bicycle in the direction of Castellino?" he asked.

"No, Don Camillo," replied the other quietly.

Don Camillo drew nearer. "Have you already been to Castellino?"

"No, I thought it over. It wasn't worthwhile. Was it my fool of a wife who put you to this trouble?"

"Trouble? Nothing of the kind . . . a little constitutional!"

"Have you any idea what a priest looks like on a racing bicycle?" snickered Peppone.

Don Camillo came and sat beside him on his wall. "My son, you must be prepared to see all kinds of things in this world."

Less than an hour later, Don Camillo was back at the rectory and went to report to Christ.

"Everything went according to Your commandments."

"Well done, Don Camillo; but would you mind telling me who commanded you to grab him by the feet and tumble him into the ditch?"

Don Camillo raised his arms. "To tell you the truth, I can't remember exactly. As a matter of fact he seemed to find the sight of a priest on a racing bike distasteful, so I thought it only kind to stop him from seeing it any longer."

"I understand. Has he got back yet?"

"He'll be here soon. It struck me that in his rather damp condition, he might find the bicycle in his way, so I thought it best to bring it along with me."

"Very kind of you, I'm sure, Don Camillo," said Christ with perfect gravity.

Just before dawn Peppone appeared at the door of the rectory. He was soaked to the skin, and Don Camillo asked if it was raining.

"Fog," replied Peppone with chattering teeth. "May I have my bicycle?"

"Why, of course. There it is."

"Are you sure there wasn't a Tommy gun tied to it?"

Don Camillo smiled. "A Tommy gun? And what is that?"

As he turned from the door Peppone said, "I have made one mistake in my life. I tied firecrackers to your bells. It should have been half a ton of dynamite."

"Errare humanum est," remarked Don Camillo.

Time: _____

Comprehension Test on THE LITTLE WORLD OF DON CAMILLO

PART I

DIRECTIONS: Circle the answer that most nearly fits the question.

1. What caused Peppone to seek revenge on Don Camillo?

   (a) a distaste for church ritual
   (b) anger at his wife
   (c) the priest's rebuke in his sermon
   (d) a temporary insanity

2. How did Don Camillo bear up under the provocation?

   (a) he railed at the congregation
   (b) he concealed his wrath
   (c) he confessed his feelings to Christ in private

3. Upon what sort of terms were Don Camillo and Christ?

   (a) they were like a father and son in spirit
   (b) so close was He to Don Camillo that He was the priest's conscience
   (c) Don Camillo was too impetuous to be restrained by divine intervention

4. How did Don Camillo humiliate Peppone so admirably?

   (a) he had a good reason for each act he executed
   (b) he gave no explanation in reply to Peppone's questions
   (c) he let divine providence intervene to chastise him

5. How did Don Camillo exhibit surprising worldliness as a venerable priest?

   (a) he occasionally indulged in cigar smoking
   (b) he made a comical figure bicycling around the village
   (c) he answered in Latin the observation of Peppone

PART II

DIRECTIONS: Define the following words according to their use in the context of the story.

1. "*pointed* allusions"

2. "picture of *fervor*"

3. "to *infuriate* a saint"

4. "no *novice* in self-control"

5. "a hasty *genuflection*"

6. "*sacrilegious creature*"

PART III

DIRECTIONS: Answer these questions briefly.

1. Do you think Peppone learned anything from this encounter with Don Camillo? Why?

2. Why was the church so crowded for the evening service?

3. Do you find Don Camillo's tendency to violence unpriestlike, or is the priest incapable by temperament of any other reaction?

4. What could have been the small object he had in his jacket?

5. What is Don Camillo's philosophy of life as evidenced by his maxims?

from GEOFFREY CHAUCER OF ENGLAND*

Marchette Chute

(1014 Words)

By the time he was seven Geoffrey Chaucer had learned his letters and was ready to go to grammar school. It is frequently assumed that there were only three schools in London in the fourteenth century and that Chaucer must have been sent either to St. Martin's-le-Grand, St. Mary-le-bow, or St. Paul's Cathedral to get his education. This list comes from a twelfth-century description of London by William Fitzstephen, who states that "the three principal churches . . . have famous schools by privilege and by virtue of their ancient dignity." But Fitzstephen adds that "there are other schools licensed by special grace and permission," and there is no reason to suppose that these other schools had vanished by the fourteenth century. It is much more likely that they had multiplied.

The medieval interest in education has been much underestimated. In proportion to the population there were more schools at the beginning of the fourteenth century in England than there were at the end of the eighteenth. One of the grievances, in fact, of a popular social critic of the period, the author of *Piers Plowman,* was that any "beggar's brat" could get an education. The Church honored education and gave it freely, without regard to class distinctions, and the fourteenth century was by no means as illiterate as it is sometimes supposed to have been.

The whole educational system was based squarely upon the time-honored proposition: "This is so because I tell you it is so." Any kind of individual initiative or curiosity was as firmly discouraged in classroom as in any other part of the medieval system, and a good memory was the mark of a good student.

Most of the classwork was oral, for books were scarce and the students worked from dictation with slates or wooden tablets. This method might have its disadvantages but it gave Chaucer a well-trained memory that served him usefully throughout his life.

If it is not safe to guess where Chaucer went to school, it is fairly safe to say what he was taught there. The Middle Ages did not believe in radical changes within a short space of time, and what was good enough for the fourth century was considered quite good enough for the fourteenth.

Chaucer learned the elements of grammar from the *Eight Parts of Speech* of Aelius Donatus, a Roman grammarian who had taught Saint Jerome. It was given to small boys in simplified form which they called, probably not at all affectionately, their Donat. The Donat ran to what would now be about ten printed pages, and consisted of questions and answers on the basic principles of Latin grammar. Geoffrey Chaucer may have owned his own copy, since a cheap manuscript copy of so small a book could be bought for threepence (the equivalent of about ninety cents in modern money). Whether he owned a copy or not, the long unbroken paragraphs of the Donat would have been his constant companion throughout his early schooldays. A twelfth-century schoolmaster attempted to make things easier for small boys by turning the grammar into rhyme for the nephews of the Bishop of Dol, and in this new form it became very popular in the fourteenth century; but the original version was not shaken from its schoolroom eminence, and Gutenberg printed a Donat before he printed the Bible.

By the time he had inched his way through his Donat young Geoffrey Chaucer would be ready for some elementary Latin reading. The average medieval textbook was as sternly moral as *McGuffey's Reader*—art for art's sake would have been an unthinkable maxim in the Middle Ages—and every young scholar had his moral nature and his Latin simultaneously benefited by what he called his Cato. This was a collection of adages and proverbs arranged in alphabetical order and supposed to have been written by one Dionysius Cato. Chaucer mentions Cato several times in his poetry, but in any case no medieval schoolboy could have escaped him.

For advanced grammar Chaucer would be subjected to Priscian, who had taught Latin grammar in Constantinople in the sixth century. He would begin with Priscian's shorter work, which consisted of a thorough dissection of the first twelve lines of the *Aeneid,* each word being analyzed as to gender, case, number and so on. Then he graduated to Priscian's larger book on grammar. The great educator believed in example as well as precept, and his book includes ten thousand lines of quotation from the Roman classics. Chaucer had a good memory and it is likely that some of his later quotations from classical authors come from no closer an acquaintance than through the standard textbooks of his youth.

The case was far otherwise with the first Latin classic he encountered at school. This was Ovid, to whom Chaucer refers in his work more often than to any other single writer and who became his friend for life. The real attraction was that both men were fundamentally alike in temperament. They both had a detached, uncritical view of their fellow man and a strong sense of fun that drew them to each other at once when they met across the centuries. Moreover, Ovid's way of writing had a clearness and facility that may have helped Chaucer somewhat in attaining his own lucid style.

Ovid was above all a storyteller, and it was as a teller of tales that Chaucer first met him in the schoolroom. There he read Ovid's *Metamorphoses,* which was a kind of biographical dictionary of the gods and proved to be a mine of stories for the story-hungry Middle Ages. Ovid had the gift of making his mythological characters come alive, the women especially, and Chaucer says that after he had read the tragic story of Ceyx and Alcyone he was upset all the following day. His friendship with Ovid was not as passionate as Boccaccio's, who almost overdid his youthful devotion, but it lasted much longer. It lasted throughout the whole of Chaucer's life and was one of his rewards for undergoing long hours of Latin grammar in the schoolroom.

Time: _____

Comprehension Test on GEOFFREY CHAUCER OF ENGLAND

PART I

DIRECTIONS: Circle the most appropriate answer.

1. The evaluation of historical evidence leads us to the belief that Chaucer's education was obtained:

    (a) at one of the leading church schools, more than likely
    (b) definitely at St. Paul's Cathedral
    (c) perhaps at one of the schools other than the leading three

2. That education in the Middle Ages flourished is borne out by the testimony that:

    (a) schools frequently closed but others quickly replaced them
    (b) the Church freely supported its belief in education
    (c) a leading social critic applauded the availability of education

3. Medieval methods of instruction were quite different from present-day methods:

    (a) small, inexpensive texts were plentiful
    (b) individual initiative or curiosity was firmly discouraged
    (c) there was emphasis on a variety of methods

4. Chaucer emerged from the medieval educational system with:

    (a) a belief that one's education should be classical
    (b) a passionate, lifelong dedication to Ovid
    (c) a familiarity with Greek writers

5. His success in mastering grammar is due to:

    (a) his training in morality along with principles of writing
    (b) his complete immersion in and training from the works of Priscian, among other grammarians
    (c) his excellent memory

PART II

DIRECTIONS: Define the following words according to their use in the context.

1. "The Middle Ages did not believe in *radical* changes"

2. "the original version was not *shaken from* its schoolroom *eminence*"

3. "which consisted of a thorough *dissection* of the first twelve lines"

4. "Then he *graduated* to Priscian's larger book"

5. "They both had a *detached*, uncritical view"

PART III

DIRECTIONS: Answer these questions briefly.

1. The first sentence suggests the demands made upon the home before the child entered a strict school. What do you surmise they were? Broaden your answer beyond the obvious one of helping the child to learn his letters.

2. What are the historian's bases for obtaining the facts of Chaucer's early schooling?

3. One emerges from reading this passage with a healthy respect for the results of the medieval scholars. Despite their disadvantages, what were their strong points as demonstrated by Chaucer's development?

4. Marchette Chute vividly describes the attractions of Ovid for both Chaucer and Boccaccio.
   (a) What did he teach Chaucer?

   (b) How might Boccaccio have overdone his early devotion?

5. (a) If you were to describe Chaucer's personality, how would you characterize him?

   (b) Judged by Miss Chute's portrayal, would he appear interesting to you?

from DELIVER US FROM EVIL*

Thomas A. Dooley

(1336 Words)

The *Montague* glided into the surrealist beauty of the Baie d'Along on August 14, 1954. On the same day several other ships anchored in the stream. By August 15th there were five ships lined up in this slit among the bay's crags and rocks. We were at Position 1; the *Menard*, another cargo ship, was at Position 5.

Anxiously we waited for our first view of the refugees. What would they be like? How many of them would there be? What kind of diseases would they bring with them? We soon found out.

I tried to imagine what conditions must be with hordes of people pouring into the city of Haiphong, beyond the bay four hours up river, waiting to be carried out to these strange ships standing offshore. Little did I realize that, just beyond that shoreline, lay an ordeal which would scar my memory for a lifetime.

Then I heard a shout and saw the men pointing to a small LCT slowly ploughing along in the angry swells. Such small craft are built to transport four or five tanks and a few dozen men. Their overall length is less than 150 feet. As this one pulled alongside, I looked down into the open deck with horror. I know horror is a strong word, but there were more than a thousand people huddled on the deck, close-packed like fowl in a crate, wet, seasick and exposed to a brutal sun. They were numb with fright. Among them was a multitude of babies.

When the LCT arrived at the side of our ship, huge by comparison, an open gangway was lowered to its deck. This was secured as firmly as possible, fighting the swells and sickening rolls of the bay. The refugees were told to come up. I could see them hesitate, in fear. I supposed that it was merely dread of the unknown. Later I learned that the trouble was more specific—they were in mortal fear of the savage, inhuman Americans against whom they had been very often and very effectively warned.

One old man, probably one of their esteemed elders, took the lead. He started painfully up. He wore a conical straw hat and in one hand clutched a slender brown-crusted bamboo pipe. In the other hand, even more tightly, he held a chipped frame—a picture of the Blessed Virgin. It was clear that these were his most prized possessions. In fact, they were nearly all the possessions he had.

For a few steps he came on bravely, then looked down at the swells smashing inches below the steps. One look was enough. He froze where he stood. When he looked up, many things showed in his wizened face. There was starvation, all too obvious; there was fright at the booming sea; there was sheer terror of what lay ahead.

He was hunched over as if heavily burdened. When,

nervously, he removed his hat, his scalp showed patches of scaling fungus. His ribs stood out sharply, stretching the skin of his chest to shiny tautness. I had never before seen such utter dejection. Could this be Viet Nam?

A white-capped sailor went down the steps; he wanted to help, repugnant as the thought of touching that old fellow must have been. But when he did touch the man, it was as if the grandfather had felt the hand of an executioner. Only the press of the people behind finally forced him to mount the rest of the steps to our deck. His trembling fingers were barely able to hold a numbered card another sailor handed him before he was urged, gently, away from the ship's rail.

We stopped the line after a few refugees had come aboard and put a canvas cover over and under the accommodation ladder so that they would not see the ocean breaking beneath the open steps. This, we hoped, would lessen their terror. Nevertheless the others, equally miserable, entered the ladder-tunnel with apprehension.

Many of them carried long balanced poles with large shallow baskets at each end. In these they carried everything they owned. Usually they had some clothes, always a rice bowl and chopsticks, invariably a religious object—a crucifix, statue or sacred picture.

On and on they came through that cavernous tunnel, some of them with eyes lowered, as if not daring to look at us. They had children on their backs and in their arms; even the older kids toted babies. The children were given a tag which, when presented later, entitled them to milk, a nearly unheard-of luxury. The little ones were sweet, and wide-eyed and grave. And very frightened. I saw a sailor, to lighten a mother's load, pick up a brown little bundle of baby and mutter, "God, this kid smells awful."

Then the last of this group of refugees was aboard and the French LCT pulled away with an obvious air of relief. A second French craft pulled alongside and the dismal exchange was repeated.

Somehow, in the confusion, our guests managed to haul aboard a huge barrel of stinking oil. I took one whiff and ordered it tossed overboard. Too late, I learned that the rancid oil was considered a delicacy, indispensable to Tonkinese cookery.

Now more than 2,000 Tonkinese were started on their passage to freedom, the first of the hundreds of thousands who would depart from this harbor before the Bamboo Curtain finally fell. They had made a wholly free choice in tearing up century-old roots and abandoning revered ancestral graves. For the right to continue to worship their God—the decisive motive in nine cases out of ten—they had given up their rice paddies, their homes, their beloved native villages. What lay ahead of them in the south, which would be almost a foreign land to Tonkin Delta folk? Indeed, would these big-nosed and strangely dressed white men ever deliver them to the south at all?

They had been told in great detail by followers of Ho Chi Minh—the fabled Ho Chi Minh who was playing ball with Moscow but whom many of them still regarded as a patriotic nationalist—that Americans were scarcely human. The whole evacuation, they were told, was a trap. American sailors would throw the old people overboard, cut off the right hands of the newborn, and sell the comely girls as concubines to capitalists. They had seen "pictures"—crude but vivid drawings on propaganda leaflets—of just such white-capped sailors as those on this big ship roasting a child alive, presumably for breakfast.

Small wonder that there was not a smiling face, young or old, among these thousands as they clambered awkwardly into the ship's cavernous belly with their sorry belongings. So it seemed a heart-warming miracle, hours later, to notice the blossoming of shy smiles here and there, first among the children, and then among their elders too. The mood of our guests was becoming more tranquil.

We now notified the galley that they would have the mammoth task of feeding these thousands. A number of comparatively clean and healthy-looking Vietnamese—and they were not easy to find—were selected to help serve the food. We planned to serve only twice a day, but since the second meal ran into the first, the lines were continuous. Vitamin deficiencies were general, and this was a chance for the Vietnamese to eat their fill, perhaps the first in months.

We cooked the rice in our own fashion, nice and fluffy. Embarrassingly, we discovered that the refugees did not like rice cooked our way. They preferred it when it looked like an inedible ball of congealed mash. When they finally got it that way, they would take extra helpings and press it into sticky chunks to be tucked into their bundles.

Finally the last refugee was aboard and the accommodation ladder hoisted. The "Ready to get underway" reports were submitted to the Skipper, the screws churned the blue-green water and the *Montague,* with its strange cargo, embarked for the south.

Time: _____

Comprehension Test on DELIVER US FROM EVIL

PART I

DIRECTIONS: Circle the most appropriate answer.

1. The Baie d'Along is a harbor:

    (a) of no interest to the average person
    (b) of strange beauty to the deeply artistic person
    (c) worth no consideration except as a commercial and military port

2. The author learned that the people:

    (a) could leave their homes easily because they had no possessions
    (b) were afraid of the unknown
    (c) were afraid of the inhuman Americans they had been warned against

3. The first battle of loading the ship which the crew members solved was:

    (a) separating the families for accommodations in each part of the ship
    (b) covering as best they could the refugees' view of the sea
    (c) welcoming each refugee so he would feel immediately at home.

4. The trip was an education in local customs for the Americans, for they learned:

    (a) how people's choices of delicacies in food were so different from their own
    (b) how little a problem it was to secure the right kind of Vietnamese assistant
    (c) how well the babies were cared for often at the expense of the parents' health

5. The experience for Dr. Dooley became momentous, for:

    (a) he had tremendous medical problems to confront
    (b) he was not prepared for the administration of a hospital ship
    (c) he had become involved in the political and religious problems of the people

PART II

DIRECTIONS: Define the following words according to their use in the context.

1. "the *surrealist* beauty of the Baie d'Along"

2. "many things showed in his *wizened* face"

3. "*repugnant* as the thought of touching that old fellow must have been"

4. "*indispensable* to Tonkinese cookery"

5. "abandoning *revered* ancestral graves"

PART III

DIRECTIONS: Answer these questions briefly.

1. How does the author make the elder seem representative of the kind of life the people had to lead? Refer to his appearance, his possessions, his reactions, his health.

2. What were the accommodations made for the general welfare of the people?

3. What does this episode tell us about the principles men hold necessary for their spiritual survival and the lengths to which they will go to live by them?

4. Why were the smiles of the guests so heart-warming and miraculous for the doctor and his crew?

5. (a) Identify Dr. Thomas A. Dooley.

   (b) What does the story tell you of his service to humanity?

from CLEA*

Lawrence Durrell

(1496 Words)

"The cloud's lifting already," cried Balthazar as I surfaced at last for air. Soon even the fugitive phosphorescence would dwindle and vanish. For some reason or other he had climbed into the stern of the cutter, perhaps to gain height and more easily watch the thunderstorm over the city. I rested my forearms on the gunwale and took my breath. He had unwrapped the old harpoon gun of Narouz and was holding it negligently on his knee. Clea surfaced with a swish of delight and pausing just long enough to cry: "The fire is so beautiful" doubled her lithe body back and ducked downward again.

"What are you doing with that?" I asked idly.

"Seeing how it works."

He had in fact pushed the harpoon to rest in the barrel. It had locked with the spring. "It's cocked," I said. "Have a care."

"Yes, I'm going to release it."

Then Balthazar leaned forward and uttered the only serious remark he had made all that day. "You know," he said, "I think you had better take her with you. I have a feeling you won't be coming back to Alexandria. Take Clea with you!"

And then, before I could reply, the accident happened. He was fumbling with the gun as he spoke. It slipped from between his fingers and fell with a crash, the barrel striking the gunwale six inches from my face. As I reared back in alarm I heard the sudden cobra-like hiss of the compressor and the leaden twang of the trigger-release. The harpoon whistled into the water beside me rustling its long green line behind it. "For Christ's sake," I said. Balthazar had turned white with alarm and vexation. His half-muttered apologies and expressions of horrid amazement were eloquent. "I'm terribly sorry." I had heard the slight snick of steel settling into a target, somewhere down there in the pool. We stayed frozen for a second for something else had occurred simultaneously to our minds. As I saw his lips starting to shape the word "Clea" I felt a sudden darkness descending on my spirit—a darkness which lifted and trembled at the edges; and a rushing like the sough of giant wings. I had already turned before he uttered a word. I crashed back into the water, now following the long green thread with all the suspense of Ariadne; and to it added the weight of slowness which only heartsick apprehension brings. I knew in my mind that I was swimming vigorously—yet it seemed like one of those slow-motion films where human actions, delayed by the camera, are drawn unctuously out to infinity, spooled out like toffee. How many light years would it take to reach the end of that thread? What would I find at the end of it? Down I went, and down, in the dwindling phosphorescence, into the deep shadowed coolness of the pool.

At the far end, by the wreck, I distinguished a convulsive, coiling movement, and dimly recognized the form of Clea. She seemed intently busy upon some childish underwater game of the kind we so often played together. She was tugging at something, her feet braced against the woodwork of the wreck, tugging and relaxing her body. Though the green thread led to her I felt a wave of relief—for perhaps she was only trying to extricate the harpoon and carry it to the surface with her. But no, for she rolled drunkenly. I slid along her like an eel, feeling with my hands. Feeling me near she turned her head as if to tell me something. Her long hair impeded my vision. As for her face I could not read the despairing pain which must have been written on it—for the water transforms every expression of the human features into the goggling imbecile grimace of the squid. But now she arched out and flung her head back so that her hair could flow freely up from her scalp—the gesture of someone throwing open a robe to exhibit a wound. And I saw. Her right hand had been pierced and nailed to the wreck by the steel arrow. At least it had not passed through her body, my mind cried out in relief, seeking to console itself; but the relief turned to sick malevolent despair when clutching the steel shaft, I myself braced my feet against the wood, tugging until my thigh muscles cracked. It would not be budged by a hair's breadth. (No, but all this was part of some incomprehensible dream, fabricated perhaps in the dead minds of the seven brooding figures which attended so carefully, so scrupulously to the laboured evolutions we now performed—we no longer free and expeditious as fish, but awkward, splayed, like lobsters trapped in a pot.) I struggled frantically with that steel arrow, seeing out of the corner of my eye the long chain of white bubbles bursting from the throat of Clea. I felt her muscles expending themselves, ebbing. Gradually she was settling in the drowsiness of the blue water, being invaded by the water-sleep which had already lulled the mariners to sleep. I shook her.

I cannot pretend that anything which followed belonged to my own volition—for the mad rage which now possessed me was not among the order of the emotions I would ever have recognized as belonging to my proper self. It exceeded, in blind violent rapacity, anything I had ever before experienced. In this curious timeless underwater dream I felt my brain ringing like the alarm bell of an ambulance, dispelling the lulling languorous ebb and flow of the marine darkness. I was suddenly rowelled by the sharp spur of terror. It was as if I were for the first time confronting myself—or perhaps an alter ego shaped after a man of action I had never realized, recognized. With one wild shove I shot to the surface again, emerging under Balthazar's very nose.

"The knife," I said, sucking in the air.

His eyes gazed into mine, as if over the edge of some sunken continent, with an expression of pity and horror; emotions preserved, fossilised, from some ice age of human memory. And native fear. He started to stammer out all the questions which invaded his mind—words like "what" "where" "when" "whither"—but could achieve no more than a baffled "wh—": a vague sputtering anguish of interrogation.

The knife which I had remembered was an Italian bayonet which had been ground down to the size of a dirk and sharpened to razor keenness. Ali the boatman had manufactured it with pride. He used it to trim ropes, for splicing and rigging. I hung there for a second while he reached out for it, eyes closed, lungs drinking in the whole sky it seemed. Then I felt the wooden haft in my fingers and without daring to look again at Balthazar I turned my toes to heaven and returned on my tracks, following the green thread.

She hung there limp now, stretched languorously out, while her long hair unfurled behind her; the tides rippled out along her body, passing through it, it seemed like an electric current playing. Everything was still, the silver coinage of sunlight dappling the floor of the pool, the silent observers, the statues whose long beards moved slowly, unctuously to and fro. Even as I began to hack at her hand I was mentally preparing a large empty space in my mind which would have to accommodate the thought of her dead. A large space like an unexplored subcontinent on the maps of the mind. It was not very long before I felt the body disengage under this bitter punishment. The water was dark. I dropped the knife and with a great push sent her reeling back from the wreck: caught her under the arms; and so rose. It seemed to take an age—an endless progression of heartbeats—in that slow-motion world. Yet we hit the sky with a concussion that knocked the breath from me—as if I had cracked my skull on the ceiling of the universe. I was standing in the shallows now rolling the heavy sodden log of her body. I heard the crash of Balthazar's teeth falling into the boat as he jumped into the water beside me. We heaved and grunted like stevedores until she was out on the pebbles, Balthazar meanwhile scrabbling about to grasp the injured hand which was spouting. He was like an electrician trying to capture and insulate a high-tension wire which had snapped. Grabbing it, he held on to it like a vice. I had a sudden picture of him as a small child holding his mother's hand nervously among a crowd of other children, or crossing a park where the boys had once thrown stones at him. . . . Through his pink gums he extruded the word "Twine"—and there was some luckily in the cutter's locker which kept him busy.

Time: _____

Comprehension Test on CLEA

PART I

DIRECTIONS: Circle the most appropriate answer.

1. The drastic incident occurred when Balthazar:

    (a) by chance entangled the lifeline of Clea's diving equipment
    (b) accidentally dropped the gun which released its harpoon
    (c) hoped to scare the hero to return to Alexandria with Clea

2. The setting of the story, Alexandria, is:

    (a) the city in Egypt named after Alexander the Great on the Mediterranean Sea
    (b) the city in Northern Virginia on the Potomac River
    (c) the city in central Louisiana

3. The hero likens his swift trip downward to rescue Clea to:

    (a) a leisurely child's game, timelessly played
    (b) a slow-motion film of endless time
    (c) a common experience, recurring over and over again

4. The hero fails to recognize himself, in his desperation to free Clea, because:

    (a) his mind is too numb to remember his actions
    (b) he is consumed by a hitherto unknown rage
    (c) the depths of the ocean so intensify a human being's normal reactions

5. Balthazar, though terrified, manages to contribute to Clea's survival by:

    (a) finding Ali's bayonet immediately
    (b) forgetting momentarily the personal loss of his teeth
    (c) attending instantly and carefully to the injured hand

PART II

DIRECTIONS: Define the following words according to their context.

1. "a rushing like the *sough* of giant wings"

2. "with all the suspense of *Ariadne*"

3. "human actions . . . drawn *unctuously* out . . . *spooled* out like toffee"

4. "no longer free and *expeditious* as fish, but awkward, *splayed,* like lobsters in a pot"

5. "suddenly *rowelled* by the sharp spur of terror"

6. "silver *coinage* of sunlight, *dappling* the floor of the pool"

PART III

DIRECTIONS: Answer these questions briefly.

1. Despite the impact, on the reader, of the tragic accident to Clea, there is a happier aspect of the story. We know that she and the hero, like children, have reveled in the excitement of the world under water. What reactions can you cite to support this observation?

2. Durrell is a master of description, especially of the extended simile and metaphor. Point out instances of his talent in this area of writing.

3. Changes in emotion and mood succeed one another in almost instantaneous succession as each new act takes place. Plot as deftly as you can their nature and sequence.

4. Unreality and improbability become commonplace in this story as a result of Balthazar's accident. What train of such distortions follows?

5. If this is your first acquaintance with Durrell, do you now wish to read more both of *Clea* and of his other novels? Make your reasons as specific as possible.

THE MACBETH MURDER MYSTERY*

James Thurber

(1574 Words)

"It was a stupid mistake to make," said the American woman I had met at my hotel in the English lake country, "but it was on the counter with the other Penguin books —the little sixpenny ones, you know, with the paper covers—and I supposed of course it was a detective story. All the others were detective stories. I'd read all the others, so I bought this one without really looking at it carefully. You can imagine how mad I was when I found it was Shakespeare." I murmured something sympathetically. "I don't see why the Penguin-books people had to get out Shakespeare plays in the same size and everything as the detective stories," went on my companion. "I think they have different-colored jackets," I said. "Well, I didn't notice that," she said. "Anyway, I got real comfy in bed that night and all ready to read a good mystery story and here I had 'The Tragedy of Macbeth'—a book for high-school students. Like 'Ivan-hoe,'" "Or 'Lorne Doone,'" I said. "Exactly," said the American lady. "And I was just crazy for a good Agatha Christie, or something. Hercule Poirot is my favorite detective." "Is he the rabbity one?" I asked. "Oh, no," said my crime-fiction expert. "He's the Belgian one. You're thinking of Mr. Pinkerton, the one that helps Inspector Bull. He's good, too."

Over her second cup of tea my companion began to tell the plot of a detective story that had fooled her completely—it seems it was the old family doctor all the time. But I cut in on her. "Tell me," I said. "Did you read 'Macbeth'?" "I had to read it," she said. "There wasn't a scrap of anything else to read in the whole room." "Did you like it?" I asked. "No, I did not," she said, decisively. "In the first place, I don't think for a moment that Macbeth did it." I looked at her blankly. "Did what?" I asked. "I don't think for a moment that he killed the King," she said "I don't think the Macbeth woman was mixed up in it, either. You suspect them the most, of course, but those are the ones that are never guilty—or shouldn't be, anyway." "I'm afraid," I began, "that I—" "But don't you see?" said the American lady. "It would spoil everything if you could figure out right away who did it. Shakespeare was too smart for that. I've read that people never have figured out "Ham-let," so it isn't likely Shakespeare would have made 'Macbeth' as simple as it seems." I thought this over while I filled my pipe. "Who do you suspect?" I asked, suddenly. "Macduff," she said, promptly. "Good God!" I whispered softly.

"Oh Macduff did it, all right," said the murder specialist. "Hercule Poirot would have got him easily." "How did you figure it out?" I demanded. "Well," she

*From *The New Yorker*, Oct. 2, 1937. Reprinted by permission; © 1937 The New Yorker Magazine, Inc.

said, "I didn't right away. At first I suspected Banquo. And then, of course, he was the second person killed. That was good right in there, that part. The person you suspect of the first murder should always be the second victim." "Is that so?" I murmured. "Oh, yes," said my informant. "They have to keep surprising you. Well, after the second murder I didn't know *who* the killer was for a while." "How about Malcolm and Donalbain, the King's sons?" I asked. "As I remember it, they fled right after the first murder. That looks suspicious." "Too suspicious," said the American lady. "Much too suspicious. When they flee, they're never guilty. You can count on that." "I believe," I said, "I'll have a brandy," and I summoned the waiter. My companion leaned toward me, her eyes bright, her teacup quivering. "Do you know who discovered Duncan's body?" she demanded. I said I was sorry, but I had forgotten. "Macduff discovers it," she said, slipping into the historical present. "Then he comes running downstairs and shouts, 'Confusion has broke open the Lord's anointed temple' and 'Sacrilegious murder has made his masterpiece' and on and on like that." The good lady tapped me on the knee. "All that stuff was rehearsed," she said. "You wouldn't say a lot of stuff like that, offhand, would you—if you had found a body?" She fixed me with a glittering eye. "I—" I began. "You're right!" she said. "You wouldn't! Unless you had practiced it in advance. 'My God, there's a body in here!' is what an innocent man would say." She sat back with a confident glare.

I thought for a while. "But what do you make of the Third Murderer?" I asked. "You know, the Third Murderer has puzzled 'Macbeth' scholars for three hundred years." "That's because they never thought of Macduff," said the American lady. "It was Macduff, I'm certain. You couldn't have one of the victims murdered by two ordinary thugs—the murderer always has to be somebody important." "But what about the banquet scene?" I asked, after a moment. "How do you account for Macbeth's guilty actions there, when Banquo's ghost came in and sat in his chair?" The lady leaned forward and tapped me on the knee again. "There wasn't any ghost," she said. "A big, strong man like that doesn't go around seeing ghosts—especially in a brightly lighted banquet hall with dozens of people around. Macbeth was *shielding somebody*!" "Who was he shielding?" I asked. "Mrs. Macbeth, of course," she said. "He thought she did it and he was going to take the rap himself. The husband always does that when the wife is suspected." "But what," I demanded, "about the sleepwalking scene, then?" "The same thing, only the other way around," said my companion. "That time *she* was shielding *him*. She wasn't asleep at all. Do you remember where it says 'Enter Lady Macbeth with a taper'?" "Yes," I said. "Well, people who walk in their sleep *never carry lights*!" said my fellow-traveler. "They have a second sight. Did you ever hear of a sleepwalker carrying a light?" "No," I said, "I never did." "Well, then, she wasn't asleep. She was acting guilty to shield Macbeth." "I think," I said, "I'll have another brandy," and I called the waiter. When he brought it, I drank rapidly and rose to go. "I believe," I said, "that you have got hold of something. Would you lend me that 'Macbeth'? I'd like to look it over tonight. I don't feel, somehow, as if I'd ever really read it." "I'll get it for you," she said. "But you'll find that I am right."

I read the play over carefully that night, and the next morning, after breakfast, I sought out the American woman. She was on the putting green, and I came up behind her silently and took her arm. She gave an exclamation. "Could I see you alone?" I asked, in a low voice. She nodded cautiously and followed me to a secluded spot. "You've found out something?" she breathed. "I've found out," I said, triumphantly, "the name of the murderer!" "You mean it wasn't Macduff?" she said. "Macduff is as innocent of those murders," I said, "as Macbeth and the Macbeth woman." I opened the copy of the play, which I had with me, and turned to Act II, Scene 2. "Here," I said, "you will see where Lady Macbeth says, 'I laid their daggers ready. He could not miss 'em. Had he not resembled my father as he slept, I had done it.' Do you see?" "No," said the American woman, bluntly, "I don't." "But it's simple!" I exclaimed. "I wonder I didn't see it years ago. The reason Duncan resembled Lady Macbeth's father as he slept is that *it actually was her father!*" "Good God!" breathed my companion, softly. "Lady Macbeth's father killed the King," I said, "and, hearing someone coming, thrust the body under the bed and crawled into the bed himself."

"But," said the lady, "you can't have a murderer who only appears in the story once. You can't have that." "I know that," I said, and I turned to Act II, Scene 4. "It says here, 'Enter Ross with an old Man.' Now, that old man is never identified and it is my contention he was old Mr. Macbeth, whose ambition it was to make his daughter Queen. There you have your motive." "But even then," cried the American Lady, "he's still a minor character!" "Not," I said, gleefully, "when you realize that he was also *one of the weird sisters in disguise!*" "You mean one of the three witches?" "Precisely," I said. "Listen to this speech of the old man's. 'On Tuesday last, a falcon towering in her pride of place, was by a mousing owl hawk'd at and kill'd.' Who does that sound like?" "It sounds like the way the three witches talk," said my companion, reluctantly. "Precisely!" I said again. "Well," said the American woman, "maybe you're right, but—" "I'm sure I am," I said. "And do you know what I'm going to do now?" "No," she said. "What?" "Buy a copy of 'Hamlet,'" I said, "and solve *that*!" My companion's eye brightened. "Then," she said, "you don't think Hamlet did it?" "I am," I said, "absolutely positive he didn't." "But who," she demanded, "do you suspect?" I looked at her cryptically. "Everybody," I said, and disappeared into a small grove of trees as silently as I had come.

Time: _____

Comprehension Test on THE MACBETH MURDER MYSTERY

PART I

DIRECTIONS: Circle the most appropriate answer.

1. The American woman was deceived in her choice of *Macbeth* as a mystery story because:

   (a) the publishers had treated it as a contemporary murder story
   (b) she was not educated enough to be familiar with the name of the classic
   (c) high school texts are not meant to be read for enjoyment

2. Although the lady's process of making assumptions seemingly was sound, she could never deduce the right answer because:

   (a) she had not read the play carefully enough
   (b) she was applying to it current principles of mystery writing
   (c) the author is spoofing the vogue of solving mystery stories

3. The final role of the narrator is:

   (a) to let himself enter into the lady's world of fantasy
   (b) to retreat before her onslaught of notions
   (c) to remain a neutral listener

4. The preposterousness of the whole story is revealed in such assumptions as these:

   (a) Shakespeare is too smart a writer for a faulty construction of plot
   (b) Hercule Poirot would have solved the mystery effortlessly
   (c) the real murderer was the least suspected, Macduff

5. As the story progresses, even the atmosphere becomes one of intrigue as:

   (a) the author probes more and more
   (b) he moves around stealthily and disappears silently
   (c) the woman becomes so British in her actions, like drinking tea, and becomes involved in the solution

PART II

DIRECTIONS: Define the following terms according to their use in the context.

1. "the little *sixpenny* ones"

2. "Is he the *rabbity* one?"

3. "slipping into the *historical present*"

4. "it is my *contention*"

5. "I looked at her *cryptically*"

PART III

DIRECTIONS: Answer these questions briefly.

1. (a) Do you see any significance in the fact that one of the two leading characters is an American woman?

(b) Do you see any significance in the changes in tone of the noun substitutes referring to her, beginning with "my crime-fiction expert," "murder specialist," "informant," "fellow-traveler," "My companion," "the American lady"?

2. Why is the title so ingenious? Connect it with other aspects of the book's resemblance to popular mysteries.

3. What is the connection between the setting of the English lake country and the line, "She fixed me with a glittering eye"?

4. Compare her version of Shakespeare's language with her American interpretations and renditions. What are the effects of her distortions?

5. As the initiative in solving the mystery shifts from her to him, what is the effect of his solutions on her? What is the apparent effect of his solutions on himself?

TABLE FOR DERIVING RATE OF COMPREHENSION

DIRECTIONS: The general procedure for calculating rate of comprehension is to divide the number of words read by the reading time. A short-cut to this procedure, however, is provided in the rate table below.

In the left-hand column, locate the figure that is closest to your reading time. Then move across the page to the column headed by the number and title of the selection read. The figure in this column is your WPM (words per minute) rate.

No. of the selection	1	2	3	4	5	6	7	8	9	10
Title	Samuel Johnson	Dry September	Cress Delahanty	Huckleberry Finn	King James I	Don Camillo	Geoffrey Chaucer	Deliver Us from Evil	Clea	Macbeth Murder
Total no. of words	596	729	775	822	881	889	1014	1336	1496	1574
Time (minutes and seconds)										
1 min. 00 sec.	596	729	775	822	881	889	1014	1336	1496	1574
10	511	625	664	705	755	762	869	1145	1282	1349
20	447	547	581	617	661	667	761	1002	1122	1181
30	397	486	517	548	587	593	678	891	997	1049
40	358	435	465	493	529	533	608	802	898	944
50	325	398	423	448	481	485	553	729	816	859
2 min. 00 sec.	298	365	388	411	441	445	507	668	748	787
10	275	336	358	379	407	410	468	617	690	726
20	255	312	332	352	378	381	435	573	641	675
30	238	292	310	329	352	356	406	534	598	630
40	222	273	291	308	330	333	380	501	561	590
50	210	257	274	290	311	314	358	472	528	556
3 min. 00 sec.	199	243	258	274	294	296	338	445	499	525
10	188	230	245	260	278	281	320	422	472	497
20	179	219	233	247	264	267	304	401	449	472
30	170	208	221	235	252	254	290	382	427	450
40	163	199	211	224	240	242	277	364	408	429
50	155	190	202	214	230	231	265	349	390	411
4 min. 00 sec.	149	182	194	206	220	222	254	334	374	394
10	143	175	186	197	211	213	243	321	359	378
20	138	168	179	190	203	205	234	308	345	363
30	132	162	172	183	196	198	225	297	332	350
40	128	156	166	176	189	191	217	286	321	337
50	124	150	160	170	182	184	210	276	310	326
5 min. 00 sec.	119	146	155	164	176	176	203	267	299	315
10	115	141	150	159	171	172	196	259	290	305
20	112	137	145	154	165	167	190	251	281	295
30	108	133	141	149	160	162	184	243	272	286
40	105	129	137	145	155	157	179	236	264	278
50	102	125	133	141	151	152	174	229	256	270
6 min. 00 sec.	99	122	129	137	147	148	169	223	249	263
10	97	118	126	133	143	144	164	217	243	255
20	94	115	122	130	139	140	160	211	236	249
30	92	112	119	126	136	137	156	206	230	242
40	89	109	116	123	132	133	152	200	224	236
50	87	107	113	120	129	130	148	196	219	230

(Continued on next page)

No. of the selection	1	2	3	4	5	6	7	8	9	10
Title	Samuel Johnson	Dry September	Cress Delahanty	Huckleberry Finn	King James I	Don Camillo	Geoffrey Chaucer	Deliver Us from Evil	Clea	Macbeth Murder
Total no. of words	596	729	775	822	881	889	1014	1336	1496	1574
Time (minutes and seconds)										
7 min. 00 sec.	85	104	111	117	126	127	145	191	214	225
10	83	101	108	115	123	124	141	186	209	220
20	81	99	106	112	120	121	138	182	204	215
30	79	97	103	110	117	119	135	178	199	210
40	78	95	101	107	115	116	132	174	195	205
50	76	93	99	105	112	113	129	171	190	201
8 min. 00 sec.	75	91	97	103	110	111	127	167	187	197
10	73	89	95	101	108	109	124	164	183	193
20	71	87	93	99	106	107	122	160	180	189
30	70	86	91	97	104	105	119	157	176	185
40	69	84	89	95	102	103	117	154	172	182
50	67	83	88	93	100	101	115	151	169	178
9 min. 00 sec.	66	81	86	91	98	99	113	148	166	175
10	65	80	85	89	96	97	111	146	163	172
20	64	78	83	88	94	95	109	143	160	169
30	63	77	82	87	93	94	107	141	157	166
40	62	75	80	85	91	92	105	138	155	163
50	61	74	79	84	89	90	103	136	152	160
10 min. 00 sec.	60	73	78	82	88	89	101	134	150	157

PERFORMANCE CHART

1. COMPREHENSION AND RATE

DIRECTIONS: To compute your comprehension score, add the number of right answers in Parts I and III of each speed-reading selection; then multiply by 10. In the appropriate space on the chart below, record accuracy of comprehension with (Δ) and the obtained WPM rate with (x). Strive to keep your level of comprehension high (above 70%) as you work to increase speed, and strive to keep above the minimal rate of 350 WPM.

TITLE		Samuel Johnson	Dry September	Cress Delahanty	Huckleberry Finn	King James I	Don Camillo	Geoffrey Chaucer	Deliver Us from Evil	Clea	Macbeth Murder
Accuracy of Comprehension	Rate (WPM)										
	1600										
	1550										
	1500										
	1450										
	1400										
	1350										
	1300										
	1250										
	1200										
	1150										
	1100										
	1050										
	1000										
	950										
	900										
	850										
	800										
	750										
	700										
	650										
	600										
	550										
100%	500										
90%	450										
80%	400										
70%	350										
60%	300										
50%	250										
40%	200										
30%	150										
20%	100										
10%	50										
0%	0										

2. VOCABULARY

DIRECTIONS: To evaluate your vocabulary performance on Part II of the speed-reading selections, use the scale below and record the results in the appropriate blank.

SCALE: Excellent = 6 correct, Satisfactory = 4–5 correct, Poor = less than 4 correct

SELECTION	EXCELLENT	SATISFACTORY	POOR
1. from *The Life of Samuel Johnson*			
2. from DRY SEPTEMBER			
3. from *Cress Delahanty*			
4. from *The Adventures of Huckleberry Finn*			
5. THE POISONING OF KING JAMES I			
6. from *The Little World of Don Camillo*			
7. from *Geoffrey Chaucer of England*			
8. from *Deliver Us from Evil*			
9. from *Clea*			
10. THE MACBETH MURDER MYSTERY			

Chapter VI

SKILLS FOR STUDYING

INTRODUCTION

Students who perform poorly on term papers or on examinations usually fall into one of two categories: those who have not studied, and those who have not learned how to study. This chapter attempts to aid the latter group, the student who may work with exceptional perseverance, but without direction or organization. Careful study skills can improve the academic performance of even the most gifted students.

In the preceding sections of this text you have examined the principles of, and actually analyzed, sentences, paragraphs, and longer selections. As you studied these units of discourse separately and then related them to the whole, you were engaged in a process of organization. By now your reading skills should have developed to the point where your concern for a writer's meaning and his method of presentation will provide the basis for continued reading improvement. This chapter will focus your attention on the use of special study skills in the reading of textbook and reference material; it will encourage you to study in an organized manner; and it will try to make you more cognizant of the role that reading plays in your writing.

OUTLINING

Perhaps the most useful skill you can acquire is the ability to recognize and construct outlines. For the practical illustration of this technique, we have chosen to outline the book review which Professor Arthur Schlesinger, Jr. wrote of *The Politics of Hysteria* by Edmund Stillman and William Pfaff. First we present the review itself, then an outline of it, and then a general discussion of outlining. Follow each carefully.

In reading Professor Schlesinger's essay, notice how promptly he identifies Stillman and Pfaff's purpose in writing their new book. Then note how he presents the main argument of the authors, that the present crisis has been engendered by the expansion of Western culture; he cites four aspects here. The results of this expansion, the authors assert, are the devastation of most of the non-Western cultures (Professor Schlesinger cites five after-effects) and damage to two more cultures, which by measures peculiar to each managed to survive. Running parallel to this havoc to the rest of the world, the authors assert and the reviewer next outlines, is the action of the apparently invulnerable West in turning to terror for its ends (three are mentioned) and the self-destruction of Europe in two world wars. Following these examinations of what the authors state, the reviewer asks, "What is the remedy?" and ends with a number of answers proposed by the authors.

The next main section is concerned with flaws of the book—of which there are quite a few, according to Professor Schlesinger—and the review ends with a general assessment of the entire book.

As you read, observe aspects of the reviewer's organizational skill that aid your comprehension: easy identification of broad segments, the furnishing of many details for clarity, the constant use of parallel structures. Note, for example, the use of similar infinitive phrases in this sentence: "The consequence was *to release the passion for destruction, to hasten the rush to totalitarianism and to destroy in the eyes of Asia and Africa lingering impressions of European moral and military superiority.*" The use of similar adjective and noun constructions is also deliberate: "Their argument is that the expansion of Europe has plunged the whole world into crisis—that the spread of *western science, western technology, western philosophy, western ideals* has forced non-western cultures into *confusion, demoralization, fantasy, fanaticism* and *revenge.*" Such stylistic devices as these facilitated the construction of the outline which appears after the review.

THE GENIE IS OUT FOR GOOD
A PLEA FOR THE WEST TO CALM THE
WHIRLWIND IT HAS RELEASED*

Arthur Schlesinger, Jr.

THE POLITICS OF HYSTERIA: THE SOURCES OF 20th-CENTURY CONFLICT. By Edmund Stillman and William Pfaff. Harper & Row. 273 pp. $4.95.

Two years ago, in "The New Politics: America and the End of the Post-War World," Edmund Stillman and William Pfaff made a lively and perceptive analysis of the American predicament in a changing world. In this new book, they are training their sights on a larger target. Their purpose is nothing less than to explain (or, as they would put it, to "explicate") the root causes of the distempers of our age and to define the mood, if not the measures, which alone can promise relief. If "The Politics of Hysteria" works less well than "The New Politics," it is surely in part because the authors had the boldness to tackle some of the least manageable and most fundamental questions of our time.

Their argument is that the expansion of Europe has plunged the whole world into crisis—that the spread of western science, western technology, western philosophy, western ideals has forced non-western cultures into confusion, demoralization, fantasy, fanaticism and revenge. A series of historical chapters describe the culture shock produced by "the explosion of European empire" from the 16th century on. Islam and Russia, the authors argue, survived the blow, the first by defiance, the second by assimilation and reaction. But most of the cultures of Africa and Asia were "devastated," their traditions and structures undermined, their cohesion and identity subverted. "Their reaction was very often the simplest and most direct—a convulsive effort to expel or kill." But nothing could hold back the onward thrust of western ideas and ideals.

Still, the West itself, despite its apparent invulnerability, had its own inner doubts and demons. "Behind the bourgeois certainties, behind the disguises of reason," as the authors put it, a little too characteristically, "there were sinister fantasies waiting to be acted out." Most sinister of all was the passion to enlist terror to bring about the happiness of man, to use violence as the instrument of a vision of truth, to seek a total solution in history. The First World War, Europe's orgy of self-destruction, was the beginning of the end. The consequence was to release the passion for destruction, to hasten the rush to totalitarianism and to destroy in the eyes of Asia and Africa lingering impressions of European moral and military superiority.

The Second World War completed the collapse of Europe. The United States and the Soviet Union then made their bids to take Europe's place, but it has become evident that neither is adequate as the inheritor

of the European destiny, and the cold war between them has declined from a real fight into a symbolic and ritualistic conflict. Meanwhile, the West, having plowed up the world, can conceive of no remedy for what it has done except more of the same—more technology, more industrialism, more modernization. It sees in the westernization of the world the only cure for disorder and revolution. But all it does is "to detribalize its victims, to strip them of one culture and give nothing in its place but a vision of limitless power and taste for ideology." Nothing is a greater mess of illusion, cruelty and nonsense, Messrs. Stillman and Pfaff suggest, than the so-called Third World.

What is the remedy? These authors do not think that the genie can be put back into the bottle: they agree that the desire to modernize is irreversible. But, if the West has caused the trouble, it also offers the only hope of resolution: "There is only the West—prodigious and guilty, creative and terribly flawed. . . . There is no true post-Western culture." At the very least, the West can mitigate the destructive process and avoid actions which make things worse (or, as the authors prefer to put it, "aggravate the crisis of the age"). More than that, just as the disruptive qualities of the West infect the world, "so a calming of the West—a resolution of its own crisis—could have a quieting influence upon those areas that react to the West." Let the West recover its civilized and humane impulses; let it eschew ideology and violence; let it not stake everything on politics; let it forsake intervention in the affairs of others; let it understand the mixed character of man and the tragedy of history; let it draw back, above all, *pas trop de zele.*

The essential thesis of "The Politics of Hysteria" is arresting. One feels about the book, however, that, like the Stillman-Pfaff theory of Europe, it is "creative and terribly flawed." It is, in the first place, awfully pretentious. It is filled with echoes of Niebuhr, Toynbee, Spengler and Freud—a wildly mixed collection; it goes in madly for slightly irrelevant quotations, perhaps designed to show the wide reading of the authors; and it is decked out with a somewhat spurious apparatus of scholarship (I say "somewhat spurious" because the footnotes lack the clinching item of documentation—the page number of the book to which reference is made).

In the second place, the authors tend to announce fairly familiar ideas with a flare of trumpets, as if no one else had ever thought them before. Thus they declare, with an air of audacity, that communism and fascism, far from being opposites, actually touch identical impulses in man and society. So, too, Niebuhr's critique of the complacent optimism and rationalism of the 19th-century West is powerful, and I agree with the authors that it is correct. But he made it a quarter of a century ago, and there is no real need to present it today as if it were a dangerous heresy. The book is saturated with Niebuhr and addicted to his key words—"demonic," "extravagant," "parochial," events are constantly "judgments" on situations, and we hear much about "the essential ambiguity of the human condition." But "The Politics of Hysteria" lacks the weight, the originality and the modesty of "The Nature and Destiny of Man" or of Niebuhr's more directly political writings.

---

* From *Book Week*, Feb. 16, 1964. Published by the New York *Herald Tribune*. By permission.

The potted history is often glib and unconvincing. In particular, one senses, as the authors would put it, an "extravagance" in their display of Western self-hatred. It is quite true that Western culture has deep and unacknowledged susceptibilities to ideological violence. But large-scale violence was not an invention of the West. It seems hardly fair to say, for example, that the West "taught the world" political terror. The annihilation of a social class or racial abstraction is surely not "impossible to a mind not conditioned by Western habits of thought"—as the authors themselves tacitly admit when they mention the Aztecs, the ancient Hebrews and the campaigns of Ch'in Shih Huang Ti in China. The history of Africa, of Asia and of the American Indians is full of other examples.

I feel, too, that they are a little glib about the character of Western, and especially of American, policy. Their thesis requires that the United States be committed to an unlimited and universal ideological crusade. Their proof lies essentially in the official rhetoric of the Dulles period. But even then, as they concede, there was a divergence between "the often sober and pragmatic reality of American foreign policy and the language in which it was clothed." Is what was said really a better clue to the nature of the policy than what was done?

Since 1961, of course, even the language has changed. Can one really say now that the "American conviction" is that "the nation's domestic society can be the prototype of a benign international order?" President Kennedy, for example, repeatedly stressed the limitations of American power and the illusion that all world problems had American solutions. He said repeatedly that we can not expect to make the world over in the American image and that our hope is "to make the world safe for diversity." Such statements contradict the Stillman-Pfaff thesis and, therefore, go unmentioned, while instead we are offered quotations from John K. Jessup, Archibald MacLeish, David Sarnoff and Clinton Rossiter—estimable gentlemen all, but something less than authoritative expositors of American policy. Nor in all the hard and intelligent words about the folly of intervention and the absurdity of supposing that foreign aid can magically heal the anguish of cultural transition do they declare themselves on the practical questions with which statesmen must deal: do they really believe, for example, that we should cancel the foreign-aid program, abandon the Alliance for Progress and do nothing but cultivate our own garden? If the United States had the Stillman-Pfaff sense of tragedy, wherein would our policies, not our words, be different?

"The Politics of Hysteria" remains a valuable book with many shrewd and stimulating insights. But it is an uneven book, in many respects cocksure and superficial. One hopes that their next essay will combine the same freshness of attack with greater sobriety and scruple in execution.

OUTLINE OF THE SCHLESINGER BOOK REVIEW

THESIS SENTENCE: *The Politics of Hysteria* by Stillman and Pfaff is an interesting and valuable but pretentious and superficial book, attributing the present world crisis to the expansion of Western culture and suggesting a solution in the reform of Western policy.

I. The purpose of the authors
  A. To explain the causes of the difficulties of our age
  B. To define the mood and/or measures to provide relief

II. Their argument on the causes of the crisis
  A. The historical effects of the "explosion" of Western culture
    1. On Islam and Russia
    2. On other cultures of Africa and Asia
  B. Inner flaws in Western culture
  C. The two World Wars as the culmination of disaster
    1. Consequences of the First World War
      a. To release the passion for destruction
      b. To hasten totalitarianism
      c. To destroy Asian and African ideas of European moral and material superiority
    2. Consequences of the Second World War
      a. To complete the collapse of Europe
      b. To leave the West no remedy except the inadequate one of more Westernization

III. Their suggested remedies for the West
  A. To mitigate the destruction process
  B. To resolve its internal crisis
    1. To recover its civilized impulses
    2. To eschew ideology and violence
    3. To renounce complete dependence on politics
    4. To cease intervention in others' affairs
    5. To acquire sympathy with other cultures
    6. To relax its overzealousness

IV. The defects of the book
  A. Its pretentiousness of scholarship
    1. Echoes of a wild mixture of authors
    2. Irrelevant quotations
    3. Footnotes without page references
  B. Presentation of familiar ideas as if they were new
    1. Similarity of communism and fascism
    2. Niebuhr's critique of the West
  C. Glib and unconvincing arguments
    1. In their historical view of Western history and culture: an exaggerated notion of Western self-hatred
    2. In their account of Western and American policy

    a. Their dependence on rhetoric of the Dulles period
      (1) Difference between rhetoric and actuality
      (2) Difference between rhetoric then and present statements of policy
    b. Lack of attention to what our practical policies should be

V. Summary evaluation: valuable book with many shortcomings

CLASSES OF OUTLINES

The outline is a tool by which the writer and the reader put things in their proper place and perspective. The writer uses it to arrange and to order the material with which he is working, whereas the reader uses it to determine the basic structure and meaning of what he reads. For both agents involved in the process of communicating ideas (sending and receiving), the outline functions in a manner similar to that of the blueprint in architecture or the recipe in cooking.

The two most common types of outline are the topic outline and the sentence outline. The topic outline consists of words, phrases, and dependent clauses; the sentence outline of complete statements. The type of outline chosen by a reader usually depends upon the complexity of the material and the purpose to which he will put the content. Classroom reading assignments frequently need to be reviewed later by the student, and the sentence or the topic outline is often helpful in taking notes on this kind of material. Either type of outline enables the reader to organize particulars about a given subject rapidly and in a form that is convenient for immediate or future reference.

The form for all outlines is generally standardized. The levels of an outline are designated by alternating numbers and letters. Main divisions are labeled with Roman numerals, subtopics with capital letters, Arabic numerals, and lower case letters in this order of importance. For class notes and the review of material read, an outline of two or three levels is usually sufficient. But for the study of detailed, difficult material, it is sometimes important to go to the fourth and fifth levels.

Other points to remember about outlining are these:

1. Indent each level so that the relationship between the parts is easily discernible. That is, major headings should be indented equally, subheadings of each new level indented even more, etc.
2. Place periods after the numerals and letters of the major divisions and the subdivisions of the first three levels.
3. Use parentheses for the numerals and letters of the subordinate ideas of levels four and five.
4. Phrase a thesis statement or summary sentence for the content of the entire outline.
5. Group related ideas, and arrange them in logical order.
6. Avoid the use of such meaningless terms as "introduction," "body," and "conclusion." Whenever these terms are used, be sure to explain them.
7. Divide only those levels that yield at least two related parts. Avoid single headings or subheadings, since a division denotes at least two parts.
8. Maintain parallelism in form between all the like items under each of the major headings and the various subheadings—that is, a noun should be parallel with another noun, a prepositional phrase with another prepositional phrase, an adjective clause with another adjective clause, etc.

FORM OF AN OUTLINE

Thesis: _____

I. _____ (used for major headings)

  A. _____ (used for subheadings of the first level)

  B. _____

    1. _____ (used for subheadings of the second level)

      a. _____ (used for the third level)

      b. _____

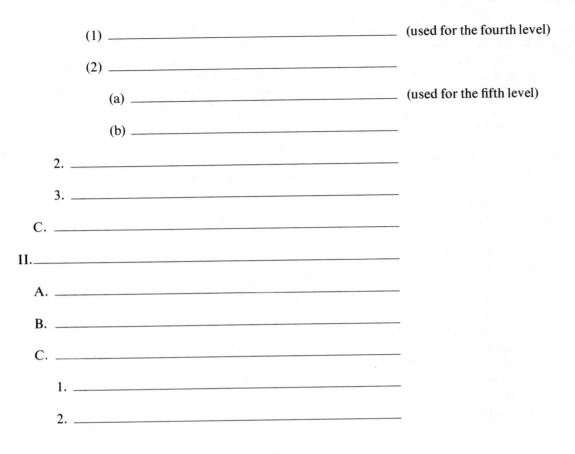

(1) _____ (used for the fourth level)

(2) _____

   (a) _____ (used for the fifth level)

   (b) _____

2. _____

3. _____

C. _____

II. _____

A. _____

B. _____

C. _____

1. _____

2. _____

READING TEXTBOOK MATERIAL AND TAKING NOTES

You do your best reading when you know the nature of the material to be read, your purpose in reading it, and the method to use to get the desired results.

Assume that you have been asked to read a chapter or two in a social science or a biology textbook. How would you approach this reading assignment? Your first step would be to establish your purpose for reading the material. Reread your instructor's assignment and note the key words; these are clues to direct your reading.

Let us assume that the chapter in your social science text is on the development of modern science. Your instructor has asked you to read the chapter so that you can answer the following questions: What were some of the major historical influences that led to the development of modern science in the seventeenth century? Following the suggestions made in the preceding paragraph, what words in the assignment would you pay particular attention to? "Major," "historical," "influences," "development," "modern science," "seventeenth century" are the words which will direct you to the answer to the question. You would then decide that your purpose in reading the chapter is to search for

and identify "influences," specifically, influences that were important, that led to the development of modern science, and that are found in history up to the seventeenth century. With your purpose in mind, take the following steps.

First, try to recall what you may already know about the question. What are some of the relevant details you might already be familiar with from other studies? You may know that during the Middle Ages man was more interested in the salvation of his soul than he was in the physical universe. You may also remember that such men as Aristotle and St. Thomas Aquinas were great logicians whose deductive system of thinking affected their possible attitudes toward science. Although their system of classification was effective, it led them to assume that the causes of things could be ascertained by logical analysis. Moreover, in their system a quantitative, experimental approach to the study of nature was not important. With this sketchy background you may wish to begin reading your assignment at this point. Later you may skim over a few pages on the Middle Ages in order to organize your thinking on this topic.

Now turn to the appropriate pages and begin to *preview* the material. Look at the title of the chapter, note its subdivisions (frequently indicated in italics or boldface print), read the captions beneath the diagrams and figures, glance at the summary at the close of the chapter, skim over the review questions listed at the end of the discussion.

These few minutes are not wasted. They serve to help you discover what the author's organization is, refresh your memory with material that may be familiar, and guide you in the crystallizing of your purpose.

Next, read each paragraph, focusing your attention on the main idea. Relate the pertinent details to the key statement. As you move from one paragraph to another, do not lose sight of the controlling theme of the total chapter. (Remember the seven steps, suggested in Chapter III, pp. 174–75, of the method for reading the long selection.) After you have completed reading a sizable portion of the material, you will be ready to take notes.

Although you may have underlined passages as you were reading, underlining is not a substitute for the value of making separate outlined notes. The value of note-taking is not only that you can preserve the information for reviews and examinations: the very act of writing the notes reinforces your comprehension of the material and makes it easier to retain. Thus, as a practical and effective means of reading, learning, and studying, the skill of note-taking is an important asset to you as a college student.

Some suggested do's and don'ts for note-taking follow:

1. Phrase the main ideas in your own words. Your ability to state concisely the main points serves as a check on your reading comprehension.
2. Use outline form to show logical and important relationships between ideas.
3. Use abbreviations, but be sure they are meaningful and consistent.
4. Be selective. Do not try to rewrite the entire chapter or book.
5. Make certain that your handwriting is legible.

Your answer to the social science question presented on p. 349 will vary in terms of the source you have used. An example of the kind of notes you may have taken is presented below:

I. Some forerunners of seventeenth-century modern science
   A. Archimedes (287–212 B.C.)—Greek mathematician and physicist who anticipated the modern modes of scientific thinking in his handling of the general principles of nature.
   B. Aristotle (384–322 B.C.)—Greek philosopher and scientist who catalogued knowledge and

increased it by his wise observations and evaluations.
   C. Euclid (450–374 B.C.)—author of *Elements of Geometry,* one of the great classics of antiquity.
   D. Hippocrates (460–370 B.C.)—father of modern medicine; contributed the famous Hippocratic oath; showed objectivity toward medical fact.

II. Some events contributing to the revival of learning (Renaissance)
   A. Invention of gunpowder in the fifteenth century; use in warfare weakened feudal bonds.
   B. Commercialization and urban development loosened ties of medieval religious views.
      1. Contact with new peoples.
      2. Incentives for wealth and pleasure.
      3. Rise of merchant and trader class.
   C. Invention of printing press (1440) and subsequent mass production of books.
   D. Fall of Constantinople (1453) and revival of interest in Greek achievements.
   E. Discovery of America and interest in new trade routes for pursuit of riches.
   F. Theory of a heliocentric universe (1543)—(formulated by Copernicus)—that affected man's interpretation of his role in the universe and his view toward other planets.

III. Some major contributors to the development of modern science (seventeenth century)
   A. Kepler (A.D. 1571–1630)—three laws of planetary motion derived from mathematical deduction.
   B. Galileo (A.D. 1564–1642)—the dynamics of moving bodies (law of falling bodies, the law of pendulum, acceleration, inertia, etc.)
   C. Newton (A.D. 1642–1727)—The principle of universal gravitation.
   D. Harvey (A.D. 1578–1657)—the discovery of the circulation of the blood.
   E. Boyle (A.D. 1627–1691)—law of gases.

IV. Some attributes of the science of the new age.
   A. Emphasis on nature, the ultimate arbiter.
   B. Use of the hypothetico-deductive method.
   C. Emphasis on quantitative, precise results.
   D. Cooperation of scientists through formation of scientific organizations.

Your final step in the preparation of the reading assignment is to review your notes. This is an important process, for it enables you to make sure that you have integrated all of the parts of the content and related them to the purpose of your assignment. From your understanding of the whole you should be prepared to make evaluations of the reading material and to relate it to other readings and academic experiences.

SKIMMING

If you know why you are reading and what you are looking for, it is not always necessary for you to read an entire book, chapter, or article thoroughly. At times such thorough reading is even pointless. For example, if you are looking for a number in a telephone directory, would you read the entire directory? Or would you sit down and read a volume of the encyclopedia from the first to the last page? No, you would skim. Undoubtedly, you have skimmed the newspaper for a particular advertisement, used the card catalog to find the complete title of a book, or looked up the definition of a word in a dictionary.

But how does one skim? You use the comprehension skills that we have aimed to develop in preceding chapters. First, decide what you are looking for. Then use one of the following devices to get the information you need:

1. *Read main ideas* of paragraphs without regard to details if you want only a *general* view of an article or selection.
2. *Use* key words to find specific details.
3. *Refer* to tables of contents and indexes to locate information and to pinpoint sections to read carefully.
4. *Note* the first paragraph of news stories and also the right-hand corner of the front page for prominent articles.
5. *Read* synopses of magazine articles to determine whether you wish to read the whole article. For example, each issue of *Fortune* carries immediately after the title page or table of contents a summary of the articles in each issue.
6. Look for the *who, what, why, where,* and *when* in a report.
7. Determine the *typical arrangement* of entries in a reference work, so that you can go directly to that part of each entry that will contain the information you seek.

EXERCISE 1: SKIMMING

DIRECTIONS: Answer each of the questions listed below by skimming the four consecutive entries from WHO'S WHO IN AMERICA.* Remember that each entry lists its kinds of information in the same order.

1. Which man is the youngest? Which is the oldest?

2. Which men hold a master's degree?

3. Which men have received honorary degrees?

4. Which men have been in the armed services?

5. Which men have studied at Harvard?

6. Which men have held public office?

7. Which men have published books?

8. Which men have been married more than twice?

* Printed with the permission of the publisher, Marquis — Who's Who, Inc., Chicago.

A.

ACHESON, Dean Gooderham, ex-sec. of State; born Middletown, Conn., April 11, 1893; s. Edward Campion and Eleanor (Gooderham) A.; A.B., Yale, 1915, M.A. (honorary), 1936; LL.B., Harvard U., 1918, LL.D. (hon.) 1950; LL.D. (hon.), Wesleyan U., Conn., 1947; D.C.L., Oxford U., 1952; LL.D., Brandeis U., 1956, Cambridge U., 1958; m. Alice Stanley, May 5, 1917; children—Jane (Mrs. Dudley B. W. Brown), David Campion, Mary Eleanor (Mrs. William P. Bundy). Private sec. to Louis D. Brandeis, asso. justice U.S. Supreme Ct., 1919–1921; with Covington, Burling and Rublee, 1921–33; apptd. undersec. of treasury, May 19, 1933, resigned Nov. 15, 1933; mem. Covington, Burling, Rublee, Acheson & Shorb, Jan. 1, 1934–Jan. 31, 1941; appointed assistant secretary of State, Feb. 1, 1941; undersec. of State, 1945–47, sec. of State, 1949–53; pvt. practice law with Covington, Burling, Washington, since 1953. Vice chmn. Commn. on Orgn. Exec. Br. of the Govt. Ensign United States Navy, World War I. Awarded Order of Vasa (Swedish); Medal for Merit; Order of Aztec Eagle (Mexico); Grand Master Nat. Order of So. Cross (Brazil); Grand Cross Order of Boyacá (Colombia). Fellow Yale Corp. Mem. Am. Acad. Arts. and Scis., Delta Kappa Epsilon Scroll and Key. Democrat. Episcopalian. Clubs: Metropolitan, Chevy Chase (Washington); Century (N.Y.). Author: A Citizen Looks at Congress, 1957. Publication: A Democrat Looks at His Party, 1955; Power and Diplomacy, 1958.

B.

ADENAUER, Konrad, chancellor Fed. Republic of Germany; b. Cologne, Jan. 5, 1876; student law univs. of Bonn, Munich, Freiburg; married twice (both wives deceased); 4 sons, 3 daughters. Law clerk, Cologne, 1902–04; became lawyer on staff of dist. atty.; on staff of mayor of Cologne, 1906; became lord mayor of Cologne, 1917; founder Cologne Univ., 1925; arrested during Hitler regime; returned as mayor by U.S. Occupation Forces, but later removed by British, when Cologne was made part of British zone; elected chmn. Christian Dem. Union in Brit. zone, 1945 in Fed. Rep. of Germany, 1950; pres. Parliamentary Council at Bonn, 1948–49. Became first chancellor of Fed. Republic of Germany, 1949; minister for fgn. affairs, 1951–55, reelected fed. chancellor, 1953, 57. Roman Catholic. Home: Rhondorf Rhein, Germany. Office: Bundeskanzleramt, Haus Schaumburg Bonn, Germany.

C.

AGAR, Herbert Sebastian, author, publisher; born New Rochelle, N.Y., Sept. 29, 1897; son John Giraud and Agnes Louise (Macdonough) A.; prep. edn. Newman Sch., Lakewood, N.J.; A.B., Columbia U., 1919; A.M., Princeton U., 1920, Ph.D., 1922, Litt. D., Southwestern, Memphis, Tenn., 1936; LL.D., Boston U., 1941; m. Adeline Scott, Feb. 6, 1918 (divorced 1933); children—William Scott, Agnes; m. 2d, Eleanor Carroll Chilton, Apr. 11, 1933 (divorced 1945); m. 3d Barbara Lutyens Wallace, June, 1945. London corr. Louisville Courier-Jour., Louisville Times, 1929–34; author of syndicated daily newspaper column, "Time and Tide," 1935–39; editor Louisville Courier-Journal, 1940–2; literary editor The English Review (London, England), 1930–34; special assistant to the American ambassador at London, England, dir. British Div., Office War Information, London, Eng., 1943–46; dir. Rupert Hart-Davis, Ltd. (London), T.W.W. Ltd. Mem. Phi Beta Kappa. Joint editor (with Allen Tate) of symposium Who Owns America? 1936. Served as seaman, later chief q.m. USNR, 1917–18. lt. comdr., 1942. Clubs: National Arts, Century (N.Y.C.); National Press (Washington); Garrick, Savile, London, England. Author: (verse) Fire and Sleet and Candlelight (with Willis Fisher and Eleanor Carroll Chilton), 1928; Milton and Plato, 1928; The Garment of Praise (with Eleanor Carroll Chilton), 1929; Bread and Circuses, 1930; The Defeat of Baudelaire (translation), 1932; The People's Choice, 1933 (Pulitzer prize for Am. history); Land of the Free, 1935; What is America? 1936; Pursuit of Happiness, 1938; Beyond German Victory (with Helen Hill), 1940; A Time for Greatness, 1942; The Price of Union, 1950; A Declaration of Faith, 1952; Abraham Lincoln, 1952; The Price of Power, 1957; Home: Beechwood, Petworth, Sussex, Eng. Office: 36 Soho Sq., London, W. 1, Eng.

D.

AIKEN, Conrad Potter, critic, poet; b. Savannah, Ga., Aug. 5, 1889; s. William Ford and Anna (Potter) A; A.B., Harvard, 1911; m. Jessie McDonald, Aug. 25, 1912 (div. 1929); children—John Kempton, Jane Kempton, Joan Delano; m. 2d, Clarice Lorenz, 1930 (div. 1937); m. 3d, Mary Augusta Hoover, July 7, 1937. Author: (poems) Earth Triumphant and Other Tales, 1914; Turns and Movies, 1916; The Jig of Forslin, 1916; Nocturne of Remembered Spring, 1917; The Charnel Rose, 1918; The House of Dust, 1920; Punch, the Immortal Liar, 1921; Priapus and the Pool, 1922; Pilgrimage of Festus, 1923; Scepticisms—Notes on Contemporary Poetry, 1919; Priapus and the Pool, and Other Poems, 1925; Bring! Bring! and Other Stories, 1925; Blue Voyage (novel), 1927; Costumes by Eros (short stories), 1928; John Deth, and Other Poems, 1930; The Coming Forth by Day of Osiris Jones (poem), 1931; Preludes for Memnon (poems), 1931; Great Circle (novel), 1933; Among the Lost People (short stories), 1934; Landscape West of Eden (poems), 1934; King Coffin (novel), 1935; Time in the Rock (poems), 1934; A Heart for the Gods of Mexico (novel), 1939; The Conversation (novel), 1939; And in the Human Heart (poems), 1940; Brownstone Eclogues (poems), 1942; The Soldier, 1944; The Kid (poem), 1947; The Divine Pilgrim (poem), 1949; Skylight One (poems), 1949; Mr. Arcularis (play with Diana Hamilton), 1949; The Short Stories of Conrad Aiken, 1950; Ushant: An Essay (an autobiography), 1952; Collected Poems, 1953; A Letter from Li Po (poems), 1956; Mr. Arcularis, 1957; Sheepfold Hill (book of poems), 1957; A Reviewer's ABC (collected criticism), 1958. Editor: Modern American Poets, 1922; Selected Poems Emily Dickinson, 1924; Am. Poetry (1671–1928), 1929. Compiler: Selected Poems, 1929. Contbg. editor, Dial, 1917–19. Awarded Pulitzer prize for best vol. of verse, 1929; Bryher Award, 1952; Nat. Book award for Collected Poems (1954). Apptd. to chair of poetry Library of Congress, 1950–52, fellow in Am. letters, 1947. Awarded Bollingen Prize, 1956; fellowship Am. Acad. Poets, 1957; gold medal for poetry Nat. Inst. Arts and Letters, 1958. Mem. Am. Acad. Arts and Letters. Home: Brewster, Mass.

EXERCISE 2: SKIMMING

DIRECTIONS: Now skim the entries one at a time and answer the specific questions listed for each man.

A. Acheson, Dean

  1. What was his last government position?

  2. What is his present occupation?

  3. What European degrees does he possess?

  4. What unusual law experience launched his career?

  5. From what countries has he received awards of merit?

  6. What is his last published work?

  7. From what college did he receive his undergraduate degree?

  8. What government position did he hold in 1946?

  9. What government position did he hold in 1952?

  10. With what service group did he see combat?

B. Adenauer, Konrad

    1. What is his most recent former position?

    2. With what city was he most associated in his early career?

    3. What academic institution did he found?

    4. What government position did he hold immediately after World War II?

    5. What was his position in 1953?

    6. How many years did he serve as chancellor?

    7. What is his official party?

    8. What was his fate when Hitler came to power?

C. Agar, Herbert

    1. What are his professions?

    2. From what institution did he receive his Ph.D.?

    3. What institutions have awarded him honorary degrees?

    4. What have been his journalistic posts abroad?

    5. What is "Time and Tide"?

    6. What are his British clubs?

    7. Who is Eleanor Carroll Chilton?

    8. What American hero has he studied intensively?

    9. What is his work of translation?

10. What is his honorary society membership?

D. Aiken, Conrad

   1. What is his profession?

   2. What types of literary writings has he produced?

   3. What is his undergraduate college?

   4. What is the title of his autobiography?

   5. What famous American poet has he studied in depth?

   6. What award did he receive in 1954?

   7. What position in Washington, D.C., did he hold from 1950–52?

   8. What prize did he receive in 1956?

   9. What is his academy membership?

  10. Where was he born and where does he live now?

READING AND STUDYING GRAPHIC DEVICES

For the college student, the ability to interpret graphs, tables, maps, and diagrams is an indispensable skill. Through these devices a large amount of material is often concisely presented to the reader. As with the prose text, you must be able to winnow out the main ideas from the mass of supporting details which are presented in graphic form.

Some suggestions for reading graphs, tables, maps, and diagrams are as follows:

1. *Note* the legend accompanying the graphical representation.
2. *Study* carefully the captions on each axis to be sure that you understand what is plotted.
3. *Determine* what major data are given. Do the lines of the graph reveal a particular trend? In the table, are the numbers statistically significant? What do the shaded portions of the map mean?
4. *Consult* the written text accompanying these devices for further explanation of the table, graph, diagram, or chart.
5. *Relate* the points presented in these devices to the overall purpose of what you are reading.
6. *Close* your eyes to see whether you can get a visual image of the main points given in the table, graph, diagram, or chart.

EXERCISE 3: READING TABLES

DIRECTIONS: Read the following table to answer the questions listed below.

COMPOSITION OF FOODS

The following table gives the approximate percentage composition of common foods.*

Food	Water	Protein	Fat	Carbohydrate	Ash
Beef (lean)	73.8	22.1	2.9		1.2
Eggs	73.7	14.8	10.5		1.0
Milk	87.0	3.3	4.0	5.0	0.7
Butter	11.0	1.0	85.0		3.0
Green corn	75.4	3.1	1.1	19.7	0.7
Potatoes	79.2	2.2	0.1	18.4	0.1
Apples	84.6	0.4	0.5	14.2	0.3

1. Which food has the largest percentage of water?

2. If you were on a "fat-free" diet, which foods would you select?

3. If you were deficient in carbohydrates, which foods would be best as a supplement to your diet?

4. What is the relationship between the water and the carbohydrate content of the foods listed?

5. Which food with much protein is also high in percentage of ash?

6. Which food high in percentage of ash is very low in percentage of protein?

7. Which foods contain elements not included on this table?

8. Comment on the effectiveness of this table. In what other ways might the information have been presented?

* From *First Year College Chemistry*, Eighth Ed. by John R. Lewis (Barnes & Noble, Inc., 1965).

EXERCISE 4: READING GRAPHS

DIRECTIONS: Study the following graph carefully; then answer the questions that follow.

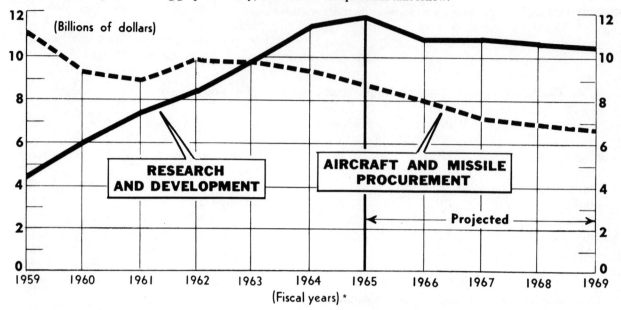

1. In which year did expenditures for research and development grow the least?

2. In which year did the procurement of aircraft and missiles increase most sharply?

3. In which year did the procurement of aircraft and missiles drop most sharply?

4. How might better performance of current aircraft and missiles affect the procurement of future-planned aircraft and missiles?

5. What might be the effect on amounts spent on research and development if competitive countries developed highly advanced systems?

6. What factors could you suggest that might cause decreased spending for research and development?

7. What are the purposes of such a graph? Are some details eliminated in order to emphasize others?

8. What are the limitations of the above graph?

* From *The New York Times*, Jan. 17, 1965. © 1965 by The New York Times Company. Reprinted by permission.

TAKING EXAMINATIONS

Examinations are not merely the means by which a teacher can establish a grade for a student; they are both valuable in themselves and valuable for what they can reveal to a student about his strengths and weaknesses. Rightly viewed, the examination is an experience in the academic process, a special kind of challenge. Here the student does not have the time or reference facilities to duplicate his performance outside class: he has a limited time and he can draw only upon his own resources, those which he has mastered. Through the results of quizzes and examinations, a student may become aware of how well he has learned the skills and content of assigned subject matter. Such knowledge is an invaluable guide for further study and continued academic growth.

Examinations, however, often do not reflect a student's full capacity or potential, for the taking of examinations requires special skills. This is not to say that there are "tricks" for taking examinations successfully; no degree of test-taking skill can compensate for a lack of mastery of subject matter. But such skills *can* enable a student to use more fruitfully all that he does know.

Try to think of an examination as a distinct and profitable form of academic experience, then recognize the special demands it makes upon you and the special knowledge it will provide. The student who views examinations as mere determiners of grades is or probably will soon become a mere crammer, one who takes in vast quantities of information at the last possible moment and hopes to make up for a semester of negligence. Interestingly, such students invariably do mediocre work on examinations. The best student is he who sees the value of the examination, who learns how to prepare and how to take examinations, and who combines these with a lively, thorough, and alert attitude toward his subject matter.

Before the Examination

In preparing for an examination, follow these basic rules: inquire about the type of test to be given; allow sufficient time for unhurried study; and come to an examination at the peak of your physical and mental strength.

It is very helpful to know whether you will be given an objective or essay examination. If the test is to be objective, pay particular attention to details. The primary purposes of objective tests are to test the accuracy with which a student knows pertinent facts of the course and to test the thoroughness of his knowledge. Precise knowledge and retention of many facts will be of particular importance here. For such a test you will primarily use your ability to memorize exactingly.

The objective type of examination is one that has great advantages for mass testing: many persons can be given the same test at one time in different areas; the test can be as inclusive or as exclusive as the tester desires; it can be quickly keyed and corrected; the results, if used judiciously, can be highly informative to the tester, although this type of examination is not as valuable educationally as the essay type.

The most familiar types of objective tests are true-false, completion, and multiple choice, examples of which, with variations, are given below.

1. Which one of the following terms should be omitted from the list:
   a. occipital   d. parietal
   b. temporal   e. cholinesterase
   c. frontal

2. Printing on cloth and parchment was practiced in Europe before the fifteenth century (*true* or *false*)

3. When wood burns, _____ and _____ are formed.

4. The author of "St. Peter Relates an Incident" is
   a. Gwendolyn Brooks
   b. James Weldon Johnson
   c. Langston Hughes

5. Identify the italic term on the blank to the left with the appropriate letter.
   (a) a gerund;   (b) an infinitive; (c) a participle.
   _____ *Extricating* himself from the conflict he had unwittingly created required all the patience he could muster.
   _____ *Releasing* his fiancée from their engagement, he left immediately for a trip to Europe.

6. Rearrange these sentences in logical order by numbering them from 1 to 4.
   _____ The bright sound of the laughter of the young girl chasing it recalled his early experience with his cousin Mary.
   _____ A large red ball shot across his path as he neared the middle of the block.
   _____ His black mood fell away as she brought back the memories of the exciting summers on her uncle's farm.
   _____ He was momentarily taken aback at the swift movement of color.

7. Insert the correct form of *who* and *whom* in the blanks.

_____ do you think will be the proper choice for class president?

He asked _____ was the visitor who had just left the office.

He asked _____ he meant when he spoke of a troubled member of his family.

If the test is to be an essay type, you should study the major points of the material and be able to support them with precise details. Your reading outlines will be of much more help here. For such a test you will need organizational and verbal skills, and should concentrate on these in your preparation. Prepare trial questions for yourself which demand an incisive grasp of larger principles; then see which of three or four possible approaches will enable you to cover all that is required. If you have particular difficulty with this type of examination, it could be very helpful to write out practice answers, timing yourself so as to duplicate actual examination conditions. Part of the skill in taking an essay-type test is to pace yourself, to know how much you can write in a given amount of time, and thus delimit and outline accordingly; too often a student will attempt so much that he becomes frantic trying to complete it all — and at other times he will oversimplify, and ignore many needed areas of investigation.

Here are some typical essay questions selected from a variety of subject matter areas:

1. *Describe* Galileo's attempts to measure the speed of light.
2. *Define* alpha, beta, and gamma rays.
3. *Identify* Sir Francis Galton and Gregor Johann Mendel.
4. *Contrast* (give differences) the British public school with its American counterpart: methods of selecting students, quality of education obtained, class status of the university-trained.
5. *Compare* (give similarities) the teen-ager of New York with the teen-ager of Tokyo: rebellion against authority; values of materialism, popularity, success, life in an age of transition.
6. *Relate* the history of the discovery of penicillin, with emphasis on the discovery by Sir Arthur Fleming.
7. *Select* two poems by Robert Frost from this list: "Two Look at Two," "Two Tramps in Mud-Time," "Birches," "Mending Wall," "The Need of Being Versed in Country Things." *Discuss* in each his philosophy of life, his rapport with nature, typically New England characteristics of diction and mood, and his development of characters.
8. *Read* the selection below from *The Merchant of Venice*, Act IV, Scene I, and *comment* upon it with reference to its universality, its lyricism, its Biblical power. [The selection is Portia's speech, "The quality of mercy is not strain'd," etc.]
9. *Analyze* the influence of the Japanese (their way of life, architecture, philosophy of nature and materials) on the architectural style and development of Frank Lloyd Wright.
10. *Review* John Henry Newman's *Idea of a University* to show, among other aspects, its salient points, its contribution to his contemporaries' ideas on British education, its relevancy to our twentieth-century institutions, and its particular message to you as a student of a university and as an educated member of society.

In preparing for an examination, it is also important to plan your review so that there will be ample time. Allow time for yourself to re-study and examine aspects of the course which have given you special difficulty. Hurried cramming, particularly for the essay examination, merely produces a garbled mass of half-understood facts. Of course there is no substitute for diligence during the entire term: knowledge must come in gradually and regularly, or it does not really become part of us. For the student who has worked steadily all semester, preparing for an examination need only be a refreshening of knowledge, or a splendid chance to gain an over-view after all the work has been mastered in its separate forms.

Finally, it is important to care for your physical needs by getting adequate rest before the examination and eating a well-balanced meal to provide adequate energy. Some tests are two or even three hours in length, and you will require all your strength to concentrate intensely for that length of time. Thinking and writing require much physical endurance! Again, studying late into the night before the day of an examination will markedly reduce the freshness and alertness of your mind during the examination.

With adequate preparation, you can enter a test with the confidence that you will do well and that you will profit from the experience itself. Examinations can be terrifying experiences for the student who neither knows his work nor knows how to take tests; for the alert, prepared, and skillful test-taker they can provide exciting challenges.

At the Examination

1. Glance rapidly over all the questions and note the value assigned to each question. Too often a student will spend as much time on a ten-point question as he will on one worth twice (or more) that amount. Jot down key words which you may use later to answer the questions.

2. Learn which way you work best: some students prefer to answer the long, hard questions first, but most find it better to complete the short easy ones before the more difficult questions must be tackled.

3. Check off each question and its parts to be sure that you have not missed any question to which you know the answer.

4. If the examination is objective, read each question carefully and slowly. Note such words as "never," "always," "all," "only," etc. Avoid wild guesses. Some examinations may stipulate that double credit will be taken off for a wrong answer.

5. If the examination is an essay type, be careful first to determine what you are being asked to do; then read the question and jot down the major ideas as they occur to you. Organize your answer in a clear, concise manner. Concision is of particular importance when you work under the pressure of a time limitation. *Make a brief outline before you begin to write.* Wherever necessary, provide pertinent supporting details; your teacher will notice evasions and circumlocutions as readily as he will a wrong answer in an objective test.

6. Reread your paper before turning it in, and make whatever changes are necessary to improve the thought, expression, and mechanics. Try to leave five or ten minutes for this. Writing quickly, you may make many obvious errors that even a cursory check will catch.

After the Examination

After the examination, while the content is still fairly clear in your mind, you will find it helpful to spend a few minutes in a post-exam review. Jot down the types of questions that were asked; note the kinds of questions you answered well and those you missed. This information about yourself you can use in future preparations for tests. Later, when your examination paper is returned, study the tests with great care. Rewrite answers to questions you did not know. Fill in any obvious gaps in your notes. Seek a conference with your teacher in order to secure advice about overcoming difficulties in that subject, or particular aspects of it. Be sure you understand *what* was wrong, not simply *that* it was.

Finally, recall the principles that dictated the production of this entire book: first, that reading is one of the most important keys to knowledge; secondly, that the enlargement and refinement of your reading skills through constant practice must be a never-ending process; and thirdly, that the virtues of good reading are its own rewards. Grades *are* important, and with work and care they will come; but knowledge and wisdom, acquired with diligence and delight, must be your first goal.